Triton College Was Just Not Any College

There is a course or program to suit virtually every student need and ability. At each level the emphasis is on careers; in fact, Triton calls itself "the Career Center of the Midwest". . . .
Time Magazine

I would like especially to commend Triton College, designated by the **Chicago Tribune** as Illinois "model junior college" and by the **Pioneer Press** newspapers as "a college for all the people." Triton, the first 2-year institution built under the Illinois Junior College Act of 1965, has become the largest junior college in the State. . . .
Charles Percy, U.S. Senator, Congressional Record

During my brief tenure as representative of the college in Washington, I recall that Triton College, under Mr. Zeitlin, offered a terrific curriculum of citizenship classes and instruction in English as a second language. I can think of no more important mission for such an institution than to strengthen the bonds of our American democracy.
Henry Hyde, U.S. Congressman

The Board was fortunate in its unanimous choice of Herbert Zeitlin as our first president. What we saw in him was his creativeness, innovativeness and vision as well as the energy and enthusiasm to carry out the task before him. He did not disappoint us.
Elmore Boeger, 2nd Chairman, Triton College Board of Trustees

I was highly impressed with Dr. Zeitlin's vision of the future of the college and his ability to convince the various governing bodies such as the Board of Higher Education, the Illinois Building Authority, the Capital Development Board and even the Governor of the State of the needs and the future of Triton College. In all cases his enthusiasm, dedication and vision impressed them to the point that his projects were approved even though they went far past the normal guidelines.
John Jay Fox, Triton College Architect

This book is available at special discounts for bulk purchases for education uses, sales promotion and fund raising purposes. Special books, or book excerpts, can also be created to fit specific needs. Author is also available for consulting or speaking arrangements.

Write or fax to:
> **Trident Consultants**
> **P.O. Box 571412**
> **Tarzana, CA 91357**
>
> **Fax: 818-884-7854**

Some names and identifying characteristics of people in this book have been changed to protect the privacy of individuals.

Published by
Jay Street Publishers
155 West 72nd Street
New York, NY 10023

Printed in the United States of America

TURBULENT BIRTH OF TRITON COLLEGE

A true story of how a California dean detects and prevents corruption in the founding of a public community college in Chicagoland

DR. HERBERT ZAKARY ZEITLIN

This book is dedicated to the thousands of students who have attended Triton College and have proven to themselves and their families that the American Dream can be achieved through higher education.

CONTENTS

Acknowledgements

I especially want to thank my dear wife Eugenia who faithfully stood by me during the most challenging year of my life. The story is now in print and it is my hope that those communities ruled by dishonest politicians or tainted trustees will profit from the experiences of the Triton College community. By developing a united front of school administrators, press and a watch-dog group, we succeeded in throwing out one bad system in Chicagoland.

To write of events that took place over 30 years ago was not a difficult task because so many vivid incidents were firmly embedded in my mind despite the passing of time.

Because I had ready access to Triton's archives, consisting of board and faculty committee minutes, news articles and letters from community leaders, the quotes used, I believe, are accurate. In the event of any errors I accept full responsibility for them.

This story is the history of Triton's beginning. Some individuals were given fictitious names. While the archive file revealed the event, it did not always mention the name of the individual involved.

Triton could not have become an outstanding college without the hard working, loyal, brilliant and experienced faculty:

Carol Bauer	Harry B. Behrman	Dr. Malcolm D. Berd
Dan Bourbulas	Lynn Carbanaro	Mamie Christoff
John Collins	Dr. George Cox	Ralph Domabil
Carl Dean	Dr. Victor Dye	Eric Fielitz
Richard Francetic	Lawrence Hassel	Garry Hinrichs
Robert F. Hlavin	Carolyn Ives	Kenneth Jakus
Shirley Jameson	Arthur Kraft	Dr. Alex Lane
Vernon Magnesen	Gerald Mathis	Thomas McCabe
Thomas Meeham	Arnold Merbitz	Doris M. Mills
Linda L. Morris	George Royce	Paul Salmon
William Semelroth	Arthur L. Shearburn	Ralph Smith
Dr. John Swalec	Susan Swibold	John Vaughns
Bernard Verweil	John Warren	Carole Widiger
Gertrude Wilson	Clifton J. Woods	

Significant Classified: Ed Sexton, Bookstore Manager; Sandy Horton, Assistant to the Librarian

The excitement of becoming part of a new college with a salary schedule second to none was a major attraction in the recruitment of a superior faculty. The board encouraged me to recruit minority staff members and to recruit a student body from all levels of scholastic ability. In other words the board wanted a college for all people regardless of race, color, religion or scholastic ability.

This forward looking board consisted of Elmore Boeger, Robert Collins, Joe Farmar, Roy Jones, Fred Knol, Ralph Serpico and Wade A. Steel, as chairman. The differences that developed between the Board and me were mainly due to my not accepting some traditional Chicagoland practices.

I shall never forget the following individuals who supported me through all kinds of adversities:

Maria Provenzano, my secretary during the first year, gave me some insight into the community and its leaders. She did a remarkable job of keeping accurate board minutes.

Dr. John Widergren, dean of admissions and guidance, first hired administrator with a strong background in guidance and adult education, gained while serving as a dean at Proviso East High School.

Dr. G. Robert Darnes, dean of instruction, musician, scholar and courageous administrator, coming from Olney Community College in Illinois where he had served as dean of the college.

Gordon Simonsen, first dean of technology in Illinois, a former faculty association president and district administrator for vocational programs in Aurora High School. He was one of the most experienced and informed vocationalists in the Midwest.

Robert Dale, dean of business management, the former business manager from Downers Grove School District, noted for his computer-sharp methods of accounting.

Bernard Verweil, journalism instructor, faculty sponsor of *The Trident,* our college newspaper, and founder of the renowned Miss Triton contest.

Neil Mehler, editor and publisher of the *Franklin Parker,* who lead the core of newspapers editors seeking the truth, even though his investigative revelations regarding questionable board methods caused the financial collapse of his own newspaper.

Citizens For Triton, a group of community leaders who

fought for honesty in government and won.

Jack Rossetter, president of the *Citizens For Triton,* a mathematics teacher who fought continuously against all odds for honesty in governance and was later elected a trustee of Triton College.

Wade A Steel, chairman of the Triton Board of Trustees, whose wise council and friendship I shall never forget. Despite all adversities and threats he kept his cool.

Elmore Boeger, the trustee who gave the college its name and who succeeded Wade Steel as chairman of the board. As a Rotarian, honest lawyer and master of diplomacy, he will always be remembered.

I am indebted to Joel Lewis, a colleague at the Paramount Company, who taught me the magic of Microsoft Word and to Yale's finest, Robert Glasser who spent endless hours proofreading and condensing history.

To my children Mark, Joyce, Ann Victoria and Clare I ask for your forgiveness. It was my firm intent to be a wonderful father. I was not! When Triton was born, as Eugenia has said, the college became my youngest and fifth child. It received my most attention. Dear kids, forgive me for not being part of your life when you needed me most, and darling Eugenia you were a superior mother, a part-time father and a perceptive adorable wife.

Preface

Eighteen years after I resigned from Triton College I was pleasantly surprised to receive a warm written invitation to the gala 30th birthday celebration from the new president.

A few days later, Florence Weese, whom I had hired many years back, telephoned and insisted that I attend as her guest, "Dr. Zeitlin, the faculty you hired love you. They want to see you. We can't have a 30th birthday celebration without its founding president."

I promised to call her back after talking with my wife. Eugenia, my partner for over 40 years, was reluctant to go inasmuch as I had just recovered from a severe pancreatitis operation that had hospitalized me for over seven months and made walking somewhat painful. After much discussion we decided to attend, since it gave us another opportunity to see our son, daughter-in-law and their two children, who lived in Ottawa, Illinois. When Florence heard of our decision, she told me she'd been in contact with my daughter Joyce, who lived in Virginia and who planned to attend with her husband and two kids, even though dinner tickets went for $75 each. I asked Florence, why such a high cost? She answered that it was a fund-raiser that the mayors of all the Triton communities promised to support, which seemed rather odd, but having been away for over 18 years, I felt I wasn't up on all the changes that had taken place.

Before landing at O'Hare airport I got a lump in my throat as we flew over the Triton campus, which, during my presidency, had been transformed from a city dump, trailer court and farm into a campus of 14 modern buildings with parking for over 4,500 cars. Instead of the few thousand cars I had expected to see from the plane's window I was amazed to find only a few hundred. I wondered what could have caused this dramatic change.

The following afternoon Eugenia and I decided to visit on our own the business, health and technology centers to see a few classes in action. Talking to one of the finest instructors I knew from the past, we learned that most classes were now being held between 8:00 AM and noon and from 7:00 PM to 10 PM, with very few from 1 to 7. In the past ten years enrollments had dropped drastically.

The decline, he said, had begun when a series of front page articles by the courageous reporter Thomas Burton of the *Chicago Sun Times* exposed vast patronage and corruption at Triton. To the embarrassment of thousands of its students the press had labeled the school "CLOUT COLLEGE." The name stuck even after Pat Naples, the chairman of the board, resigned upon threat of a strike by the faculty. Later Triton lost its accreditation.

"What's the enrollment today?" I asked.

"13,000."

"And what was it 10 years ago?"

"27,000."

"That's a drastic decline. How do you explain it?"

"Dr. Zeitlin, haven't you heard? Since you left, Triton has become a political cesspool. We didn't realize it at the time, but when you were chief, Triton was Camelot. Since then, we've had six presidents, all leaving under pressure. It got so bad that the better communities have stopped sending us their students. We're all praying that our new president, Dr. George Jorndt, can make some improvements."

As we walked from building to building we were pleased to find the original carpet, layed over 25 years ago, in relatively fair shape, thanks to the brilliant purchase made by our first business manager, Robert Dale.

When we arrived at the president's office Dr. Jorndt welcomed me with the crisp, enthusiastic greeting, "Dr. Zeitlin, you look great. I'll always remember the day you hired me. You were such a lively, stern and creative president. You can rest assured I will carry on in your best traditions."

"How are your board members? Are they working well together?"

"Absolutely! We are a team and we're going to revitalize the college and get the enrollments up pronto. That's my number one priority."

"How will you do it?"

"It's a matter of attitude. The faculty and the community in the past have been rather critical of previous boards, but under my administration that will change. Let me give you this positive attitude pin. Wear it with pride. Those seeing it will know that you're a positive person."

"How many of these pins do you have?"

"A few thousand. The trustees and administrators will give them to those who believe Triton has a bright future. You know we have several hundred suppliers and dear friends here at Triton. They all purchased ads in this 30th Anniversary Commemorative Book without any pressure from the administration. It's a real money maker. Now, what do you think of this 104-page masterpiece?" Dr. Jorndt gave each of us a copy.

"It's a wonderful job of printing," I said, flipping through the pages. "The photos, beautiful ads, Triton Trivia and the special features make this booklet very special. This short history of the college is unique. Congratulations on selecting such a fine editorial staff."

"The press has been rather cruel and continues to label us *Clout College.* Well, as of today that's going to change. We have a different board with a totally different outlook. Triton shall shine once again."

As we left I told Eugenia that with Jorndt at the helm I had high hopes Triton would regain its fame. She had reservations about the outcome as we looked forward to the big dinner party Saturday night We had been told it was a complete sellout, with 60 reserved tables of 10 seats each.

When we arrived at the student center on Saturday night, we were surprised to see a red carpet from the parking area to the main entrance. How nice! Hundreds of well-dressed individuals were moving quickly to the large dining area, several of them in formal attire. Before we found our table I ran into a few veteran faculty members. We embraced and exchanged news like relatives. I was so pleased and surprised at their warm welcome after my 18-year absence.

I asked Florence, who was on the planning committee, how many teachers were attending.

"Fifteen out of a total of 650. Most of them were reluctant to spend $75 to hear speeches by the trustees and their political friends. I tried to get more to attend but was not very successful."

"Are these politicians Republicans or Democrats?"

"Some of both, but this year mostly Republicans. The biggest promoter of this affair is Don Stephens, Mayor of Rosemont, and the father of our board chairman, Mark Stephens."

"What ever happened to Michael Bakalis?" (Dr. Bakalis had been Triton's immediate past president.)

"He was fired for political reasons after serving only 16 months. He's now suing the board for over a million."

"Do you think he'll win?"

"Not likely, even though he was once our State Superintendent of Schools. He's a Democrat and they are out this year."

"It makes me so sad to hear that. After we cleared it of the politicians way back, the Triton board went on record never to endorse a politician for trusteeship."

"Well, Dr. Zeitlin, all that has changed. The politicians are now running the college."

"I knew of Dr. Bakalis. In educational circles he was ranked as an eminent scholar and administrator. To be publicly fired may mean the end of his career. It will be extremely difficult for him to get another job. Why did they fire him?"

"He was fired because he refused to hire several incompetents recommended by the political trustees."

After a superb dinner prepared by the restaurant training students, I congratulated Jens Jenson, the food manager in charge, for doing such a splendid job when he came over to greet us with a gracious welcome. My spirits picked up when Tom Bondi, the auto mechanics teacher I'd hired many years before, was selected to be the Master of Ceremonies. Through his and many of other teachers' efforts, I was put on the list of individuals to be introduced.

The program opened with remarks from the president of the Triton Foundation, followed by the chairman of the governing board, Mark Stephens. Mr. Stephens made it a point to thank each mayor and his respective entourage for their help in creating and supporting Triton for the past 30 years. I barely managed to keep a straight face at that remark, knowing that most of the people he was thanking had opposed the creation of the college. I remembered well not being able to get a single city council to go on record approving the bond election in 1965. My, how history changes when the second generation takes over.

It was strange indeed to hear the audience give the Rosemont mayor, Don Stephens, Mark's father, the loudest applause for his continued help to Triton. I seriously asked Florence, "What has Don Stephens given to Triton?"

With much laughter she responded, "Besides giving us Mark, he's given Triton Casino Nights. I guess you weren't there last night. The entire student center became Las Vegas at its best or worst, take your choice."

"Florence, you must be kidding! Since the day Triton opened any student caught gambling on the campus would be subject to suspension. Has that changed?"

"Well, Dr. Zeitlin, times have changed. Let me show you the invitations that were mailed to thousands of citizens under the postmark of NON-PROFIT ORG. U.S."

I was shocked when Florence pulled out of her bag a green post card invitation urging people celebrate Triton's 30th birthday with blackjack, poker, roulette, dice, money wheel and much more. Admission was $5 per person. Maximum winnings at each cashout was $250.

"Florence, it's hard for me to believe this has happend at Triton. Did many students show up last night?"

"It seemed like there were thousands there. Where they came from, I don't know, but I didn't see many Triton students. The faculty didn't think promoting gambling was anywhere to be found in the college's objectives or philosophy. They encouraged the students to boycott this event. That's another reason why so few teachers are here tonight."

"How will Dr. Jorndt justify all this when the accredition process comes up again?"

"I'm sure someone from Nevada will help him out. Here, take a look at these red booklets giving specific instruction on how to gamble. There are thousands of them. Notice how Dr. Jorndt and all the trustees are listed. Isn't that a sign they approve of the event?"

"Yes, it is. I can't understand why the college president and the trustees would support a Casino Night. Don't they realize they're gambling with the future of thousands of students? What if Triton lost its accreditation?"

"I'm not sure they're aware of it. But Mark told me that Casino Nights are sponsored by the Triton Foundation in an effort to raise money for scholarships. The board has nothing to do with the Foundation."

"Oh, come on now. Isn't the Foundation really an extension of the board?"

"I know that, but the North Central Accrediting Association doesn't."

"There's more to this than I know. So what's the real reason Mark Stephens established Casino Nights?"

"It's no secret. Everybody knows he did it to please his father. For years his Dad has wanted open gambling in Rosemont or on the nearby riverboats. He feels his city, next to the busiest airport in the world, could become the gambling center of the Midwest. If he could get the Triton community to support his dream, it would be the first step toward meeting his goal."

"Do you think it will happen?"

"If Mark or his father gets into the governor's office, I think it will. However, right now there are many state legislators who strongly oppose open gambling in the state of Illinois."

"Are there any other groups opposed to gambling?"

"I've been told all the school superintendents are opposed to it, including the six fired Triton presidents."

"Does that mean for Dr. Jorndt to remain president he has to support Don Stephens's dream?"

"I am sorry to say, yes."

"Can't Dr. Jorndt get these men to change their mind?"
"It's possible, but not likely. Tonight's audience are all followers of Don Stephens. He holds all the right cards."

Hearing all this from Florence I wondered why I had bothered to come, when suddenly my name, as the founding president, was called out by Tom Bondi. I was delighted to receive an ovation equal, if not better, than that given to Mayor Stephens. As I was about to sit down Malcolm Berd, an early faculty association president, asked me to pose for some pictures with the Triton faculty. In all, 12 teachers sought me out. We hugged each other and nothing but beautiful remarks were heard. I couldn't get over it. Although I knew all of the faculty, some well and some slightly, I was overwhelmed by the respect and honor they paid me. My daughter caught a picture of us as my eyes watered.

Eighteen years had passed. The faculty now referred to the good old days as "Camelot with Zeitlin." At that moment – which I'll never forget – I knew Triton would remain in my blood forever. Florence later told me that the old faculty would never forget me for my 12 years of fair, honest and creative administration, completely free of political conniving.

Just before the dinner program ended Mark Stephens announced that last night's Casino evening was such a success that it had been extended for another night. All the tables and wheels of fortune would be opened again immediately for another great night of gambling. To my surprise Eugenia said, "Let's go and see what the great life is all about."

Out of curiosity we observed the professional gamblers, imported from who knows where, cut the cards, move the chips, roll the dice and spin the wheels as people of all ages lost to the house. We were in Las Vegas and hadn't realized it!

Eugenia remarked, "If Jimmy Stewart's George Bailey hadn't been born, this is what would have happened to Bedford Falls." I swallowed as Eugenia's words make their impact, and I felt a surge of guilt for leaving Triton.

After we left Chicagoland, my dear wife urged me to write about my experiences at Triton to set the record straight.

"What good would it do?" I asked.

"You knew Chicagoland was tainted before you went for the interview," she pointedly reminded me. "Within a few years you untainted it, and that in itself is a small miracle worth writing about. You've proven that some communities, regardless of past reputation, can change for the good."

"Do you think the public would be interested in reading about it?"

"I'm sure they would, since there are thousands of cities in the U.S. that have been tarnished by corrupt politicians. The citizens feel helpless. You licked city hall and managed to survive. I'm sure there are many who'd like to know how you did it."

"Sweetie, it wasn't me alone. I received lots of unexpected help along the way."

"And that's reason enough for you to tell your readers how the unsolicited help came to you."

And so the story of the most challenging years of my life shall begin.

PRINCIPAL PLAYERS

Dr. Herbert Zakary Zeitlin, President of Triton College, previously Dean of Instruction at Southwestern College. Stanford graduate.

Eugenia F. Zeitlin, English professor, New York University graduate, wife and mother of four children.

Wade A. Steel, President of Triton Board of Trustees, Superintendent of Leyden High School District. University of Illinois graduate.

Robert M. Collins, Secretary of Triton Board, Supervisor at Illinois Telephone Company, Republican Precinct Captain. Wright Junior College graduate.

Roy Jones, Vice President of Triton Board, Supervisor at Commonwealth Edison, 24 Years' Experience as a School Trustee.

Fred Knol, Trustee, Supervisor at Lindberg Steel, Sunday School Teacher, Republican Precinct Captain. Morton College graduate.

Elmore Boeger, Trustee, Lawyer, Banker, Past Rotary President, law degree from Valparaiso University.

Joe Farmar, Trustee, attorney for Bekins Moving Company, Democratic Precinct Captain, law degree from Notre Dame University.

Ralph Serpico, Trustee, Supervisor of Cook County Assessor's Office, Head of Coalition, Proviso Democratic Party leader, All-American Football Star. University of Illinois graduate.

Donald Dunahow, Attorney for Elmer Conti, City of Elmwood Park and Triton College. Graduate of Crane Junior College.

Dr. John Widergren, Dean of Admissions & Guidance, former Dean at Proviso High School. Doctorate from University of Wyoming.

Dr. G. Robert Darnes, Dean of Instruction, former Dean of Olney Community College. Doctorate from the University of Oklahoma.

Gordon Simonsen, Dean of Technology, former Director of Adult & Vocational Education at Aurora High School District. Master's from Bradley University.

Robert T. Dale, Coordinator of Business Management, former Business Manager of Du Page Elementary School. Master's from Northern Illinois University.

Jack Rossetter, President of Citizens for Triton, Mathematics Teacher at Oak Park-River Forest High School. Master's from Illinois State University.

John Jay Fox, Architect for Triton College, Chicago, Illinois. Graduate of Illinois Institute of Technology.

Towns and villages in the Triton district:

ROSEMONT*

HARWOOD HEIGHTS*

NORRIDGE*

SCHILLER PARK

FRANKLIN PARK

NORTHLAKE RIVER GROVE

STONE PARK ELMWOOD PARK

MELROSE PARK

RIVER FOREST

BERKELEY BELLWOOD MAYWOOD OAK PARK

HILLSIDE FOREST PARK

WESTCHESTER BROADVIEW

NORTH RIVERSIDE

LaGRANGE PARK*

BROOKFIELD* RIVERSIDE

*Only portions of these communities are located in District 504

OTHER CAST MEMBERS

A.   Qualified political job seekers recommended by college president:
Maria Provenzano, Secretary to College President
Virginia Sybilla, Secretary to Dean of Admissions
Jim Tarpey, part-time Community Relations Specialist

B.   Unqualified political job seekers rejected by president:
Ellen Atkinson, Clerical Worker (Recommended by Mayor Daley's office)
Joe Pulitano, Purchasing Agent (Recommended by Babe Serpico)
Neil Neuson, Business Manager (Recommended by Joe Farmar)
Lewis Case, Chief of Security (Recommended by Bob Collins)

C.   College president recommendations rejected by board:
William Roetzheim, Director of Athletics & P.E., U.S. Olympic Star
Dale Alexison, Business Manager from Du Page County
John Moody, Business Manager, Wellston, Missouri
Robert Dale, Business Manager *(later approved)*
Gordon Simonscn, Dean of Technology *(later approved)*

D.   College president's recommendations accepted by board:
12 classified
89 faculty

E.   Political bosses:
Democrat *Mayor Richard Daley* (Ralph Serpico's political boss)
Democrat *Jim Kirie* (Joe Farmar's political boss)
Republican *Mayor Elmer Conti* (Bob Collins's political boss)
Republican *Mayor Dick O'Connor* (Bob Collins's uncle)

F.   Supportive educators:
Dr. Leroy Knoeppel, Superintendent of Proviso High School District
Dr. George Cox, Principal of West Leyden High School
Dr. Elmund Gleazer, Executive Secretary of American Assn. of Jr. & Community Colleges
James Hannum, Assistant Superintendent of Cook County Schools

G.   Supportive press:
Neil Mehler, *Franklin Parker*
Kingsley Wood, *Chicago Sun Times*
Allen Pilger, *Maywood Herald*
Greg Mahoney, *West Cook County Press*
Robert Newman, *Proviso Herald*
Jack Spatafora, *The Times*
Carol Swatos, *Mont Clare, Leyden Herald*

H.   College president's children:
Mark Clyde Zeitlin, Age 14, Freshman at Elmwood Park High School
Joyce Therese Zeitlin, Age 10, 5th Grader at St. Vincent Ferrer School
Ann Victoria Zeitlin, Age 7, 2nd Grader at St. Vincent Ferrer School
Clare Katherine Zeitlin, Age 6, Special Education, Martin Enger School

Reprints of Triton History

. . .in the beginning

1
It's An Emergency

It was a sunny Friday afternoon in early August 1964 in Chula Vista, California, and I felt great. As the dean of instruction at Southwestern College I had just approved the final copy for the new college catalog, interviewed several candidates for teaching positions and left my recommendations with the college president, Chet DeVore. I had worked very hard this past semester and was ready for the vacation with my family in Ensenada, Mexico. All that remained to be done was a tune-up, oil change and lubrication of my old Ford station wagon at the Sears Motor Center.

It was great living in Chula Vista. Some of the advantages: tropical climate, a small town with the big city of San Diego nearby, 15 minutes to the smooth blue Pacific ocean, 20 minutes to the world famous San Diego Zoo and 22 minutes to the exciting border town of Tijuana. After living over 12 years in the desert towns of Lancaster, California and Phoenix, Arizona, beautiful Chula Vista was a paradise! What kind of fool would want to leave? All was right with the world as my beautiful and talented wife, Eugenia, was packing the rented 15-foot trailer. The four kids were looking forward to fishing, boating, horseback riding and visiting at Estero Beach, plus shopping and visiting in Ensenada.

As I was about to pay my bill at Sears the service manager on the speaker system called out, "Is there a Dr. Zeitlin here? Please call your wife immediately. It's an emergency!"

My God! something has happened to one of the kids. "An emergency!" I thought the worst. Was it Mark, the eighth grader who loved all sports, or was it Joyce, the beautiful creative artist who'd reached fourth grade with a straight A average? The two older ones were very solid, quite dependable and very active. They loved life and every day was a new, exciting beginning. It had to be petite and precocious Ann Victoria or her younger sister, Clare. We all worried about Clare, our lovely Down Syndrome. Everyone knew of her handicap and watched her closely. Could she have run out onto our busy street and gotten hit by a car? Quite possibly. I always told Mark and Joyce to keep the side gate closed. Was this going to be another case of everyone watching her but no one taking responsibility for her safety? Oh, heaven forbid. I told myself, "Stay calm, Herbert. Stop thinking the worst." I called Eugenia back.

"Eugenia, tell me slowly. What happened?"

"You just got a call from a Mr. Bob Collins, secretary of the board of a new community college district in Melrose Park, Illinois. He wants you to come for an interview for the college presidency, Tuesday night. I didn't tell him you'll be in Mexico – or should I have done so? Damn it, are you going to cancel our vacation plans?"

"Don't worry. It can wait."

"I sure hope so. Don't forget–we've been planning this vacation for months. The kids will be heartbroken. We're all set to go tomorrow at 8:00 A.M. Where is Melrose Park?"

"I don't know. I never eard of the place. It must have been the application I sent to Dr. Frank Endicott at the Northwestern University placement bureau several months ago. I'll check it out when I get home."

My mind was on Melrose Park as I paid my bill and was eagerly homeward bound.

The *Rand McNally Road Atlas* showed Melrose Park to be a western suburb of Chicago, population 19,900. Among the other suburbs: Lincolnwood, Park Ridge, Harwood Height, River Grove, Elmwood Park, Oak Park (birthplace of Ernest Hemingway) and Cicero (workplace of Al Capone). I was ready for my call to Bob Collins.

"Hello, this is Herb Zeitlin, dean of Southwestern College in California, returning your call."

"Congratulations, Dr. Zeitlin. You have been selected by the presidential screening committee to be one of three candidates to be interviewed for the presidency of our newly formed community college and technical institute. Can you come for an interview with the board this Tuesday night? All your traveling and hotel expenses will be paid for upon your arrival."

"Mr. Collins, thanks for the happy announcement. I am interested in the position but I have a conflict in scheduling. The family and I are leaving for a Mexico vacation tomorrow morning. Could we make it two weeks later?"

"Oh, I don't know. . .well, I guess it's OK. We'll interview the president from Arkansas Tuesday night and the president from Michigan a week later. We'll reserve the third Tuesday for the dean from California. Say, you don't sound like a Californian. You have a strange accent. Where are you from?"

"For the past seven years I've lived in California. Prior to that, seven years in Phoenix, Arizona. During my three years in the Army Air Force I was influenced by natives of Texas, Wisconsin, Tennessee and Illinois. But I suppose the most lasting regionalism is from Queens, New York, where I graduated from Jamaica High School and New York University."

"You're really a New Yorker, aren't you?"

"Yes, for the first 27 years."

"You sound like some people I know from the Big Apple. But accents make no difference to the board. We want to get the best president possible. Can I tell you anything about our district?"

"Yes, please do so–I'd like to know everything about the district, such as population, total assessed wealth, tax rate, communities served, election results and the enrollment projections. Was a feasibility study made prior to establishing the college?"

"Why, of course. Actually, we had two rather extensive studies made. I'll have our part-time secretary mail them to you tomorrow. When you arrive at O'Hare Airport, take a 15-minute taxi ride to the Leyden Township High School in Franklin Park. Report to Wade Steel, a high school superintendent and president of the college board. He'll make all the arrangements for your hotel and the dinner meeting with the board."

We exchanged views about the weather, the coming presidential election, the good life in Southern California and the need for a community college in Illinois. As I hung up, Eugenia breathed a sigh of relief. "You said you'd do it and you did it." The kids applauded.

Nothing was going to interfere with our vacation plans. The trailer was packed and we left promptly the following morning.

The normal driving time from Chula Vista to crossing the border at Tijuana is 21 minutes, plus a five-second slowdown as the Mexican customs officer waves you through the border entrance. However, this time, for some unexplained reason, we were asked,

"Where are you going?"

The instant reply, "Estero beach in Ensenada."

"Pull over to the side, unload all your bags and wait," commanded the heavyset mustached officer.

And wait we did. About an hour later he reappeared with his overweight and heavy-breathing supervisor and had us open all six suitcases. They slowly felt their way through the contents of each suitcase. What were they looking for? It's well known that much dope and liquor find their way to California surreptitiously over the Mexican border, but not the other way around. The two authorities retreated to the back of the station wagon, wrote down our license plate number and spoke in whispers.

"What are they talking about?" snapped Eugenia.

"They think this is a stolen car," responded smiling Joyce.

"You shouldn't have worn the squaw dress with all that Indian jewelry. They may think we're rich," I rationalized.

And so we waited another 30 minutes until a clean-shaven Caesar Romero type appeared. He stared at Eugenia, focusing not on her jewelry but on her good points. Eugenia got a little red in the face. I got out of the wagon and stared back at him intensely. I slowly took out my yellow pad and wrote down the number on his badge. He took a deep breath, looking slightly annoyed, and reluctantly said, "OK, you can go now."

"Well, what was that all about? What did they want?" Mark asked.

"They wanted a tip. Helen DeVore told me the going rate is now two dollars a bag when you get stopped. For $10 we could have been on our merry way," Eugenia retorted.

"That's a bribe! Those officers are well paid by the Mexican government and I'll be damned if I pay anything extra," I shouted as we hit the open road.

The kids were quiet after Dad's sudden outburst and Eugenia was dead silent as I thought about the corrupt Mexican border patrol. Precocious Ann Victoria broke the silence. "Mommy, what's a bribe?"

"Sweetie, that's when corrupt people take money from you that they haven't earned," Eugcnia responded.

Ann Victoria thought a while and then popped the question, "Who are the corrupt people?"

"They're bad people! They're dishonest. They want you to do things that are not right. Mommy and Daddy try to avoid them."

The vacation in Ensenada was filled with swimming, fishing, boating, card playing and monopoly. Eugenia and the girls collected seashells while Mark and I went horseback riding along the ocean's edge. They admired our mild-mannered horses and everyone except Clare petted them.

Several times during dinner, Eugenia looked deeply into my eyes and said, "Come back, dear Herbert, you're in Mexico with your family. I know what you're thinking about"

Every day my mind went off to distant places and things. Melrose Park, Oak Park and the city of broad shoulders–Chicago. I wondered what kind of a mayor Richard Daley really was. Would Chicago, with its reputation as the city of clout, have much effect on the city of Melrose Park? What would it be like to be president of a community college and technical institute? One out of three interviewed. Were the odds with me or against me?

My mind flashed back to a previous interview in April in San Marcos, California, where I was one of seven interviewed for the presidency of Palomar College. The 60-minute interview had gone so fast. Fifteen questions in 60 minutes. It was like an express train, with such questions as:

> Where were you born? Describe the city.
> How did you do in elementary school, high school and college?
> Any honors or special achievements?
> Describe your life in the military.
> What does your wife do?
> Is she aware of the role of a president's wife?
> What do you know about Palomar College?
> What changes would you recommend?
> Are you for or against tuition in California community colleges?
> How would you go about solving Palomar's financial concerns?

Give us some examples of your leadership abilities.

Leave us the names and numbers of three individuals who would recommend you for this job.

It was awkward facing the nine well-dressed white males inviting me into the "hot seat"–and hot it was. There were five trustees, plus the retiring college president, the faculty association president, the classified president and the honorary mayor of San Marcos. All were straight-laced, stoic, totally lacking in laughter or humor. Only once, when I was describing my enjoyable teaching experience in the Air Force, did the committee chuckle, when the college president said, "Teaching in the military is good training for future college presidents. They all become Little Napoleons."

The very first question, "Where was I born?" was a little irritating and unnecessary since all the committee members had copies of the confidential papers from New York University that firmly established me as a "New Yorker." I never have been able to quite figure out why non-New Yorkers laugh when you say you're from Brooklyn or New York.

Maybe too many movies and TV shows have portrayed New Yorkers as uncouth smartasses. I spoke out.

"I feel I received a superior education in the public schools of New York, rich in mathematics, science and the humanities. During my four years in high school I was elected president of seven different student organizations and was the only sophomore ever elected president of the entire student body. It took me eight years to complete the baccalaureate degree in industrial education at New York University since I was also working 20 hours per week in a New York office as a purchasing agent and shipping clerk, and served Uncle Sam for another three and a half years. The wonderful G.I. Bill of Rights paid all my expenses for my master's in guidance and the doctorate in education at Stanford University."

I'd expected my comments to open up some kind of dialogue, but there was nothing from the stone-faced governing board and staff.

"Next question, Dr. Zeitlin. Tell us about any special achievement or honors of yours in the past."

"When I was a student in an Air Force Technical School at Madison, Wisconsin, the radio kit I'd constructed was selected as the best engineered kit from a class of about 150 students. After receiving accolades from the squadron leader, I accepted an invitation from the officer in charge of instruction to become a teacher. It was an ideal teaching situation. Class size was always less than eight students, usually washed-out cadets from the flight school. Our equipment was superior, and the visual and audio aids were always in good working order. Most instructors would serve a few months, or at most one year, and then would be shipped overseas. But I served for almost two years, until the war's end, because my students obtained the highest grades in the military *sweat box.*"

I had hoped that at least one of the stoic trustees would ask about the sweat box, the ordeal faced by a student as a panel of experts grilled him closely for an hour on his knowledge of electronics. Alas, not even a murmur.

The meticulously dressed, gray-flannel-suited chairman thumbed through the dossier labeled "Dr. Herbert Zeitlin–Stanford" and testily cried out; "There's a lot to read here. How many recommendations do you have?"

Feeling a little embarrassed, I meekly responded, "Seven or eight, plus some statements from my major professors and a few colleagues in the education world. You have in front of you my work history for the past 17 years. As I advanced on the educational ladder I'd receive a positive recommendation from each former employer."

"That's all very good, Dr. Zeitlin, but what did you actually accomplish as the president of the Arizona Vocational Guidance Association to make Dr. Delbert Jerome, the State Supervisor of Guidance, say your leadership was superb and will be long remembered?"

"I was lucky to be at the right place at the right time. Arizona, as one of the newer states, lagged behind New York and California in the licensing of counselors. Anyone could open an office and offer testing and counseling services. There were no requirements! Pseudo-counseling spread. The public was beginning to judge these therapists as money-grubbing quacks. This had to stop."

"And how did you stop it, young man?" the chair asked, intrigued.

"Through the joint efforts of my fellow counselors, the office of the state superintendent of public instruction, the governor's office and the university president, we managed to influence the state legislature to pass a law requiring a master's degree, plus an internship, for counselors. This is another example of a professional group requesting more state control to protect the best interests of the public. During the first year of licensing, the number of fly-by-night therapists diminished while university enrollments in guidance and counseling sky-rocketed," I proudly declared.

The elderly man at the end of conference table, also in a gray flannel suit, yawned, got up, poured himself a cup of coffee, ate a cookie and then asked me, "Would you like coffee and a cookie?"

"Yes, I would," I responded. He filled my cup and went around the table filling all the others. The three-minute refreshment break energized the group. All eyes were open and the chair continued to speak up.

"I'm a little confused. What's the difference between the Arizona Vocational Guidance Association and the Arizona State Vocational Association? They sound a lot alike. What do they have in common?"

Holding my right hand up with all the fingers spread apart I pointed out that there were six distinctive divisions in the Arizona Vocational Association, all receiving federal money for teacher salaries, supplies and equipment under the Smith-Hughes and George-Barden Acts.

"The teachers specialize in agriculture, trades, homemaking, apprenticeship training, distributive education and vocational guidance. And I predict in the very near future there will be a seventh division, probably to be called 'health careers.' The hospitals today are begging the colleges to train more nurses and other health specialists. Each division has its own president and the full membership elects a state president to serve as the spokesperson for all vocational teachers and counselors."

"This is very revealing, Dr. Zeitland. I didn't know the federal government gave money to community college vocational teachers. How much do they generally give?"

I thought to myself, is he putting me on, or does he just not know about this aspect of federal aid?

Suddenly, the college president burst out, "Jim, you may have forgotten, but this college has a long-standing policy against seeking any kind of federal assistance. You know that with federal aid there's always federal control."

"Well, I think it's time to review our policy. Perhaps it's one way Palomar could solve its financial problems. Again, Dr. Zeitland, how much money is available?"

This was the second time he'd misprononnced my name. Should I correct him? I thought, don't be stupid Herbert. All eyes around the table were on me to answer this very important question. Don't break the fixation. Placing my hands together as if in prayer I slowly moved the fingers back and forth and said, "I can't give you an exact figure other than to say that hundreds and hundreds of millions have been given to public schools and colleges that have vocational approved programs, and one day I hope it will be in the billions. Each year since 1916 Congress has increased the amount. Each state in the union has a vocational department that sets up the guidelines on how its share of money is to be distributed. I know of no public school or college that's withdrawn from the program once it's become part of it."

"And, why is that so?"

"Mainly, because the graduate gets almost instant placement and a beginning salary above that of the liberal arts graduate. When I was at Phoenix Technical School, many of our students in nursing, electronics, auto servicing, computer science, drafting, air conditioning, and several other programs were placed with good firms, even before graduating."

"That's all very interesting. You've given our board something to think about We've taken pride in our outstanding liberal arts program. Now, according to your dossier you were editor of the *Arizona Vocational Review.* What was that all about? I never heard of the publication."

The chairman, opening his mouth wide while compressing his lower lip with his thumb and index finger, made two kissing sounds and asked, "How did you like being editor-in-chief of the *Arizona Vocational Review?*"

"I liked it very much. I made many friends while soliciting articles from teachers and administrators."

"How much did it pay?" the chair inquired.

"The money amount was zero. I spent many a weekend on my own time editing and writing, and planning the state convention. In order to tap state and federal money for vocational-technical programs the instructors had to file applications requiring up-to-date information about the ever-changing local, state and federal laws. Once that was done the dollars began to flow in."

"How much money, Dr. Zeitland?"

"At Phoenix Tech we received several hundred thousand each year through direct grants, start-up aid, scholarships and fellowships, plus funding for equipment and supplies. More recently, last year to be exact, when I started up the police science and electronics programs at Southwestern College, the college received 50% reimbursement of the teachers' salaries. Business and industry, through local advisory committees, became full-time partners with vocational-technical schools. As chairman of these committees I felt I played a good part in the communication process. My being president of the Arizona Vocational Guidance Association, editor of the *Vocational Review,* and, later, president of the State Vocational Association provided me with some of the richest experiences of my life."

"What were some of these rich experiences?"

"Well," I replied, rubbing my chin twice and waiting half a minute, "what happens in Washington, D.C. is of major importance to all of us in these United States. In the year I served as president of the state vocational association there was a strong movement in Congress to eliminate all federal aid to education, particularly vocational education. The Democrats had been in power for 20 years when suddenly a Republican general appeared on the horizon. He campaigned vigorously with a young, energetic California Senator promising to phase out or eliminate all federal involvement in education. They called for a return to the good old days where 'that government is best that governs least.' The politicians cited time and again proof that government support was not needed for a college to become great. Hillsdale College in Hillsdale, Michigan was cited as the best example of an independent college that had existed for over 100 years without a penny from government sources and still ranked as one of the best in the nation."

"Is that true, Dr. Zeitland?"

"Yes, it is. Hillsdale is a fine, small, liberal arts college serving a rather affluent student body. It would never accept the goals and objectives of a public community college. Open admissions would never fly in Hillsdale!"

"Continue, Dr. Zeitland."

"For a while it looked like the Smith-Hughes, George-Barden and other vocational acts would be repealed, just like Prohibition. The House and Senate had the votes – all that remained was to take an official count. It never took place."

The chairman, with both hands behind his head and a frown on his face, muttered, "How come, young man?"

"Thanks to the U.S. mail and AT&T, Washington legislators were flooded with the message: cut anywhere else, but leave vocational education alone. That year vocational education became a sacred cow, like Motherhood. The partnership between business and industry with vocational education was sealed in concrete. The people had spoken and no politician goes against the voice of the people.

"That November I attended the national convention of vocational educators in Boston. Dr. M. D. Mobley, the executive secretary of the association, congratulated me for the 1,000 letters, telegrams and phone calls I'd solicited from the general public and VIP's in Arizona. In no uncertain terms they'd told their lawmakers not to touch funding for vocational education."

The spirit of the interview picked up as I continued to speak and all the committee members scribbled on their yellow pads. The quiet and sedate group became noisy. The chairman called for order and commented, "Fifty per cent reimbursement of a teacher's salary is a big hunk of money. Where has Palomar been all these years? The first order of the day for our new president will be to prepare a list of the pros and cons pertaining to federal aid."

I thought much but said nothing as the board talked among themselves. Seven highly intelligent and respected men, but so ignorant about the benefits of federal aid. What an enigma! If only my old professor William Sears from the New York University Vocational Education Department could have been here. He wouldn't have believed this, but how proud he would have been of his A student with his master's degree in vocational education and guidance!

Several more questions followed but this time the interviewer wrote down my responses. I felt I had scored. When you talk about money and how to get it, everybody listens. As I left each board member got up to shake my hand and several said, "You'll be hearing from us soon."

The chairman gave me a lingering handshake, slowly placed his left hand on my shoulder and said, "We have two more candidates to interview and then we'll get back to you, Dr. Zeitland."

"I look forward to hearing from you," I added. "By the way, my name is Zeitlin, not Zeitland, but you came pretty close. I hope the day will come when you call me Herb."

The next day upon arriving in my office at Southwestern College I was greeted by the smiling president, Chet DeVore.

"Congratulations, Herb. I think you got the presidency at Palomar. The board chairman called me early this morning and asked me what you've accomplished this year as the dean of instruction. I told him you did a bang-up job in establishing the computer science and law enforcement programs."

"Was that all?"

"He also wanted to know how well you were liked by the faculty. I told him the faculty was charmed by you and your lovely wife when you gave the summer session windup party at your home."

"Anything else?"

"Oh yes, you're in, Herb. He wanted to know when you could be released from your contract at Southwestern. I told him after 30 days, subject to board approval."

I gave Chet a brotherly hug and thanked him for his wise counsel during the past two years. We both agreed it would be better not to mention this happening to anyone until that important phone call came in or upon receipt of a contract in the mail.

Chet's parting word was, "I told Joe Rindone that we weren't big enough to keep a hold on a Stanford man for long. They all rise to the top. Good luck, Herb."

The next week at the Southwestern instructional office was busy, since we were moving to a new campus and adding many new faculty. The phone was constantly ringing, with all the reference checks and interview scheduling, but there was no call from San Marcos, home of Palomar College. Finally, after a four-week wait, the Palomar board president wrote and thanked me for a splendid interview. But the job had gone to an internal applicant, their dean of instruction.

While walking along the beautiful Estero Beach waterfront with Eugenia, I replayed the Palomar interview several times. What had gone wrong? Had Chet DeVore exaggerated his dialogue with the Palomar board president? No, I think not. He wasn't one to joke. The sure thing just had not been sure.

A big wave forced us to retreat up the beach. We sat down and I asked my dear one, "Why didn't I get the job at Palomar?"

"You may never know! You can only speculate. Maybe you said too much in praise of New York. You know the conservative west doesn't like New Yorkers. They may have thought of you as just another smart aleck."

"That's possible, but when I left, several trustees stood up, shook my hand enthusiastically and said they'd be seeing me soon."

Eugenia frowned a little and said, "You probably came on too strong as a vocationalist. Boards and faculty want their college president to come from mathematics, science or the humanities–not industrial education.

"Do you really believe that?"

"Yes, I do. You got a clue when the question came up about Hillsdale College, the so-called great liberal arts college that's free of federal aid or control. Some of their trustees may think like the Hillsidale trustees."

"If that's so, then what chance does an industrial education major have?"

"Very little chance in that environment. I don't know of a single college president who came from a background in industrial/vocational education. Do you?"

"No, but get acquainted with the first. I'm going to get that job with the Melrose Park Community College and Technical Institute. Besides, the industrial/vocational education issue may have had nothing to do with my unsuccessful bid for the presidency. Their dean of instruction was on the inside track. Quite often boards do window dressing just to please the faculty and the public. So they go through the interesting motions of interviewing many."

I had to know more about Melrose Park. How did the city get its name? Mel-Rose–sounded romantic. Could it be that some guy by the name of Mel fell in love with a lady named Rose while meeting in the park? Sounds logical. Or could it be a beautiful park-lined town where everybody grew roses? I just didn't know, but I was curious to find out. Why had a town of 20,000 residents select the name of Melrose Park Community College and Technical Institute?

Would the suburbanites of Chicago accept me. with my Eli Wallach accent. I grew a little scared. My suspicion of midwesterners having an antipathy against New Yorkers reappeared. I recalled what my renowned Professor I. James Quillen of Stanford had once said, "The greatest collection of intellects and humane people meet regularly at the United Nations Building in New York City, where accents flourish and help to nourish the mind.

I had to stop my obsessive imaginings and get at the real facts. Here I was in Ensenada, Mexico without access to the university or city library of San Diego. I closed my eyes and went into deep thought as the family ate dinner. Suddenly Mark burst out, "Wake up, Dad! What are you thinking about?"

"Son, you caught me off guard. I was thinking about Melrose Park and wondering if they had good schools. By the way, have you seen any cars or trailers with Illinois license plates?"

"Well, today, Joyce and I saw plates from Alaska, Texas, Arizona, Montana and Maine, plus many other states. I don't remember seeing Illinois."

"Mark, I have a special job for you. Tomorrow morning I want you and Joyce to go up and down each line and roadway and find a vehicle from Illinois. We're looking for one from Chicago, Melrose Park, Oak Park or Elmwood Park. Even if you don't find any of those cities, please make note of anyone from Illinois."

And so my two eldest had a mission to fulfill for their Dad. The next afternoon Joyce ran up to me and shouted, "We did it, Dad! We found two, one from Joliet and one from Elmhurst." They gave me the site numbers.

Immediately, I checked the location of the cities in the road atlas and decided to visit the family from Elmhurst, six miles west of Melrose Park. After dinner Eugenia and I located the site and saw a mature couple sipping wine and talking sedately, outside of one of the most deluxe and largest trailers in the park. Parked nearby was their brand new Cadillac Coupe de Ville. Retired and rich, I thought I hesitated in my approach but Eugenia said, "They won't bite you. They look like very nice people, ask them."

Smiling and with confidence the Herb Zeitlins introduced themselves to the Richard Andersons with the remark, "We're both teachers from San Diego County and are thinking about moving to Illinois. Could you tell us something about your state?"

"I can but I won't. . .unless you agree to one condition."

"Pray tell. . .what's that condition?"

"That you and Eugenia join Florence and me in sitting down and sampling some of this Italian wine."

Laughingly I accepted as Richard poured and said, "You've come to the right party. My wife and I were born, bred and educated in the state of Illinois and so were both our folks. Before retiring last year, during 40 years with the State Farm Insurance Company as an adjuster, I traveled throughout the state, so I know the good and bad communities. What city are you interested in?"

"Have you heard of Melrose Park?"

"My God, you surely picked a humdinger!"

"Why is that?"

"It's the most politically corrupt city in the state."

"Why, what did they do?"

"They loaded the ballot boxes for John F. Kennedy. He never would have made the Presidency if it weren't for Mayor Richard Daley and his gang of precinct workers from Cook County, including Melrose Park. The state Republican Committee investigated voter fraud in Melrose Park and were shocked at what they found. Chicago and many of the cities in Cook County take pride in their corruption and their ability to get away with it."

"I find that hard to believe in this day and age."

"Herb, let me tell you this. Chicago and its suburbs for many generations have been known for nice homes and many factories, lovely churches and nearby vice centers, great entertainment and vulgar night spots, and always talk of Mafia-connected businessmen."

"Richard, that was in the good old days. It can't be happening today. The people are too educated. Chicagoland has some of the nation's greatest universities and most renowned professors. They wouldn't allow corruption to flourish."

"If you're thinking of moving to Illinois, pick Du Page County, where we're thinking about building a community college, not Cook County. Although the two counties are adjacent they're as different as day and night. Cook County suburbs and Chicago are predominately Democratic with many minorities, while Du Page is mostly white and one of the strongest seats of Republicanism in the nation."

"Are you really telling me I shouldn't take the job in Melrose Park?"

"Absolutely. . .unless you're someone who wants to put his hand in the cookie jar, and I don't think that educators are built that way."

"No, we are not." I turned to look at Eugenia. By now her forehead was wrinkled with disillusion and disappointment.

Saddened by the news she angrily said, "I don't think Melrose Park is the place for us."

We thanked the Andersons and left.

The trip back to Chula Vista was quiet and relaxing, except for the kids suddenly getting excited as they saw several people falling from a plane overhead. There was a Mexican Sky Diving Club nearby. Ann Victoria excitedly asked, "What would happen if the parachute didn't open?"

Mark, the eldest, brilliantly responded, "Instead of making a safe landing, he would hit the earth with a big bang and probably enter Saint Peter's garden. Those guys take a gamble on life every time they jump."

"Now listen, kids, this is one family that doesn't gamble on life. Your Mom and Dad want you all to go to college, develop high moral standards, get good jobs, get married and have children. And that will happen as long as Dad and I continue to work."

Then Eugenia, looking directly at me, slowly emphasized, "And that means *WE ARE NOT MOVING TO CHICAGOLAND EVEN IF DAD IS OFFERED TWICE HIS PRESENT SALARY.*"

"I agree with you completely, my dear. As soon as we get home I'll call Bob Collins and cancel the appointment. It's settled. It's all over! We are not leaving beautiful sunny California," I loudly proclaimed.

Never did our rented home look so good as when we drove into the driveway at 9 Sierra Way. The row of "Birds of Paradise" were ready to fly, a bird was biting on the fruit of the peach tree and the avocado tree was ready for picking. Our next door neighbor welcomed us back and presented us with a near ton of mail. We unpacked the trailer, put a hold on the mail, returned the trailer and became rejuvenated by eating double hamburgers at McDonald's.

Upon returning home I went into the family room to sort out the mail. Half of it was junk, several bills to be paid and letters from our parents. Last was a large brown, legal-sized envelope with several dollars worth of stamps on it, from Melrose Park. This was it! I sliced open the envelope, which contained a large blue book of 109 pages and a smaller gray book of 23 pages, both entitled, *A Proposed Community College.* I was impressed by the authors: Dr. Jack Childress, Dean of the School of Education, Boston University, and Dr. Frank Endicott, Director of Placement and Professor of Education, Northwestern University, both renowned educators from prestigious universities.

I started to read at 6:00 PM but couldn't put the material down until eight hours later. At two in the morning all the kids and Eugenia were sleeping, but I was so stimulated by the survey report that sleep was impossible. While a student at Stanford I'd read many an educational survey, but this one was superior in content, style and documentation, with a remarkable plan of action. I had to talk it over with Eugenia. I decided I was going to Melrose Park for the interview.

"What made you change your mind?" Eugenia asked.

"Melrose Park is only one of 20 or more communities that will comprise the college district. Surely a community of 20,000 can't control a district of 500,000 well-educated citizens."

"They can if the 480,000 other people are lethargic voters. Just remember, many a fine community may become corrupt when a few evil ones are able to operate without restraint."

"Not likely, my dear. Let me summarize my eight-hour analysis of this blue book. First, we have over 20 small cities in West Cook County, with a population of approximately 500,000 and an assessed wealth of almost $1.6 billion, wanting to form a community college. The proposed district is 19 miles long and the widest section is 7.5 miles. The district is saturated with light and heavy industry between highly populated areas. Secondly, they project a maximum going rate of 1.6

per cent, which in my opinion is extremely conservative."

"Back up a little. Just what is meant by the going rate? Is that in any way related to the prime rate of interest paid to depositors?"

"No, no, no. The going rate is simply the number of students going to college, divided by the total population of the district. When we lived in the remote desert area of Lancaster/Palmdale, 3,600 students attended Antelope Valley College from a total population of 50,000, a going rate of 7.2 per cent. This extremely high rate was due to the extensive evening programs, which attracted over 3,000 evening students. While I served as the dean of the evening division, we had over six times as many evening students as the day enrollment."

"And most of your students came from Edwards Air Force base, McDonnell Douglas, Northrup, Boeing and other aerospace companies. I think we should keep in mind that the Lancaster area, once a sleepy agricultural oasis, suddenly became inundated with brilliant scientists, engineers and computer tracking specialists who had little to do after work hours – and that's why the college became the center of challenging activities. Antelope Valley College was not a typical college and you can't use that as an example."

"You're right, Eugenia. However, if I can find a satisfactory site, with plenty of parking, and offer comprehensive programs taught by top-notch faculty in modern buildings on attractive grounds, and with low tuition, at least five per cent of the population will flow to the new college. That means 25,000 or more full and part-time students within a 10-to-15-year growth period. I'm amazed that the state of Illinois does not have a single public technical institute. With my experiences at Phoenix Technical Institute, Antelope Valley College and Southwestern College, I'm ideally suited for this new and challenging position. What do you think, Eugenia?"

"Go for it! Just remember, none of our kids have seen or felt snow or cold weather. We have, but they haven't! I wonder how they'll adjust and how long it will take. By the way, what did the gray book say?"

"The gray book talks about forming a smaller college about half the size that the blue book recommended."

"What brought that about?"

"I can't explain it fully, but for some unknown reason three of the most affluent school districts withdrew from the intended college."

"Why?"

"Maybe they didn't like Melrose Park being part of them, or perhaps the wealthy felt there was no need for a community college and technical institute. Their kids wouldn't go to a public college."

"You mean that in order to avoid another civil war the southern aristocracy this time peacefully withdrew from the union?"

"Yes, that's about it. What it means is that the new district will be cut in half. Eight hundred million assessed wealth instead of $1,600,000,000. Population will be reduced from 500,000 to 250,000, and maximum enrollment may be 12,500, not 25,000. If they're smart, and I think they are, they'll reconsider. It's a shame, however, that they won't be part of an historic beginning."

2
Drinking with the
Happy Board

When I landed at O'Hare Airport at 3:00 PM, I hailed a cab and was at the East Leyden High School within 25 minutes. Even though the weather was hot and muggy, I was fully charged with confidence as I greeted Wade Steel with a smile and a hearty handshake. We looked each other over. Mr. Steel was my height; we were both wearing white shirts and gray suits. There was perhaps a 25 years' difference in age, I with much brown and wavy hair and he with thinning gray hair that once was black. He was solemn and stoic, and in a dignified manner announced, "Dr. Zeitlin, we'll be having dinner with the board at the Red Steer Restaurant at 7:00 PM; following that we'll adjourn to the Melrose Park office for the interview."

He then pulled out an envelope from his desk and said, "The board will pay for your hotel and meals tomorrow, but I'll reimburse you now for your plane and taxi trips."

I showed him the ticket stubs and he counted out the amount to the penny. A strange sinking feeling came over me – he's paying me off even before the interview. Could it be that I waited too long? They've already hired their president and this will be another wasted interview. I hope not. I must think positively and go along with his script.

As he drove me to the Embassy Hotel on Manheim Road I wanted to ask him about what the board was going to quiz me on, but thought it inappropriate at the time. Instead I lightly asked, "Can you tell me something about the board members and their backgrounds?"

"Why of course. We have two lawyers. There's Democrat Joe Farmar, a precinct captain from Elmwood Park with a degree from

Notre Dame, who is now working for Bekins Moving & Storage as a labor attorney. Then there's Republican Elmore Boeger, a third generation resident of Hillside, graduate of Valparaiso University, and now a banking and probate lawyer. We also have four big supervisors: Robert Collins, born and bred in River Grove politics, is our board secretary and one of Illinois Bell's top supervisors. His uncle is mayor of River Grove. Fred Knol, a Sunday school teacher and precinct captain from Westchester, is our second supervisor. He's the boss of all heating treatment at Lindberg Heat Treatment Company. The third supervisor is Roy Jones from Hillside, party affiliation unknown, an executive with Commonwealth Edison Company. Roy also serves as a school board member of the Hillside School District. He won't be present because he just got married for the third time and is now on his honeymoon."

"Do you know what happened to Roy's first two marriages?"

"Yes, both his wives died, one from cancer and the other from a heart attack. He's now married to a dean of a small liberal arts college that his daughter is attending."

"I imagine the daughter had something to do with their getting together."

"Yes, she made it happen."

"Now, who is the fourth supervisor?"

"Babe Serpico. He's the top man in the Cook County Tax Assessor's Office. Babe is the boss of Melrose Park. a former All-American football great and presently the Democratic committeeman for the entire Proviso Township. His supervisor is Mayor Richard J. Daley."

"Excuse me. Does that mean that Chicago's greatest mayor will be calling the shots on this new college?"

"Oh no, we've been assured that he's not in the picture. He's so busy running Chicago and the Democratic Party that he won't have time to oversee the workings of a little college."

"Oh, Mr. Steel, this college may become a big college given the right circumstances. I think the survey was very conservative – the school has far greater potential than the experts predict"

"Dr. Zeitlin, we cannot predict the future. Time will tell and we shall see."

"Tell me about the seventh board member. What party is he a member of and what subject did he teach?"

"As the superintendent of schools I thought it best not to reveal my party affiliation since I had to work well with the Republicans and Democrats in order to get things done. Over 35 years ago I was hired by the Leyden High School District to teach biology, which I liked very much. I've seen good and bad times throughout the years. During the bad times, I organized the first teachers union in the Leyden District. Later on I was invited to become vice principal and finally superintendent."

"That's very impressive, a labor leader becoming a superintendent and later president of a college board. Now, the big question is how well these three Republican politicians will work with the two Democratic chiefs."

"Especially well. As a matter of fact they formed a coalition known as 'the committee for sensible school tax administration' and helped each other get elected. They forced out the independents and League of Women Voters candidate. You'll meet this fine working coalition in a few hours." He dropped me off at the hotel.

As we approached the front entrance to the Red Steer Restaurant four men wildly waved to us. They wore no jackets, were tieless and in shirt sleeves. As I got out of the car one of them popped out, "Welcome to Melrose Park, Dr. Zeitlin. How was your Mexican vacation? I'm Bob Collins, I spoke to you on the phone two weeks ago."

What a friendly guy, I thought, as I shook hands with a young, short, lively Mickey Rooney type, and responded, "Your directions were on the mark. It's a real pleasure to meet you, Mr. Collins. Our vacation in Mexico was great. The fish were biting and my daughter Joyce caught several big ones."

"Please just call me Bob."

"I will if you call me Herb."

Bob introduced me to the three other trustees as if he'd known me for a long time. All of them came forth and gave me a hearty welcome with a heavy handshake.

Fred Knol, the Sunday school teacher, looked and sounded like

Gary Cooper from *High Noon.* He asked, "Is there much technical education in the California community colleges?"

My immediate reply was, "There is some but not enough."

Standing next to Fred Knol and about the same height (6' 3") and weight was the thin man, attorney and banker, Elmore Boeger, a Gregory Peck prototype, who asked, "What's the size of the Chula Vista Rotary Club and what are some of their projects?"

I rattled off, "Eighty-five members, who strongly believe in service above self by raising money for college scholarships and providing meals and clothing to the unfortunate."

Next came heavyset Joe Farmar, the Notre Dame law school graduate, weighing in at around 260, whose voice and stature compared favorably with Jackie Gleason's of *The Honeymooners.* Grasping my hand and looking me straight in the eye he said, "Dr. Zeitlin, you are the first Stanford graduate I ever met and I'm pleasantly surprised. You don't fit the stereotype of a distinguished scholar. Your answers were short and direct. I thought you'd be a tall, thin, slightly bald, nervous type with eyeglasses, and verbose. Instead, you're just the opposite. You're good-looking with short and honest answers. I like you. We must talk more."

At this point stoic Wade Steel interrupted us with, "Fellows, we have a board meeting tonight after the interview, so let's get started."

Joe, having sensed a reluctant look on the faces of the other trustees, called out loudly, "Wade, we can wait. We promised Babe we wouldn't get started without him. . .so let's wait. We want to chat further with Dr. Zeitlin."

At that moment Joe was the officer in charge of the ship. Wade backed down a little. Around ten minutes later a short, dark-haired man with extraordinary presence, wearing an expensive suit and shirt, arrived in a big black Buick. All the fellows ran up to greet him enthusiastically. There was no question; he was the power behind the board. His iron grip while shaking my hand nearly cracked my bones. He relaxed the hand a bit, put his arm around my shoulder and said, "Sorry I'm late, Dr. Zeitlin. Let's all get to dinner."

Babe Serpico sat next to me during the dinner and asked me many questions about my family, what the kids were doing and did they like sports. I told him I had four children, ages five to fourteen. The oldest liked football a great deal but needed to gain a little weight before getting into the lineup. Babe had the same concern about his eldest, Joseph. As we continued to talk about sports Babe suddenly asked, "How many sports do you think the new college could field?"

"As many as the students and community want and are willing to support," I instantly responded. "Football, basketball, baseball, golf, swimming and hockey would be a good beginning if we can find the facilities and coaches. As the college grows in enrollment we would consider many other sports, both for men and women."

"That sounds like a good idea to me, Dr. Zeitlin. Women should have an equal opportunity for all sports. However, I don't think they should go into weight lifting. I like my women soft and gentle. I don't want to roll over while I'm sleeping and touch a muscle-bound rock."

Joe Farmar nodded his head in agreement, signaled the waiter and asked him to take the orders for drinks before presenting the menu. Then he looked at me and said, "You do drink – don't you, Dr. Zeitlin? If you don't, you're with the wrong party."

"I'm a beer man, Joe, and I do enjoy a Budweiser with steak and potatoes, but tonight looks like a special one so I'll join you with a Manhattan."

After the waiter took the orders for two Manhattans, two scotch and sodas, two martinis and one double martini the group settled down a bit as they perused the menu. As the drinks arrived the happy hour began with shouting and laughter. When the final dinner order was given Joe stood up and said, "Let's all have a second round."

Everyone responded positively except Wade Steel and Herb Zeitlin. We were the sober ones. I couldn't believe it. These boys made it a point to have fun before getting into the serious business of selecting a college president. What a contrast from the bland trustees from Palomar. Everyone enjoined the rapidly made epicurean dinners and spirits from the Red Steer. When the time came for dessert Joe and Bob ordered their third Manhattans. Wade and I had ice cream and coffee. And then we eagerly staggered to the small attorney's office a few blocks away at 1829 Broadway for the interview.

3
Three Day Interview

Wade called the meeting to order and apologized to me for the rushed affair. Everyone got very quiet when Wade asked in a low voice, "Dr. Zeitlin, we have a few questions we would like to ask you. First, tell us why you want to be a college president."

"To create something new, like a college, is very exciting both to a board and its president. A human being may live to be 70, 80 or 100 years old, but a college may live forever and I'd like to be a part of a good beginning. The two feasibility studies researched by the eminent scholars, which I read thoroughly, made some rather conservative forecasts. I feel this new college has far more potential than the experts have predicted."

As I finished answering the question several trustees hurriedly wrote on their yellow pads. Wade Steel continued with, "What past experiences have prepared you for these new challenges?"

"For over two years I've served as dean of instruction at Southwestern College in Chula Vista, California. The total enrollment is over 3,000, assessed wealth about $300,000,000 and the district population, 150,000. Although Southwestern College has half the population and one-third the assessed wealth, nevertheless it achieved an enrollment of over 3,000 within a three-year period, twice the number that the Endicott team has predicted for the Melrose Park college during the same time span."

Joe Farmar interrupted us with, "How do you account for this vast difference?"

"Californians take great pride in their tuition-free community colleges. Even though it hurts at times, they're willing to pay higher property taxes in order to build superior facilities. In my district fifty per cent of the high school graduates attend the community college. Given the right beginning this could happen here."

Wade continued, "Next question, please. What are your major duties as dean?"

"I recommend to the president the hiring of all full and part-time teachers, chair the curriculum and instruction committees, organize and chair the occupational advisory committees, conduct research, write news articles, edit the college catalog and serve as acting president during his absence."

Wade looked down at his paper, started to tap his fingers on the table, looked up and then sagaciously asked, "Now Dr. Zeitlin, should you be selected as our founding president, what would be first thing you'd do?"

I rubbed my hands over my forehead, hesitated a few seconds and then said slowly, "First and foremost I would develop procedures and policies with the board's approval so that we could have a good working relationship."

"Dr. Zeitlin, what would be your major priorities in getting this college started? Take your time."

"I can't predict the unexpected but I certainly would give a lot of time to the following major items of concern: surveying the community to determine its educational needs, publishing a first-class college catalog, locating temporary and permanent sites for the college campus, selecting a top-notch administration and faculty, passing a big bond issue, keeping the public informed, selecting an architect, building bridges of understanding with high school and elementary school principals and superintendents, developing articulation agreements with the universities, and maintaining an informed and positive relationship with local, state and federal officials. You may ask, which item is the most important? All of them are of equal importance; if I fail on any of them, it would be a drastic setback."

We all waited for Wade, Joe and Bob to finish writing. I expected one of them to quiz me further about some of the ten major concerns. None of them did. They looked at each other and waited. . .nothing came forth. Finally Wade in a pedantic manner asked, "Did you know that the Endicott team recommended a two-year planning period before opening the college? The board would like to start the college in a year. Do you think you could do it?"

"Yes, I'm sure we could do it if we all worked together. Presently in the U.S. an average of one new college district is formed per week. Some start off meekly, some slowly, hopping along aimlessly. Others plan well and become a dynamic influence in the community. I've read much about the founding of Stanford University and I would like to imitate their first president by hiring the best faculty, wherever we may find them."

"And where will you find them, Dr. Zeitlin?"

"Anywhere in the United States. California isn't the only state with great community colleges. Florida, Texas, Virginia, and New York are new pacesetters."

"And how does Illinois compare with these pacesetters?"

"Not very well. The surprising thing here is that the first public junior college opened in Joliet, Illinois and was well received around the turn of the century. Other states picked up the ball and advanced it down the field. Illinois in its reflected glory has stood still for the past 30 or more years. To stand still while all your neighbors are advancing is really going backwards, but there is new hope on the horizon if your Governor Kerner can get a new community college bill passed."

"In the meantime, where would you obtain high-caliber teachers?"

"Being adjacent to metropolitan Chicago is a godsend! You have some of the finest colleges, universities and high schools in the nation, plus a myriad of industry and commerce. We would recruit from them. We should have no trouble finding gifted, talented and superior teachers for the university transfer studies but might find it a little difficult to obtain acceptable vocational/technical instructors."

At the mention of vocational/technical Fred Knol leaned forward, pointed his finger at me and asked, "Now, Dr. Zeitlin, how serious are you about developing vocational/tech programs? At a recent conference that Elmore Boeger and I attended we were told that vocational/tech studies are the most neglected areas in almost all of the colleges."

Looking me straight in the eye Mr. Knol barked out, "You highly-educated Ph.D.'s are always promoting the liberal arts, the humanities and math and science. Now, tell me, am I right or not?"

I swallowed a little before replying, waited and said, "Yes, Mr. Knol, you are correct. However, I am the exception. I guarantee you if I get this job you will have a strong and varied voc/tech program, sometimes called 'industrial, occupational or career education.' You select whatever name you like. One thing all these names have in common is that the student upon completing the training has a job waiting for him or her. I'm amazed that none of the nearby colleges offer anything in electronics, auto mechanics, welding, machine shop, computer science, beauty culture, or law enforcement."

"And I suppose you would offer all of these programs if you became president?"

"Yes, I would, and right from the beginning. This new college must create the image from its opening day of a community college and technical institute for all the people."

Fred Knol continued, "That's all very good, Dr. Zeitlin, but can we afford it? I've heard all these programs are very expensive. Am I correct or not?"

"The answer is a big *yes.* They are expensive because of the small class sizes and the high-cost equipment, and that's why the federal government way back in 1916 passed the Smith-Hughes Act granting financial assistance to high schods and colleges offering these kinds of programs."

"I've never heard of the Smith-Hughes Act. Did Al Smith, the Democratic presidential candidate, have something to do with this law?"

"No, but historically the Democrats have supported federal aid to vocational and special education, starting with Woodrow Wilson, then Franklin Roosevelt, Harry Truman, Kennedy and Johnson. There's a lot of money out there, if only you go after it."

"Who is stupid enough not to go after it?"

"Well, many boards of education refuse to accept any financial assistance from the federal government. If the board will permit, I can explain in greater detail the myriad of sources."

Wade Steel got back on track with, "This board has as yet not adopted any policy with regard to accepting dollars from Washington, and we don't have time to listen to all the possibilities. Now let's get back to the next question. Dr. Zeitlin, what's the average cost per square foot for constructing college buildings in California? Do you think that here in Illinois we could build for $15 per square foot?"

"Maybe, but I wouldn't recommend it because they'd be the cheapest quality possible. These constructions, commonly known as butler buildings, would probably be made of sheet metal or aluminum, cold in the winter and hot in the summer. They're good for storage but not suitable for a college, plus being very expensive to heat or air condition. Today, we just completed a new campus for Southwestern College for approximately $35 per square foot."

"Could you do the same for our new college?"

"I can't answer that. Construction costs are determined by many factors, such as materials used, single level versus high rise, site preparation, landscaping, parking facilities and architectural style. Costs vary considerably among different states. I'm not an authority on Illinois construction costs. An Illinois school architect would be the best source of information on costs."

"After we hire our college president we'll start interviewing for an architect. Now, Dr. Zeitlin, for our last question, you may take as much time as needed to answer. How would you describe yourself physically, mentally, emotionally and socially?"

I hesitated, thinking about how best to reply. This was a new one for me. Should I blow my horn, hold back or unravel the pertinent points. I decided on the latter. "Physically, I am average height and weight, in excellent health, enjoy swimming a lot, was a lifeguard once, like to gallop when I go horseback riding, earned a letter in handball in high school, enjoy playing touch football or volleyball whenever I get together with my four brothers and wives, and way back passed the rigid 64 examination when I got my private pilot's license renewed."

"And how smart are you?" Wade Steel asked.

"In high school I was a member of the Arista honor society and was especially strong in math, science and history. While in college I worked over 20 hours per week in a New York office, did limited homework but managed to get mostly C's and B's and a few A's. As a graduate student in summer college I earned mostly B's and A's. At Stanford I worked very hard and was awarded mostly A's. My doctoral dissertation was featured in the *New York Times* as a scholarly contribution."

"How well can you control your emotions?"

"After serving over seven years as a school administrator, I can take it when it gets hot in the kitchen. Emotionally, I'm stable, orderly, practical, visionary and always striving for peaks of excellence in everything I do. My greatest pleasure is being with my wife and our four lovely children."

And then Wade Steel added, "Socially, how well do you get along with people? I mean the little guys as well as the big boys?"

"Very well, I feel. I like people. I like to joke with the janitors, kid with the clerical staff, drink beer with the faculty and administration and have tea or coffee with community members. During my four years in high school I was honored to be elected president of eight different student organizations and clubs. While an educator, I was selected by my colleagues to serve as president of the two different professional organizations. And more recently the Lancaster, California Rotary Club elected me as their president."

"Well, Dr. Zeitlin, you certainly have a very impressive record and you've given this board something to think about. I don't mean to be curt, but we have a meeting in ten minutes so we have to end this interview. We want to thank you for coming here and wish you well on your return trip to California."

So that's it! Thank you and so long – and all the time I thought I was doing well. I was impressed with this group's unusual questions. I wanted to be part of them but the ball had bounced in the opposite direction. Another Palomar experience, I thought I got up from my seat slowly, looked around, grabbed the blue and gray feasibility booklets, thanked Wade for the interview, and then gave a farewell wave to the rest of the board, when Ralph Serpico stood up and abruptly called out, "Hey, wait a minute, Dr. Zeitlln. I've got a question to ask you."

"Fire away, Mr. Serpico," I responded, while placing my hand on the doorknob.

"I want to know, how well do you work with politicians? You know, Dr. Zeitlin, you have a coalition of two leading Republicans and two top-notch Democrats on this board. Can you work with us?"

"Yes, I would always strive to keep the two parties together for the betterment of the college. When there's a team approach, you can produce miracles."

At this moment Joe Farmar and Bob Collins stood up together and accosted Mr. Steel. "Wade, if Herb can stay over for another night,

Bob and I would like to get his professional opinion on the selection of the River Grove site for the college campus. We could pick him up at the hotel at 9:00 AM and spend a few hours showing him the alternatives. I'm sure he would like to get a feel of the land."

"Can you, Dr. Zeitlin?" Wade asked.

The room became very silent again. Everyone was waiting for my response. I suddenly felt I was in again. Joe, Bob and Ralph were nervously smiling at me. I put my two booklets down on the table and loudly proclaimed, "I would be delighted to. I came here to get this job and I would like to see and learn more about the communities. That may take more than a day."

"Good, then it's settled. We'll see you tomorrow," proclaimed a happy Joe Farmar as he and all the others hurried to their cars to get to the board meeting. Wade dropped me off at the Embassy Hotel as he proceeded to East Leyden High School, where the board was scheduled to reassemble.

Shortly before nine the next morning Bob and Joe arrived at the Embassy. Bob insisted that I take the front seat while Joe did the driving. The view of the community was better from the front than from the rear, Bob proclaimed. They really treated me like an honored dignitary instead of an applicant for a job. The conversation flowed easily about our families. As we slowly drove south on Manheim Road Joe told me that the busiest and largest airport in the world, O'Hare Field, was adjacent to the college district. The nearby hotels, motels, shops, restaurants, all in the district, profited tremendously from the influx of the tourist and business trades.

When we reached North Avenue, we went east and Joe called off the many manufacturing plants along the way, adding that they were the biggest taxpayers and were all prosperous and expanding. Unquestionably, there was a great need for industrial workers for the thousands of companies in Chicagoland, the number two city in the nation.

When we reached Fifth Avenue and Palmer, Bob cried out proudly, "This is my hometown. I was born and have lived here all of my twenty-seven years, and I never intend to leave. My uncle is the mayor, but these days I'm at odds with him. He wants to see all of these

40 farm acres sold to light industry, which would produce more taxable income for River Grove than residential property. I told him we're going to build a college here and he said, 'No way. We don't need a college, and besides that colleges are tax-exempt. So, dear nephew, secretary of the board, go find a site anywhere else in the district, but not in River Grove!' Right now there's very little conversation between the mayor and his nephew. We communicate through my mother, his sister."

"That's a tough family situation."

"You're telling me. It gets tougher each day. I admired, respected and applauded him for many years. He's the most liked man in River Grove. He knows more about good and dirty politics than anyone I know. He was my idol. I wanted so much to be like him. Now, I'm not sure."

"Bob, you're the one to be admired. You have more foresight than your uncle. You can see the positive effects of having a college in your community. I'm sure your uncle will feel differently once the college is built. Time heals wounds and one day he'll reflect with pride as River Grove becomes known as the home of a great college."

"You're sure it's going to be a great college?"

"I am positive!"

"Well, I hope so. Now, Herb, what do you really think of this site? Is this a good beginning or not?"

"I like it. It's a good location with easy access, and faces a wide highway. Does that Des Plames River across the street ever overflow onto this land?"

"No, that is, I don't ever remember it happening in my lifetime."

"Being across the street from a beautiful forest preserve is a positive ingredient. You know, 40 acres is not much for a campus. What are the chances of expanding to the south, west and east?"

"It would be quite possible to add another 12 or more acres on the east side by acquiring the River Grove dump site and the small landlocked field. But it would be almost impossibly expensive to acquire the 20-acre trailer court on the south side."

"Why?"

"I found out that the trailer court is making big money for its owners and they don't want to sell. They'll fight us all the way."

"That's understandable. Now, Bob, look across the street. I see a possible paradise ahead. I see a large and beautiful green golf range, an old Outdoor Theater and a summer kiddieland. To acquire all those sites would be wonderful."

"Herb, those three grounds are untouchable. The original survey team was smart enough not to mention them."

"Who owns them?"

"They're owned by special interests."

"What are special interests?"

"When you live in Chicagoland you learn after a while not to ask about special interests – so drop it."

His answer disturbed me. I didn't like his curt response but since I was the applicant I followed his direction and left it at, "Hmm, that's interesting."

Joe Farmar interrupted our dialogue with, "Another possibility is the 18-acre Maywood dump yard. Let's drive over."

We drove south on Fifth Avenue. After we passed over North Avenue Joe announced we were now entering Maywood, an old community with many traditions. He stressed the fact that property values had been dropping for several years and we could obtain the 18 acres at a very low cost. A group of realtors had made a board presentation pointing out the possible benefits of this land to the college. They'd even offered to cut their commission in half if the college had difficulty in financing. After we got out of the car to look at the dump, Joe stopped me, put his hand on my shoulder and asked, "How would you advise the board to handle this situation?"

I looked at the dump and was distressed to see old refrigerators, washing machines, dryers, furniture, files, kitchenware, miscellaneous trash and papers piled up in a pyramid. A few rodents appeared as we walked around and stepped on the debris. As we retreated from the smell of sewage I remarked to Joe, "You don't want to offend the realtors. They're an important asset to every community. Thank them for their generous offer and expression of keen interest in the college's development. Tell them no decision can be made until the president and architect are hired."

"Herb, you must be psychic! That's exactly what we said. Well, I'm hungry. Let's go to lunch. We need to talk some more. This time we'll take Herb to Horwath's, the best restaurant in Elmwood Park"

Joe ordered Manhattans for all three of us before the waiter took our orders. He then proceeded to talk about his wife, Ceil. First, she was beautiful and intelligent. Second, she was a remarkable mother to his children and third, she was a terrific social asset. She was great at entertaining and charmed all his clients, including many lawyers. Joe proclaimed that marrying Ceil was the smartest thing he ever did.

Suddenly Bob burst out with, "I can say the same thing about my Beverly. She's the greatest! However, we can't afford to entertain much in our humble bungalow. Joe makes a lot more money than I do and owns a big house in the elite section of Elmwood Park. The only difference between the two women is that my wife is a better cook. Wouldn't you say so, Joe?"

"Yes, I have to agree. Beverly prepared a wonderful meal for the Farmars recently. Now, Herb, give us the full story about you and Eugenia. How did you first meet?"

I felt a little awkward, not knowing what to reveal. In California, where fifty per cent or more of the marriages end up in divorce, it was so refreshing to hear two Illinois husbands go into ecstasy about their lifelong partners. Can it be for real? I wondered, and accepted what I heard.

Thinking back 15 years I readily recalled a most pleasant moment in my life and said, "I was strongly attracted to Eugenia's beauty and intelligence when the principal first introduced her at a faculty meeting. Shortly after, an enterprising PTA president and principal's secretary talked us into taking small but romantic parts in a school play. We started to rehearse during the lunch hour in my shop. We continued to practice our lines as I drove her to the Long Island Railroad Station. I had difficulty doing the kissing scene and had to practice a lot.

"Opening night we reached perfection, and brought down the house with a sustained embrace and kiss. The principal reprimanded me for the smooching. He was jealous, but his wife said bravo. After the show she insisted that the most romantic couple at the Merrick School have dinner at her home. In the months that followed we discovered that we had many things in common. We both wanted to travel, advance in the educational profession, make a contribution to society, help our families and have many children together. When I got nominated for a counseling position with the Phoenix Technical Institute, which later I took, we decided the time was ripe to form a permanent alliance. And here we are, 15 years later, with four children, ages five to 14."

"How long did you live in Phoenix?"

"I served as a counselor and director of testing for over seven years and between babies Eugenia taught eighth grade and high school English, and later became a counselor at West Phoenix High SchooL"

"How are the summers in Phoenix?"

"Natives and old-timers never talk about the weather, while newcomers always do. It's hot enough to fry an egg on the sidewalk; temperatures vary from a cool 90 to a maximum of 128 degrees. Fortunately, we spent most of our summers in northern Califoruia."

"Herb, I don't think my family or I could take it in Phoenix. Did you enjoy your summers in California?"

"Very much so. I worked very hard during the summers at Stanford keeping up with the best graduate students in the nation and becoming part of the school plant facilities lab. Eugenia helped me greatly with some of the research work for my doctoral dissertation. After obtaining my degree, I worked for five and half years at the Antelope Valley High School and Junior College District in Lancaster, California, first as dean of the evening college and director of adult education and later as principal of the largest high school. During that time Eugenia taught English 1A two nights a week at the college."

"What made you move to Chula Vista?"

"Well, after thirteen years the desert was finally getting to us. When the offer came to live in paradise land, the San Diego Coastal area, we took it. I enjoy my job as dean of instruction at Southwestern College very much. The community, climate, facilities and faculty are delightful and after three years of holding classes in a local high school from 4 to 10 PM, we're about to move onto a sparkling new college campus."

"So, why leave?"

"To create a college from the very beginning is a terrific challenge, and with my specialized training and experience I am ready, willing and able to produce. Fred Knol made a very accurate and significant statement about the lack of voc/tech programs in colleges. The higher education family is responsible for this predicament. If I am hired, I guarantee you this western suburb of Chicago will become the technical training center of the midwest."

"Herb, Bob and I support you for the presidency, but we're only two from a body of seven. I need to speak to Wade and the Babe. Can you delay your flying back to California another day?

"Yes."

"Good. I'll take you back to the hotel and call you before 4:00 PM."

At 3:45 Joe called back and said, "Here's the deal. The board likes you but they will make no offer without seeing your wife. Can you get her out here tomorrow for an 8:00 PM dinner meeting with all the trustees and their wives? It's important that you do this. Can you do it? Call her now and get back to me as soon as possible."

"I'll try to reach her. It's 1:45 PM California time and she may be out."

"Keep trying. I'll be home in an hour but you can call me up to 11:00 PM. I hope she can make it."

"I hope so, too. I'll call you back as soon as I have an answer."

I immediately called Eugenia. No answer at 3:45 PM Chicago time. Tried again at 4:15, 4:45, 5:15, 5:45, 6:15. Where, oh where is Eugenia? The kids are usually home at this time and Mother is preparing the evening meal. Where can she be? The mind takes you on long journeys when you are impatient. I saw some beautiful scenery along the way, then suddenly a horrible auto accident God forbid, she had an accident!

On the seventh call she answered. "Hello, darling. How are things going?"

"Fine. Where the heck have you been? I've been trying to reach you for the last three hours."

"Today was a hot one. The temperature reached 88 degrees, so we all packed the car and went to Silver Strand Beach. It was great. Sorry you couldn't join us. Well, what's happening?"

"The interview went rather well. The board is interested in me but can't make any offer until they meet you. Could you hop on a plane and be out here before 8:00 PM for a dinner meeting tomorrow night with all the trustees and their wives?"

"You must be crazy. I can't do it."

"Why not?"

"It's impossible. Too short a notice. I'd have to get someone to watch the kids. Get food in the house before leaving, get plane tickets – and all within the next hour or two. No, no, no. I can't do it. You're asking too much. And besides, if you don't get the job, you'll blame it on me."

"No, I won't. Think about it and call me back within the hour. I know you can do it."

"The answer will still be *no*." She hung up with a big bang.

I waited and waited. Would she call back? I thought so but I couldn't be sure. After an hour had passed I accepted her "No" as the final answer and decided to call Joe back. What should I tell him? The truth, of course. Joe would then realize that Eugenia carried the weight in our family. Oh well, wasn't it true in most families? I called Joe and his line was busy. I thought and thought. Maybe all those stories about Chicago, the Mafia and corruption were true. It was so good to know that I still had my job in Chula Vista, the best place in the nation to live.

As the phone rang my thoughts immediately shifted to a more positive picture. Alas, it was the hotel manager wanting to know if I was going to stay over on Friday. I told him I would let him know the next day. I tried calling Joe again. His line was still busy. He must have a teenager in the family. It was 8:15 PM. Joe's line was still busy. My phone rang. Eugenia!

"Sweetheart, I got a morning plane to O'Hare, arriving at 5:05 PM. Can you meet me there?"

"That's wonderful. I'll rent a car and meet you. How did you do it?"

"I was lucky. Mrs. Manning is available up to Sunday evening and she'll take me to the airport tomorrow morning. Now, I have to get some food in the house. I don't know what I'm going to do with my hair. What should I wear for the evening affair?"

"Wear something nice."

"Thanks a lot, that really helps me. What's the temperature?"

"A sticky 90 degrees with no wind."

"Tell me about the trustees. What are they like?"

"I've met six very intelligent gentlemen who drink a lot and love to have fun. They're always joking but can get serious when an important issue is discussed."

"Describe them to me."

"You have the likes of Gregory Peck, Gary Cooper, Jackie Gleason, Mickey Rooney, Mr. Straight Lace and *On the Waterfront's* Marion Brando."

"What do they do for a living?"

"Brando is a Cook County Tax Assessor. He takes his orders from Mayor Richard Daley. Mr. Straight Lace is the superintendent of the Leyden High School District, and the energetic Mickey Rooney is a young supervisor for the Illinois Telephone Company."

"Tell me more about these twin Hollywood stars."

"Jackie Gleason is a middle-aged attorney for Bekins Moving and Storage Company, while Gregory Peck is a banker and attorney specializing in probate cases. He's also a Rotarian – that's a good sign. Gary Cooper is a Sunday school teacher and a supervisor for a large steel heating plant."

"That's a very impressive board. I'm getting nervous."

"Don't be. I'll go into greater detail about these fellows when I pick you up at O'Hare. We've got to cut these long distance calls short. They cost me a small fortune. Good-bye, my love."

When Eugenia got off the airport ramp I greeted her with a big hug and a lingering kiss. This mother of four, wife of a small-town college administrator, was absolutely the most beautiful woman in the world. Her beauty had improved with each passing year of our 15 years of marriage. I'd said she could do it and she had. I reflected on the vicissitudes of our years together. Two adventurous teachers hailing from the big city of New York settling down in the small town of Phoenix, population 90,000 and 2,700 miles away from our families. What would the future hold?

The birth of Mark, our first child, weighing in at 9 1/2 pounds, the heaviest baby born at the Good Samaritan Hospital at that time. His early rash problems finally solved by substituting goat's milk for regular milk. The easy birth and lovely beginnings of Joyce.

Eugenia had been so happy when we bought our lovely first home with nothing down, thanks to the G.I. Bill. Her early success as a trade journal writer and the moving up from eighth grade English teacher to high school English teacher and then high school counselor had made her feel much appreciated.

Packing and unpacking for five summer sessions at Stanford had been stressful, but she had adjusted cheerfully. Working together in the research phase of my doctoral dissertation was challenging and fun. After 7½ years in Phoenix, I accepted a big promotion to dean of the evening college and director of adult education at the Antelope Valley College in Lancaster, California. Eugenia stayed behind in Phoenix with the two kids in order to sell our home. I was amazed that she did it within 60 days and with a profit of over 20 per cent above our purchase price. That's when I began to realize that buying and selling real estate was another way to get rich.

With the profit from the sale of our Phoenix home, we immediately purchased a lovely three bedroom, two bath tract home on a large site in an up-and-coming area of Lancaster. Real estate values were climbing at the rate of five to ten per cent per year in southern California, so we decided to rent our Lancaster home when we moved to Chula Vista. And here we were in Chicagoland, anticipating another move so that I could advance professionally and accept the challenge of starting a new college.

What a wife! To think that within one hour's time she'd worked out the details on how to get to Chicago and leave the kids with a good housekeeper. I confessed to Eugenia that I thought she was remarkable and if I didn't get the position I'd be happy to stay in Chula Vista as long as she was with me.

Millions of novels have been written about love and words expressing love have inspired people throughout the world. But the trust test of love is when one has to walk the extra mile to please the partner. Eugenia did more than walk the extra mile, she flew 2,000 miles on very short notice.

As we drove to the hotel I updated her on the background of the trustees. It was a political board with two big Democrats and two grand Republicans working together for the benefit of the college.

"How can that be?" she asked. "I thought they were natural enemies."

"Not in this case, my dear. These men are astonishing and appear to be united in wanting to create a great college."

Poker-faced Wade Steel, wearing a well-tailored suit, arrived at our hotel with his wife Mildred two hours later. His mood had changed from stoic to charming and gracious. He opened the back door of his car and waited for Eugenia to enter. He apologized for the board's unusual request to see the presidential candidate's wife and complimented her on her beautiful dress. What a contrast from the way he'd treated me at our initial contact, when he'd paid me off. Could he have changed that much in 48 hours, or was it Eugenia's presence that had caused the change? I didn't care. It was just great seeing him in this fine frame of mind – maybe it was a good omen.

Gray-haired Mildred, in her sixties, was exceptionally pleasant and cheerful. She asked so many questions about our children and Eugenia responded with enthusiasm and humility. In the past Mildred had been a social worker and teacher in the slum area of Chicago, where she first met Wade. The Steels had no children of their own but felt that all the graduates of Leyden High School were their family.

When we arrived at the elegant Red Steer Restaurant, Wade jumped out of his car and helped Eugenia out of the rear. I, on the other hand, wanting to show my good breeding per Vance Packard's Status Seekers, rushed over to Mildred's door to open it and escorted her to the entrance of the restaurant. Eugenia took Wade's arm and followed us. We switched from the middle class practice in car seating where married couples go arm and arm to the upper class practice of shifting partners. It was rather nice chatting and laughing with Mildred.

As the couples entered the lobby of the restaurant a sudden round of applause and cheers went up with Joe Farmar proclaiming, "Hurrah, you're here! What took you so long? Now let's get acquainted."

I looked around. There were five other couples. All beautiful, active people and dressed to kill. The ladies all seemed to be wearing big diamond rings, dazzling earrings, stunning gold necklaces and glittering gowns. I felt I was among the rich and famous. Wade and I wore our conservative gray and the other men wore well-tailored blue and black.

Several of the ladies simultaneously came up to Mildred and me and one of them said, "Welcome to Illinois, Dr. Zeitlin, and a hearty welcome to you, Eugenia."

Mildred was startled and immediately responded with, "I'm Mildred Steel, Wade's wife. The beautiful girl behind me is Eugenia, Dr. Zeitlin's wife."

The spokeslady for the trustees' wives felt embarrassed, her light skin turning red, but she recovered quickly, "Well, Fred told me that Dr. Zeitlin's wife was mature, intelligent and beautiful, and that fits you, Mildred."

They all laughted as Mildred found Wade and Eugenia found her life partner. Wade then proceded to introduce Eugenia and me to each trustee and his wife. They all seemed so gracious, kind and considerate. This was not the usual interview. This was a party and we were going to have fun. And so the drinks flowed as we feasted on the gourmet food and delightful conversation about families, sports, movies and the differences between Chicago and San Diego.

There was no question about it. This big happy family of 14 positive personalities was enjoying each other's company. There wasn't a negative individual in the group.

After two and a half hours of frolicking Babe Serpico approached Wade Steel from the rear and whispered something in his ear. The whispering continued between the two for several minutes. Finally Wade asked, "Are all the boys in agreement?"

Babe nodded. Wade then stood up, clicked his empty Manhattan glass with a spoon and announced, "Sorry to interrupt these festivities but we've got important business to accomplish this evening, so let's all go over to the college office right now."

Ten minutes later we all reassembled at 1829 Broadway. The ladies were asked to wait in the small outer office while the men flocked together behind the closed doors of attorney Gus Taddeo's place of business, next door to the college office. Silence again became golden as Wade started to speak

"Dr. Zeitlin, I am happy to inform you that this board wants you to become our first president. It was a unanimous decision. Now, can you get released from your contract and start work for us on or before October 1st?"

"Yes, I can. The Southwestern College board has a policy of releasing any administrator that's offered a promotion within a 30-day period. However, I won't make this request until I have a written contract from you. Can you do this within a week?"

"Yes, I'm sure we can. We'll talk to Don Dunahow, our attorney, on Monday and he'll draw up the terms and conditions to be included in the contract, such as salary, length of contract (one year to start with), vacation time of 30 days per year, relocation expense account, plus all the other details."

I kept a poker face and thought deeply. In starting up a college there would be many pleasures and pressures right and left. If I took a wrong turn during the first 12 months, I could be dismissed promptly. There'd be no tenure with a one-year agreement. With no job and no income, how could I support a wife and four kids?

"Gentlemen," I said, "I like you all very much and would like to become part of your team in a long-term relationship, not just for a year. To begin with it would have to be a three or four-year contract."

Wade hadn't anticipated this response and didn't know how to handle it. He first looked at Babe, then Joe and then all the rest of the boys. We were at an impasse. I was determined not to speak. In previous negotiating sessions I had learned that the first one to speak when you're deadlocked will make a compromise suggestion. Finally, after a long silence, Elmore Boeger, the experienced legal university advisor, got the picture. "I think Herb's request is reasonable. You can't accurately judge a president's performance within a year. Therefore, I recommend we give Herb a three-year contract. At Valparaiso University that's the usual pattern."

Wade surveyed the land and all the trustees nodded approval or sounded off with a loud "Yes."

"That's fine. Now, that's settled. You'll be mailed a three-year contract within the week. Are there any other matters to discuss?"

"Mr. Steel, we haven't discussed salary yet."

Wade read off the beginning and maximum salaries of the high school superintendents within the suburbs of Chicago and then said, "You have 7½ years of administrative experience so that puts you in the middle range." He pointed to a figure on his paper. "Is that satisfactory?"

Without blinking an eye I said, "Yes."

"And of course, Dr. Zeitlin, you can expect a raise every year after we evaluate your work each April."

I'd recently received a $500 raise from Southwestern, so I could hardly believe my ears when I realized I'd be making $7,000 more by working in Illinois. At last, I could buy Eugenia her own car. I waited to scream with joy and say yes indeed, but held back, not wanting to appear too anxious. I realized how right my old professor at NYU, Bill Sears, had been: "The Chicago suburbs have the best high schools in the nation and the people are willing to pay the price."

Before adjourning the meeting Wade spoke to me in a low and melodic voice. "I must say, Dr. Zeitlin, you have a beautiful, intelligent and charming wife. We all enjoyed her company very much. She'll be great at entertaining. The board wishes you and Eugenia much success as you become our first president and she our new first lady."

Joe Farmar, picking up Wade's line, opened the door and announced, "Ladies, meet the new president of our college and his first lady."

Cheers and applause came forth from the wives. Eugenia congratulated me with a short tender kiss. Congratulatory handshakes, hugs and kisses became the order of the day. This was one happy moment in the life of a college administrator.

I wondered what my blue collar immigrant father would have said had he suddenly awakened after resting for over a year. Probably, "Only in America could a shop teacher become a college president"

As Eugenia and I got into Wade's car, Cecile Farmar called out, "When are you two flying back?"

Eugenia responded, "Sunday after 2:00 PM. We're planning on spending all day tomorrow looking for a home. Herb wants to live close to the college so I guess we'll start looking in Melrose Park?

"What are you looking for?"

"Four bedrooms with two baths and a nice backyard on a quiet street."

"Try Oak Park or Elmwood Park. I don't think you'll find it in Melrose."

Mildred turned to Wade and asked, "Do you know of any homes in Franklin Park that the Zeitlins might like?"

"I'm not aware of any, Mildred. Most of our homes are modest two or three bedrooms. It's going to be hard to find a four bedroom. Eugenia, check the newspapers."

"Thanks for the tip." We drove off to our hotel.

Before going to bed Eugenia grabbed a *Chicago Tribune* and a *Sun Times* and started to check off the homes for sale. We talked a lot; we couldn't get to sleep for all the excitement, enthusiasm and joy. A new job with a big raise, a new home, new schools for the kids, new doctors, new dentist, plus new friends. What would our new life be like? What did the Almighty have in store for us?

After finishing an early breakfast Eugenia got on the phone and made several appointments with enthusiastic real estate agents. We looked. They showed. No go. We were not "looky lews." We wanted to buy. There wasn't anything like our 9 Sierra Way, Chula Vista home. The homes we saw were small, dark, no yard or little yard and built 40 to 50 years earlier. It was going to take more than a Saturday to find our new dream home. The agents recommended Oak Park for big homes or the distant suburbs of Du Page County for newer ones. Eugenia lit up at this spirited advice. I objected: our new residence had to be in the college district. What kind of president would I be if I didn't live with my larger college family?

We said so long to the Melrose Park agent and started to look on our own. I drove to the River Grove site and surveyed the area. Small and unpretentious bungalows without a single "for sale" sign. I quickly moved along to the village of Elmwood Park, Joe and Cecile Farmar's residential area. The houses were newer, more attractive and bigger, and the curb appeal was great. This was the region we liked.

I rang the bell on a home with a large sign that read "for sale by owner." He welcomed us and was exceptionally cordial. Eugenia liked everything about the 3,000 square foot home and I agreed with her. At 6:30 PM we'd found it. Eureka! Illinois, here we come. But then the good news turned sour when we heard the price. He was asking two and a half times the price of our California house. I couldn't believe it. It was sticker shock. Even with the $7,000 raise it would be difficult for me to finance it.

Saddened by the news, we felt the need for a pick-me-up and decided to have dinner at a Chinese restaurant to refocus on the last 24 hours. As we were drinking our tea Eugenia laughingly asked me to open my fortune cookie. I said, "You know I don't believe in that stuff. It's silly and just another way to make money for the cookie maker."

"Please open it. . .No lectures, please."

"Well, OK, if you open yours first."

"Oh, this is great! It's a good omen – *The best is yet to come.* What's your fortune?"

"It will probably say I'm going to win the lottery or go on a long cruise. Well, here goes. *You should be able to undertake and complete anything.* Well, how do you like that? I'm going to glue this in my appointment book for posterity."

"Darling, just you wait. Everything is going to turn out fine. I don't know why you still have reservations. I particularly liked talking to Bob Collins. He asked so many questions about you. He's so young, yet so mature. All the trustees and their wives like you and you made them quite excited with your optimistic forecasts for the new college."

"I agree with you fully, my dear, and I do feel fortunate in connecting with such fun-loving and intelligent gentlemen. I'm sure they're for real. If they're not then they truly gave 'Oscar' caliber performances."

4
Southwestern Faculty Reaction

It was exhilarating returning to the Southwestern campus. I had a secret, and I told no one. I didn't want a replay of the Palomar fiasco. My president, Chet DeVore, greeted me. "Welcome back, Herb. Start packing, we're moving to our new campus in three days. By the way, how was the fishing?"

I wondered if he knew. Had someone contacted him about me? After all, "How was the fishing?" could mean many things.

He was a very smart man and his subtleties were not always easy to detect, so I replied, "Great! Joyce caught three little ones, Mark caught one big one and Eugenia, Ann and Clare caught sunburn," and left it at that. I decided to wait for the signed contract before informing him.

With the announcement of the movement to the new site there was a surge in enrollment, forcing me to add several new class sections in mathematics, English, reading, police science and computer science. Fortunately, in record time I found the part-time teachers to cover them.

On Wednesday the college staff moved to the new campus. No grass, dusty roads, some clogged plumbing – but the excitement was great. At last, our own campus. No more sharing facilities with the high school. We were now truly a community college, ready, willing and able to join the prestigious colleges of southwestern California. My office was light and bright with many bookcases, ample room for my secretary and a large and attractive reception area. My newly-appointed assistant dean had an office adjacent to mine. I felt wonderful. Again I asked myself, why should I leave? It was still not too late to change my mind and live the good life with my family.

Finally, late afternoon on Friday, August 28th, Eugenia called to tell me that a large brown envelope had arrived from the Melrose Park Community College. When I arrived home around 6:00 PM, my gastric juices started to flow as I opened the large holder of good news. There, on five legal-sized sheets, spelled out in detail in ten separate paragraphs, were the duties and responsibilities of the college president. What a contrast from my one-page agreement with Southwestern. The contract was signed by the president of the board and its secretary and approved as to form and legality by attorney Don Dunahow. I wondered what kind of attorney this Don Dunahow was. He certainly covered a lot of ground, was even verbose in some areas. But he was very thorough throughout. I particularly liked the sentence, "He shall be entitled to thirty calendar days of annual vacation with full pay."

I accepted as an oversight the omission of relocation expenses for the president and his family that Wade Steel had agreed to during the interview. The 30-day deadline notice to Southwestern was approaching and they had to be informed the following week at the latest. I signed the contract and put it in the mail.

On Saturday morning I went over to Chet's house, a block away from where I lived, and submitted my resignation, to be effective 30 days later. Chet congratulated me, wished me well and asked if he could announce my promotion at the faculty meeting before school on Monday morning. I reluctantly agreed and then told him I might be a little late for the meeting, as I had to orient two new instructors.

I arrived at the faculty meeting a half hour late. As I entered the assembly hall, President DeVore asked me to introduce the two new staff members. Upon completing the introductions I asked the faculty to give the attractive young sociology lady and the handsome electronics instructor a hearty welcome.

I had no sooner stopped talking when the entire faculty stood up, applauded, cheered and whistled. I was shaken by this strange and unusual behavior of the usually sedate Southwestern faculty and said to the newcomers, "From the welcome you've just received you can truly see what a friendly faculty we have here."

Instantly, Waddie Deddah, a faculty spokesman, stood up and said, "Dr. Zeitlin, congratulations. Chet just told us about your big promotion. We were fortunate to have you for two and a half years.

Now Chicago will get California's best."

I smiled with joy and felt a lump in my throat as Chet continued the meeting with reports from the other deans, division chairs, counselors and the athletic director. Gee, I loved this group. It was going to be harder to leave than I thought. The final speaker was Joe Rindone, the superintendent and chief administrator of the district.

When Joe walked up to the podium he started to unload material from his attaché case and said, "I won't be long."

Instant laughter followed with a remark from the rear, "Don't bet on it."

"I want to briefly tell you about how this college district was formed. Over three years ago we mailed to all our taxpayers this brochure, which pointed out the advantages of having a college within the community, and what it would cost. Chet and I spoke to every service club and PTA that would listen to us during an intensive three-month campaign period. An election was held and the people gave us a strong Yes vote. Herb, do you think you could use this brochure?"

"Yes, I'd be delighted to have it"

"Here, catch it. If it worked for me, surely it will work for you. Now, once a college district is formed a major problem is how you find out what courses and programs of study it should offer. Yes, you guessed it, you make a survey. Here's catch number two, the 12-page survey form – the basis for the first Southwestern catalog."

"Mr. Rindone, I'm waiting for three, four and five."

"Number three is this Board Policy Handbook It's urgent that you, the teacher, develop cooperatively the procedures, rules and policies with the board under which the college will operate. Avoid the horrible practice of developing policy as you go along."

"Why is that a bad practice?"

"Experience will give you the answer. The fourth giveaway is this large book of over 100 school job descriptions with pay scales for southern California. Add 20 to 30 per cent to bring the salary rates up to Chicago's. Southern California prides itself on the good life where you work harder for less money."

The faculty was tuned into every word between the superintendent and the dean of instruction. It was like the wise father talking to his young son. I was so thankful he'd taken time out of his busy schedule to pass on some of his wisdom.

Joe finalized his pitch. "Herb, here's a good book on Chicago, the city of broad shoulders and the city that works for Mayor Richard J. Daley. Despite its frigid winter weather, Chicagoland is a great place to live. Several of my friends and relatives live there, and they love it."

In response I praised Joe and Chet for getting us on a new campus within four years, the division chairpersons for their creativity in developing new curricula, the counselors for getting the students in and then out with a degree, the cafeteria staff for keeping us alive with their good food and the maintenance crew for protecting us from the nasty elements.

In closing I said, "I will be here for another four weeks. However, I bid thee farewell today. When in Chicagoland, give us a ring. Eugenia and I would love to have you stay over, providing you give us the latest on what's happening at Southwestern. Now, let's prepare for the grand opening of our new campus with a hearty welcome to the 3,000 students."

Joe stood up and asked, "Dr. Zeitlin, will you grant one reasonable request?"

"The answer is *yes,* without even knowing what it is. What is it, Mr. Rindone?"

"Just promise me you won't recruit any of the Southwestern faculty."

With much hesitation I said, "I promise not to recruit any of the Southwestern faculty…for at least two years."

The meeting ended and everyone went dashing about doing something very important. Later that day history instructor Waddie Deddah and the new sociology teacher came into my office with much concern on their faces. Waddie spoke first.

"Dr. Zeitlin, our superintendent gave you one false steer. Chicago is *not* a good place to live. Believe me, I have friends there. I've also researched it thoroughly for my own unit, *Chicago, the Captive City.* Since 1837, when the city was first incorporated, Chicago has been systematically looted and seduced by crooked politicians, mercenary businessmen and sadistic gangsters. It's been said that the ties between mobster and politician are closer in Chicago than anywhere else in the world, including Sicily."

Lori, the new sociology teacher, added, "There have been more than one thousand gangland killings in this city and only two convictions. The Mafia/politician/businessman corporation has existed in Chicago for over a century, but never as openly as today. If you don't cooperate with these partners in corruption you become another 'hit.' The newspapers will play along and report you as missing, killed in a car accident drowned, drunk or overdosed. I beg you – don't go to Chicago."

"Hey, wait a minute. I'm not going to Chicago. I'm going to 14 suburban communities west of Chicago. The suburbs are quite different from the big city."

"Are you sure?" Waddie asked.

"Well, no, but, generally speaking, people move to the suburbs for a better life. Isn't that correct?"

"Yes, but they take with them their old ways. Now isn't that right?"

"Some do and some don't. The board I'm joining consists of seven professionals, including an attorney from Notre Dame, another attorney from Valparaso University, a county tax assessor from the University of Illinois, a high school superintendent and three supervisors from the utility companies. Eugenia and I met six of these gentlemen and their wives and they are all intelligent and enthusiastic about creating a new college."

"Are they honest?"

"I think so."

"For your sake I hope you're right. You're intelligent and nice but, I fear, a little innocent. I just hope you're not led astray. Your educational career may come to an end. If I were in your shoes, I would not accept the offer, even if it carried a terrific salary increase. Wait it out a little. There will be plenty of new colleges opening in California."

"Waddie, you have to have faith in humanity and believe in each other. That's part of the American dream. I have two big Republicans and two major Democrats on the board who have vowed to work together for the benefit of the college."

"Did I hear correctly? You have four very important politicians on the board? If that's the case, you're doomed. They'll drain you with demands for favors. A politician's life is filled with requests for jobs and contracts. Their survival is based on keeping their supporters happy by giving them what they want The longer they stay in office, the more corrupt they become. Believe me, it's true."

"Waddie, I admire and respect you very much, but in this case I think you're wrong."

"Dr. Zeitlin, you have guts but you refuse to read the signs."

"That may be true, but I'm a teacher first and teachers always strive for positive changes in the behavior of their students."

"That would be true if these board members became your students, but I think you'll be the student and they'll be the teachers."

"Maybe so, only time will tell." I thanked my two deep-thinking colleagues.

Waddie shook my hand and patted me on the shoulder while Lori, a slight tear in her eye, kissed me gently on the neck as if I were headed for the gas chamber.

5
Coalition Score: 5 to 2

How long does it take to drive from San Diego to Chicago, a distance of 2,100 miles? A conservative traveler would take seven days, while a moderate one could make it in five. However, a certain speedy college president did it in three and a half days with short overnight stopovers in New Mexico, Oklahoma City and St. Louis.

I arrived at 1829 Broadway around mid-afternoon on a sunny Wednesday, two days earlier than expected. Bob Collins told me to pick up the office keys from Maria Provenzano, the board's clerical helper, who lived in the same apartment complex with her husband and child.

I once knew an Angelia Provenzano while a student at Jamaica High School in New York. She'd been short, smart, lovable and food-loving, so I pictured this Maria as middle-aged, short and fat. Instead, I was pleasantly surprised to see before me a young, thin and attractive brunette. She looked like "Maria" from *The Sound of Music,* a la Julie Andrews. Her first words to me were, "So you're Dr. Zeitlin – I can't believe it! You're 30-something, not mid-40s, balding, and wearing glasses, as Bob Collins described you to me. What a joker he is. I'll never believe another word he says."

We chatted freely as we crossed the courtyard to the office. She'd graduated from Proviso High School over two years ago, got married and now had a one-year-old son named Joseph. Her husband Tony, formerly a professional baseball player, was now in college, hoping eventually to become a lawyer. Babe Serpico, her brother-in-law, was helping them out financially. She hoped to return to work full-time real soon. In the meantime she was available for part-time work if I had a need for her. To which I replied, "I have a need for you right now. Find me a nearby studio apartment today."

She told me there was nothing available in her complex at that time but there would be a few units available the following month. Our dialogue was interrupted by the frequent honking of a horn as a big touring sedan pulled up in front of us. Out came Babe Serpico, who gave me a hearty welcome to Melrose Park: "Call me psychic or something, but I knew you'd arrive here a day or two early. Is there anything I can do to help you?"

"Yes, you can. Find me a one bedroom or studio apartment today."

We followed the Babe to the office. He immediately got on the phone, made several calls and on the third one his clout paid off. Mrs. Camille Cucignaro, one of Babe's precinct workers, was the manager of an exceptionally large apartment tract. She had a small furnished suite that had just become available. Maria gave me the address and directions for an immediate appointment. Before leaving I asked Maria if she would be available for some temporary work starting the following day at 8:30 AM. She was startled by my request and hesitated answering. Babe interrupted with, "You said you wanted to work, now is your chance. If your mother can't baby-sit Joseph, I'll get my wife to do it."

Maria, overwhelmed, replied, "I need to catch my breath. Dr. Zeitlin, I'm a little rusty on my typing and shorthand, but I'm willing to try it out, if you are, for a couple of days. OK?"

OK it was, as I left for my appointment with the apartment manager.

Mrs. Cucignaro was short, plump with glasses and approaching senior citizen status. She greeted me very pleasantly with, "Any friend of Babe is an instant friend of mine. The Babe has done so much for me. I'll never be able to repay him."

She then showed me a luxuriously-furnished two bedroom, two bath penthouse, which I immediately backed away from when I heard the price. We then took the elevator down to the first floor to look at the studio apartment. It was quite small but clean and neat with complete furnishing, including dishes, microwave oven, garbage disposal, dishwasher and refrigerator. The price was right. I gave her one month's rent in advance and told her I would be staying two or three months at the most.

After unpacking the car I drove to a nearby grocery and purchased six frozen dinners, a dozen eggs, cereals, fruits, vegetables, coffee, tea and milk. I intended to make my own meals most of the time. Later that evening I called Eugenia, gave her my new address and office phone number and promised to spend all day Saturday and Sunday house hunting. We were hoping to get the family to Chicagoland by the Thanksgiving holidays. All the kids got on the phone and we had a great long distance family reunion.

Joyce promised to write me a long letter to keep me updated on the happenings of her two little sisters and Mark, her big brother. Her father, in return, agreed to answer all her questions and give her much-needed information about the schools, churches, parks, theaters, libraries, shopping centers, etc. Before hanging up Eugenia reluctantly asked, "Darling, I have one important question to ask you."

"What is it?"

"How in the world could you drive 2,100 miles in three days?"

"I didn't. I flew. I pushed the inner button on the horn and the wings came out. Then I gave it two pumps and with full throttle the car was airborne, thanks to 007."

"How many tickets did you get?"

"None. With you on my mind I flew through the clouds gently, avoiding all turbulence, and made a three-point landing at Miegs Airport. Good night, Eugenia, I love you dearly."

The next day I arrived at the college office at 7:30 AM. I carried in many of the college catalogs, course outlines, board policy book, professional books and forms used at Southwestern College. I intended to revise these forms to satisfy the new college's needs. There was no book rack or file, so all the material had to be laid out on the floor. I started to open the three dozen or more letters addressed to the college president when Maria arrived at 8:25 AM, five minutes early. I gave her a warm welcome, complimented her on her lovely dress, settled on the lunch hour for each of us so that the office would be covered at all times from 8:30 to 5:30, reviewed telephone etiquette and then gave her an 8½" by 13" yellow lined pad.

"Maria, would you take an inventory of everything in this room that the college owns and give me an estimate of its value? Type it up and make a copy so that we can review your findings this afternoon. In addition, make a list of everything an effective office needs regarding supplies and equipment. Be sure to include two secretary's desks and chairs, two legal-sized four-drawer metal files with locks, two electric typewriters, file folders, paper, pens, etc. and anything else you can think of. After you've typed this list, get hold of the suburban yellow pages and get quotes for each item from the three largest office equipment/stationery houses in this area. Any questions? Hearing none, full speed ahead."

Maria started to work immediately as I got on the phone to Wade Steel. He suggested that we meet for lunch at the East Leyden High School to discuss some items. I agreed and told Maria to remind me to move out at 12:30 PM.

As I started to read my mail, I was suddenly interrupted with, "Hello, there. You must be Dr. Zeitlin. Babe told me all about you. I'm Gus Taddeo, your Melrose Park attorney, who will be sharing this reception area with you, I hope, for just a short while. I would appreciate it if you'd keep your voices down whenever I have a client and I'll do the same for you."

He wished me good luck as he departed, smoking a big cigar. I wondered what his specialty might be. As a Melrose Park lawyer he certainly was well-dressed, accessorized with golden cuff links and tie clasp. His clients must pay him well, I thought.

Driving over to the industrial area of Franklin Park, home of the East Leyden High School, was a matter of 14 minutes. Wade greeted me pleasantly, turned over to me a large brown envelope containing inquiries and requests for job applications, and uttered with finality,

"Answer these people as soon as possible. From now on I'm referring all inquiries about the college to you, the chief administrator."

I took his statement to mean that the changing of the guard was effective immediately. He must have been snowed with requests for everything and anything and wanted to be relieved of these administrative responsibilities.

"Wade," I began, "the office is short on supplies, equipment and personnel. How much money is available to date?"

"The state legislature has provided us with a start-up grant of

$100,000, which you now can use. Upon my recommendation the board decided to collect the full tax rate of 15 cents per hundred dollars on the assessed wealth of the district. Around December tax income of over $1,000,000 should start to flow in."

"Wade, that's wonderful. I assure you we'll use every penny wisely."

On the way to the school cafeteria Wade introduced me to Dr. Byrne, the high school principal. He was very tall, stately and poised. He volunteered to help in any way possible as the new college developed. The cafeteria was well over 40 years old and was certainly beginning to show its age, as very few improvements had been made over the years. I thought money, or the lack of it, must be the problem for the Leyden district. The services and meals, however, were exceptionally good and I enjoyed meeting a friendly and talkative faculty. During the luncheon Wade informed me that an executive meeting of the board was scheduled for Saturday at 10:00 AM in our office to decide on a site for the campus.

I asked Wade if there was any possibility of using one of the high schools from 3:00 to 10:00 PM as a temporary campus until new college facilities were built.

"It's possible," he replied, "but I don't think East Leyden is the one because of its age and lack of parking. Have you considered the other four?"

"I certainly have, and I wonder if you could help me get an appointment for 2:30 PM with the principal of West Leyden."

Using the phone in the faculty dining room Wade immediately arranged for me to tour West Leyden with its principal, Dr. George Cox. Upon arrival at 1000 Wolf Road in Northlake one was impressed with the new blacktopped curved driveway leading to the main offices. The buildings were mostly glass and steel separated by columns of light brick and were two or three stories high with seven distinctive wings. The top view symbolically looked like a Rotary wheel with seven heavy spokes. I wondered if the principal was a Rotarian. If he was, would it mean instant friendship? Puffing heavily as he ran out to my car, Dr. Cox's first statement was, "Welcome to Northlake. Now, what would you like to see, Dr. Zeitlin?"

"Every important feature of this campus that can be seen within an hour's time."

And we traveled fast starting with the science facilities, moving on to the light and cheerful classrooms, to the shops, gyms, swimming pool, cafeteria and athletic field, and ending up in the parking lot for 500 cars.

"How many of these facilities do you think could be made available to the college after 4:00 PM?" I asked Dr. Cox.

"Everything except the pool, gyms, library and the athletic field, and those could be made available after 5:00."

"Dr. Cox, I like West Leyden High School. It's a good possibility but I have to inspect several other school plants. Oh, by the way, could you free up five or more classrooms for conversion to a counseling center, library, bookstore, faculty center and administrative offices?"

"No, we can't do that. Every single classroom is being used between 8:00 AM and 3:00 PM. As a matter of fact we're operating well beyond capacity. Can't you find a few empty stores or homes for that purpose?"

"I suppose we could but I'm trying to avoid a split campus situation. Mesa College in California operated that way for several years and it was one frustrating experience for both the students and the faculty. I'm going to try my darnedest to avoid it."

As Dr. Cox walked me to my car I thanked him for an excellent tour and wished him bon voyage. After starting up the engine I called out,

"Where and when does the Northlake Rotary Club meet?"

"We don't have a Rotary Club."

"How come?"

"Northlake is a workingman's town and I'm proud to be a Kiwanian."

"Hmm, that's unusuaL Most high school principals I know join a Rotary. I need a make-up. Where do I have to go?"

Coming closer to the car Dr. Cox replied, "Try Elmhurst, Hillside, Chicago or Oak Park. Do you know what Vance Packard said about service clubs?"

"No, what did Vance Packard say about service clubs?"

"All service clubs provide a good outlet for successful people to do good things. However, the Lions always have the most fun in the towns where the Kiwanians work, and of course everyone knows the town is owned by the Rotarians."

When I got back to the office Maria was busy on the phone writing down the bids from the Office Discount Company, which appeared to be the lowest. I was amazed she'd been able to accomplish so much while I was gone. We reviewed each item and I checked off those that were urgently needed. We put a hold on some equipment until we could obtain a larger office. A pad of the standard purchase order forms used at Southwestern College was given to Maria to type the order immediately. She changed the heading from Southwestern College to Melrose Park Community College and Technical Institute.

I got on the phone and made an appointment to visit Superintendent Dr. Leroy Knoeppel at 1:30 PM the next day at East Proviso High School and Ed Stubbs at West Proviso High School at 3:30 PM. While Maria was typing, Joe Farmar and Bob Collins unexpectedly popped in, surprised to see Maria and me at work.

"What gives here?" exploded Joe Farmar. "Here it is, Thursday. You're two days early. Did your Skylark fly like a Mercedes? Don't answer. Bob, make sure that Herb gets paid for these two precontract days. We were surprised last night when Babe called us to announce your arrival. Now, tell us, how are things going?"

"Well, I made contact with a friendly Melrose Park landlord last night, got Maria to work today and tomorrow, saw Wade Steel, just got back from visiting Dr. Cox at West Leyden High School and tonight after dinner I start to work on the college catalog. Tomorrow, I'll visit with Dr. Knoeppel and Ed Stubbs and start answering these letters."

"That sounds like a short work day to me–14 hours. Right, Herb?" remarked Bob Collins. "You're not going to burn the candle at both ends, are you?"

"No, of course not. When you like what you're doing the hours move fast."

"Let me save you some valuable hours, Herb, and give you a briefing on Knoeppel and Stubbs. Don't get into an argument with Kip. He's an uncompromising autocrat and you can't win with him even if you're right. Did you know that he ran for the college board and then suddenly withdrew?'"

"No, why did he do that?"

"His dear friend Roy Jones wanted him to be our first college president, and we had to kill that idea from the very beginning. That's why our coalition had to do something about it."

"What did you do?"

"We hired a highly paid professional search team to seek out candidates throughout the United States. We were lucky they found you."

"Very interesting. Now, what can you tell me about Ed Stubbs?"

"Kip and Stubbs are two of a kind. Ed is a little younger, less dictatorial but more pedantic. He's an emphatic talker but really says very little."

"Thanks a lot for the info. Now, what's on the agenda for Saturday's executive board meeting?"

"We must settle on a site and authorize our attorney to negotiate a good deal ASAP. My uncle is working hard in soliciting the industrial VIP's to buy off the River Grove site in small parcels. If we don't move fast the best available sites will be gone. Secondly, we must find a more acceptable name for this college. Even Babe agrees with me that Melrose Park Community College and Technical Institute is not the best choice. Any ideas, Herb?"

"I can't recommend any names at this time. I haven't been here long enough to get the feel of the community. However, I do like your idea of getting the community involved. Perhaps we can brainstorm your idea this Saturday?"

"Fine, we'll do it. Oh, here's another two dozen letters you'll need to answer pronto. See you Saturday."

After the two men left I slowly dictated two short letters to Maria. As she started to type there was a light knock on the door and slowly it opened. In front of me there appeared a very tall, thin, dark-haired, handsome young man who introduced himself, "I'm Tony Provenzano, Maria's husband and Josephine Serpico's kid brother. Welcome to Melrose Park, Dr. Zeitlin. If you ever need an auto mechanic, barber, dentist or doctor I can help you get the best."

"Thanks, Tony, I appreciate your help."

We chatted briefly. I looked at my watch and it said 5:13 PM. I insisted that Maria call it quits for the day and go home. She asked Tony to come back in 30 minutes so she could finish the letters. I protested, "Go home, Maria. You have a family waiting to be fed. You did a good job. See you tomorrow at 8:30."

With much anticipation I started to read the letters that Bob had dropped off, and stopped at 7:00 PM. Before going home to my frozen dinner. I bought a newspaper to catch up with the news and reflected on Day One. It had been a good day. Everyone I'd met had been pleasant to me and shown much interest in the college. I wondered what Day Two would bring.

After washing the dishes I started work on the college catalog and stopped at revised Page 6. The board had to decide soon on an opening date and the calendar for the school year. I fell asleep around midnight, thinking about how to survey the community for its educational needs and the challenge of finding a suitable architect.

Day Two started again at 7:30 AM, except this time I grabbed a *Chicago Tribune* and studiously studied the classified ads. I was very pleased to see many openings for auto mechanics, electronics technicians, nurses, secretaries, machinists, accountants, security personnel, real estate agents, teachers, etc. I knew that I was on the right track insofar as what educational programs the new college should offer. When Maria arrived, I asked her to telephone the Chicago state employment office and obtain copies of the weekly inventory of job openings in metropolitan Chicago, the monthly report on jobs filled and unfilled, the employment outlook for city, state and nation, and the name and telephone number of the head of the service.

After Maria dialed 411 for information I waved good-bye and told her I was going to the Office Discount House to pick up our supplies and equipment. The drive along Grand Avenue was slow, cars galore, trucks loading and unloading and long red lights. Parking was tight but nevertheless I enjoyed the feeling of being in a big city. The car radio news reported there had been no bombing incidents in Chicagoland during the past month. Gangland had quieted down a bit, another good sign.

The salesman at Office Discount filled the college order quickly and efficiently and helped load my car trunk with the much-needed supplies. An IBM Selectric typewriter and a legal-sized metal file would be delivered Tuesday morning. Nearby was an instant printing store, where I discussed with the manager the college's immediate needs. He quoted a very low price, which I accepted at once, for revising many of the Southwestern forms for use at our college. Included were teacher, classified, maintenance employment and evaluation forms and the purchase order pads. I was getting hungry so I stopped off at a McDonald's for a double hamburger with iced tea.

When I returned to the office, Maria said she'd made contact with the assistant director of the state employment agency. He wanted to meet me when he dropped off the requested material. I asked Maria to call him back and schedule a 10:00 AM appointment for Wednesday morning. On my desk she had left the two letters for me to sign. I was shocked when I saw one misspelled word, one strikeover and one incomplete sentence in letter number one. The second letter had two messy corrections.

I immediately called her into the inner office, closed the door and said, "Maria, these letters are not ready to go out. This is the office of the president and this type of work reflects badly on both of us. Redo both of them and get it right this time."

She accepted my criticism without blinking an eye, swallowed hard as her lips tightened and said, "I once was an A student but I've lost my skills since having a baby. I'll practice this weekend with Janet LaDere. She lives in my apartment complex and has an IBM Selectric. I'll do much better Monday."

"I sure hope so, but in the meantime polish up these two letters so they'll shine picture perfect. Use the Webster's dictionary in my top drawer."

As I was about to leave for my 1:30 appointment with Dr. Knoeppel a trio of unshaven, rough-looking young men wearing black leather jackets asked for Gus Taddeo. Maria took them into Gus's office as I wondered whether they were members of the Marion Brando motorcycle gang. Could they be boys in trouble in need of a lawyer?

Proviso East High School, located at 1st Avenue and Madison in the Village of Maywood, built in the 1920's, had an enrollment of over 3,500 and parking for about 1,000 cars. The beautiful stone structure, large hallways and big classrooms gave one a strong feeling of tradition. I waited in Dr. Knoeppel's outer office for about 10 minutes as his two secretaries busily typed without a word to each other or to me. When Dr. Knoeppel came out to greet me he apologized for the delay and ushered me into a large office with traditional furniture. He seated me at a large conference table in front of his huge desk and asked, "How can I help you, Dr. Zeitlin?"

"I'm looking for a site to set up a temporary college campus to operate between the hours of 4 to 10 or 11PM. Do you have any classrooms available at East or West Proviso for that purpose?"

"We have nothing at West Proviso. It was built for 2,500 and we now have over 3,000."

"How many at East Proviso?"

"Maybe six or seven classrooms. Dr. Zeitlin, you have to realize that our high school population is growing each semester and our adult education program is very large. We can't help you much. Have you considered building butler buildings on the Maywood site?"

"Yes, but I feel it wouldn't be a good beginning."

"Why not?"

"Butler buildings are generally good for storage but definitely not suitable for student learning."

"You could hold your shop classes there and the academic classes here at East Proviso. You know the Endicott study was overoptimistic about the future of this junior college. As a long-time educator I predict your opening enrollment will be around 200, plus or minus 50. Junior colleges in this area do not have a good reputation. They're dumping grounds for weak students. They have no luster."

"Well, I'm here to change all that. They shine in California and they will become brilliant in Illinois if the people are willing to pay."

With that I got up to leave. Dr. Knoeppel was obviously from the old school, and it wouldn't pay for me to try to change his mind. It was annoying to hear him say "dumping ground for weak students" and "hold shop classes" in butler buildings. Once again, I'd run into an educator with a doctorate degree who couldn't accept the idea of a community college as a college for all the people, superior, average and weak students. As I said goodbye to Dr. Knoeppel he asked, "How is Wade Steel doing?"

"I saw him yesterday. He's doing fine. Why, does he have a health problem?"

"No, but he may have one in the months ahead."

"How is that?"

"He's the president of a board of four crooked politicians affiliated with special interests. Did you know that?"

"I met the coalition of two Democrats and three Republicans and they all seem to be fine gentlemen wanting to work together to build a college."

"You just wait...you and Wade are going to run into some troubled waters in the months ahead. Call me when the goings get rough if you need some help."

I smiled, thanked him, discussed several other educational matters and then headed over to West Proviso High School for my appointment with Ed Stubbs. Along the way I reflected on my dialogue with Kip. How much weight should I give to his remarks about the four crooked trustees? Not much, I thought. He was blackballing those trustees because they wouldn't consider him for the presidency. It's not unusual for a disappointed office seeker to attack those who thwart his ambitions. However, he'd warned me about four crooked politicians, not five. Did that mean one of the politicians was honest? Which one? I supposed it was the least educated one. All of them appeared refined and cultured gentlemen. I doubted any one of them was evil. Again, only time would tell.

When I arrived at the West Proviso High School campus, a good stone's throw from the Eisenhower Expressway, I was impressed with the near-new buildings and the large parking lots. I said to myself, this is what I want!

Ed Stubbs greeted me pleasantly, meekly shook my hand and said, "Before you start looking around I must warn you we have no room for any college classes. We're operating day and night way above our capacity. Have you tried the Hillside Shopping Center? They have a few empty stores."

"No, I haven't. I left Dr. Knoeppel a short while ago and he apprised me of the tight situation at both Proviso schools. He also told me that you're an excellent educational researcher."

"Kip really said that about me?" His eyes popped out

"Yes, he told me that you annually do a follow-up study on the graduates as to what colleges they attend and their majors. You also keep track of those who go to work, their salaries and job titles."

"This is the first compliment I've received from Kip in years. Would you like a copy of last year's follow-up study?"

"Yes, I would."

"Here it is, Dr. Zeitlin. You'll see that for the last several years, 60 to 68 per cent of our graduates have gone on to colleges and universities throughout the nation. Many of them attend the University of Illinois and other Illinois schools, with majors in business, engineering, liberal arts, teaching, psychology, sciences, medicine and law."

"How many go to the community college?"

"Very few, less than seven per cent. It's a known fact that the sad sack students go to the junior college as a last resort. I think the numbers will go up in the future since the universities are running out of room."

"Mr. Stubbs, could you help me on a little research project?"

"Try me."

"I'm in the process of preparing a questionnaire that I'd like all high school seniors to fill out in February or March. I need to know what vocational/technical programs they'd be interested in taking. Could you get the cooperation of the senior teachers to administer this questionnaire?"

"Yes, of course, but I don't think you'll get much interest from this college preparatory high school. Our students want to go to the real colleges, not trade schools."

I didn't bother to explain to Stubbs that community colleges are real colleges and that trade/technical programs are of collegiate caliber.

We parted. Ed Stubbs was relieved that the new district college would not use his facilities, and I was fascinated by his detailed research study.

I was surprised upon returning to the office to hear a lot of noise emanating from Gus Taddeo's inner sanctum. Maria told me it was the usual Friday afternoon of poker, twenty-one and other Las Vegas attractions. Profanity flowed freely. I was greatly disturbed. This was certainly not the right image for the college. I had to talk to Babe the next morning about getting a new office ASAP. The three visitors eventually left with Gus.

On his way out Gus asked, "Would you like to join us next Friday? We could use another hand."

I wanted to say, hell no, but being the gentleman that I was, I responded with, "Thanks for asking me. I like poker but I'm just getting organized and a bit short on time. Maybe sometime in the future."

Before leaving Maria presented me with the letters I'd dictated to her the day before. This time she'd done it right. She said, "I'm not accustomed to this manual typewriter. I'm anxiously awaiting the arrival of the IBM Selectric. I'll be practicing my shorthand and typing skills all this weekend with Janet. You just wait. I'll do much better Monday."

After she left I started to clean up the office and noticed the waste paper basket was filled with crumpled paper. I read the contents. It had taken Maria 14 tries before she'd gotten it right. Now I had a real challenge – she couldn't type! Woe is me. What would I do with her now?

She was the sister-in-law of the most powerful member of the board. Should I fire her or was there another solution? I looked skyward and said, "Heaven help me!" I decided to put it on hold until next week.

I called Wade Steel to ask about the agenda for the next day's executive board meeting. He stated there was no agenda. The main purpose was to decide on a site, and other items might come up. I told him Bob had suggested we brainstorm the group on procedures to follow in naming the college. He thought that was a good idea.

I asked him, "Should I take minutes?"

"We don't take minutes at executive meetings, but I think we should make a note of what we agree on. It's sometimes difficult when everyone is talking at the same time to obtain a general consensus. So when I repeat what we agree on please write it down and read it back to the group."

I went home to another frozen dinner, studied Stubbs's excellent follow-up report and before retiring wrote down some key points to make in naming the college.

Day Three started with a breakfast of two soft-boiled eggs, ham, toast and coffee. I arrived at the office at 8:00 AM. I arranged the chairs in a circle and placed a legal-sized yellow pad on each one. This was to be my first official meeting with the full board, and I was excited thinking about these fine, educated gentlemen. I wondered about Roy Jones, a simple, ordinary name, but probably an unusual person, now with his third wife. What aphrodisiac had the daughter used to get Roy and Ruth together? As I was thinking the front door opened gently and there appeared a smiling, meticulously dressed, middle-aged gentleman who looked and sounded like Nelson Rockefeller. He introduced himself.

"I'm Roy Jones. You must be Dr. Zeitlin. Ruth and I checked you out in the *Who's Who in American Education.* You have quite an impressive background. Tell me about Stanford University. Is it as great as they say it is?"

"Everything they say about Stanford is correct. I was just lucky enough to get in and out with an advanced degree. Now tell me, how does it feel to have a wife again?"

"Great, just great. I was very lonely until I found Ruth. Well actually I didn't find Ruth, Sandy did. She was Sandy's college counselor for several semesters. We hit it off beautifully for over four months so we decided to get married. It's wonderful to come home every night and have a sparkling conversation with a caring wife who is also a great cook and superb housekeeper."

As we exchanged tidbits about our families, in walked Elmore Boeger. In his Gregory Peck manner he said, "Herb, the Maywood Rotary Club meets every Thursday at noon at the Grace Lutheran Church. May I pick you up at 11:45 this Thursday? Please consider joining."

"Elmore, we're on. I'll put it right down in my appointment book. However, I would like to make-up in several other clubs before reaching a decision on which one to join. Is that OK?"

Before he could reply Wade Steel and Babe Serpico entered. Hearing my response Wade called out, "Herb, don't ignore the Franklin Park Rotary, which meets every Monday at the Embassy Hotel. Their membership reads like a *Who's Who in Manufacturing.* You'd make some excellent contacts with leaders in industry."

Babe blurted out, "The best club for Herb is the Melrose Park Club, just two minutes away from here."

Roy Jones responded with, "If you ask me, Herb should join the Hillside Club, the one farthest away from the office. A president must reach out to the outward areas."

"Roy, shut your big trap, no one is asking you. Herb is not required to join any club, least of all if an asshole like you recommends it."

Everyone stopped talking after Joe Farmar's outburst. He, Bob Collins and Fred Knol joined the group.

A few seconds later Babe walked up to Roy, waved his finger at him and said, "Why the hell are you against the River Grove site? What's going on in that demented mind of yours?"

"He thinks we're all getting a kickback when the River Grove property is sold," Sunday school teacher Fred Knol murmured.

"In the meantime," Bob Collins continued, "He's preventing the college from moving forward. Yesterday, they put up a very large 'for sale' sign. My uncle is doing his darnedest to solicit industry to buy small parcels. Accurate Springs bought one of the sites and will be building soon. We need to act now, not tomorrow or next month or next year."

"Roy, why are you against this site?" asked Wade.

"Fellows, I'm not against anything. I just feel that we're moving too fast. I've been a school board member for many years. Most trustees are deliberating groups of wise men, but this board wants to act without facts."

"What would you like to see done, Roy?" Wade asked.

"I think we should consult with the Citizens' Committee on Buildings and Sites. This has not been done and I want to know, why not?"

This time Elniore Boeger volunteered an answer. "Roy, the citizens of this community elected us, the trustees, to decide on a site. To resurrect a dismantled committee would take many months and we don't have that time to spare."

"Well, I'm not going to vote for the River Grove site until we have a legitimate investigation of all the other possibilities," Roy snapped back.

The arguing went on for about 15 minutes, all six trustees trying to change Roy's mind. But firm he stood, not giving an inch. He's a tough cookie, I thought. I said nothing throughout the ordeal but wondered about Roy's hidden agenda. He knew something about someone but was afraid to let it out.

Finally Babe Serpico announced, "Roy, you are one stupid jackass. This board has got to communicate unity among the trustees to the community as we prepare to pass a big bond issue and you're generating dissension. Fellows, let's not waste any more time with this son-of-a-bitch. Now, Mr. College President, what have you been up to?"

I briefly summarized my activities for the past few days and ended with, "Babe, I need a larger office and later on offices for three deans and a business manager. It was rough yesterday afternoon when Gus played poker with his buddies for four hours. It creates a bad image for the college. Can you help me out?"

Bob Collins interrupted us, "Babe, join Gus and his cronies at some other place. Herb is right. Gambling in a smoke-filled room next to the president's office has got to go."

"OK, I got the message. I'll get the apartment manager out in two weeks. Now, Bob, how are you doing in finding a better name for the college?"

That remark opened a big door. Every trustee called out several names rapidly. The leading presidents were John F. Kennedy, Dwight Eisenhower, Harry Truman, Herbert Hoover, Teddy Roosevelt and Woodrow Wilson. Also mentioned was Mayor Richard Daley.

Joe Farmar suddenly stood up and in disgust called out, "Gentlemen, we're on the wrong track! If we name the college after a Democrat we anger the Republicans and if we name the school after a Republican we will infuriate the Democrats. We want to unify the community, not divide it. So let's act like intelligent men and not like a bunch of idiots."

Dead silence fell again after Joe's outburst. Seconds later in his Gary Cooper style Fred Knol proclaimed, "As a long-standing Republican I agree completely with Joe. So let's drop the damn thought of naming this college after a president, governor or mayor. Do you agree with me, Wade?"

"Yes I do, Fred, but we do need to find a new name soon. As a new president, do you have any suggestions, Dr. Zeitlin? How did Southwestern College get its name?"

It was nice to be brought back to the circle of thinking men as a resource person. I then cited the great community involvement before the Southwestern trustees reached its decision. I felt we should do something similar by getting the future students, future educators, PTA's and community leaders to participate in the search for a name. To begin with, I recommended that we hold an informal press conference in the month ahead in which each trustee would briefly discuss some aspect of the college's development. I stressed the urgency of favorable press coverage right from the very beginning through making the press partners in leadership and in communication. Some prize or award could be given by the press or board to the individual or organization that produced an acceptable name.

The board then authorized me to go full speed ahead in contacting the principals, PTA presidents, service clubs, church groups, industrial, health and commercial leaders personally, by phone or writing, asking for their help in finding a college name. I was pleased by the enthusiasm displayed by the trustees on my first recommendation. Elmore Boeger read back to us the several dozen names already mentioned. Which one would be the winner, or was there a new one on the horizon?

Before adjourning the meeting Elmore gave a progress report on the search for an architect and I was asked to develop a list of colleges to visit that had recently constructed new buildings.

The group broke up after three hours in a spirited mood, with some joking, but continued abusive remarks directed at Roy Jones. As I was putting my notes together Bob Collins and Joe Farmar came back and said firmly, "Herb, meet us in 30 minutes at Horwath's Restaurant. We've got to talk."

The command was very forceful and threatening. I wondered what was up.

When I arrived at Horwath's Joe had just ordered his second Manhattan, Bob was sipping his martini and they had ordered a Manhattan for me. After we placed our luncheon order, Joe declared, "We've got to get rid of the son-of-a-bitch Roy Jones. Babe agrees with us that bastard must go. We'll show him that he can't buck the coalition's decision. He'll be gone in six months, if not sooner. We've asked Don Dunahow, our attorney, to check the legality of his serving on two school boards. There's a conflict of interest here. He can't serve on two boards, especially at the same time. What do you think?"

"I can't say at this time. I'll have to check with the Illinois School Board and Junior College Board executive secretaries."

"You don't have to be part of the dumping process. All we ask of you is to ignore him. Whenever he says anything or asks a question, don't respond. The silent treatment really works. Bob and I have done it many times in the past. Roy will get the message real soon and maybe we can get him to resign."

"You know, I met him for the first time this morning and we had a rather pleasant conversation before the fellows arrived. Perhaps I can convince him to change his mind. May I take him to lunch?"

"I think you'd be wasting your time, but if you want to try, go ahead and produce a miracle. We'll give Roy his last chance. Get back to us immediately after your lunch with him."

We continued to eat drink and talk for two and a half hours. Joe and Bob did a critical analysis of almost every remark made by everyone at the morning session. They particularly liked Elmore Boeger's support of not resurrecting the original site committee. Bob claimed the only reason Elmore got on the board was to prevent the college from ever considering his Hillside golf course for the site. Boeger owned the land and he had future plans to sell it off in small parcels and make a million or two. By getting on the board he had obtained a degree of control; he could claim a conflict of interest should the college attempt to buy his land. I was amazed at the talent of the Bekins attorney and telephone supervisor for instant recall. It was phenomenal how accurately they quoted the recent dialogue.

Bob and Joe reminded me that the coalition had the votes for anything they wanted to do, hire or fire anyone! Babe had put together five solid voters, led by Farmar, Collins, Knol and Boeger. I was emphatically told the coalition was unbreakable, so don't dare to touch it. Hearing that I ordered a second Manhattan. I canceled my real estate appointment. Bob and Joe were on their forth or fifth round and their speech became slurred. I was beginning to feel sleepy so I left and went home to take a nap.

Sunday was spent looking at homes with two different realtors. Winston Park, adjacent to Melrose Park, had a lovely four bedroom, plus two baths at a reasonable price. I liked it and was ready to make an offer but decided to talk to Eugenia first. Late Sunday night I discussed the pros and cons about the home with my dear wife. We finally ruled it out because it was on a main drag and we feared for our darling Clare's safety. We would just have to wait. There was no waiting on the line to hear progress reports from Mark, Joyce and Ann Victoria.

A big lump developed in my throat when all three kids said how much they missed me and asked when we could all be a family again. I tried to explain. They listened, even if they didn't understand. I'd hoped we could all be together again by Thanksgiving, but knew it might not be until Christmas.

As I went to bed I thought of the very exciting past five days. The biggest surprise of the week was the discovery that three of the trustees were not the gentlemen I'd thought they were. Serpico, Farmar and Collins were rough and tough, quick to use profanity and threats to intimidate Roy Jones. I certainly would not want to face that trio as my opponents. Joe Farmar's declaration, "We have the votes and can do anything we want" frightened me and raised several "what ifs" in my mind.

I finally focused on the challenges of the coming week:

1. What should I do with Maria? She can't type but she is the sister-in-law of boss Babe Serpico.

2. Where and when will we hold our classes?

3. How do I get the community involved in naming the college?

4. We need some guidelines or criteria in selecting an architect.

5. What colleges have been built recently that we can visit?

6. What approach shall I use to get Roy Jones to accept the River Grove site? Will my 24 graduate units in psychology be of any help?

7. I desperately needed to know the motive of each trustee.

I finally fell asleep and saw in the dreamland distance a baseball scoreboard that read 5 to 2. The fans were cheering as Elmore Boeger came up to bat. Would this Rotarian strike out or get a hit? The fans jumped up, blocking my view as he hit the ball. I dozed off, not knowing what happened.

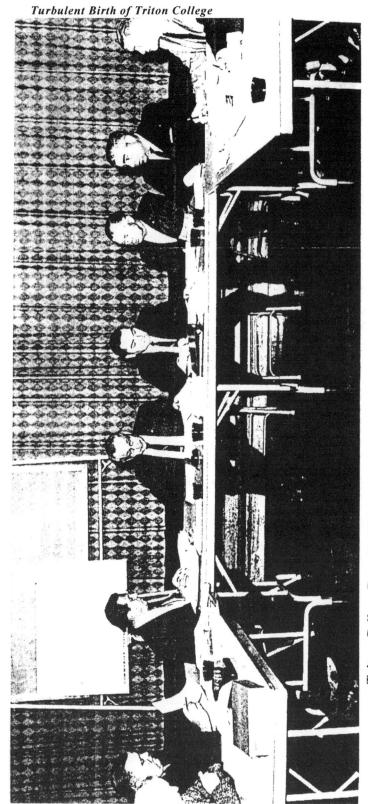

Triton College Board of Education. Seated left to right: Fred R. Knol; Joseph E. Farmar; Dr. Herbert Zeitlin, president; Wade A. Steel, board president; Robert M. Collins; Roy C. Jones; Ralph Serpico; Elmore Boeger.

6
The Seven Challenges

When I arrived at the office Monday morning, a beaming Maria was seated at her desk behind a new IBM Selectric typewriter. "Try me out, Dr. Zeitlin. This is my new baby and I love it. Start dictating."

"OK, here goes: 'Dear Maria, I'm happy when you're happy. If you like this typewriter, we'll get you one just like it. Tell me, how was your weekend? Very truly yours, H. Zeitlin."

She typed as I dictated rapidly. Within minutes she finished the letter and answered my question, "I borrowed this typewriter from my neighbor Janet and had Tony dictate to me all weekend. I'm back to my A rating. Here's the letter, now what do you think?"

"It's perfect, a near miracle! Now, let's start answering some of these inquiries piled up on my desk."

Within an hour I dictated ten letters. Maria caught every word and without hesitation proudly fine-tuned the feedback. I was amazed at her high spirits and confidence. We agreed that every morning at 8:30 we'd spend at least one hour together planning the day's agenda and promptly answering all correspondence.

After a coffee break together I asked her, "How did you do it? You're an A+ secretary today."

"Dr. Zeitlin, for a secretary trained on an IBM Selectric, typing on your old Royal manual was like shifting from a Mercedes to a four-ton truck. The equipment we secretaries use does make a difference. I hope you remember that when you hire future employees."

And remember it I did. I vowed to myself that no college employee would be forced to use obsolete or secondhand equipment or supplies. I was determined that starting that day everything purchased for the college would be the latest and proven best on the market.

At the Office Discount Store I picked up some literature on Chester Carlson's new copying machine. It used nothing moist in the process, only dry powder, electric charge and light. It was called xerography. Maria told me this machine could reproduce copies superior to traditional carbon copies. I immediately placed an order for the first Xerox machine to be used in Melrose Park.

Partly from Maria's sudden turnabout my adrenaline was flowing rapidly. Due to her remarkable performance, what had seemed my number one challenge Friday night, the cause of much loss of sleep, had evaporated by Monday morning. She was one intelligent lady, with a positive outlook, excellent secretarial skills and a willingness to walk many extra miles. After all, she'd just sacrificed a weekend of pleasure with her family for one of hard work in retraining and practice. And practice did make perfect!

I presented her with a job description outlining the duties and responsibilities of the president's secretary and asked her, "Do you think you can do it? Any questions?"

Maria studied the paper for several minutes and meekly replied, "I think I can. This is one of the most detailed job descriptions I've ever read. Boy, I'm a little scared. There's so much to do. But I certainly will try."

"Great, fill out this job form right away. Your application should be approved and your salary determined by the board at its next meeting." She was beaming, and so was I. I had gotten an excellent secretary who'd spent her whole life in Melrosc Park. She knew her way around town and would be an important link to the head of the political coalition, her renowned and respected brother-in-law, Babe Serpico. He and the rest of the board would welcome and accept her as my first official personnel recommendation.

As Maria was typing, I picked up from my desk the legal-sized yellow pad where I had listed in red ink my seven challenges of the week.

CHALLENGE I: What should I do with Maria? I had thought this would be the toughest and it had turned out the easiest.
CHALLENGE II: Where can we hold classes? Unresolved, many choices. I had held talks with the two principals from Leyden and the two from Proviso. Thus far Dr. Cox's West Leyden offered the most

promise, though there were some serious drawbacks. Elmwood Park High School, one of the newest and smallest, remained to be visited. I got on the phone and called Clem Loew, the third superintendent who'd been instrumental in creating the college district. He suggested that I meet with him and his principal, Ray Libner, at 2:00 PM. I agreed.

CHALLENGE III: How can we get the community involved in selecting a name? I took the first step by dictating a letter addressed to all the elementary and high school principals, asking for their help. Step two was to visit all local Rotary clubs, starting with the Melrose Park Rotary, seeking their suggestions for a college name. And step three was to put the item on the agenda for the upcoming press and media conference with the college trustees.

CHALLENGE IV: What guidelines should be used in selecting an architect? Sounded simple; just use the recommended criteria established by the American Architectural Association. Simple it was not! The AAA urged boards to pick an architect with experience in recent junior/community college construction. But even though the junior college movement had started in Illinois in 1902, not a single junior college building had ever been built in the state. All the campuses were hand-me-downs from high school or elementary school districts. In some cases even discarded military barracks or other government facilities had been used. To find an architect with a background in junior college construction we would have to go out of state. Politically astute Joe Farmar frowned upon the idea of importing an architect from California or Florida, where the great junior colleges were firmly established. He felt it would jeopardize his reelection. Much more dialogue between the college president and the board would be needed before this concern could be resolved.

CHALLENGE V: What colleges or universities should we visit? Due to phenomenal growth in enrollments, three universities, Illinois, Northern Illinois and Southern Illinois, had recently been forced to construct new buildings. I, therefore, immediately wrote to their presidents seeking assistance. While the space requirements of a community college and a university differ, much could be learned about new construction methods and materials from a visit with an informed administrator. I hoped most of all for the trustees and our architect to see the wonderful college campuses in California, but decided to hold back on this recommendation until the architect was hired.

CHALLENGE VI: How do I get Roy Jones to accept the River Grove site? Putting aside my 24 graduate units in psychology, I just picked up the phone and asked Roy if we could have lunch together Wednesday afternoon. He readily agreed and suggested a small restaurant in Du Page county. On Saturday, Roy had withstood an onslaught of insults and intimidation from the coalition leaders. He wanted to talk and I was ready to listen and learn.

CHALLENGE VII: What does each trustee want? They'd convinced me during the interview they all wanted a community college and technical institute for all the people and that I'd been their unanimous choice from a field of 36 candidates. To date, I had lunch with Wade Steel, our board chairman and the superintendent of the Leyden district, who, I believed, was sincere, honest and a conservative moderate.

Bob Collins, the secretary of the board, had three children. Joe Farmar, the voice behind the board, had six children. Each thought in terms of low-cost college benefits for all their kids. It was fun to have lunch with these two gung ho fellows. They were spirited, imaginative and comical even though they'd been rude and insulting to Roy.

I was looking forward to my luncheon with Elmore Boeger at the Maywood Rotary Club on Thursday. A true Rotarian generally is a successful professional or businessman who believes in service above self for the benefit of his community, state, nation or the world. I found it hard to accept Collins's and Farmar's comment that Boeger was on the board only to prevent the college from buying his Hillside land.

I had always thought a luncheon was a good way to get acquainted with someone. I also planned to dine soon with Fred Knol and Babe Serpico. To keep communication alive I would encourage all the trustees to visit with me in the office and arrange frequent luncheons together. It was still too early to pass judgment on the political coalition. I wondered if I had the skills needed to change Roy Jones's mind on the site selection.

Shortly before noon I left for the Melrose Park Rotary meeting at the Melrose Park National Bank on nearby North Avenue. The club was relatively new, with a membership of 26 young and active fellows who all seemed to know Babe Serpico. The club president was also the manager of the bank. He seated me between a real estate broker and an insurance broker. The catered lunch was excellent. Between bites I made an appointment with the realtor to show me another four bedroom, two bath home on Saturday afternoon. He also gave me the address of a good barber.

Since their speaker did not show, the club president, seated across the table, asked me many questions about the college; the member listened attentively. I suddenly realized that here was an opportunity to become the substitute speaker. With permission from the chair, I stood up and continued to discuss the future of their new college, promising that classes would be held in September in a temporary facility. A rapid-fire question and answer period followed. Thirty minutes later I ended my talk with a request for their help in naming the college. As I sat down I was surprised by a good round of applause. Some of the members hadn't even known a new college was on its way. The club president extended an invitation to me to join the club. I thanked him, put it on hold, and hurried off to Elmwood Park High School.

Of the five high schools in the college district, the Elmwood Park school was built on the smallest site, 22 acres, and had the smallest enrollment, 1,150. Clem Loew and principal Ray Libner greeted me with enthusiasm. As we toured the plant, everything we saw was clean, neat and modern, including an updated science building. Available to the college were 10 classrooms from 4:00 to 10:00 PM and some science facilities from 5:00 to 10:00. The two administrators projected the beginning college enrollment at 200 to 300 students at the most. Any surplus could be sent to the East Leyden school. I was elevated by their expressed cooperation but felt downcast by their projected limited enrollment. Could they be wrong? Here were two experts who knew their business, and I didn't want to waste time trying to convince them of the community college's potential. I felt that time would prove them wrong. When they showed me their limited parking area, I knew for certain that Elmwood Park was not the place to go. However, the banter between the superintendent, the principal, the faculty and staff was amusing, cute and marvelous to behold. It didn't take me long to realize that this school had high morale. I thought my son Mark would love this place, if only I could find a suitable home in this community.

7
Job Needs of Chicagoland

I returned to the office at 5:00 PM. As Maria left she introduced me to a tall, blond, thin gentleman who'd been waiting for me almost an hour.

"Dr. Zeitlin, this is the Bob Curtis I spoke to at the state employment office. He has all that information you requested."

"This is great, Mr. Curtis. Such service is deeply appreciated. Please sit down and give me a rundown on the labor shortages in Chicagoland and in the state of Illinois."

"Dr. Zeitlin, with all our busy factories working full blast, we need more skilled workers in drafting, tool and die specialities, welding, numerical control, computer science and electronics. As you know, Chicago is the midwest's largest health care center. The hospitals are calling for nurses of all different degrees, plus a dozen other classifications. Will your technical center be able to help us out?"

"Why, of course, that's my job."

"I read about you in the newspapers. I think you're the first shop teacher in the state to become a college president. Maybe Illinois is finally getting on the right track."

"What do you mean?"

"I had a long discussion with Ernest Clements, the dean of Wright College, with an enrollment of over 12,000 the largest community college in the state. I tried to get him to offer some vocational/technical courses in cooperation with our office but was unsuccessful."

"Why was that?"

"Well, he was for it but his faculty was totally against it. The many Ph.D.'s leading the Wright faculty felt their academic status would deteriorate if trade courses were offered."

"Don't tell me. . .the eminent scholars hope to make Wright

College the Harvard of the midwest. Right?"

"Yes, how did you know that?"

"Mr. Curtis, I've been in vocational/technical for almost 25 years and have fought the battle of liberal arts versus practical education most of that time. I'm still fighting it. My oldest brother Lester, who took courses at Columbia University in New York City, is brilliant when it comes to discussing the world's greatest philosophers, the latest books, the politics of the day. But show him the oil stick or air pressure gauge of his car, and he's a dunce. And that also goes for my wonderful wife, whom I love dearly. They have an antipathy against oily, greasy and dirty things."

"And yet, oily, greasy and dirty things are the lubricants that made this country great. Look at World War II, when the arsenal of democracy under FDR produced more planes, tanks and weapons of war ever before imagined by mankind."

"It's a sad fact of life that Americans tend to forget how united this country was during the war, when millions of women and men got their hands dirty to produce our great victory. People greatly respected those who used their hands, coordinated by their mind, to make things. Today, the blue collar worker is considered lower class, and who wants to be seen as lower class?"

"No one, unless he's the town plumber, driving a Cadillac and owning the best house in town."

"Bob, I got news for you. The number of blue collar workers is decreasing. The last time I visited the IBM plant in San Jose I saw thousands of men and women in white coats manufacturing all kinds of computers. Many of them were technicians with one or two years of training beyond high school. For every hardworking engineer, we need 10 to 15 technicians to help him – and help him we will at this new community college and technical institute."

"Dr. Zeitlin, how can you recruit a faculty that will support this philosophy? Dean Clements tried and failed."

"Bob, it won't be easy, but I have something that Dean Clements doesn't."

"Pray tell. What's that?"

"It's known as the board of trustees. I have seven aces . . . two highly respected attorneys, three industrial supervisors, a county tax collector and a perspicacious high school superintendent of schools. They're a great mix and they're all united in support of the 'People's College' concept. We intend to offer something for everybody, with special emphasis on technical education. We won't have academic rank among the faculty. They'll all be considered equal in status, though those with training above the master's level will be given additional compensation. With over one million dollars as start-up money thanks to Wade Steel, I feel I have a once-in-a-lifetime opportunity to build a dream college."

"Be more specific, Dr. Zeitlin. How will having a good board help you recruit a topnotch faculty?"

"Mr. Curtis, when you have a board with integrity and vision instead of a penny-pinching and conniving one, a creative chief administrator can produce miracles. This board and I think alike. We both endorse fully the 'People's College' concept – something for everyone. I'm now working on a proposed faculty salary schedule that will be second to none in the state of Illinois. The trustees realize that if we're to attract the best, we have to pay them well. Your office can help by advertising this fact when we recruit those technical and academic instructors. Can I count on you for help?"

"You surely can. I'd like to be part of your dream, but how can you prevent those misguided academicians from changing your direction?"

"By carefully screening all candidates. We'll hire only those who show vigor and passion for the people's college goals and objectives. Secondly, those hired must love teaching and not be interested in the 'publish or perish' method of advancement practiced at so many universities. Of course, we have no intention of hiring beginners. Students are not awakened by instructors who are just learning. All the educators who join our faculty will have presented evidence of successful teaching elsewhere."

"Sounds good to me, but will it work?"

"It's got to work. If we let one lemon in, it will sour our entire future."

"Suppose a board member's wife, sister, brother, son, daughter or dear friend, who may not be qualified, wishes to join the faculty. Would you bend and make an exception? Your job future may depend on your decision."

"*May* is a small word with major significance. I will make no exceptions to this policy. Every trustee is fully aware and supportive of this procedure. Colleges are evaluated by the public on the quality of its faculty and not on how many patronage workers get jobs."

"Are you tough enough to withstand the pressures that'll be put upon you?"

"Yes. . .I think so, but only time will tell."

"Your political coalition is under immense pressure to return favors with jobs and contracts. How are you going to cope with that?"

"Bob, I have a three-year contract. It's my intention to work closely during that time with a board that is honest and dedicated. Together we'll give the public what it wants – higher education for the masses. After the college is opened the public will be so pleased that all the trustees will be reelected."

"Sounds good to me, but will it really happen? You intend to eliminate 'clout' at the college level?"

"Yes, clout at any level is not good. It's inefficient, it's costly and it's based on whom you know rather than what you know. My board has mandated me to assemble the best faculty possible within the next eleven months, and it shall be done. We'll be going all out to recruit experienced, successful teachers from the great universities of the nation."

"Well, good luck to you, Dr. Zeitlin. Your time has come. Maybe the Melrose Park college will be a facsimile of the great community colleges of California we've read so much about."

"No, no, Bob, not a facsimile but better. And it can happen if Governor Kerner comes through with an improved financial plan for Illinois community/junior colleges."

"It's looking good right now; both Republicans and Democrats promise to support his proposal, even if it means increased taxes."

"That says a hell of a lot for the people of Illinois. This is a state that cares for the betterment of its people. I pray that the governor's bill is passed."

The more I talked to Bob Curtis, the more I liked him. Besides giving me encouragement he displayed insight into Cook County politics and was a storehouse of information about labor needs. We continued our dialogue over dinner at a nearby restaurant. When the check arrived, we split it equally. I promised to give him a list of all our job openings in the future and he, in return, promised to screen personally all the applicants before sending them to the college.

8
Jones Tells It As It Is

On Wednesday afternoon I met Roy Jones at a quiet and sedate restaurant in Elmhurst, a city known as a Republican stronghold of Du Page County. Roy welcomed me with a hearty handshake, seated me at a table in a quiet corner, placed a Manhattan in front of me and whispered, "Herb, do you know you've been hired by a bunch of crooks?"

I took a big gulp, swallowed and said, "Do you have any proof?"

"The proof is in Babe Serpico's pockets. They're stuffed with bills of every denomination willingly donated by traffic violators. He's an easy ticket fixer, and for two or three century notes he'll get you a job at city hall. Residents of Melrose Park have labeled him *The Boss* and some even call him *The Godfather.*"

"I can't believe that."

"You've just got to believe it. One of the candidates for the presidency dropped out when his private investigator did a background check of this so-called political coalition of trustees."

"What did he find out?"

"The big lawyer from Notre Dame, Joe Farmar, takes his orders from Jim Kirie, the Leyden Democratic committeeman and restaurateur of River Grove. Since he has a pact with the Mafia, Kirie's restaurant has never been bombed or threatened. Farmar does Kirie's dirty work secretly, and sometimes uses bodily harm as his weapon."

"Is there more?"

"I'm only beginning. That little weasel Bob Collins is the trickiest one of them all. He's a master of electronics, and bugging is his specialty."

"Aren't all telephone technician specialists good at bugging?"

"Some are and some are not. Bob Collins takes his orders from

Elmer Conti, the Leyden Republican committeeman, state legislator, mayor of Elmwood Park and Franklin Park banker with Mafia ties. Conti is the epitome of businessman/politician/mobster. Bobbyboy admires his boss Conti and some day hopes to be his successor. In the meantime you should assume that your telephone calls from your office and home are being monitored by Bob and his associates. You just wait, Bobbyboy will be sure to supervise the installation of your phones."

"I still find it hard to believe. What's the dirt on Fred Knol and Elmore Boeger?"

"There isn't any. They were recruited to give respectability to the coalition. Fred is a hardworking supervisor at the Lindberg Steel Healing plant. He and his wife Betty and son Russell are avid church members. Fred regularly teaches Sunday school. Phyllis and Elmore Boeger are also devoted Lutheran churchgoers. His name has been one of the most respected in the commanity for over three generations. Elmore graduated from Valparaiso University law school, has a private practice, is trustee for Melrose Bank and is a past president of the Maywood Rotary Club."

"Roy, what do you recommend I do?'"

"Get out as fast as you can. Get your old job back and return to sunny Chula Vista. This gang is bad; they'll ruin your health and reputation."

"I can't do that, though my old job is still vacant. They all seem like such enthusiastic trustees. What you said is unbelievable, but even if it's true I'll try to reform them. Just like Joe and Bob asked me to reform you."

"Now tell me, just what do they want from me?"

"They want you to vote for the River Grove site publicly. They feel not doing so will create doubt about the board's integrity."

"Dr. Zeitlin, there's no doubt in my mind that Kiddieland, Golfland or the Drive-In theater would be far better for a college campus than the low-level Carey farm that's been soaked in water for years. If and when the Des Plaines River overflows again, the college structure would be in grave danger."

"Have you talked to the other trustees about this?"

"Yes, but they refuse to listen."

"Why don't they listen?"

"Well, Bob and Babe said the other sites are too expensive and the special interests would fight a sale endlessly."

"Who are these special interests?"

"Don't you know by now?"

"No."

"The land is owned by the fruit and vegetable King family, friends of the Mafiosi."

"This is new to me. Who is the King family? Where do they live?"

"Well, I call them the King family, but it's actually the Naples family, who live in Melrose Park."

"And who are the Naples?"

"An old man named Tom with twin sons, daughters and assorted relatives. If they're forced to sell through condemnation proceedings their profit for the land sale would be huge. They don't want to pay big capital gains taxes to the federal and state governments. Therefore, they'll resist selling."

"So it's really a case of how to cheat the government. Is that it?"

"Yes, whatever they'd say, it's really protecting their profit on a good business deal."

"How much did Tom Naples pay for this land?"

"I can only guess. Rural land in Melrose Park and River Grove in the twenties was selling for $50 to $100 an acre. If Tom acquired 200 acres, multiply that by $100 and you get a total of $20,000. Now, 40 plus years later, the land is worth about $60,000 per acre. Multiply that by 200 and you have $12,000,000 – a profit of $11,980,000. That's not bad for an Italian immigrant who could barely speak English when he came over."

"Roy, from what you tell me I think Tom Naples was a brilliant visionary who had faith in America and his community, and deserves a lot of credit. His family should be immensely proud of him. He exemplifies the only-in-America rags to riches Horatio Alger story."

"Like so many immigrants, in order to protect his investments, Tom Naples sought protection. He found it with one of the Godfathers. Which one, I don't know. Take your pick: Tony Accardo, Elmer Conti or Babe Serpico."

"Well, Roy, I'm not qualified to know who is protecting whom. My

major challenge right now is to restore harmony among the trustees. You can help me by not fighting tooth and nail when the board votes on the River Grove site. Otherwise you'll only get hurt and your days on the board will be curtailed
. . . Can't we reach a middle ground?"

"Like what?"

"Like your voting your feelings, which I accept is a no vote, but keeping quiet about your speculative reasons. Everything I heard from you is based on hearsay. The press would have a ball reporting, day after day, on all the hearsay from different sources. Your informants could be handing you a bunch of garbage, and garbage is not evidence."

"Dr. Zeitlin, this is not a bunch of garbage. But to please you I'll vote no, state that I think the trustees are moving too fast, and then shut up. Now, how's that for a step toward harmony?"

"Fine, I think the boys will like that. I'm hopeful they'll show more respect to you. A six to one decision is not a divided board."

Roy seemed more relaxed now that a decision had been made. So was I as we ate a light lunch. Roy went into ecstasy describing his newly acquired wife's cooking and how delighted his kids were to have Ruth with them. Sadly, he told me about his oldest daughter Sandy, who was in the process of getting a divorce. I told him she should consider taking some classes at our college and make a fresh start in meeting some eligible bachelors. Roy, in turn, promised to keep his eyes open for a four bedroom and two bath home in Westchester or Hillside. He dashed back to work and I returned to the office to call Bob and Joe. They suggested we meet at Tom's Steak House in the early evening to discuss Roy and one other important development. This took me by surprise. I wondered what that other development was all about.

When I arrived Bob and Joe were already on their second martinis and they had a Manhattan waiting for me. Bob announced that he had the keys to my office, which I could move into next week. The manager needed two more days to clean out his records. We agreed to check it out after dinner.

Both boys were in high spirits and you could smell it. They showed me the *Chicago Tribune's* headline: *"Martin Luther King Wins Nobel Peace Prize."* I was surprised and pleased when they encouraged me to do an intensive campaign to recruit black students and faculty. What a contrast from when I was 17 and working as an usher at the Jamaica theater in Queens, New York The manager had directed me to keep the "niggers" out of the orchestra and send them up to the second balcony for seats. I quit the next day.

It was so refreshing to hear Joe say, "America is great because of its minorities. Dr. Z, we want you to give equal service to all students, regardless of race, color, creed, sex, handicap or national origin. If they can't afford it, President Johnson with his Great Society program will help them out. . . And now, what happened with Roy Jones?"

I proceeded to summarize the highlights of our luncheon, stressing the fact that Roy was going to vote no but would not go into detail, if asked, on why. He had agreed with me that it was desirable to accept the board's decision and promised to cooperate in obtaining the preferred site.

"Did he tell you why he was against the River Grove site?" Joe asked.

"Yes, an engineer friend told him that the Carey farm was lowland with water a few feet below sea level. If the Des Plaines River were to overflow again the college buildings would be flooded. There's also the danger that when the buildings are on a water foundation cracks in the walls will develop sooner than expected."

"That's a bunch of bull," was Joe's instant response.

"In his heart Roy felt the Kiddieland playground would be an ideal campus site because of its location and higher altitude. He also felt the drive-in theater spot would be suitable for a football field or parking lot."

"Did you explain to him that the cost of Kiddieland is completely out of our range and we would face a long legal battle?"

"Yes, but he thought we could overcome both obstacles."

"So, what made him change his mind not to fight the coalition?"

"He wants to be reelected and seeks your support."

"Hmm, we shall see. What do you think, Bob? Don't answer, I know. Well, congratulations, Mr. President, you drove some sense into what I thought was an incorrigible son-of-a-bitch."

After dinner we drove over to 1829 Broadway and Bob opened the manager's office. When I walked through I thought I was at a Las Vegas night club den. The office consisted of a thick white carpet, a well-stocked bar with refrigerator, four bar stools, a large half-moon white desk with four black armchairs in front of it, a large boss's chair similar to a Supreme Court justice's seat, four inlayed ceiling lights projecting over the desk, red amber lights over the bar, a microwave oven, long white drapes with black stripes, and an extra large black leather couch. Outside the main office was the reception area with two secretarial desks, a mimeograph machine, bookshelves, two end tables with Playboy magazines on them, cabinets for supplies, a coffee machine with six sexy cups and a bathroom nearby. I sauntered into that room and saw mirrors to the left of me, to the right of me and above me. I counted ten images of a familiar figure. The beautiful tub was fully tiled with gold accessories.

I held my breath until Bob asked, "Well, what do you think of it?"

"Quite unusual, to say the least It must have cost a fortune."

"Right on. It's yours starting on Monday. Anything you want changed, just tell Babe. He'll fix it."

"This bar is a connoisseur's paradise, but it doesn't fit in with a college president's goals. Or maybe it's just for a retired one who wants to enter dreamland. There's a fortune here in liquors alone. Can the bottles be removed along with the sexy cups and the Playboy literature?"

"Consider it done. How do think Maria will like this place?"

"She'll love the thick white carpet and heavy drapes because it will reduce the noise level, and there's more than adequate space for additional personnel. It certainly is glamorous. I'm sure she'll adjust to the new setting. How can we thank you for moving so fast?"

"It's nothing. Just typical service from the coalition. We always aim to please our friends."

As I left for home I felt a little embarrassed – such a big office for a beginning college president. I really wanted to reject it, but was tuned into the feelings of these three hardworking trustees. To say no to their efforts might end any help from them in the future. I decided I must concentrate more on finding a temporary facility soon and a more suitable administrative office.

9
Rotary

Rotarians strive to create order where there is chaos, beauty where there is ugliness, fellowship where there is loneliness and misunderstanding, and health and happiness where there is poverty and disease.

Elmore Boeger called me at 11:00 AM and asked that I meet him at the Maywood Rotary at 11:45 instead of noon. Wayne Thorne, the president, thought it would be a good idea if I greeted each member as he arrived with a handshake. Rotarians generally are not shy. One can never overemphasize the importance of fellowship. A warm handshake can develop into a lasting friendship. It was delightful exchanging greetings with the town mayor, pharmacist, police chief, fire chief, dentist, stockbroker, banker, printer, lawyer, realtor, car sales manager, minister, jeweler, artist and 26 other professionals. Each exchange lasted about 30 seconds of tidbits.

President Thorne, principal of an elementary school, called the group together at exactly 12:10 PM. A flag salute and invocation was followed by the entrance of four rather attractive and efficient waitresses, members of the Women's Guild of the church. (The luncheon fee would go to the Guild.) With eager and prompt readiness the ladies placed on all three large tables big bowls of fried chicken, mashed potatoes, vegetables, bread and beverages. Just before dessert the president called upon a member to lead in the singing of a few Rotary songs. Next came the introduction of guests, fining announcements, committee reports, discussion and then assignments. At exactly 1:00 PM the president turned over the meeting to the program chairman, who introduced the speaker of the day.

Silence fell. All joking and laughing stopped and full attention was given to the guest speaker.

"This afternoon it is with great pleasure that I introduce to you the coroner from Gottlieb Hospital, Dr. Joseph Goldsteine," the program chairman remarked. "I know you've enjoyed the splendid meal prepared by the Women's Guild especially for you stronghearted Rotarians. But now that your gastric juices have settled down, I must warn you those juices might erupt swiftly when Dr. Goldsteine takes exhibits one, two and three out of his refrigerated carrier. I recommend that those prone to fainting in the face of gory organs should leave."

Dead silence fell again. Each one of us looked at his neighbor and made some murmuring sounds. One Rotarian got up to leave, expecting others to follow, but no one did. As he got to the door he suddenly turned around and said, "Oh hell, I'll stay. If you fellows can take it, so can I. Wayne, just in case I pass out call my wife."

"I've given this talk several times before, usually without incident But last week at the junior chamber of commerce one of the youngest did go out like a light. It took a few minutes of smelling salts to bring him back."

With that Dr. Goldsteine unzipped his case and placed on a table a wobbly reddish plastic bag with three compartments. We couldn't tell what we were looking at. All three sections were bright red. One man said it was a heart, another said it was a liver and a third thought it was lungs.

Dr. Goldsteine explained, "The brightest red is a lung from a 25-year-old killed in an auto accident, the middle one is from a 48-year-old and the third one is from a 89-year-old woman who died of heart failure. All three deceased had good lungs and could have lived longer if some other organ had not deteriorated. The rich redness is an indication of a non-smoker. Now let's look at the moderate smokers, those who smoked a pack a week or less."

He proceeded to show lungs specked with black, from the young, middle-aged and senior. He noted that the young pups, if they'd immediately quit cold turkey, could still have had extended life. The senior, with many more black spots, was in more serious condition but might have lived another five or more years had he stopped smoking at once.

"And now the condemned, those who smoked a pack or more a

day." Dr. Goldsteine displayed lungs with little redness remaining. "This senior's lung is almost completely black. I suspect he would not have lasted out the year. The others had one to three years left."

As the doctor put his exhibits away a Rotarian from the rear called out, "What do you recommend for us smokers who can't quit?"

"Putting it bluntly, you quit or you die. I've no sympathy for those who claim they can't do it. You're a selfish group, with no love for those who brought you into this world or those whom you associate with daily. If you've an ounce of intelligence, you'll quit today."

As I looked around the room the dozen or more smokers had stopped smoking. I wondered for how long. After Wayne thanked him for his vivid demonstration the doctor came over to me, put his hand on my shoulder and said, "Mr. College President, you face a big challenge. You must educate the students and faculty on the evils of smoking and develop programs for those who want to quit. This will be a better community once smoking in all schools, restaurants and public gatherings is prohibited. I don't know if I'll ever see that day. The tobacco companies are big and rich and will fight tooth and nail to prevent it from happening. Our only hope is to have the state and federal governments do something about it."

At precisely 1:30 Wayne hit the Rotary bell and the meeting was over. Forty middle-aged men and seniors left, thoroughly shaken, upset, agitated and distressed.

Elmore turned to me and said, "Wow, what a program! I only wish I could get my wife Phyllis to quit. I've tried everything, including a special request to the Lord every night.

She hasn't delivered as yet."

"I empathize with you. I've the same problem with my older sister Betty, who lives in Florida. She's beautiful and highly intelligent, but lacks that special ounce of sense that says no to smoking, even though our father died a miserable death from cancer last year. He was a copious smoker – two packs daily."

"That's sad. Well, what do you think of my Rotary?"

"Elmore, your club is a wonderful mixture of friendly and competent members. I enjoyed so much the chitchat with everyone, but was surprised to see no black members. What gives?"

"Dr. Z, you've touched on a sensitive area. We have invited several black leaders to our meetings but they've declined."

"Why?"

"I really don't know. I guess we have to try harder."

"Did you know that Bob Collins and Joe Farmar recently urged me to actively recruit black faculty and students?"

"Collins and Farmar aren't the only ones. Shortly after we were sworn in as trustees we all attended a conference and learned about the *People's College* concept. And then you came along and preached the same sermon. Dr. Zeitlin, I can guarantee you that you'll be working with a forward-looking board that intends to open doors of opportunity to all people, regardless of color, religion, sex or nationality. You, like Moses, were selected to show us the way."

"Your remarks are music to my ears. Together we'll make it happen. Now, why did you run for the board?"

"Vernon Forgue, an attorney who shares office space with me, was invited by Babe Serpico to run. He declined but offered me the opportunity."

"What happened next?"

"I'd already been tinkering with the idea for several weeks, so I accepted. The political parties were not about to let the so-called 'educators' take over without a fight. They formed a coalition of three Republicans and two Democrats."

"Did you actively campaign?"

"No, I didn't have to lift a finger to get my name on the ballot. It was all done by the politically active men in the township."

"And what was the result?"

"Twenty persons ran for the board. In the end five politicians and two educators were elected. When we organized the board I was offered the chairmanship, but even though I had the highest number of votes, I declined in favor of Wade Steel, who had more experience in school matters."

"I've heard a lot about Serpico's political coalition. Are those boys honest?"

"Absolutely. I'd never be part of them if they weren't. I've been a Rotarian for over 20 years, like my father before me. He served with distinction and taught me that honesty is the only policy. The Four Way Test has been a way of life for me and most Rotarians. I'm a firm believer in that famous 24-word statement"

"Elmore, I've heard so many Rotarians express their faith in the test, but I haven't met one yet who can recite it accurately. Can you?"

"Herb, you're speaking to the past chairman of the Four Way Test committee. Did you know that my friend, Herb Taylor, a Chicago Rotarian, conceived the test back in 1932, at the height of the Great Depression? He decided to leave his top executive position at the Jewel Tea Company, based in Melrose Park, to accept the job of chief executive of the failing Club Aluminum Products Company. He miraculously saved the company from bankruptcy by having all the employees memorize the test. It gradually became a guide for every aspect of their business. It's been said that Taylor's four department heads –one a Roman Catholic, the second a Christian Scientist, the third an Orthodox Jew and the fourth a Presbyterian–all agreed that the test not only coincided with their religious beliefs but provided a model set of values for their personal and business life. And last year all members of the Maywood club vowed to post the test in their office and near their home phone as a reminder to practice the test daily."

"Elmore, there's no doubt in my mind that you're a good lawyer. But like most lawyers you've recited an interesting history while managing to avoid answering the question. Can you recite the Four Way Test?"

"Why, of course. But first I think you should know that this test has played a major role in reducing car accidents and fighting drug abuse. It's been chiseled in granite. It's even been the subject of a master's degree dissertation and translated into more than 100 languages, including Russian. Did you know that Japan has led the world in practical use of the test? I predict that whatever country has the most people following the test as a way of life will be the happiest and most prosperous. America must awaken to this Rotarian belief. Do you accept that?"

"Yes, I do, but if you don't recite the Four Way Test in plain English, I'll report you to Wayne and he'll fine you a big one."

"OK, the four simple questions it asks of everyone are:

1. Is it the truth?
2. Is it fair to all concerned?
3. Will it build *Goodwill* and *Better Friendship*?

4. Will it be beneficial to all concerned?"

"Well, well, well – you said you could do it and you did. Congratulations, you're one of the rare few who can say it accurately. How come?"

"Herb, as the immediate past district chairman of the Four Way Test committee, I know the test inversely or conversely, take your choice."

"What did you accomplish as the chairman of the committee?"

"First, we attempted to make it known in the community that any business or professional organization displaying the Rotary sign was a place of honesty. You know that Chicago is a paradoxical city. For over 100 years it's been known as a city of 'corruption with grace.' We needed something to counterbalance the good over the evil; thus Rotary was born out of necessity.

"And, secondly, most of the high school and elementary principals encouraged us to address their classes on the Four Way Test in order to instill good conduct and ethical standards among the city's youth."

"Elmore, did you lecture in any of the schools?"

"Yes, I did. On three different occasions I stressed the merits of the test in West Proviso High School business law classes. Other Rotarians met with students in history, English, political science and philosophy classes."

"That's remarkable. Did you get any flak from the students?"

"Not really. Well, sometimes there was resistance, but on the whole I felt good carrying the message that honesty is not just the best policy...but the only policy. I have great faith in our youth. They'll do the right thing as long as they know what's right. And it's the responsibility of all elders, not only Rotarians, to teach their kids the vast difference between right and wrong. I only wish I had more time to devote to this project."

"And so do I. Of equal importance, if not more so, is the instilling of honesty and proper ethics among adults. That should be another goal of the college."

With that we said good-bye and parted.

It had been especially nice talking to Elmore Boeger. I felt that here was a lawyer with unimpeachable integrity. I had found one honest man and I was not going to let him go. He was positive toward the Serpico coalition, while Roy Jones was negative. If you put the right conductor between the negative and positive, current would flow and energy be released. As the chief executive officer of the board it was now my responsibility to become the right conductor. With renewed electromotive force I returned to the office to prepare for my first public board meeting.

10
October Board Meeting

Wade Steel and I agreed on the following action items for the board agenda of October 14th:

1. Request to join the Illinois Association of School Boards at a fee of $250 per year
2. Need for additional office space and clerical help
3. Authorization to pay bills
4. Authorization to pay college president's moving expenses
5. Authorization to set up an Impress Fund to be controlled by the college president, board president and board secretary
6. Authorization to seek any and all federal funds for educational programs and buildings

Other items listed for discussion included working with the state employment office in developing a curriculum to address job shortages, devising a procedure to find a new college name and reviewing the architectural selection process.

I arrived at the Little Theater of the East Leyden High School, site of the board meeting, before eight o'clock. Five trustees were laughing and joking with an audience of eight concerned citizens and two reporters. Bob Collins grabbed me and introduced me to what appeared to be the oldest man in the group, Don Dunahow, the board attorney.

Dunahow said, "Welcome to Melrose Park, Dr. Zeitlin. How did you like the contract I sent you?"

"It was the longest contract I've ever received."

"That's just a small sample of how thorough I am in all legal matters. I look forward to working with you on all contracts with administrators, teachers and contractors. Have you found your home yet?"

"No, it's been difficult finding a modern four bedroom, two bath home in an acceptable area."

"Dr. Zeitlin, when you do, I'd be happy to assist you in the closing at no cost to you. That's a special favor I do all college presidents. You know, of course, that in Illinois we have no escrow companies. You have to have an attorney to close a deal."

"Thanks very much, Mr. Dunahow. I appreciate your concern."

Standing next to Bob Collins was a tall, handsome, upbeat gentleman by the name of Jim Tarpey, who introduced himself as Bob Collins's high school buddy. He said, "Dr. Zeitlin, you have a big job ahead of you. If you need any help with the press, I'm your man. Public relations is my specialty."

I thanked him just as Bob Collins called the meeting to order at 8:00 PM sharp with the announcement, "Wade Steel and Babe Serpico will not be here tonight." In Steel's absence, Joe Farmar moved to name Fred Knol president pro tern. The motion was seconded by Roy Jones and carried on a voice vote.

Fred called upon Roy Jones to introduce me to the audience. In a loud, spirited voice aimed at the assembled group Roy said, "Welcome, Dr. Zeitlin, we've been waiting for you. I just found out today that you're the first Stanford man to become a college president in the state of Illinois. Good luck to you and may your dreams of building a great college coincide with those of this governing board of seven dedicated citizens. We're here to build a better community through education, and with mutual respect we'll do it."

I couldn't believe what I heard from Roy. A week ago he had called these same men a bunch of crooks, while tonight he was describing his fellow trustees as a league of dedicated men. Seeing is not believing! Joe Farmar stood up and said with gusto, "On behalf of my colleagues, Roy, we appreciate you're the most experienced trustee here tonight, with over 15 years of dedicated service to the Hillside district. We all look to you for guidance. This board is indeed fortunate to have you."

Could these two arch enemies have changed so much within one week? I doubted it. "Which one was the better politician, I didn't know. Their goal had been to show amiability within the board, and it had worked.

In a business-like fashion, Fred Knol went down the list of action items. They all passed without a dissenting vote. Here I was, concerned about possible fireworks, and the meeting had instead turned out heavenly. They'd given the public what it wanted – a board working in harmony for the benefit of the people. I didn't know it at the time, but I was married to great showmen.

The meeting ended 90 minutes later with Joe Farmar declaring, to my surprise, that while the board was considering five possible sites for the campus, no decision had been made. All the men nodded in robotic unison. He moved to have the meeting adjourned to the night of October 20th for a full discussion about sites.

I then realized how naive I must have appeared to these experienced politicians. The battle between Roy and the Serpico coalition had not occurred. On the previous Saturday morning at the executive session the trustees had already decided on the River Grove site by a vote of six to one. And here, a week later, the group was proclaiming to the public that no decision had been made.

Why had they lied? Was I now an unwitting part of a cover-up? Boeger and Jones left the circle immediately after Knol adjourned the meeting. Left to talk to the press and a few remaining citizens were lead spokesmen Joe Farmar, Collins and Knol. Had these three met previous to the board meeting? It seemed so, since they were so united in their denial of a site selection. But why?

I wondered, who'd devised these tactics?

Shortly before noon the next day, Bob Collins popped into my office and suggested that we have lunch. As he sipped his martini and I milked my Manhattan, he whispered, "Herb, we owe you an explanation."

"Please, Bob, tell me, what gives?"

"Last night I got a call from Don. He asked me to set up a dinner meeting with Babe and the boys with a request to change the game plan. Les knows Carey's attorney, who's hoping to get old man Carey to cancel his listing with his broker. If that happens, the real estate agent won't get his usual ten per cent commission for a land transaction. Simply put that means the college will be able to purchase the property at ten per cent below the fair market value. Don's genius will save the college several hundred thousand dollars. Now, what do you think of that?"

"Is that legal? Is it ethical?"

"The hell with ethics. Don has done it hundreds of times. He makes it legal. He's a brilliant lawyer, and always finds loopholes that help his clients. I'm so glad Mayor Conti recommended him to Babe. He'll save us millions."

"Isn't there a danger the realtor will sue the college?"

"No way. Don will give him a little pocket money to keep his mouth shut. It always works."

"Bob, I just don't like being part of this."

"Herb, just stay out of it. Don will handle it. All he needs is a little time to get the cancellation. If old man Carey hears about this prematurely, he'll want to up the price. That's why the board postponed voting lasting night. In addition, Don has to convince Carey that it's in his best interest to sell the whole site at once and retire in luxury now, rather than sell the farm in bits and pieces over a long period. Otherwise he might not live to enjoy the fruits he's earned."

"Sounds logical. What's the time schedule?"

"The two lawyers and their wives are having dinner with Carey and his wife this Saturday night. I expect to hear from Don sometime Sunday."

"I've a lot to learn about real estate deals."

"You stick with us and we'll help you make a million."

That line disturbed me. What did he really mean? I left Bob with mixed feelings. It was right to try to save tbe college money, but wrong to cheat a real estate agent out of his earned commission. If the agent sued, win or lose, it would tarnish the image of the college and its board. Secretly, I hoped Carey would not sign the cancellation. I objected to Bob always calling Carey an old man and Don trying to scare Carey about his future. I had to talk to Wade about the new plan. He'd probably tell me to wait it out and let the board decide.

The next day I went to the East Leyden High School for lunch with Wade. My prognosis was correct. Upon leaving he said, "Herb, wait it out. It just may not happen. Carey is not that dumb. Time will tell."

The weekend passed quickly, with no luck in finding a home. Monday morning Bob called and reported, "I got sad news for you. The old buzzard says no on kicking his broker out, and what's more he wants to sell it slowly and in small parcels. He figures he'll save over a million in federal taxes."

"How does Don feel about it?"

"He's stewing. God help Carey when Don is finished with him."

"What does Don want the board to do?"

"He wants a unanimous vote for the full Carey farm tomorrow night. Serving notice to all concerned that the college is serious about this site will stop industry from edging in on our campus."

"Bob, do you think it will work?"

"The big shots in this community know well enough not to mess with Donald Dunahow. The law is with us through condemnation proceedings. Herb, we're really going to get you a big site."

After talking to Bob my mood changed radically and the adrenaline flowed copiously. I was so relieved that the board was not going to try to chisel Bennett & Kahnweiler, the real estate agents, out of their commission and that the securing of the site would be done legally. I immediately called Wade to prepare the agenda.

The adjourned meeting of October 14th was reconvened for October 20th. Nine determined-looking men on stage faced a larger than usual audience. Wade Steel called upon Ralph Serpico, the chairman of the site committee, to make his recommendation. Serpico reviewed the positive and negative aspects of all the sites and concluded with a firm recommendation for the 57.8 acres on Fifth Avenue and Palmer.

Five other trustees made comments supporting the Serpico motion. Roy Jones stood up and made a motion to table Serpico's, in order to allow the hoard to form a citizens committee to help in the selection. Since there was no second the Jones motion died.

A vote on the question resulted in six ayes and one nay. The audience applauded; eight men behind the table were beaming and one was sullen.

"At last the college is moving ahead," voiced one concerned citizen.

Before adjourning Wade asked me to give a brief report on my recent activities. I informed the trustees of my visits to the three local high school districts and the cooperation received from the five principals. Enthusiasm for the college was high even though space for classes was very limited. Boeger suggested I make a survey of the

2,800 graduating seniors to find out what courses they were interested in taking at college. I predicted that up to 20 per cent of the seniors might enroll during the first year of our operation.

Farmar moved and it was seconded and carried that we meet again on November 11th, even though it was a national holiday. I felt this was indeed a good board and much had been accomplished that night. Imagine giving up a holiday for public service! The mood was so good that a member of the Franklin Park press suggested we all go out for a late snack, which we did, with the exception of Jones, Boeger and Dunahow.

This district of hardworking people, with limited education and homes a generation or two old, had come alive with enthusiasm as we awaited the birth of a college. It was good to be part of it. My only regret was that my wife, who'd come from a similar background, was not there to share the moment.

11
Crisis Over Business Office

The following three weeks were busy, with more letters of inquiry and calls from future students, faculty and solicitors. Every time I left the office I returned to answer three or four new calls. I needed help. Interruptions were the order of the day, so I decided to work every night after dinner. Surprisingly, I made progress. The draft of the college philosophy and objectives, the senior survey, the roster of colleges to visit and the organizational chart of the college with administrative job descriptions were readied for board presentation.

One evening at 11:00, in a euphoric mood, I decided to call Eugenia. She was delighted to hear all the news but was upset with me for working all alone in a small office at such a late hour on a Saturday night

"It's not safe there. Get home immediately," she urged me, "and find us a home in Elmwood Park tomorrow."

As I started to gather my things together I heard someone trying to unlock the door, which I'd bolted from the inside. In his frustration at not being able to open the door the intruder hanged his fist and called out, "Open this door, goddamn it, I know you're in there. I can see the light."

I said nothing, quietly picked up the phone and called 911 to report an attempted break-in at 1829 Broadway. There was dead silence for several minutes, each one waiting for the other to make the next move. Quite unexpectedly a low voice bellowed, "I'm going to report you to Dr. Zeitlin."

"And who are you?"

"I'm Ralph Serpico."

I opened the door instantly and we looked at each other in utter disgust. Not a word was spoken. As Ralph walked in I heard a police siren close by. I opened the door again to face a bright light in my eyes. I took a few steps backward and suddenly heard the command, "Come out with your hands up high or we'll shoot."

I must be dreaming, I thought. This couldn't be happening to me. The two Melrose Park officers forced me to bend over the railing as they frisked me from head to toe.

"We got him, boss," the officer in charge said to Babe.

"Let him go. He's Dr. Zeitlin, the guy we're trying to protect It's all a mistake. Thanks, guys, you got here in minutes."

"When you call, Babe, we can make it in seconds," the sergeant said as he departed. As we walked back to the office Babe asked, "Well, what do you think of our police force?"

"I think they're terrific. I don't know if they answered your call or mine. Which one?"

"Neither, it was Maria who called. She and Tony were walking me to my car when she noticed the light on in your office. I thought someone had broken in, so I asked her to call the police while I investigated. She said the Babe was in danger. That police action shows you how much respect and protection I get from my friends."

"You're one remarkable person. This community loves you."

"Now, Dr. Zeitlin, what in hell were you doing here at this late hour?"

"I was working for you."

I took Babe by the elbow and led him to a white 3' x 4' tablet labeled *Organizational Chart* resting on a tripod stand.

Babe's first remark was, "Hmm…What's this hodge-podge of little and big squares? Can it be this checkerboard has had several abortions?"

"No, no, Babe. This is a chart outlining how the organization works. Each square shows who does what and who the responsible one is. Each box represents an office, an individual or a group."

"Who's the most important person or group?"

"The top box is the most important because it represents the people in this district. The second box represents the board. They voted you and the other six trustees into office to do a job, and if you don't do it right, they'll vote you out!"

"How are we doing so far?"

"Rather well. You got the third box filled after a six-month search for a college president. I'm now serving the board day and night, as you've just seen. In addition, you've already passed a budget, established a tax rate and last week joyfully selected a site. All that remains is to pass a big bond issue, develop the curriculum, build a campus and staff the college with well-qualified and experienced administrators, who in turn will select the teachers and counselors. Please note that on the fourth line are three deans and one coordinator, all directly reporting to me as the chief administrator."

"Which dean is the most important?"

"They're all of equal rank, and on the same salary schedule. We're going to have the first dean of technology in the state. Since there are no tech deans in Illinois, we may have to go out of state to find one or settle on a coordinator of technology, a division chairman or director of adult and vocational education. He or she will recommend to me all the occupational instructors, including business, health, trades and industry. In addition, he'll chair all the advisory committees and be responsible for filing all applications for federal, state and local grants."

"What will the second dean do?"

"The dean of instruction will recommend the hiring of all instructors in the university transfer programs and will develop articulation agreements with the universities so that our students will receive full credit upon transfer."

"Isn't this the job you had at Southwestern College?"

"Well, not exactly. My title was dean of instruction, but I also served as director of adult and vocational education. That was the traditional California way of combining these two functions into one. But usually the transfer program prospered to the neglect of the vocational. Since our college is a technical institute as well as a two-year transfer college, we must give equal status to the occupational programs."

"Will it be difficult to find a dean of instruction?"

"There'll be many applications, but finding the right one will be hard. This job is the most frequent steppingstone to a college presidency. If I'm lucky I may find a dean or president from one of the small Illinois colleges who'd like to transfer to the big city."

"Why would a dean of a small college leave his home base to become part of another small college? You know the Endicott team predicted a total enrollment of 500 if we opened in two years. You promised to open nine months from now and my guess is you'll have 250 students."

"Babe, despite what the Endicott team and several local principals have said about low registration, I'm preparing to greet 1,000 or more live bodies on opening day. You give me the four administrators I want and it will happen."

"Hmm...OK, we'll give you what you want, but if you don't hit that magic number you may be forced to return to California. Do we understand each other? Now, tell me about this third administrator."

"The third one is the dean of admissions and guidance. His or her major responsibility will be to get the students in and make sure they take the right courses to graduate. This person will supervise two counselors, one coordinator of student activities, one coordinator of the data processing center, one school nurse and the director of athletics. I'm hopeful we'll find a local high school dean or counselor to take over this position. The students will feel good if they find a familiar face on the campus."

Babe pointed to the last box on the line. "What gives with this fourth administrator? Why is he called a coordinator instead of dean? Doesn't a coordinator get paid less than a dean?"

"Yes, he does, and it was deliberately planned that way. One of the problems in higher education is that many a business manager of a college or university wants to run the show. They tell the deans what they can or cannot do since they control the flow of money. I don't want it that way. Every dean must feel he has the right to be creative and make recommendations that build the college upward rather than be restricted by edicts from the business office. The job of obtaining enough money to run the college efficiently rests with the board and the college president."

"Dr. Zeitlin, let's get something straight right now. I don't care what title you give this person, but he reports to the board and NOT YOU. YOU STAY OUT OF THE BUSINESS OFFICE. Your job is to hire the teachers, make speeches, cut ribbons and kiss the babies. But the board will run the business office. It's been that way for years within the

Chicago schools, and look how great they are. Your board has four politicians and we are committed to those who got us into office by getting them JOBS AND CONTRACTS. You said you know how to work with politicians – now DO IT!"

"Babe, it just doesn't work that way in higher education. You're surrounded by the most intelligent people in the community, so good business procedures must be observed at all times. There shall be no hanky panky deals at the taxpayer's expense and all job placement shall be based on merit and not on whom you know. That's the only way to go."

"Dr. Zeitlin, I have one word to say to you."

"And what is that?"

"Bullshit, bullshit. I'm really pissed off at you. Now, listen up and get this straight. For the Wednesday night meeting, I want the business manager's title to be changed to vice president, controller or, better still, advisor to the board."

In a rage Babe left, slamming the door with thunderous impact. I ran after him but he sped away like a jackrabbit. The head of the coalition was incensed and I felt bad. He'd been the first to want me as the president, he'd found me an apartment pronto, gotten me a wonderful secretary and bent over backwards to relocate me into a luxurious office. What should I do now? I walked the floor for over an hour, spit out some cold coffee, drove home and had a sleepless night, unable to stop the sizzling juices in my stomach.

Early Sunday morning I called Wade Steel to describe Babe's outrage. "Wade, what does this mean? I've been on the job only six weeks and the top boss of the coalition says my main function is to hire the teachers and kiss the babies. He was emphatic about my staying out of the business office. Is that how you see it?"

"No, no, Herb. As I see it, we have serving as trustees four local politicians with no previous school board experience. They need to be educated and you and I must be the teachers. Jones and Boeger have been there and they can help us out. It will be hard but it can be done. The neophytes must accept you as the chief administrator responsible for all the hiring and firing. We're not going to take on the worst features of the Chicago system.

"That sounds good to me. In California we have over 100

community college boards and not a single one has the business manager reporting directly to the board. I know. I studied all of them while a graduate student at Stanford. Whoever controls the flow of money must take his or her direction from the college president. We cannot obtain the best staff and merchandise by repaying political lackeys. Do you agree?"

"Yes, I do. I'll talk to Babe the first thing tomorrow morning. You prepare the agenda as you see fit for the Wednesday meeting."

I hung up, slightly relieved that the board president agreed with me. I also had a certain ally in Roy Jones, and maybe in Elmore Boeger. Still, I was greatly concerned that if the issue came to a vote my organizational chart would be defeated by a vote of 4 to 3. I didn't like the thought. A second or third no vote might mean I would be out. There had to be a better way.

What do I do now? Stay calm and think. . .I decided to test the Serpico turbulence by soliciting a reaction from Bob and Joe. On Monday morning I called the boys. We agreed to meet in my office in the evening to discuss thoroughly the organizational chart.

They arrived together, not in the usual jovial mood, but in stoic silence. They listened attentively as I detailed every position. Joe, the Notre Dame law graduate, led off the cross-examination. "Where will you find these great administrators?"

My immediate response was, "We'll look everywhere for the most qualified. But for this first round of recruitment we'll concentrate on Illinois candidates and give special consideration to those interested from the five local high schools."

"How many will come from California?"

"None. I promised President DeVore and Superintendent Rindone at Southwestern College that I would not recruit any of their faculty for at least two years."

"That pleases us very much. Bob and I were sure that your right- or left-hand man or woman would be a Californian. Now, how much are we giving to these deans?"

"The salary range for deans will be about 15 per cent less than for the president, and for the coordinator approximately 20 per cent less. All department chairpersons will be on the teachers' schedule plus receive an additional stipend for the chairmanship."

"Is that the usual in higher education?"

"Yes, most deans in community colleges get paid slightly less than presidents and a little more than principals of large high schools. After the organizational chart is approved, I will submit to the board schedules for administrators, teachers and classified staffs."

"Where will these administrators be housed?"

"Babe has assured me there will be two additional apartments available after the first of the year. The dean of admissions and two counselors will be housed in one while the dean of technology and dean of instruction will occupy the other."

"Well, you seem to be on the right track. Maybe we can get the Babe to cool down a bit if you answer this last question correctly."

"And what is that?"

Joe popped his eyes at me, stood erect, put his hands on his hips and stated, "Dr. Zeitlin, I want to make it perfectly clear in good old-fashioned slang that the board is the boss and we have the final say in all hiring and firing. Is that understood?"

"Yes, I accept that policy completely. It's standard procedure with over 3,000 college boards throughout the United States. The college president shall solicit and recommend to the board only those candidates that are most qualified."

"And what happens if we don't accept your recommendations?"

"Personnel matters are generally held in executive sessions with the board. You tell me what's wrong with the candidate. I make note of it and make sure that the second candidate I present to you satisfies your new requirements."

"Now, hold on a minute. Suppose we don't accept your second or third recommendation? What happens next?"

"I hope it never reaches that point, but if it does I'll get the message and we'll mutually agree to separate on peaceful terms."

"That sounds good enough for me. What do you think, Bob?"

"I'm sure Babe would accept that agreement. He's busy as hell tonight but I'll call him tomorrow morning."

"I'm satisfied. So, Dr. Zeitlin, go ahead and present your organizational chart and any other stuff that needs to be acted upon. I'm hungry. Aren't you? Let's go out to dinner."

The crisis meeting over, we agreed to meet at the Red Steer. When

I arrived at the restaurant, Joe was all alone guzzling his Manhattan with gusto. Bob had gone to the phone to invite his friend Jim Tarpey to join us. Upon his return Bob said that Jim would be joining us shortly. Then smilingly he asked, "Herb, what do you think of the minutes I've given you after every meeting?"

"It's wonderful to get them the day after, even if they're not letter perfect. You must stay up late at night to get it done."

"No, I don't do them. I don't have the time. Jim Tarpey does them for me for free. He's a great supporter of the college."

"For free? He should get paid."

"I was hoping you'd say that. You're really on target tonight. Could you use a part-time public relations specialist?"

"'Why, of course, particularly if he's had experience working with newspaper people. Has he?"

"Yes, he has. I believe he personally knows most of the local reporters. I'll have Jim fill out a job application when he gets here."

As we were having dessert Jim Tarpey arrived in a jovial mood. He greeted everyone and gave me one hearty handshake. He was meticulously dressed in a grey sharkskin suit, imported black pointed shoes, clean-shaven, recently doused with a heavy touch of after-shave cologne.

Bob said, "Whew, whew. . .settle down, Jim. Now tell us the latest story at your office."

"Well, the fellows are all talking to the girls about psychoceramics."

"What the hell is psychoceramics?"

"You know that psychiatry is the study of the mind, and psychology is the study of human behavior. Now everyone is studying psychoceramics."

"Out with it, Jim. What is psychoceramics? Can it be taught at the college?"

"Yes it can, if Dr. Zeitlln can find a qualified instructor."

"Can you, Dr. Zeitlin?"

"I'm sure we can because Chicago, like New York and Los Angeles, has a large supply."

"A large supply of what?"

"Crackpots. Psychoceramics is the study of crackpots."

With that Bob threw his olive at Jim while Joe squeezed his cherry and pushed it into Jim's mouth, and we all laughed.

The following morning I spoke to Tarpey's boss, who highly recommended Jim and any member of the Tarpey family. He described the Tarpeys as long-time residents of River Grove, hardworking, intelligent, honest and well-liked by everyone. I called Jim and told him he could start the following night by getting to the board meeting early, giving a warm greeting to the arrivals and distributing copies of the agenda to the public. Later, we would plan the press conference together. He thanked me profusely for the job and made a few positive suggestions.

12
Progress at Armistice Meeting

In the old days, prior to 1956, November 11th had been known as Armistice Day. On that day in 1918 the Allies and Germany had stopped fighting in World War I in order to negotiate a lasting peace (which lasted until 1939). On the same day in 1964, a smiling, affable college president greeted each arriving trustee with a warm handshake. It was marvelous to behold the rousing reception given to Babe. They all respected and liked the Boss of the coalition. As he gave me a strong hug Babe's rage was nowhere to be found, while the others laughed and joked. I wondered what had brought about this 180-degree change.

Collins and Farmar listened attentively as Jones expounded on why Barry Goldwater had lost to Lyndon Johnson in the presidential election. Knol and Boeger analyzed the fear of tomorrow evoked by the movie *Dr. Strangelove*. Wade, arriving late, called the meeting to order at 8:15 PM with a request to hear reports from the various committee chairs.

Babe, as chairman of the site committee, informed us that attorney Don Dunahow had been authorized to enter into negotiations with the attorney of the Carey farm. Don would periodically give the board a progress update.

Architectural chair Elmore Boeger stated that 20 architects had responded to his inquiry to the American Architectural Association, with each one following the criteria he had given. The next step was to evaluate the achievements of the architects and narrow down to the four or five of the most qualified; then a visit by the board to the site of the last building completed by each architect would be scheduled. All the trustees responded positively to Jones's suggestion that Dr. Zeitlin obtain confidential statements from the construction firms on their working relationships with the architects.

The meeting and the spotlight progressed to Roy Jones's report on the annual meeting of the Illinois School Board Association. Each trustee asked him several questions, which he answered immediately, precisely and accurately. Inasmuch as Roy was already the representative from the Hillside school district Fred Knol moved that his boss, Ralph Serpico, be appointed delegate from the college and Elmore Boeger the alternate. The motion was seconded and carried unanimously without discussion.

Wade turned to Bob Collins, pulled out a yellow legal-sized pad from him attaché case and dramatically declared, "What I have here is the talk of the town..."

His colleagues were taken aback What's up? It must be something big! Wade frowned, Joe popped his eyes and Fred and Roy opened their mouths wide. Elmore remained poker-faced while Babe smiled, awaiting a surprise announcement. Wade only said, "Everybody and his uncle has a suggestion for a college name. God only knows what it's going to be. I can't stop the flow. God help us if we select the wrong one." He called out a dozen or more possibilities and set November 23rd as the deadline date for any additional suggestions, with a final decision to be made in December.

With great dignity, Wade then announced that the press conference would be held on Saturday, November 18th at the West Leyden High School faculty cafeteria at 12:00 noon. Thirteen editors of Chicagoland newspapers had been invited. The purpose of the conference was to exchange ideas and to let the press know what progress had been made thus far. All the trustees realized that help from the press was urgently needed in promoting a successful bond issue.

At that point I mentioned that Jim Tarpey, a public relations specialist, had been writing the minutes regularly for free. He had also volunteered to do other press releases on a weekly basis. I felt he should be paid and recommended that he be hired on a part-time schedule. Bob beamed when I said, "The college would indeed be lucky to have such a high-caliber individual as Jim serve as Community Relations Associate."

With those remarks Bob Collins moved to appoint Mr. Tarpey as Community Relations Associate, to be directly responsible to the college president at a salary of $100 per month. The motion was seconded by the Babe and again carried unanimously.

I felt good. I had pleased the board secretary by hiring his best friend. Four weeks earlier the boss of the coalition, Babe Serpico, had expressed his pleasure with me when I recommended his sister-in-law as my secretary. I recalled the prediction of Bob Curtis, the state employment authority: "In order for a chief administrator of a school district to stay in office he must hire a relative, family member or best friend of each trustee."

It seemed my first two appointments were in line with the Curtis prophecy. Two down and five to go. But Curtis had implied trustees' kinfolk were, almost by definition, incompetent or lackeys. Yet in this particular case he'd been dead wrong. I'd gotten two very well-qualified, supportive employees waiting for my direction. If the next five trustees' kin were of the same breed, I'd be a very lucky administrator.

Under "new business," Wade asked me to read the tentative statement of philosophy and objectives of the college. I was well-prepared, having spent over two years at Southwestern College reaching an acceptable consensus with the faculty. I sounded off with the first aim, "To provide superior-quality collegiate instruction for ALL OF THE PEOPLE within the limitations of their ability to profit from instruction."

Joe Farmar immediately asked, "Those words 'for all the people' –do they include such minorities as blacks, browns, yellows and reds?"

"Yes, color shall never be a factor at our college. All staff members shall be trained to be color-blind. If they're not trainable, out they'll go."

"How about sex, age, nationality, religion or political affiliation?"

"Our doors will be continuously open to all groups, including rich and poor."

It was refreshing to receive incessant questions from the sagacious board as we went through the remaining five aims. The audience seemed to love the stimulating dialogue between the college president and his bosses.

I pointed out to the trustees that in order to implement the philosophy the institution would seek to fulfill the following major objectives:

1. To provide TRANSFER EDUCATION paralleling the

freshman and sophomore studies at the University of Illinois, state colleges, private colleges and universities.

2.   To provide OCCUPATIONAL EDUCATION in technical, vocational and semi-professional curricula to meet employment opportunities in business and industry.

3.   To provide GENERAL EDUCATION for local residents desiring to broaden their intellectual and cultural experiences.

4.   To provide GUIDANCE AND COUNSELING services to assist students in self-appraisal and in the determination of realistic educational goals.

5.   To provide COMMUNITY SERVICES through cultural, intellectual and recreational activities with the use of college facilities and encouragement from the college faculty and staff.

After I explained the significance of each objective Joe Farmar asked, "Dr. Zeitlin, I don't mean to be personal, but did you write this wonderful philosophy and objectives yourself, or did you borrow it from some other catalog?"

"Joe, like so many other college presidents, I borrow from the best wherever I find it The philosophy that I presented to you tonight is modified from the catalog of Southwestern College in Chula Vista, California. I added the 'FOR ALL THE PEOPLE' in capital letters and changed 'vocational/tech' to 'occupational,' a better word at present. Later the term may change to 'career education.' While a graduate student at Stanford, for a research project I analyzed every junior/ community college catalog in the state of California, so you might say I'm a specialist in this area."

Elmore Boeger interrupted with, "This philosophy and objectives sounds good to me. Let's put it down as an action item for the December meeting. Now, I'd like to know how you're coming along with the pending visits to other college campuses."

"Elmore, I've written to 22 college presidents, and thus far nine have responded to my questions. Most of these new colleges are just a step ahead of us, with the exception of Flint, Michigan. I'll try to arrange an all-day visit to Flint for some Saturday soon."

"Let's do it real soon, Mr. President," Wade Steel added. "Please tell us what happened at the higher education conference you attended at Monticello last week."

"I, along with several other new presidents, was given a warm welcome into the higher education family. We were told that a new master plan for higher education is in the works. Governor Kerner believes that junior colleges should be separated from the high school board and become part of the higher education division. I feel that we're indeed very fortunate to have such a forward-looking governor."

"What difference does it make if the junior colleges are governed under the high school board or under a separate junior college board?"

"It makes a great difference. Under the high school board the junior college is of secondary concern, with the major attention and money going to the high school. By joining the higher education family, better articulation with the universities will follow. In addition, each community will vote on its own tax rate for the community college. The signs are all positive that this will happen."

"How do the universities feel about the pending change?"

"They welcome it. They feel that the time has come for universities to concentrate on upper division and graduate work, leaving the junior colleges to handle all incoming freshmen and sophomores."

"Do you think it will happen?"

"It's happening today in California, where more than half the freshmen are enrolled in community colleges and the students are proud to be part of a system that saves their parents thousand of dollars. It will happen in Illinois if proper state financing is provided. The way to save taxpayers money is to expand community colleges rather than to strain the facilities of the universities beyond capacity."

"What does the renowned Dr. Henry have to say about the new master plan?"

"He was the featured speaker and was enthusiastically received. After all, he's president of the prestigious University of Illinois, the university with the largest number of full-time day students in the nation."

"What's that number?"

"It's over 30,000. Dr. Henry emphatically stated that UI is bursting at the seams and cannot take any more students."

"So he really supports the new master plan."

"Oh yes, and his faculty is 100% behind him, or close to that! As a matter of fact, after he delivered his remarks I spoke to him about our college using his lower division courses and programs. He heartily endorsed the idea and promised to have his academic vice president contact me to sign an articulation agreement. Upon leaving he asked me to convey his best wishes to Wallace Sterling, the president of Stanford University. Again I felt good. It was wonderful to be the simple messenger between the two biggest giants of the university world."

Wade stood up, stretched his arms, took a deep breath, sat down and announced, "You know, fellows, I have a very dear friend, Assemblyman Bill Clayborne, on the Higher Education Committee. He'll tell me what it's all about and when I know I'll tell you. Dr. Zeitlin, I see this large tablet in front of me labeled 'Organizational Chart.' I know you're dying to tell us what it's all about, so you're on!"

"In order to carry out the goals and objectives of the college I need help, and that help will come when we hire four top-notch, experienced administrators."

I then reviewed the duties and responsibilities of each dean and the coordinator of business management, all reporting directly to me. Several questions followed. Fred asked, "Of the three deans, which one is the most important?"

"They are all of equal rank and will be on the same salary schedule."

"Why is the dean of technology listed first?"

"This is a technical institute, and to give recognition to that fact we'll list the technical or occupational programs, which this dean is responsible to develop, first in the college catalog. This will be a hard position to fill, since there are no tech deans in the state of Illinois."

Elmore Boeger interrupted, "How about the other deans?"

"We should have no trouble finding a dean of instruction and a dean of admissions and guidance. The concern will be to get the right one from a large field of candidates."

"Why is the business manager called a coordinator instead of a dean?" said Roy Jones.

"In my experience I've seen too many business managers limit or stifle a college's development. They tend to make too many decisions on how the money is to be spent, and that is wrong. As the chief administrator of the college the president is in charge, not the business manager. The deans must be given the opportunity to grow, and such growth should not be controlled by the business manager. That's why his salary level is below that of a dean."

I turned to look at Babe, Bob and Joe and they all smiled, returning the look with a "yes" nod. Several more questions were asked. I ended saying that a more complete chart would be worked out as staff positions were developed. Before adjourning at 9:40 Wade stated that a vote would be taken on the chart at the December meeting.

As I picked up my paraphernalia Joe stole up behind me and whispered, "Herb, get your ass over to Nielsen's restaurant ASAP. Don has called a special meeting."

I was tired but the adrenaline started flowing again at this big-voiced, quiet but firm command. I responded with an OK. I looked around. All the trustees but Wade were gone. I asked him, "What's up, Wade?"

"I don't know. Bob told me that Don is angry and has called an urgent meeting with the coalition. He wants the two of us to join them. Did you notice the heavy scorn on Don's face before he left? There's no doubt about it. He's very upset. I don't know if it's with you or me."

"We'll know shortly." I felt it was me. He hadn't liked my comments about the business manager reporting to the college-president. Well, I guessed this was showdown time. I was determined not to yield an inch.

When I arrived at the restaurant, I saw six men in a corner all smoking, drinking and talking surreptitiously. They stopped talking as I approached Don and loudly asked him:

"Are Boeger and Jones coming?"

"Boeger's little Phyllis was not feeling well...so he had to get home to look after his little Mommy. Jones wasn't invited, nor will he ever be."

While we were talking Wade unzipped his portfolio case and handed Don three handwritten legal-sized pages with the comment, "Here is the list of the invited newspaper editors. I know several of them to be highly respected individuals."

"But you don't know all of them, do you, Wade?"

"No, I don't know all of them."

"Well, I know most of them, particularly the smart-ass ones. They're known to exaggerate and build nothing into something with their prolific use of words. They can't be trusted."

"Is there anyone you object to, Don?"

"Could you scratch Neil Mehler?"

"No, I can't do that The invitation is already mailed. Not only is he a friend but he's the owner and editor of the *Franklin Parker*. He did some very fine articles on East Leyden High School."

"Mayor Conti and I think he's a scumbag. He spells trouble to me. You'll be sorry for what you've done. You hire me as your lawyer for guidance and then you ignore me on the important items. Next time, ask me before you do any other crazy things."

Silence fell over the group as Don, the lawyer for the city of Elmwood Park, reprimanded Wade. I didn't think it was justified and was quite surprised to see all the trustees appearing to support Don.

Wade, the most respected and loved superintendent of schools, stayed quiet and swallowed hard. I wanted to say something as he stood alone facing the coalition's aggressive attorney.

I raised my hand and when it was not acknowledged, I started to move it about. Finally Don said, "Dr. Zeitlin, what are you itching to say?"

"Don, we just can't hold a selective press conference. If we only invite those we like and reject those we dislike, then we're not being fair to all concerned. The unacceptable press may form a coalition of their own, a de facto opposition. That's a bad beginning."

Babe Serpico instantly came to my defense with, "I think Dr. Zeitlin is right. As a long-time politician I think we should avoid creating adversary groups. If we don't have the press with us, the tax referendum will definitely fall. As Mayor Daley has taught me, I'd especially make it a point to woo Neil Mehler."

"Fellows, I agree with Babe," interrupted Bob Collins. "We would be a stupid board if by our actions we created foes instead of friends. Therefore, I'm recommending we postpone naming the college until after the bond election. The community is divided. The leading choices are West Suburban, West Towns, Suburban, Kennedy and combinations of Leyden-Proviso, and I don't like any of them."

"Then sound off when you meet the press, just like you're doing right *now,*" Don retorted. "I'm telling you gentlemen that you're not prepared to meet the press unless... *YOU DO SOME IMMEDIATE HOMEWORK!*"

"What do you propose, Don?" Wade asked.

"You're dealing with a bunch of smart-asses. You have to be as smart as them, if not smarter. Remember, you've been trustees for over six months. Haven't you learned anything? I don't want to hear anyone say, 'I don't know.' If you really don't know refer the question to the specialist here, our eminent college president. And, Herb, if you don't have a good answer, I'll take over."

I said, "Les, don't you think we should have a dry run before meeting the editorial staff?"

"Definitely, and the sooner the better. I'm willing to start tomorrow night at seven in your office and again Friday night, if necessary. What do you say to that?"

The men looked at each other in dead silence. After 60 seconds Joe said, "I think it's a good idea, and you're brilliant to bring it up. Bob and I can make it. How about you, Fred?"

"No, I can't. I'm on the swing shift and can't get away, or else Lindberg Steel will collapse. But I certainly feel you should invite Jones and Boeger. Not to do so would be asking for disaster. We all want a successful bond election and the board must appear united. Do you agree, Babe?"

"Why, of course. I'll be there, provided you order a pizza with pepperoni and olives. I think Wade, Les and Zeity should grill us with whatever questions the press might possibly ask and tell us how good or bad our answers are. After all, they're the experienced ones. Am I right or am I right? Take your choice."

"I agree," Joe said. "Prior to the great debate between Kennedy and Nixon, Jack's boys shot questions at him for a grueling two days. We must question each other closely and severely. If the Irish Mafia can do it, so can we."

And so for two nights the six trustees were cross-examined avidly, until Wade said, "Fellows, we're ready for the smart ones."

On Saturday, surprisingly enough, all thirteen editors or their representatives arrived on time. After they munched on doughnuts and coffee, Wade gave a brief welcome and introduced all of us, making sure to name the community in which we resided, the job we presently held and a few words about our fine families. He said there would be no long speeches and hoped for a free exchange of ideas and viewpoints about the college. Babe smiled broadly when Wade mentioned that the college president was now living in Melrose Park.

Wade opened with, "Now, fellows, what can we tell you about the college?"

In an orderly fashion Wade went around the room and allowed each newsman an opportunity to respond. Then the questions flowed in nonstop. Among the highlights were:

Where and when will the classes be held?

What programs and subjects will be taught?

Will the college have any trouble getting accredited, and by what agency?

How are you doing on the naming of the college?

How much will the River Grove site cost the taxpayers?

Where will you get the money to buy it?

How much will you ask the taxpayers to approve for the bond issue?

What is it going to cost us?

How much will the tuition be?

How many students do you expect to attend on opening day and 10 years later?

Where will you find the teachers and how much will you pay them?

What is the difference between a community college and a technical institute?

How much parking will you have?

What are the goals and objectives?

Will you have programs for the able and ambitious as well as for those needing remedial work?

Will the architect be hired from California or Illinois?

When will construction begin?

WHAT CAN WE DO TO HELP?

All questions were answered to the satisfaction of the press. They loved the wholesome exchange and pledged their support for the up-and-coming bond election. It was marvelous to behold the spirit of the unified trustees in their instant response to all the inquiries. I gave all the trustees and Jim Tarpey an A+ for their outstanding performance. Again I felt fortunate indeed to work with such a highly intelligent and diverse group of personalities.

Before leaving Neil Mehler approached me and said, "Dr. Zeitlin, I enjoyed reading your 17 reasons why a student should attend a community college, but I'd like to know which one you think is the most important."

"All of them are important! If I were a father or mother I would be delighted to save thousands of dollars each year by having my son or daughter attend the local community college. If I were unemployed or unhappy with my present job, I would jump at the opportunity to try something different by enrolling in one of the occupational training programs to learn a new skill and do something I'd like better."

"How can you say you'll offer similar or better instruction than that at the University of Illinois?"

"I recently received approval from President Henry to offer any of his lower division courses. It's my opinion, based on research, that our freshmen and sophomore transfer students will receive better instruction with us than at the university because we will not use untrained teacher assistants. The 'publish or perish' philosophy prevalent at so many universities will not operate here. We intend to recruit experienced master instructors from Chicagoland, where there is a gold mine of talent"

"Dr. Zeitlin, to be truthful, your goals seem unrealistic and impossible to fulfill. You're just dreaming."

"Neil, I believe a goal is just a dream with *a* deadline. I'll try in the months ahead to meet all the deadlines. Given the right climate, everything I said can happen. Can I count on you for help?"

"Surely I wish you good luck. You'll certainly need it. Now, where is my old friend Don Dunahow?"

"He's right behind you. Don, can you help Neil out?"

"What's on your mind, Neil?"

"Mr. Dunahow, I heard you're a specialist on the sale of general obligation bonds. Is that correct?"

"Yes, I am. What would you like to know?"

"What is the average interest rate of double A rated bonds with a twenty-year maturity, and will they be easy to sell?"

"Tax-free general obligation bonds are always easy to sell, especially if Standard & Poor's or Moody's rates them AA. Presently these bonds are earning 3.1 to 3.2 per cent but that's not guaranteed. The rates change every day."

"Why are they so easy to sell?"

"People who make big money hate to pay federal and state taxes. In order to avoid paying taxes they put their hard-earned savings in bonds instead of banks or thrifts."

"Do you think the interest paid may go up to 4 or 5 per cent in the near future?"

"Not in my lifetime, but if you have a minimum of $25,000 to invest I can get some worry free ones."

"Well, thanks, but I'm not ready yet."

As Neil left Dunahow muttered something under his breath but I couldn't grasp his grumble. Bob and Jim Tarpey called out, "Come on along, Herb. Let's all breeze away to the Red Steer. See you all in twenty minutes."

I was the last to arrive at the restaurant. Smith loudly announced, "Late again, Dr. Zeitlin. Sit here next to Bob and me. If you had a Lincoln you'd have been here ten minutes earlier."

"I'm not too sure of that. I had a lot of stuff to pack into my small trunk and it takes time."

"You did well today and so did the rest of the gang."

I was surprised to receive a compliment from Don; his mood had changed from critic to supporter. It was refreshing to see such a happy and harmonious board drinking away.

All the boys were trying to please each other with compliments. Babe thanked Roy Jones for saying, "The River Grove site was the best possible choice for the board to make."

It looked like the two archenemies wanted to be friends. Elmore praised Fred for his strong stand on having many vocational/tech programs. In return, Fred said, "It was very smart of Elmore to assure the public that the architect would probably come from Illinois, not from California."

Joe Farmar suddenly popped in, "Let's all give Wade a big hand for his masterful job as chairman. He kept everyone under control and on track." Light applause followed.

Jones complimented Collins on his splendid explanation why naming the college was delayed. Why choose a name that would make half the community unhappy? We had to find one satisfactory to all concerned.

I ordered a big steak with plenty of onions and mashed potatoes with oodles of gravy. With each bite positive juices flowed within me. Why? After eight weeks of division the trustees had suddenly appeared to respect and admire each other.

Their goal had been to solicit the press's help in passing a bond election, while the press, in a nice turnaround, had actually volunteered it.

In addition to Neil Mehler several other editors requested copies of my paper on the advantages of a community college. The press had arrived in a lackadaisical mood but left as new disciples to carry forth the gospel of the college. The dry run had paid off in big dividends; the trustees had responded to each question as experts. From the nature of their questions the reporters seemed to sincerely want to learn. I welcomed the opportunity to inform them, and promised weekly college releases. Jim Tarpey had listened in and responded with his usual nodding of the head.

As I was eating my dessert Bob asked, "How are you doing in your search for a home?"

"I've found a beautiful four bedroom, two bath home with a large backyard in an excellent, quiet location in Elmwood Park. There's only one problem."

"And, what is that?"

"We settled on the price but I can't finance it unless I put 20 per cent down. The best I can do at present would be ten per cent. The owner will not go for a lease option to buy; therefore we're at a stalled position. I may have to go for a lease option on a smaller home down the street."

Hearing that Joe interrupted us, "Herb, give me the details. I may be able to help. I have a lot of banker friends."

I readily supplied Joe with the particulars. "I'll get back to you one day next week," he said.

As I headed for my car Bob stopped me. "Herb, are you flying back to San Diego for Thanksgiving?"

"No, I can't afford it, but I'm hoping to get my family back here before Christmas."

"If that's the case, then Beverly and I want you at our home for Thanksgiving at 6:00 PM. You're not eating alone on this special day. You're joining the Collins family."

"Bob, that's especially nice of you. I would be delighted to be with you."

On Wednesday, the night before the holiday, I went to Dominick's on Ninth Avenue to purchase a fine bottle of wine and a two-pound box of chocolates for Beverly and the kids the following day.

13
Thanksgiving
With the Collins Family

The Collins lived on Davisson Street, a tree-lined, quiet road of brick bungalows of modest means. I managed to squeeze my little Skylark into a tight parking area at the end of the street. As I entered the Collins vestibule Bob gave me a brotherly hug. Beverly pecked on my cheek as I presented her with the wine and chocolates. The kids grabbed the candy and ran with it. Bev chased after them, caught them, grabbed back the sweets and admonished them with, "Not now, you can have two each after dinner." I chuckled, remembering my children.

Bob introduced me to his especially warmhearted mother, who expressed much concern for my wife and four children in faraway California. "Is this the first time you've been separated for Thanksgiving?"

"Yes, the first time in fifteen years."

Bob joined in. "Well, Dr. Zeitlin, after dinner we're going to bring the Collins and Zeitlins together through modern technology. I make my living by bringing folks together. The bells between Illinois and California will be ringing a happy tone soon."

"That sounds good to me."

We all sat down at a lovely decorated table. Bob requested that we all hold hands as he delivered a short prayer thanking God for our families, good health and continued prosperity. As soon as Bob said "Amen" the little one yelled out, "Squeeze, Uncle Herbert."

I was flattered to be called Uncle Herbert and pleasantly surprised to be part of the ritual Bob had taught his offspring. Bob's mother said she had taught Bob, and she had learned it from her own mother. And so, it had been practiced in the Collins family for three generations, with a fourth on the horizon.

Beverly opened the large oven, pulled out a huge, sizzling turkey and placed it in front of her husband to carve. In rapid order she rushed in a large salad bowl, mashed potatoes, cranberries, beets, peas and carrots, cauliflower, yams and freshly baked rolls. Bob kept filling my glass and his with white wine as we ate an epicurean feast prepared solely by a superb chef, Bev. Even Mother Collins declared that she never could duplicate her daughter-in-law's menu. Pumpkin pie with decorative fluffy cream was our dessert, served with coffee or tea. A continuous flow of conversation started with Mother Collins, who focused on her son's early beginnings, his high school days and his job with Illinois Bell. With pain she mentioned the conflict Bob had with her brother, the mayor, and with pleasure she expressed great admiration and respect for the top man at Illinois Bell, Jim Olson. Bob entertained us with short accounts of his relationship with Olson. He was always the one ready to do special jobs for his boss.

Bob's mother and wife cleaned the table, washed the dishes and sent the kids to their room to watch TV while Bob and I relaxed with B & B cordials and pfefferneusen cookies. True to his word my youngest trustee placed a long-distance call to Eugenia and told me to talk as long as I wished; he had no-cost long-distance privileges with the company.

I told Eugenia that I had a wonderful friend in Bob Collins. He was just like my brother Arthur, a skilled technician, always willing to help, with a marvelous wife and well-behaved kids. At that remark, before leaving the room Bob cried out, loud enough for everyone to hear, "Tell Eugenia she can call me Brother Bob, and so can you."

"Eugenia, he's a real pal." I told her about the pending decision on one of two homes in Elmwood Park. I promised to return to Chula Vista before Christmas so she should prepare to move after the holiday. The two-hour difference between Chicagoland and Southern California was in my favor. Eugenia had been about to serve the Thanksgiving spread just as we'd finished, so she asked me to keep it down to 15 minutes. Mark asked about the weather in Chicago. He was shocked when I told him it was snowing and the temperature was in the upper 20's while San Diego had a high of 75°.

Joyce wanted to know what snow felt like. I told her nice and clean. Ann Victoria expressed concern about her new school; would Joyce be going with her? The kids kept rattling off many questions and I tried to accentuate the positive aspects of moving. It would be an adventure traveling on the Sky Chieftain to the Midwest. Chicagoland meant ice skating, skiing, sailing on a big lake, museums, art exhibits, baseball at Wrigley Field, plays and great educational opportunities. Finally Clare got on the phone and managed to say, "Miss you Daddee, come home for Christmas, kiss, kiss." I returned Clare's kiss, kiss with many hugs and squeezes and I heard Eugenia announce, "Hurry up, dinner is served."

As I hung up Bob put his hand over my shoulder and said, "Herb, I can see you're a great family man with traditional values, just like me. The most important thing in the world for Bev and me is our kids. Every cent I earn goes for their betterment."

"And what part will education play in their betterment?"

"It's the prime factor for a better life. What I could not get I'll give to my kids. And that's why the board will have to work day and night to promote the sale of bonds."

"How will your uncle the mayor vote?"

"He'll vote 'NO', just like he did in the formation of the district."

"Why?"

"He thinks we're overeducating the masses. If everyone received a college degree, we would have a country of smart-asses and no one to do the necessary dirty work. He used to cover up his lack of a high school diploma, but lately he boasts about it. He managed to succeed in business and polities without wasting a lot of money on college, so who really needs it?"

"Is he happy?"

"No, he's a grumpy old man and fights tax increases at every turn."

"When do I get to meet him?"

"Next week at the Leyden Municipal meeting. I assume Wade told you all about the organization."

"Yes, he did. The league consists of mayors, council members and all other governmental officials running the villages. Is that correct?"

"Correct. They say the main purpose is to have better informed politicians, but I say their hidden agenda is to keep taxes down, particularly school taxes! My uncle was very angry with me when we hired you."

"Why?"

"Because you came from California. He felt the president should be someone local. He dislikes Californians and described them to me as suntanned egocentric SOB's with low moral standards and many crackpot ideas."

"That's sad."

"Yes, it is, and that's the element we'll be fighting in the bond election. Now, let me tell you about my old high school buddy, Harry Smith, who'll be dropping in soon. His parents were a lot better off than mine, so upon graduation he went off to six years of college to become a lawyer while I went to work for Illinois Bell. He married a young and beautiful business girl named Marilyn. They had a healthy baby that died a year ago through a tragic accident."

"What was the accident?"

"They hired a 14-year-old babysitter to watch their 9-month-old child. When they came home late at night they found the baby dead."

"Oh, my God, what happened?"

"After feeding the baby the sitter placed her in the crib face down. The little one wiggled her way to the space between the mattress and pad and could not get out. The sitter couldn't hear her crying because she'd closed the door and was glued to TV's *Bonanza.* When the Smiths came home around midnight, Harry asked, 'How's our baby?'"

The sitter had replied, "I gave her one bottle and she fell asleep right away. I haven't heard a peep out of her all night."

Bob continued the story. "When Harry and Marilyn went into the bedroom they saw the child caught between the mattress and the pad and not breathing. Harry tried CPR and every other conceivable method to revive her, without success. With fury, Marilyn lashed out at the sitter, who'd suddenly become catatonic. Within minutes the fire department and an ambulance with a doctor arrived and tried to revive the baby, to no avail. When the sitter's parents arrived, the doctor sedated Marilyn and the sitter so they could go into a long sleep. When Marilyn awakened the following day she told Harry she'd had a horrible dream. She broke down again when Harry told her it hadn't been a dream!"

"How long ago did this happen?"

"About a year ago."

"Have they recovered?"

"They never will recover fully but they're trying desperately. The neighbors have helped tremendously."

"How so?"

"Florence Youngman and her husband, who live in the house next to them, organized a sort of a hospice committee of 14 wonderful neighbors, who cooked, answered the phone, cleaned the house and engaged the young bereaved couple in positive conversation every evening. They were not left alone for 14 consecutive nights. Every evening a different neighbor brought over a hot dinner for the Smiths and talked them into fixing up their old home. Their blacktop driveway was crumbling, so a neighbor who specialized in concrete work took the initiative and replaced it with four inches of solid concrete and red brick borders. Harry and Marilyn loved it and were amazed when the contractor refused payment. He said it was a gift from God.

"The next day the kitchen refinisher showed the couple a variety of photos of modern kitchens and gave Marilyn 24 hours to make her choice. The job was completed in four days and Marilyn was overjoyed. She had a kitchen better than her parents'. Again the craftsman refused payment, claiming he got a message from God's Wife and She had to be obeyed.

"A third contractor, specializing in landscaping, put in a new lawn with automatic sprinklers. His message had come from God's Child, so he'd moved with alacrity. Harry was overwhelmed and at the beginning didn't know what to do. To distract them from the tragedy, the neighbors, many of them skilled craftsmen, had gotten the Smiths to focus on the many paths of rebuilding."

Bob hadn't quite finished the story when the Smiths arrived. I was surprised to face a couple that looked like Mr. and Mrs. America plus. They were two very attractive, beautifully dressed, vivacious and articulate young individuals. Harry's handshake was strong and firm, just like a football player's. Marilyn gave me a tender hug and a little peck on the cheek with the comment "Bob told us all about you, and we're dying to meet your beautiful wife."

"Hopefully you'll meet her after the Christmas holidays. I know she'll be delighted to see you folks. Please tell me, how's the construction going at your home?"

Harry shook his head in disbelief and slowly voiced his feeling. "Herb, you won't believe what I'm about to tell you...When our baby died last year, it seemed like God immediately commissioned 10 of our neighbors into angels to help us through our pain. When we first moved to River Grove I didn't know anyone on the block. Now, a year later, we're just like one big happy family."

"Pray tell, how did that happen?"

"I'm not really a very religious man, but St. Paul was right when he said you have nothing when you don't have charity, and charity in the finest sense is *love*. Our neighbors gave us faith, hope and charity. When Clare died, they forced themselves into our lives every night at 6:00 PM by appearing at our doorstep with a home-cooked meal for four. Every night a different couple appeared. As we ate these wonderful meals we talked a little about the past and much about the present, and speculated on the future. Our friends included hardworking blue collar technicians, craftsmen and clerical workers with educational levels ranging from eighth grade, to high school graduate, to college graduate. The one common denominator was faith in God and love of people. They turned Marilyn and me on with their many suggestions for improving the physical condition of our house. We were overwhelmed with enthusiasm when we saw the new driveway go in, followed by a new kitchen, drapes and beautiful landscaping. The laborers refused any money from us, claiming that God's orders had to be obeyed. I couldn't believe it was happening to us. Had I read about this in a novel, I'd have dismissed it as an author's fantasy! Such a thing just doesn't happen in real life."

"But it really did happen?"

"Yes, it did. On the eleventh evening Marilyn cooked a grand dinner for six and we surprised Florence Youngman just as she came home from her work at the post office. I'd found out surreptitiously that she'd been the controlling power behind the hospice movement, with her husband, John, as a general contractor, coordinating the reno-vation of our residence. A tall, rugged, unshaven individual in workingman's clothes, his neighbors called John a diamond in the rough with a heart of gold. He had just purchased bikes for his two birthday kids, ages 12 and 14. As we talked Florence and John mentioned their long-term goal of sending their sons to a prestigious college. But something was always coming up to drain their finances. It looked to them like their goal would never be achieved."

Harry then told me how he'd used his legal expertise to help John and Florence with their financial troubles.

Harry had asked John if he had any unpaid accounts, and John had retorted instantly, "A dozen or more lingering debtors. If only I could collect, I'd be able to buy some much needed new equipment and maybe get Florence a new car."

"I think you need the services of an attorney," Harry had said. "Why don't you turn over those bad ones to me and let's see what will happen. I have a reputation of being tough with Sad Sack Sams and Sallys."

John had replied, "But I can't afford an attorney. Besides, many of these homeowners are my friends and I hate to put pressure on pleasant people."

At that point Harry had stood up and sweetly sounded off, "John, listen to me. Your friends are milking you. You're a nice guy and nice guys finish last or go bankrupt! Let me put the heat on them and you may see some immediate results."

Florence had suddenly injected, "I've been telling John for years that the good friends he's helped so much are avoiding him at socials because they owe him money. John, won't you please consider Harry's proposal?"

John had been taken aback by his wife's remarks. He said nothing for a few awkward minutes and then reacted, "Harry, in the past we've heard so many nasty things about scheming lawyers that we were reluctant to touch one. However, since we've met you, Florence has renewed her faith in the legal profession. We'll assume you're different from the rest. We have a wonderful marriage because I recognize that Florence is a better judge of character than I am. I'm a gullible jerk at times. I'll get the names, addresses and amounts owed over to you tomorrow morning."

Harry continued his story. "In the first 30 days I collected $29,476.13 and forwarded the check to John with a postscript that the check was a gift from God, and refused any attorney's fees."

I interrupted him. "Now stop right there, Harry. You can't make a living working for nothing."

"For the balance of the collection, which took over three months, I settled with the deadbeats for a sum total of $147,711.17."

"How did you feel when that happened?"

"Satisfied. My tough approach had worked."

"Just what is this tough approach all about?"

"I let John's welsher friends know, via certified mail with a return receipt requested, that I meant business: either pay up or suffer the legal consequences."

"And what would the consequences be?"

"I clearly spelled out to the defaulters that unless the account were settled pronto, I would place a mechanic's lien on their property. That, of course, would mean that their home could not be sold."

"So what, the owner might never intend to sell."

"Herb, that would be only the first step. Next I would serve notice to the credit agencies that Mr. Bad Wrench was evading his financial responsibilities. Down, down would go his credit rating to a level so sunken he could not get a loan anywhere."

"Would that be the final act of pain?"

"No, there's more. Let's say the delinquent owner owed John $20,000. John would be entitled to interest on the unpaid account, which in today's credit card market is 1.5 to 2 per cent cumulative monthly. A low rate it's not."

"What would that amount to annually?"

"Around $4,000, increasing the total due to $24,000."

"Let me get this straight. Is it possible that the $20,000 could increase to $40,000 in 5 years, or over $80,000 in 10 years?"

"Not only is it possible, it's another fact of life. Many a contractor won't push for immediate payment. He just waits for his Golden Day when his long-term investment pays off better than a bank. For his part, the debtor gets the shock of his life when he has to pay up in order to sell his house."

"Is this procedure legal?"

"Absolutely. When I file a mechanic's lien I state that the lien can be removed upon payment of total amount due plus interest and legal fees."

"What do you charge the poor homeowner after he recovers from his initial shock?"

"$100 per hour."

"What do you charge the general contractor?"

"Twenty per cent of the settlement. In John's case I informed his welshers that the interest charge was to begin on their account upon receiving my certified letter. That really made them cough up fast. Shortly after the settlement I mailed John the check for $147,711. Two days later, unannounced, John dropped into my office and presented me with his personal check in the amount of $29,542 and said, 'A messenger from God instructed me to deliver this to you. It's the 20 per cent of the wonderful settlement you reached with my many lost friends. Florence and I feel you're the best attorney in Cook County. Whether you like it or not you're our lawyer for life."

"Did that statement surprise you?"

"Yes, it did, especially since Cook County attorneys have been taking some hard knocks from the press. I don't like Bill Shakespeare's line that in order to make this a better world we should shoot all the lawyers."

"Come now, that was said over 300 years ago. It's different today. Don't you think so?"

"No, I don't. At every service club meeting I ever attend eventually someone comes along and makes a caustic, not a joking, remark about lawyers, usually something like St. Peter always rejecting attorneys when they arrive at the Pearly Gates. I don't like being the brunt of those nasty jokes. Ours is really the least-respected profession. People, in general, just don't like us. John was at first reluctant to go with me until Florence pressured him to change his mind."

"Harry, I'm not too sure your feelings are correct." Marilyn entered the room.

"Every year when people go to the polls, more lawyers are elected than any other professionals. Do you know how many United States presidents came from the legal profession?"

"Quite a few."

"Twenty-four of the last 36 presidents were lawyers."

"Maybe that's why the country is in such sad shape," Harry said. "However, starting this Thanksgiving I'm looking forward to the future with optimism. I'm willing to bury the ugly past. John Youngman has given me a new beginning. Helping him was a pleasure, and there are many more John Youngmans out there who need legal guidance. As a matter of fact he's referred two other contractors to me for help."

"Are you going to help?" I said.

"Of course I will. Since I wanted to repay the favor that John did for me, I decided to take his referrals for free."

"Again I say to you, you can't make a living by taking cases for free."

"Oh, yes I can. I'm willing to take cases for nothing, provided that I get 20 per cent of whatever I collect. When that gets out in the community, I believe my caseload will increase. One way to get ahead in this world is do something for nothing. All favors are returned sooner or later. Don't you agree?"

"It all depends upon what the favor is. I don't believe there's such a thing as a free lunch. Sometime after the gratis meal there'll he a request for a 'little' favor, and 'little' may not be defined to everyone's satisfaction."

Bob joined in. "My uncle's success in business and politics was mainly based on his ability to help his friends get jobs and contracts. They in turn always made generous contributions to his election campaign. The system has worked for generations and it still works exceptionally well."

Harry added, "The Chicago system was built upon favors to friends and relatives. It's a known fact that Chicago businessmen and lawmakers cooperate better than in any other city in the nation."

"Did I hear the word 'cooperation'?" Marilyn said as she sat down on the big sofa. "I heard you talk about worldly matters but don't you think it would be a better world if men and women were treated equally?"

We all instantly replied, "Yes, of course."

"Well then, next Thanksgiving you men set the table, buy the flowers, cook the meal and wash the dishes, and we women will discuss the affairs of state."

We were all stunned by Marilyn's sudden outburst and wondered what it was all about. The group was speechless for many seconds. Finally, I said softly, "Marilyn, for centuries in almost every country in the world women have been treated as second-class citizens. But we're on the brink of great changes and the United States will lead the world in greater opportunities for women."

"Those are pretty words, Mr. College President. We heard them sometime ago. Just what are you personally going to do when you open this new college?"

"I'm glad you asked that because the board is scheduled to adopt a philosophy and goals for the institution at the next meeting. When that's adopted it's our hope that everyone in the community will benefit from additional knowledge, skills and appreciation of the arts and sciences. Presently throughout the United States there are more male students enrolled than female, but in the decades ahead we hope to reverse that, or at least equalize the enrollment by sex."

"Sounds good to me, but how will you do it?"

"First, we'll provide child care and pre-school centers on the campus so mothers can drop off their little ones while they attend classes. Secondly, we'll hire professional counselors and librarians to enable women to develop to their maximum. And third, we'll encourage women to enroll in any course or program. One of the good things that World War II proved to us was that women in the labor force could handle successfully all kinds of equipment and machinery, and in some cases better, than men. Therefore, we'll have no restrictions in enrollment based on sex."

"Dr. Zeitlin, what are some of the problems preventing all of this from happening?"

"Presently, we have no campus, no buildings, no equipment, no faculty and no students. All we have is a college president, his secretary and one of the most enthusiastic and forward-looking boards I've ever seen. Nine months from now we hope to open with a beginning enrollment of over 1,000 students."

"One thousand? Really?"

"Yes, I have faith in the future and we will make it happen despite the negative feelings expressed by the mayor of River Grove and other government officials. River Grove will be the site of our campus, and Bob is to be admired for standing up to his uncle. One day I hope Mayor O'Connor will recognize his shortcomings. We're now preparing for a bond election for money to purchase the site."

Harry jumped in. "Let me give you my thoughts on that subject. I'm sure you'll win the election because you've got the support of all the thinking people."

"That won't help. We need a majority..."

For more than an hour Bob and I provided answers to the many questions raised by Harry and the three women. They all volunteered to help in the election campaign in any way possible. I left feeling exhilarated by a superb dinner and the exchange of viewpoints among five positive believers in the community college movement As I was putting on my boots in the vestibule Marilyn suddenly entered, closed the door, handed me an envelope and whispered, "Please read this, Herb. It helped me get through the most difficult days of my life."

While I was still slightly bent over, she impulsively grabbed me around the neck with both hands and gave me a big wet kiss. I drove off with a taste of green creme de menthe in my mouth, straight from the lips of a most beautiful bereaved mother. What did it mean? What was in the letter? I wondered.

14
Harmony and Hope

On Saturday, December 1st, I drove over to 7919 Cortland Parkway to talk to Mr. and Mrs. Herb Johnson, the owners. He'd just finished shoveling the snow from the driveway when I arrived. He greeted me pleasantly and invited me in for a cup of coffee. We talked. He and his wife were retiring, moving to Tucson, Arizona after the Christmas holidays. I offered to rent his home for 18 months at the going rate with an option to buy when the lease was up. To arrive at the selling price, since the listing date had expired, he decided to deduct the usual 6 per cent paid to the brokers. I requested a $200 credit per month for 18 months, giving me a total of $3,600 credit toward the down payment. He objected unless I gave him $1,000 in non-refundable option money up front. I agreed, and that made both lessor and lessee happy. Johnson was happy because he didn't have to leave his home vacant and I was happy because at last my family would be living under one roof within four weeks.

Johnson said he would have his attorney draw up the lease and have it for me to sign by Tuesday. The whole transaction took place within 38 minutes over coffee and doughnuts. After we shook hands on the verbal agreement he openly expressed his disappointment with his real estate agent, who had held only two open houses in six months, done little advertising and brought him only one ridiculous lowball offer. We hit it off so well that before leaving he offered to leave behind three double beds for us until our moving van arrived from California. I thanked him profusely.

As I started my car up he called out to me, "Can you use a TV?" I answered, "Of course."

He ran towards me and said, "The TV in the den is yours. It's my Christmas gift to your family."

What a wonderful landlord, I thought, as I stopped for a red light on North Avenue. It was no wonder. When two Herbs get together, they produce fine medicine.

As I arrived in the office on Monday morning Maria alerted me to a call that had just come in. "It's Mr. Farmar," she said, as I picked up the phone.

"Herb, I've got good news for you. Can you meet me at the Red Steer at one for lunch?"

"I love good news. You're on, see you then."

The morning sped by with calls, dictating and interviewing. I kept searching for clues as to what Joe's good news might be all about. When I arrived at the Red Steer, Joe was at the bar sounding off to his friends about the rebellious kids at Berkeley. He insisted the college president was a softie. If Father Hesburgh, the president of Notre Dame, were in charge the rebels would be kicked out.

"This free speech movement is nothing new. That should be allowed but the taking over of buildings is unlawful and those responsible should be expelled. And furthermore we need college presidents with guts, not the jellyfish we have at Berkeley," Joe claimed.

When he saw me his tone changed a little, and he introduced me to his fine drinking buddies. He took his Manhattan with him as he ordered me a martini. After we placed our orders for liquid refreshments, he opened his attaché case, took out several legal-sized papers and said, "I have it all here, Herb. Now all you have to do is sign."

"Joe, what is this?"

"You said you wanted the Gross house. It's yours. Now all you have to do is fill out this loan application and put 10 per cent down. With an interest rate of 6 per cent fixed for 30 years I got you a good deal. I have a banker friend who owed me a favor so he bent the regulations to please me. What do you think of me now?"

"Joe, I greatly appreciate your efforts, but on Saturday I reached an agreement with Herb Johnson, and tomorrow will sign an 18-month lease with an option to buy."

"As long as you haven't signed you can get out of it if you wish. A verbal agreement in a real estate deal means nothing."

"I don't want to withdraw. Herb Johnson is a prince of a guy, and I have a wonderful deal. You know, Joe, you're a remarkable person. I tried three lenders and they all demanded 20 per cent down payment. Now, how did you do it?"

"I worked my ass off for you, Herb. I hope you appreciate it. Nick Pullizzi, the president of the Melrose Park Bank, owed me one"

"You have some real good friends. How did things go with you today, Joe?"

"Rotten, I don't want to talk about it. Why don't you loosen up a bit and have another drink with me?"

I wanted to decline, but Joe apparently was in need of a drinking companion, so I agreed.

Joe was on his third Manhattan, and for the first time I violated my own golden rule and had two strong ones without eating anything. I have to admit, I began to feel a little foggy and my speech became a little slurry. Then it came to me. Joe wanted to get me drunk. I called the waiter over again and insisted that we order.

I ordered an open corn beef sandwich with mashed potatoes. Joe ordered his fourth manhattan. We continued to talk about Joe's rotten day. He felt bad because his boss had reprimanded him when he felt he should have been commended. After all, he had gotten the complainer to sign a release. His boss just didn't like the methods he'd used.

I asked him, "What did you do?"

"I don't want to give out my secrets. In the future you may want to use them."

I didn't know what his methods of persuasion were all about, but imagined if I probed long enough it would come out. Joe was in no mood for a cross-examination by a college president, though I began to suspect something was wrong with his relationship with his boss at Bekins. His medicine for exasperation and depression was *alcohol*. What antidote should I use to get him out of his feeling of dejection?

"Joe, you've got to pass over the bad events of the day and concentrate on the future. I know you have great natural abilities and it's easy for me to see why your Notre Dame graduating class voted you most likely to succeed."

"And they also predicted that I would be the attorney general or governor of Illinois in 20 years. Here I'm at age 41 and what do I have to show for it? My old friend of yesteryear, Oliver Wendell Holmes, was right: if you don't make it by age 40, you probably won't make it at all."

"Oh, come on now, Joe. Justice Holmes said that over 50 years ago. It doesn't apply in today's dynamic world. Just look at where you are today. You're married to a gorgeous woman, she's given you five bright ones and you have a lovely home in Elmwood Park. Aside from being a decorated executive officer on a navy destroyer during the war, you've held office in the St. Vincent Ferrer Holy Name Society, the South Elm Little League and the Knights of Columbus. You have all the qualifications necessary to climb the ladder. What more can you ask for?"

"Money, I need more money! It takes money to advance in your profession and I don't have it. Keeping up with the Joneses is a very expensive habit. It makes business forge ahead, while the head of a household slides toward bankruptcy. My childhood wish was to own a home in River Forest–not likely at this time if I continue to work at Bekins. When I first started, the salary was great, but it hasn't kept up with modern day demands. I need to find a job that pays more and will lead to a judgeship or some other political office."

We continued to talk about possible jobs in the local and state governments. I ordered coffee and pie a la mode for dessert while Joe ordered his fifth Manhattan. Despite his heavy drinking Joe was lucid, red-eyed and loud, at all times in complete possession of his faculties. Before my leaving he asked me to call his wife and have her pick him up. As he ordered his sixth invigorating dose of medicine, he was fully aware of the consequences should he be caught in a traffic violation.

When I spoke to Ceil she said, "Oh no, not again. Where is he? I'll be there in 20 minutes!"

I returned to the table. Joe had gone to the bar to join his friends to assimilate another whiskey and sweet vermouth. I paid the bill and told Joe that Ceil would be over shortly. His response was, "My darling doesn't have to hurry. I feel fine, maybe she can make the time to join me."

Driving back to the office I reflected on the reasons for Joe's depression. How long had this been going on? Seven Manhattans within 90 minutes. Whew! What had caused it? A straight A graduate from Notre Dame with so much to offer. What had happened? Was the real problem lack of money, an unsatisfactory sex life or dreams unfulfilled? Probably all three. What could I do to raise his self-esteem?

Back at the office Maria informed me that Dr. Lund, principal of the Oak Park River Forest high school, had invited me to the Oak Park Rotary Club for lunch the next day to hear a talk on the contributions of Hemingway.

Ernest Hemingway, one of America's finest authors, had almost been the subject of Eugenia's master's thesis at New York University. She'd decided against it because so many other English majors were researching his life and contributions. America loved Hemingway, known for his free and simple style of writing about so many intimate details of life. I phoned Eugenia about the event and she requested that I take avid notes and mail them back to her. She promised to put the notes in *For Whom the Bell Tolls*, the first of many books she'd given me to read.

When I arrived at the private and exclusive Oak Park Club, Dr. Lund greeted me pleasantly and introduced me to six of his associates at his table as the president of the newly formed Technical Institute in Melrose Park. They appeared surprised at the mention of a Melrose Park Institute. I heard such comments as: "What are those hoodlums up to now? What's it all about, Lund? Oak Park is not part of it, are we?"

When the time came for the main introduction, Dr. Lund introduced mc as the first president of the future community college. No applause, some quiet comments and whispers. The Rotary president then went on with several introductions of prominent guests, and they all received much applause. I felt a little embarrassed. Was I being shunned at what I was told was the best Rotary Club in the Chicago suburbs? This certainly was not in the spirit of Rotary.

Folding my arms across my chest I boldly asked Dr. Lund, "Weren't Oak Park and River Forest part of the survey team that looked into the formation of a college district last year?"

"Yes, we were, and the committee voted unanimously to withdraw from forming a public junior college district. It might have succeeded if the vote had been for a private four-year college. Junior colleges, as we know them, have a bad name in this area. They're for the dummkopfs and incorrigibles. As you've probably heard by now, this high school is one of the best in the nation, with over 85 per cent of its graduates going on to elite universities. Our students, in general, come from good, well-behaved middle-and upper-class families. To be perfectly frank with you, our citizens don't believe in ethnic mixing."

"Isn't that a snobbish approach? Can it be that Ernest was right when he said that Oak Park was a community of big lawns and people with narrow minds?"

"Yes, it is, but people move into our community because of the excellence of the educational system, and, what's more, they're willing to pay for it."

"And you don't think a junior college can give a superior education, do you?"

"There may be some exceptions in California, but here in Chicagoland it just doesn't happen. We studied the communities to be part of the college district and they were so different from Oak Park that we didn't want to try to mix them. When you mix the extremes in education you produce chaos. The low achievers can't keep up with the high producers and the high achievers become bored; they goof off and their level of achievement is lowered."

"Do you really believe that?"

"I personally may or may not, but it's the true feeling of our board. They didn't want a junior college, and it's lucky for you that Oak Park withdrew. Otherwise their large no vote would have prevented your district from being formed. Elmwood Park, a notch below Oak Park, is, in some ways, similar to us, and they also overwhelmingly voted no. Isn't that proof enough?"

"No, it isn't. You just can't give labels to communities, ethnic or racial groups, or to sons and daughters of immigrants. This is America and every group must be given the opportunity to reach its maximum potential. The shift from lower class to middle class is not only a possibility but a goal for a better life."

"Dr. Zeitlin, your words are good for a PTA speech, but they're not realistic, as you'll soon find out"

"I appreciate your up-front comments. It's nice to meet someone who truly knows his community so well. I feel my new challenge is to try to change the attitudes and behavior patterns of your political leaders."

"Mr. President, I'm quite interested in the technical aspects of the college. Will you offer training for the trades?"

"Yes, we expect to have programs in the auto and refrigeration trades, building construction, electronics, computer science, nursing and health fields, beauty culture, printing, police and fire science and many others."

"That sounds good to me. For those of our students who drop out or don't go on to college there may be a spot for them in your trade classes. Lately we've been seeing a small influx of a racial group that may end up in jail unless we do something about it. While our high school is judged one of the best in the nation, we don't provide sufficient vocational education. Did you know that recent polls show that most Americans regard crime as the number one social problem?"

"No, I didn't know that. I thought providing equal educational opportunities for all the people was our country's biggest challenge. It's a wise taxpayer who invests his money in schools rather than in jails. Jails try hard to rehabilitate the inmates by giving broad job training. I say schools should train them, give them a salable skill, and they won't go to jail. Our biggest social concern is that we don't have equal opportunity for all the people. I'm appalled that so many sagacious trustees have antipathy towards vocational education, even if the federal government pays for it. Do you have that problem at Oak Park?"

"Oh yes, we have. Our board is solid Republican and we don't like to accept funds from the wild-spending Democrats. They're going to bankrupt this nation. Had Goldwater been elected he would have balanced the budget and stopped federal aid to education."

The other six Rotarians, like a chorus line, all nodded approval of Lund's remarks. Why had he invited me to the Rotary meeting? It wasn't Hemingway! He was searching for a solution to the disciplinary problems at the school. Send them to the new tech! I thought back to my seven and a half years at Phoenix Tech. We readily accepted the incorrigibles, the rough and ready, and in four years turned them into well-respected parents and citizens. And we could do it again at the first technical college in Chicagoland.

The meal at the Oak Park Club was superior. I would change Hemingway's statement about Oak Park from "Oak Parkers have big lawns but narrow minds" to "Oak Parkers eat good meals but they don't nourish the mind." The so-called best Rotary Club, in my opinion, was far from the best. Oh well, all Rotarians were not alike.

As we were finishing our dessert the guest speaker, Willie Butler, turned out to be one of the oldest Rotarians in the area. He knew Dr. Clarence Ed Hemingway, Ernest's father, very well. He went into great detail about what a wonderful family physician Dr. Ed had been. He'd delivered over 2,000 babies, had been available at any time for the sick and elderly, and had been a great Rotarian loved by all. What a contrast to his son Ernest, the wild one, who had gotten so excited about World War I that he had volunteered his services to Italy as an ambulance driver, got wounded and returned home as a little hero. For many years Ernest had a reputation with women–love them and leave them. And Oak Parkers would never forgive Ernest for his famous disparaging characterization of the good people of his home town.

Butler stressed that Ernest and his father never got along well. Dr. Ed wanted his son to follow in his footsteps as a doctor, and sent him to Northwestern University as a pre-med student. Ernest was bored with his classes and dropped out during his first year. He did not want to live in the shadow of his famous father.

Throughout history there have been families where renowned fathers reared sons who, unknown to them, were jealous of Dad's achievements. The most famous one in history was Phillip of Macedonia, whose son Alexander cried every time his father returned from conquering a country. Alexander was afraid there would be no countries left for him to fight and conquer. And in modern days the Bing Crosby sons–all of them–rebelled against society. Many claimed it was just to get Dad upset

"Every time Dr. Ed was honored, Ernest withdrew further from his father," Willie Butler continued. "Finally, in desperation, Ernest left home to become a reporter, and ultimately a writer. Some felt Ernest's attacks on Oak Park were his way of getting even with his father. The community was shocked beyond belief when Ed, its most respected doctor and citizen, shot his brains out. Did Ernest's behavior contribute to his father's suicide? I think so, but one never knows what's in the mind of an individual just before he pulls the trigger. Several Oak Parkers felt that the bullet went into the wrong Hemingway."

Butler concluded by saying, "Rotarians and guests, I want you to know that while the nation's literary folks are constantly praising Ernest and his books, I and many others feel that it's really Dr. Ed who most deserves Oak Park's respect. He actually saved lives, while his son just created imaginative, salacious stories, and time and again showed disrespect to his neighbors. This is just another case of a rotten son driving his parents crazy, ending with the father's death."

A few moments of silence followed and the speaker sat down. No applause. The Rotary president stood up and asked, "Any questions?"

One solo response. "Mr. President, this is not a question, but I think we owe Mr. Butler our deepest thanks for revealing some unknown facts about the Hemingways. Let it be known that this club shall always remember Dr. Ed as the good one and Ernest as the ungrateful son who contributed to the demise of his parent."

The tremendous applause that followed startled me! I knew Eugenia would be troubled by Willie Butler's conclusion. The President rang the bell and the most influential and affluent citizens of Oak Park returned to their daily routine.

I left the meeting with mixed feelings. It was nice hearing from a primary source, but were his conclusions correct? Had Hemingway been responsible for his father's death? Eugenia would research this subject when she came to Chicago.

The more I thought about Ernest's famous remarks about Oak Parkers the more I tended to agree with him. No wonder he stayed away. I hoped the day would come when this community's vision and scope would broaden: Forty years had passed, with no signs of forgiveness of youth. The vast majority of these people still refused to acknowledge Ernest as one of America's great writers. And I wondered how long it would take Oak Parkers to recognize the community colleges as one of America's greatest social inventions for advancement up through the classes.

The two and a half hour board meeting of December 9th was packed with positive signs of harmony and respect towards each trustee and attorney.

Serpico, reporting for the site committee, stated that the Carey farm of 40 acres was the definite choice. Smith then added that a separate adjacent parcel of 10 acres could be acquired at a later date. The board unanimously nodded approval and Smith had the authority to negotiate for the full 50 acres.

Wade Steel summarized his visit to Wheeling High School and Fred Knol discussed his tour of Cannel High School. The architect of each school had accompanied the visiting trustee. I mentioned that while it was nice to see the latest in high school construction, it would be more significant to see community colleges. The first community college to be visited would be in Flint, Michigan, that Saturday, December 12th.

Bob Collins announced that based on the letters he'd received, such names as West Suburban, West Towns and Suburban were the leading candidates for a college name. Silence followed, a few negative comments were made, then a general negative consensus was reached. Keep trying, broaden the field, consider other possibilities.

Joe Farmar pointed out the many fine aspects of the recent press conference. The press was just as excited about the birth of a college as the trustees. Our common goal was to change a negative voting public into a positive block. The press as a whole was commended for its forward-looking viewpoint.

Elmore Boeger reviewed his contact with the many architects. He hoped the board would make a selection soon, stressing that it would be in the public interest to select one from Illinois.

I slowly read the philosophy and objectives of the college. Several trustees interrupted me to request further explanation. It was finally moved by Collins, seconded by Jones and carried unanimously to adopt the statement.

Since we intended to pattern the university transfer courses after those offered by the University of Illinois, I recommended the same starting dates, with two semesters of equal length and one summer session of eight weeks. Carried without any discussion.

The dialogue on the organizational chart was quite lengthy; several changes were agreed upon, and carried.

We devoted much time on the proposed salary schedule for instructors and deans. While the board agreed that for a high-quality faculty it had to pay above-average rates, I argued that above-average was not good enough. If we were to attract a superior teaching staff, we needed to offer the highest beginning salary in the state; not to do so would have an adverse effect on the image I was striving to create.

"And what image are you trying to create, Dr. Zeitlin?" Jones quipped.

"Roy, sometime ago you asked me to tell you about Stanford. Tonight, let me tell you and the other trustees that Stanford would never have achieved its greatness had it not had a glorious beginning."

"What was so glorious about it?"

"With Senator Stanford's many millions behind them their board of trustees approved the highest beginning salaries in the nation at that time. This enabled them to recruit one of the most talented and respected faculties ever assembled for a new university."

"But Senator Stanford put his vast wealth behind his university. We don't have that kind of money."

"Roy, I feel exceptionally lucky. Thanks to you and the other trustees we have over one million to start up with. Let me put it to the best use possible, the instructors' salary schedule. Today Stanford's standing with other universities is very high. Give me a decade and we'll have a similar position in the community college family."

"Do you really believe that, Dr. Zeitlin?" Wade Steel asked.

"Yes, I do. Please give me the chance to prove it."

The trustees expressed mostly reservation. Roy Jones suggested that before we accept the proposed schedule I should seek the advice and counsel of the three local high school superintendents. I agreed.

When the administrative salary schedule was presented it was readily approved. With a big smile on his face Roy commented, "I like it because the maximum instructor's salary far exceeds that of the beginning administrator."

"That's designed so teachers can advance in salary by obtaining more education and becoming the best-informed instructors in their respective disciplines. They don't have to become administrators in order to make more money."

"Will you have difficulty getting administrators?"

"Yes, since the beginning salary is not all that great. That's my hardest job right now. I have to recruit the administrators first so they can help us find a superior faculty. No instructor will be hired until the proper administration is in place."

"When will that happen?"

"I start tomorrow by mailing all these job descriptions to the university placement offices and the local high school districts. Hopefully, we'll have one or more administrators on the job by February or March."

The next item on the agenda was informational bulletin #3, entitled *Advantages of the Community College*. Babe called out, "Dr. Zeitlin, how many of these bulletins are we getting at each meeting, and do we have to memorize all this stuff?"

"I can't give you an exact number, but you can expect to receive one to four bulletins prior to each meeting. No, you're not required to memorize the contents, but every good board member should read and digest the contents."

"Dr. Zeitlin, that's asking me to do too much. You're worse than my U of I history professor. I just don't have the time to read all of it."

"Babe, get Josephine or your son, Joseph, to do it, or if you wish I'll summarize them to you prior to the meetings," interrupted Joe Farmar.

"OK, OK, you can do that but I think Dr. Zeitlin should keep them short. I just don't have three or four hours to spare for every board meeting."

"Babe, you did beautifully at the press conference, and you gave up several evenings for the intensive training sessions. You just have to make the time. Otherwise you won't be informed."

"Where did these 16 advantages come from?" asked Joe Farmar. "They're good!"

"It's an accumulation of knowledge gained during my four years as a community college teacher and five years as an administrator. With the board's approval I intend to include all these items in the survey form to high school seniors and adults."

"By all means, include it in the survey," Wade said. "It's very enlightening, and should help us sell the referendum to the public."

My last item was a request to add additional part-time clerical help due to the increased activity in the office. It was readily approved without a formal vote.

As I drove home I felt exceptionally good about the meeting. All my goals had been approved with the exception of the instructors' salary schedule, which, knock-on-wood, would be accepted in January. Equally significant was the frankness and respect each trustee had shown each other and the college president. Nine weeks earlier the board had been divided. The Serpico coalition had wanted Jones out. Now he was part of the team. How and when had this change happened? It had all started when Donahow said the board was not prepared to face the press. They met the challenge head-on with the extensive training sessions coordinated by Steel, Dunahow and Zeitlin. Perhaps Collins was right in describing Dunahow as a brilliant lawyer. He irritated the board. He provoked them. The board had worked to prove him wrong. Donahow's strategy had been successful; they all showed up for the training sessions. I looked forward with enthusiasm to flying with the coalition to Flint, Michigan.

Saturday morning I picked up Wade in Franklin Park. He told me that Mildred had gotten up early to prepare him a hearty breakfast. When we arrived at the departure gate at O'Hare, we were surprised to find Collins, Knol and Farmar at a nearby bar having a liquid tonic for breakfast. We declined to join them since the passenger boarding was announced. Despite the early hour and the crisp cold December weather everyone was in a jovial mood. I mentioned that Dean Charles Donnelly, the chief executive of the college, would give us a brief orientation prior to conducting the tour.

When we arrived on campus, we were ushered into a large and very impressive boardroom with many portraits of past and present board members. The table had 15 judge's chairs facing an audience space for over 100 visitors. Dean Charles invited us to an alcove for coffee and doughnuts. He started his presentation by saying Flint College had an enrollment of 6,378 students, with more than 4,000 males and over 2,000 females. Using a slide projector he showed us all the major buildings on the campus and ended with, "What building would you like to visit?"

I was pleased when Joe Farmar burst out, "Everything! We're all new trustees and need to be educated on what one of the best community colleges has to offer."

Dean Charles was taken aback and responded, "That would take more than a day or two. Could you shorten it to two or three hours?"

Laughingly we all agreed as we gulped our coffee, stuffed down the doughnuts, grabbed our coats and followed Charles. He was an exciting guide, well-informed, ready, willing and able to answer questions as he opened doors to the many shops, labs and classrooms. There were only a few classes in session on Saturday, so our movement was fast and furious. We picked up brochures along the way and chatted with a few instructors and students as we took pictures. At 2:00 PM Charles led us back to the boardroom, where his boss, the superintendent of schools, presented us with a student newspaper and a college catalog. He expressed much interest in our district. He had heard our college was one of the first in the nation to have elected an independent board with no connection whatsoever to the high schools. His board of nine members had gone on record opposing any attempt to separate the city school district from the college because in the long run it would cost the taxpayers more money. He presented me with a large book, entitled *Board Policy,* and called particular attention to the last ten pages, devoted to the college.

In parting he ordered his security chief to drive us to the best restaurant in town and wished us well in the coming years. After a gourmet meal we had three hours to kill before our flight. We used the time to rerun the positive and negative aspects of the tour. Each trustee opened up with his comments.

Fred Knol was impressed with the many industrial and technical shops and wondered if we could duplicate the equipment without the help of General Motors. I assured him that we would not duplicate, but would do even better, since we were starting fresh and had Zenith, Motorola, International Harvester and the federal government behind us.

Fred smiled and said, "Dr. Zeitlin, I'm writing down what you said in my little book. You better make it happen."

Joe Farmar couldn't get over the college's unique method of raising money: placing contributors' names on plaques mounted on the honor walk. The more money you gave, the larger the plaque. Surprisingly, there were not hundreds but thousands of people who gave $100 to $100,000.

Joe estimated that over one million dollars had been raised. "I think we can outdo Flint by making it known that anyone giving a million to our college would have a building or facility named after him."

Bob Collins said, "Fellows, did you notice that some of the buildings were named after trustees? Herb, whatever architect you find better come up with a campus of over seven buildings."

"Bob, I assure you our college will have many more than seven buildings. Nothing would give me greater pleasure than to be around five or more years from now, when the business complex is named after you, the science building after Wade Steel, the football stadium after Ralph Serpico and the technology building after Fred Knol. The other trustees can take their choice of buildings."

"Why five or more years? I may not be around that long," Joe said.

"That's just a random number. The length of service would be a factor, but the major criteria should be the contributions made by the trustee. We need to develop a board policy on the naming of buildings."

"I disagree with you on that one, Dr. Zeitlin," Joe immediately responded. "The best policy is no policy. Circumstances change so rapidly in this day and age that a set policy would put the board in a straightjacket position. We need flexibility so that our power is used wisely. I'm sure the others would agree with me." The four trustee heads nodded yes.

"I agree with you totally, Joe," responded Bob. "Just think., seven buildings named after the founding trustees. Boy, oh boy, I love the idea. The Robert Collins School of Business! Eat your heart out, Mayor O'Connor. Your nephew is doing better than you. Herb, do you really think you can make it happen?"

"Yes, I do. As the executive officer of this board I would love to place your name on the agenda for such action. And, Joe, you won't have to cough up a million to have a building named after you. It's not dollars that count. It's what you do during your time on the board."

"We shouldn't put a price tag on the honor of naming buildings after someone," Wade said. "I'm sure the buildings at Flint were named for trustees out of respect, admiration and love for the achievements made by the individual. And that's worth more than money can buy. The children and grandchildren of those trustees so honored have been offered a lifetime of service to the community. One of the greatest things in life is the giving of yourself to help others."

"I'll drink to that," shouted Bob, as he ordered another round of drinks for all of us. Joe stopped the waiter and requested two Manhattans for himself, stood up and in a serious voice offered a toast: "To Dr. Zeitlin, who arranged this trip, who will arrange several more, perhaps to Florida or California, and from this day forth will set the stage so our college will have seven buildings named after us."

Shouts of "Hear! Hear!" came forth as Joe sat down. I stood up and proclaimed, "I'm not joking. This will happen if we have a successful bond election and continue to work as a team."

There were cheers as I sat down and the laughing continued. Bob, Joe and Fred were almost stoned, if their slurred speech were any indication of their condition. Wade and I, on the other hand, were quite sober, since we'd had only one drink each, eaten a full meal and had coffee and pie. The others had had two drinks at O'Hare, two before lunch and two while waiting for dessert. A total of six. Could I believe what they said?

What appeared to be a drinking contest was beginning to fizzle out. Joe ordered number seven, Bob started on his sixth and Fred, while nursing number five, sleepily asked, "Herb, tell us what you want us to do next year. January is only nineteen days away."

"For January it's urgent that we adopt an instructor's salary schedule and start hiring the professional staff."

"Consider it done. Just put it on the agenda again and this time it will pass unanimously."

As Fred talked I felt my action items were gaining speed. This late luncheon session was much better than the regular board meetings. When the trustees are on stage, you never know what they're really thinking. They play a role, each one vying for a star rating from the public. At a happy drinking luncheon or dinner meeting the true personality of the board member comes into focus.

As Wade paid the bill he commented, "This was a very good day. We all learned something and we're starting to adopt policy. Joe is right. We need flexibility in naming buildings. By not having a written policy, we open a big door to the most deserving individuals. That shall be our policy."

When we arrived at the Flint airport Joe headed for the bar for number eight while Bob slowly trailed behind him. Fred stumbled

My boss predicted that the sixties were going to be the best decade of the twentieth century because of LBJ's pledge of a Great Society. "All the way with LBJ" meant a war on poverty, civil rights to all, free medical care for seniors, financial aid to college students and greater federal aid to higher education and public schools."

I added that with one new community college opening every week, at last America would be offering realistic training for all job-seeking youth. Greater emphasis on occupational or career education was just another way to reduce poverty and unemployment. Some day people might judge a skilled mechanic or plumber as important as a doctor or lawyer. With equal pay for attorneys and mechanics we would be approaching a classless society. Could this happen in America? We now had an oversupply of lawyers and an undersupply of auto mechanics. Balancing the two would be the way to go. There would be fewer bad jokes about the legal profession and more respect toward auto mechanics. The sixties were bound to be the great turning point in American society.

On the morning of December 23rd I got up early, packed my car with all my belongings, gave Camille Cucignaro, my landlord, a small box of chocolates and thanked her for her kind services. I was leaving 1952 North 17th Avenue, Apartment 4, my Melrose Park home for three months, for a larger home two miles away in Elmwood Park.

When I arrived at the office, Maria informed me that Bob and Joe were taking me out for lunch at noon, leaving me plenty of time for my 3:00 O'Hare departure. It had been snowing all morning, with three inches of that beautiful white powder on the ground by the time the boys arrived. Bob was carrying a beautiful gift-wrapped package about two feet long and four inches in diameter.

"What's in the package, fellows?" I asked.

"Can't tell. It's Eugenia's Christmas present from the families of Bob Collins and Joe Farmar. Beverly picked it out," Joe responded.

I felt the gift. It was rather heavy, ruling out a Chicago sweatshirt or an umbrella. My curiosity got the best of me. "Is it a salami?"

"No, no, it's nothing you eat, but something she'll find very useful. And you might occasionally use it yourself. Eugenia will love it. It's something new on the market."

Bob left it on my desk as we raced over to Tom's Steak House for the usual. Our discussion focused on family ties during the holidays. Both trustees had almost completed their shopping for the wives and kids. I hadn't even started.

"Bob and Joe, I'm a little embarrassed. I don't have a gift for you."

"Don't be silly. You're our gift from sunny California. When you return give us some of that warm and beautiful sun."

"Fellows, my plane leaves at three o'clock, which means I'll have to leave here by 1:30. Hopefully, that should give me enough time to give Maria her Christmas present and drive to O'Hare. Babe didn't know it at the time but he gave me a wonderful gift when he talked Maria into working for me. I have a perfume set for her."

When we got back to the office, I opened my luggage and gave Maria her present. She kissed me first, then Joe and Bob, and proudly stated, "It's very exciting to be working for Dr. Zeitlin and the board. I feel I'm part of creating something great. You guys are going to give new life to Melrose Park and all its suburbs. I can't wait until the college opens."

With that I grasped my bags and Eugenia's gift and said, "Adios."

I wiped the snow from my car and turned on the key to start. No go on the first attempt. The engine was cold. No go on the second try. It started on the third try, and then I noticed a red light on the voltage panel. Was the generator out or was it something else? As I lifted up the hood there was the smell of burning rubber. The fan belt was broken. What do I do now?

I had an hour and fifteen minutes to make the plane. Should I call AAA? No point, they didn't make repairs. Should I call Buick service or should I leave the car and call a cab to O'Hare? That sounded sensible, or should I ask Bob or Joe for help?

I ran back to the office as the fellows were about to leave and explained my new challenge. Bob said, "No problem, Herb, I'll drive you to the airport. Give me your car keys and I'll get the belt replaced before you return. I'll call Bev and tell her I'll be a little late to the shoe store. We're buying all the kids shoes at wholesale prices."

The tension eased when we arrived at O'Hare with 35 minutes to spare. As the plane took off I reflected on what a great guy Bob really was. He reminded me so much of my kid brother, Arthur, who also was a terrific mechanic and always willing to help his family and friends.

There was no doubt about it. Bob treated me like a brother, and Joe was just as accommodating. I was indeed lucky to have two such friends as bosses.

Three and a half hours later the plane landed in San Diego, a city so different from Chicago. I shed my coat, scarf, gloves and big rubber boots and flung them over my arm as I left the plane. It was difficult walking down the gangplank but I was overjoyed when I spotted Eugenia and the kids from behind the gates waving at me with fire and furor. I raced over to them, overtaking several slow-moving passengers. I gave the black overcoat to Mark and the gloves and boots to Joyce, grabbed Eugenia and gave her a big hug and a lingering kiss, followed by hugs to Mark and Joyce. I finally lifted up Ann with the left hand and Clare with the right and whirled them around together. At last the family was together.

As we walked to the luggage claim area, Eugenia said, "You look a little thinner. Let's hurry home. I have a great meal waiting for you."

"This coat is heavy," my 14-year-old son said. "Will I have to wear something like this when we get to Chicago?"

"Don't you like it?"

"No, it's dark, heavy and long."

"Well, then, you don't have to wear it. But tomorrow all of us will be going shopping to outfit the family for the great climate of Chicago."

"Who are you kidding, Dad? I read the Chicago climate is one of the worst. Isn't that the truth?"

"It has its ups and downs but try to think of the positives. I'm going to get Joyce and you a pair of ice skates. You'll love the invigoration of skating."

"Will I have to wear gloves all the time?" Joyce asked.

"No, sweetie, only when the temperature goes below freezing."

"How often does that happen?"

"Only two or three months of the year. The spring, summer and fall are great."

When we arrived at the luggage section, Mark suddenly gave Joyce my overcoat and Joyce gave my boots to Ann and gloves to Clare. She and Mark raced over to the revolving unit to snatch my valise. I regained my coat from Joyce as my two older ones lugged the bag to the station wagon parked nearby.

Eugenia gave me the car keys. I became the designated driver to Chula Vista, a short 20 minutes away. It was twilight, the temperature was 74 degrees, 50 degrees warmer than Chicago, and I felt great. When we got off the freeway the kids demanded that I go down Santa Claus Lane, Joe Rindone's Street. His home was beautifully decorated with twinkling red and green lights outlining the front view of his home. As we drove down the street I was awed by the great variety of decorations of Joe's neighbors. Eugenia commented, "Will we see anything like this in Chicago?"

"Well, not exactly," I sheepishly replied as we drove to 9 Sierra Way, "but the spirit of Christmas is just as great."

"Dad, wait until you see the beautiful tree Mom bought," Joyce said. "We all had fun decorating it last night; even Clare helped."

Arriving home, I again had second thoughts about leaving California. The house looked so beautiful with its green lawn, red roses on the side and the sparkling birds of paradise at the front entrance. But too late to change now. Focus on the positive future, my brain quietly responded.

The front door, solidly covered with shining silver paper and crossed by wide red ribbons, looked like a Christmas package. Another facet of Eugenia's creativity.

In the living room was one tall, gorgeous tree adorned with ornaments gathered from 15 years of a happy marriage. The large dining room table in the family room was all set. Eugenia announced, "Wash up, dinner will be served in five minutes."

After we sat down I asked my family to join hands. I led them in a short prayer, concluded with postscripts from Eugenia, Mark, Joyce and Ann. Following Bob Collins's lead at his Thanksgiving dinner, I asked God to bless my family and the college trustees as we squeezed each other's hands hoping that our prayers would be answered.

I listened attentively to the kids' stories. Our plans called for completing our shopping the next day and then packing for three days before boarding the Amtrak train to Chicago. It was wonderful and exciting being back with the family, asking and answering trigger-like questions. Later that night in bed, Eugenia expressed much sympathy for the Farmar family, whose father had a drinking problem. She felt good when I told her the trustees had approved the hiring of three deans aud a business manager. She immediately suggested Anson Hayes, Southwestern business leader, for the position of business manager. I reminded her that I had promised Joe Rindone not to recruit any of his faculty for at least two years. She felt that here an exception should be made. Anson Hayes had a BBA and a master's in business administration, several years' junior college teaching experience and a wonderful wife and family. She added, "I know him and he is *honest.* Darling, I've been reading a lot more about Chicago. It's not a city of brotherly love. Most of the corruption takes place in the business or personnel offices."

"Eugenia, my dear, your concerns are without substance. This board is different. They're seven honest men, all trying to build a better community for themselves and their families. In the future they'll all be honored."

"What do you mean?"

I told her about the visit I'd made with four of the trustees to Flint Community College, where we'd finalized the policy on naming buildings.

"And what is that policy?" she asked.

"The policy is that there shall be no policy."

"Oh, come on now, that doesn't make sense."

"Oh, yes it does! The board wants the freedom to name buildings anytime and for any reason. A firm written policy would put them in a straightjacket position, with a great loss of power."

"Has a decision been made on who gets what building named after him?"

"Oh, yes. The science building will be named after Wade Steel, the business center after Bob Collins, the tech building after Fred Knol and the gym or stadium after the all-American football star, Ralph Serpico. The other trustees will have their choice."

"Has any of this been approved by the whole board?"

"Yes it has, not in an open board meeting but in an executive session with Serpico, Jones and Boeger. Each trustee will need to serve with honor for at least five years before his name is bestowed on a building. I was directed as the chief administrator and executive officer of the board to make sure it happens. Farmar added that my job is to convince the students, faculty and public that it's right."

"I can't believe this. Is that legal?"

"That's a good question. The answer is not that easy. Joe Farmar and Bob Collins, as sophisticated politicians, tell me that in Chicagoland all boards of any worth settle the serious money or personnel matters in private executive session prior to the public meetings. Though this violates state law, in reality it's done most of the time. Again, Mayor O'Connor boasts to his nephew Bob Collins that secret meetings are the best way to go."

"Is there any way the public can tell when a board is acting illegally?"

"Oh yes, there are grounds for suspicion when all the action items are moved, seconded and carried with little or no discussion and the meeting is short and sweet. We should also be suspicious when a surprise item not on the agenda is brought up and approved without discussion."

"Are there any other signs of misconduct?"

"It smells when only one bid is presented and unanimously accepted; also, when the trustees stretch a meeting into the wee hours of the morning hoping that no one from the general public will be there to see or hear an illegal operation."

"How can we prevent a board from operating illegally?"

"Attend the meeting from start to finish. Always get a copy of the agenda and be sure to ask questions. Politicians will not get away with murder if the public is watching. Unfortunately, most people don't accept their responsibilities and hardly ever attend the public meetings or hearings."

"Will Bob Collins imitate his uncle?"

"No, he's just the opposite in almost every way. He proved that during the press conference by putting on the table all the vital concerns of the college board. I'm happy to call him brother Bob. In due time, once his uncle retires, he'll reach his goal of becoming mayor of River Grove."

"Did your brother Bob ever mention naming a building after you?"

"Yes, he did. It was agreed that the first seven buildings would be named after the founding trustees. Bob promised the eighth one would be named after the founding president."

"Do you think it will ever happen?"

"It's possible, but it's low on my priority list. More important right now is the planning for a successful bond issue. Without money we can't build a campus."

"May I make a suggestion?"

"Please do."

"I've been thinking. I know just the right building that should be named after you. It will reflect your spirit."

"You're joking with me on a serious matter. So tell me, what building should it be?"

"You're so filled with fire I'm certain the boiler room would fit you to a 'T'. It would be your place to let off steam."

Hearing that quip I grabbed my beautiful wife and kissed her passionately. We rolled over together and went into a deep sleep.

The next morning we got up early, packed the kids into the wagon and drove over to Marstons to complete our Christmas shopping. We had fun outfitting the kids for the 50 degree change in weather. While Eugenia was having lunch with Mark and Joyce, I slipped away with Ann and Clare to buy ice skates for the two older ones, a gold Seika watch and the latest Hemingway book for Mom. The little ones promised not to tell the others about Dad's purchases. Eugenia had already made up several gift packages for all of us and placed them under the tree.

On the way home I stopped off at two used car dealers to solicit an offer for our Ford wagon. *Honest Jim* offered $365. Q*uality Motors,* after test driving the vehicle, suggested $295, stating, "That's a good offer, since I think your wagon will be needing a new transmission soon."

While I was negotiating with *Quality Joe*, Eugenia motioned me to go. As I left him I said, "I'll think about it," and drove away.

With anxiety Eugenia sounded off, "Wbile you were spouting away I wrote a classified ad. If we hurry over to the *San Diego Union* we'll be able to get it in for Thursday and Friday."

"What does it say?"

"*Ford Station Wagon. Low Mileage. Runs Great. Must be sold today or tomorrow. Leaving state. Anything above $500 will take* *it. Phone: 884-1917.* How does it sound to you?"

"Great. Let's do it and hope for the best." We zipped over to the classified office of the newspaper.

The next morning Christmas arrived when Ann and Clare started chanting at our bed, "Mommy and Daddy you must get up. Christmas is here! Mommy and Daddy you must get up. Christmas is here!"

I moved quickly as Eugenia prepared an early breakfast of crêpes suzettes, cereal and eggs. For over three hours we opened the presents. No one was disappointed with the new clothing or any of the personal gifts. Eugenia loved her watch and said, "Now that I have time on my hand I promise you never to be late for any appointments."

When I opened the box that said, "To the finest husband and father in the world," I swallowed. I was taken aback by what I saw. It was an expensive suede jacket, dress shirt, cuff links and tie with a little note, "Wear these on those very important occasions, Mr. College President — ILY — EFPZ."

The last gift to be opened by Eugenia was the one from Bob and Joe. As she slowly tore the paper, out sprung an electric cord. Then, as she got down to the core, a black handle with a doubled-edged metal blade appeared.

Joyce said, "It's a curling iron for Mom's hair."

"No it isn't," Mark said. "It's a hedge cutter for Dad."

I took the appliance, plugged it in and turned it on. My arm started to vibrate. "It's a hair cutter for animals," I stated.

"You're all wrong," Eugenia emphatically declared. "It's for animals, only not to trim their hair, but to slice their meat. It's an automatic meat cutter! I saw it demonstrated at Sears last week but I never thought I'd be the first in the neighborhood to own one. I must write a thank you note to those men for their thoughtfulness."

At dinner that night Eugenia was thrilled to slice the baked ham with the most modern kitchen instrument of the day.

Early the next morning we were awakened by phone call from a buyer, named Jerry, who immediately wanted to see the Ford. When he arrived an hour later, he kicked the tires, opened the hood, started the engine and asked, "Mind if I take it on the freeway?"

"Not at all, but I'll go with you."

Before reaching the freeway Jerry tried out the brakes, lights and radio. Once on the freeway, he zoomed up to 70 miles per hour in seconds, stayed there for several miles, and said, "Do you hear that?"

"No, I don't hear anything unusual."

"I thought I heard a little knock"

Back at 9 Sierra Way the buyer opened the hood again, advanced the carburetor, checked the exhaust and made a decision. "I'll take it right now. Here's four bills."

He showed me four $100 bills. That was $35 above Honest Jim's offer. Not bad, but not good. I said nothing, thinking of the old trite real estate adage, "The first offer is usually the best." So, I'd better take it and get on with the packing.

Suddenly Eugenia called out, "Herb, there's another buyer on the phone who wants to talk to you, and a third one left his number."

"Tell him I'll call him back in a few minutes." I decided on how to handle this first prospective buyer. "Jerry, you know value when you see it, and so do others. Here it's only 9:30 and I've already gotten three calls. I'm going to stick to my ad. The first one that gives me $501 or above gets this perfect Ford. Is it going to be you?"

He said nothing and walked away to his car. Oops, had I misjudged him? Within a minute he returned with a large white envelope and counted out $101 in small bills. He said, "We got a deal."

I gave him a receipt for his money and told him he could pick up the wagon and registration on Saturday at 7:00 AM.

After Jerry drove away, Eugenia congratulated me on obtaining $136 above the highest bidder. I also congratulated her for her splendid ad writing and wonderful timing in announcing those important telephone calls.

With enthusiasm we continued to pack, and finished late Friday night. Before going to bed for our last night in Chula Vista Eugenia set the table for breakfast and made up a bunch of sandwiches for our luncheon.

At 7:00 AM on Saturday I transferred the title on the wagon to Jerry and wished him good luck. He was surprised to hear we were going to Chicago and commented, "People come from Chicago, not go to."

We were startled to see Ann and C!are kissing the wagon good-bye. They'd loved the back compartment where they'd had freedom to play, and started to cry as the wagon disappeared down the road.

"Will we get a new one when we get to Chicago?" Joyce asked.

"Not right away," I replied.

At the scheduled time the Bekins crew arrived in an extra large van and loaded the truck in less than five hours. They promised to deliver our furnishings to Elmwood Park early Tuesday morning.

After the truck left we ate our sandwiches in the backyard at the big round table. Several neighbors dropped by to give us bon voyage gifts of candy, cakes, wine, books and toys for the little ones. Eugenia and I were touched by the graciousness and warmth of our neighbors. We loved them all and it was getting hard to say goodbye. Finally, in the afternoon, Gregory Cullison, the grocery store owner and dear friend, arrived with his nine-passenger station wagon to take all of us to the Amtrak station in San Diego.

Boarding the train was exciting as we prepared for the 45-hour trip. Our kids had never been on a train and asked many questions:

"Is it coal, gas, oil or nuclear power that makes this train go?"

"Where do we sleep?"

"Where does the garbage and other waste material go?"

"When does the driver sleep? Isn't 45 hours too long to drive?"

"Where does the electricity come from?"

"How fast can this train go?"

I answered all the questions as best I could. I described how much better this train was than the one from New York to Chicago that I'd traveled on so long ago when I won a free trip to the Chicago's World Fair as a newspaper boy. That train had been slower, dirtier and jerkier and the only food on board had been sandwiches, hot dogs, coke or coffee. There were no sleeping cars and we had stayed up most of the night, arriving at our destination exhausted.

I told the kids we'd be eating in a special train known as the dining car as soon as the train started moving. No sooner said than the train started to accelerate and hit 65 miles per hour in minutes. The dinner gong sounded and we wobbled our way through three cars to a beautiful dining car filled with tables covered with white cloths, shining silverware and fresh flowers as centerpieces. The younsters took a long time to order as Eugenia explained the choices on the menu. A wholesome meal was promptly served with pie a la mode for dessert.

Refreshed and excited, we enjoyed the scenery as the train zipped along the oceanside.

Ann called out, "Good-bye beautiful and calm Pacific. Daddy, will we ever return?"

"Oh yes, when Mark graduates from Stanford, we'll all go to his commencement."

When we returned to our roomette we were surprised to find it converted to four bunk beds. Eugenia and I took the double one on top while Ann and Clare selected the one on the bottom. On the other side of the room Joyce grabbed the bottom and Mark was left with the top. In rapid order we brushed our teeth and changed into our sleeping wear. This was the first time that all six of us slept in the same room. Although exhausted after getting up at 6:00 AM, we continued to talk into the night until Mark's silent trombone erupted and I received a kick from Eugenia with the words, "Turn off in the halls of the mountain king, darling." I obliged.

In the middle of the night, so it seemed, Ann awakened Eugenia with, "Mommy, Mommy, look outside, it's so different. Are we entering Heaven?"

"No, darling. We're slowing down because we're climbing the mountains of Flagstaff and are moving into a blizzard."

"What's a blizzard?"

"A high wind filled with fine snow."

"What's snow?"

"A mass of white petals. When you taste it, it turns into water."

"Is that one of God's miracles?"

"Yes dear, now go to sleep and tomorrow we'll get off the train for a short while and taste one of God's miracles."

Morning arrived. The sun was shining bright and God produced another miracle. All the snow was gone; we were passing through New Mexico. The family was in a euphoric mood as we enjoyed the quiet but mysterious beauties of the state. After breakfast I got out my 8-millimeter movie camera for some action shots of the kids. My mind immediately turned to some 35 years earlier when my father, a movie buff, had purchased a QRS 16 millimeter camera to capture the important events in the lives of his hardworking wife, five sons and two daughters. Before dying he gave me the films, which I'll treasure forever. Now it was my turn to nab the young and carefree children. I hoped they'd cherish the action record as much as I did and *their* kids would thank Grandpa for his vision many years later. The film captured the zealous look on the faces of all the Zeitlins as the locomotive zinged along into a new time zone.

While they were in such a happy state, I asked my kin, "What day is the most important day of the year?"

Mark's instant response was, "Christmas, because we get lots of presents."

Joyce jumped in, "My birthday, since besides getting presents I don't have to do any work around the house."

Ann added, "The first day of school, because I learn something new every day."

I studied their faces. "Thus far we've had three guesses. but though they're all good, they're not right. Start thinking. Think! What's the most important day of the year?"

Clare started clapping her hands while Mark rubbed his forehead. Finally, Joyce said, "Clare is clapping her hands because she's so happy today. So I guess today is the best day."

"You're absolutely correct!" I said.

Eugenia joined in with her own twist of wisdom. "Every day is important, because you never know how it will come out. Every day is filled with opportunities to do good. If yesterday was a bad day, you can make today better. Make up your mind to change it and it will happen."

All the kids nodded their heads as I raised a second question. "What's the best feeling in the world?"

Without hestitation, Mark sounded off, "Hitting a home run or catching a forward pass!"

Joyce started to hit my hand and then blurted out, "Daddy, remember when were in Mexico last summer and on my first casting, I caught a fish? I felt great then."

"And so did I." I looked at Ann for her answer.

"Reading a good book," popped out.

"All your answers are good," I commented. "It tells me what you like to do. But I'm probing for something that all of us would agree makes us feel good on the inside for a long time."

"I have the answer," Mark said. "If I've learned anything from my parents all these years, it's that helping others creates the best feeling within us. That's why you're both teachers."

"Mark, you get an A. You're excused from the final examination. Now I have a third question for you all. Who is the most disagreeable person you'll meet when we arrive in Illinois?"

A long silence fell over the group...no one said anything. Finally Mark asked, "Is it our landlord?"

"No, Herb Johnson is a prince of a guy," I responded immediately. "He gave us his old TV set and left behind three beds and a couch so we won't have to stay at a motel if Bekins is delayed."

"I give up," Joyce said.

"Sweetie pie, don't ever give up. Quitting is so easy, and generally one of the biggest mistakes someone can make. Think hard. I'll give you a little clue. What kind of kids at school do you dislike the most?"

"The ones who use cusswords, disobey the teacher or are always complaining."

"You've got it."

"Which one is it?"

"The complainer. He or she becomes the most disagreeable person in any group. Avoid them if you can. It's a sad fact of life that they get a lot of attention, and negatives attract negatives. If you want to feel good, always associate with the optimistic students–not the negative ones."

Talking, listening, reading, sitting and sleeping together in the little roomette for over 45 hours gave me an opportunity to know each one a little better. We played cards for many hours. I taught them 21, regular and stud poker. Mark and Joyce did most of the winning. To keep them on their toes Eugenia and I won a few. Ann won two and Clare always had the honor of cutting the cards.

A day later we arrived in Chicago. The sky was gray, temperature in the 30s, with a little leftover snow as I hailed a taxi to Elmwood Park The drive along Eisenhower Expressway was stop-and-go most of the time. The kids said nothing, but stared at the old tall buildings. We got off at Harlem and headed north to North Avenue, where the scenery changed to a more modern mode. When we arrived at 7919 Cortland Parkway, the family cheered from curbside. The clean, neat and light house on a tree-lined street was appealing. Eugenia immediately went into the small but modern kitchen. I heard a big hurrah. She really did like it, and gave her robust approval as she inspected the rest of the home. Mark compared the smallest bedroom with the den and instantly chose the former. I got on the phone and called Bob, who said he'd deliver the Skylark shortly.

Within the hour two cars showed up at the house, Jim Tarpey in one and Bob in my Skylark. They gave Eugenia and me a big welcome back as they greeted the rest of the Zeitlins with zip and zest. The kids felt at home with Uncle Bob and his pal Jim as we toured the near-empty home.

"What's the good news on the car repair?" I asked Bob.

"It's nothing. No cost. A friend of mine fixed it."

"Oh come on now, Bob, I owe you for parts and labor. I insist on paying right now."

"Well, if you insist, it's $15 for the fan belt, $10 for labor and no charge for delivery."

"Bob, that's exceptionally reasonable. If you hadn't helped me out when you did, it would have been $50 for towing, plus a $100 or more at a Buick service station. Thanks a million." I gave him $25.

Bob picked up a receiver and said, "Sean, I'm at Dr. Zeitlin's home right now and the Johnsons have moved. So can you find me a snappy new number for our college president?"

He waited. "Yes, he has a full house...Give me the number: 453-4525. Thanks."

"What is this full house business?" I asked.

"You just got it! Three fives and two fours is a winner." The two friends drove away.

Eugenia's glazed look disappeared when Mark shouted, "Mom, don't you get it? Three fives and two fours is a full house. It's a great poker hand!"

Later that evening we drove over to the Wagon Wheel for a relaxing dinner. We then hopped over to Dominick's Market on North Avenue, where Eugenia was pleasantly surprised to find such a variety of epicurean foods. We loaded up, drove home, turned the heat on, unpacked and went to bed in our new partly-furnished home.

The next morning the Bekins truck arrived as scheduled and

unloaded all our belongings in less than four hours, and not a single broken item!

As we were eating lunch Eugenia looked me straight in the eye and said, "I know what you're thinking."

"You do? My, you are psychic. Well, what shall it be? Red wine or white wine for our New Year's eve celebration tonight?"

"That's not what you were thinking. When Maria called this morning, you were all aglow and couldn't stop asking questions. Why don't you go to the office right now so you can find out what's happened these past 10 days? Mark and Joyce can help me get things in order, So go!"

I kissed my dear wife and dashed off to Dominick's to make the wine purchases. With a full throttle I accelerated to 1829 Broadway. Maria was getting ready to leave for a New Year's Eve party but stopped to update me on some important activities.

"The phone was very busy. Mostly calls about the different administrative positions. The mail reflects high interest in the future college. Also, for the first three Saturdays in January Mr. Boeger and Mr. Collins had me confirm luncheon dates with the full board to interview different architects."

I thanked Maria for running the office so well during my absence, wished her and her family a happy New Year and insisted that she leave pronto, although she did so reluctantly as she handed me about two dozen message slips.

After she left I spent several hours studying the applications that Maria left on my desk in three different piles: dean of admissions, dean of instruction and coordinator of business management. There were no applications for dean of technology. I spent several hours reviewing each one until I was interrupted by a call from Eugenia. "Let's start the New Year right by you having dinner with your family before 7:00. No excuses."

I agreed and started to gather up several applications to take home with me. Just before leaving I got a call from Wade Steel. "I heard you were back from Bob Collins. Herb, I forgot to tell you that next week the Leyden Municipal League will be having a rather important meeting and I want you to attend. My old friend Assemblyman Bill Clayborne will be discussing a bill that will affect all the junior colleges in the state."

"Wade, I would not want to miss it. I heard that Governor Kerner has some great ideas about advancing the cause of higher education. Let's hope it's good news all the way."

"It's going to cost money to advance his ideas and we'll probably hear objections. You don't have to make a speech but I want to introduce you to the group."

"I'll pick you up at your home a half hour before dinner time." I said goodbye.

By the time I returned to 7919 Cortland Parkway the weather had turned bitter cold, with a zero degree forecast. My suntanned kids had gone outside to explore the neighborhood, but hastily returned with red noses and numb toes and cheeks. Joyce, breathing hard, called out, "This is so different from California. I'll dress warmer tomorrow."

Ann and Clare were sitting on the kitchen floor close to the double oven defrosting their anatomy. Mark called out, "Has the Pasadena Tournament of Roses parade been called off because of this freeze?"

"You must be kidding. You know darn well that it's warm there and they've never cancelled a parade or football game. Tomorrow we'll watch both on TV."

I couldn't get over the progress Eugenia had made while I was gone. The kitchen tools were in place, all beds made and the furniture properly arranged. In the distance we could smell the cornish hen percolating a delightful flavor as we sat down to our first dinner in our new residence. Afterwards, Mark and Joyce washed and dried the dishes and we all gathered around the TV in the den to watch Guy Lombardo and his Royal Canadians from the New York Waldorf Astoria usher in the New Year.

Clare and Ann started dancing. Mom and Dad joined them and danced to Guy's romantic numbers as the two older ones watched. A few minutes before midnight all the young ones dressed warmly and with their pots and pans and noisemakers marched outside to stir things up, expecting to see others doing the same. Five minutes after midnight they returned. Mark was disappointed. "Gee, nobody was there. These people are different. They don't know how to have fun."

"On the contrary, Mark," I replied. "They're having fun indoors. They're smart. They know enough not to go outdoors in freezing weather, and in time you'll become as smart as they are."

After retiring, while lying in bed Eugenia asked, "I noticed you brought home a folder filled with applications. Are there any good ones?"

"They're all good, but I'm looking for the exceptional ones, especially those with recent training in computer science. There are no applications for the dean of technology, but I think I found two special ones for the coordinator of business management."

"Tell me more."

"The top one has a B.B.A. and a master's with a specialty in computer science, plus three years' experience as the business manager of an elementary school district in Du Page County."

"How old is he and what's his name?"

"He's 29 and his name is Dale Alexison. I hope he's as good as his papers show. I'll have Maria try to schedule an interview as soon as possible. The second best is 39 years old. He has a similar educational background, but with 13 years' experience as the assistant superintendent in charge of finance and business in a large high school district in Missouri."

The following day, a holiday, we relaxed and watched TV and read the local newspapers. Later on in the afternoon the kids and I drove over to the Elm School and the Elmwood Park High School, where the oldest three were looking forward to enrolling. Mark loved football and I told him he could try out for the junior varsity this fall. Joyce and Ann wanted to know if they could continue to take piano lessons, and who their teacher would be. I told them I didn't know but we'd find a good one.

Clare pulled on my arm and managed to get out, "What about me?"

I told her I didn't know, but would find out about her school on Monday.

15
Search for Architect
And Business Manager

January started out as an exceptionally cold month but soon heated up. The trustees and I planned to visit several campuses where various architects had recently put up buildings. We were determined to select an architect before the end of the month.

When I arrived at the Moose Hall in River Grove for the Leyden Municipal League dinner on the first Thursday in January, the boys were at the bar describing their campus visits. Joe, who had taken a trip to Bloom High School, discussed how exciting it was to see bright colors used in classrooms and halls. It had moistened his palate for learning. He was surprised at the low building costs made possible by the use of new materials. Wade, on the other hand, expressed sorrow for the president of Carthage College, where he noticed several cracks in the walls of the newly constructed main building. To stay within budget the president and his board had ignored the architect's recommendation of soil tests before starting construction.

Bob, Joe, Babe and I had a great time visiting the University of Illinois, where as a freshman Babe had supported himself as the campus shoemaker. We all vowed not to repeat the university's biggest mistake.

"What was their biggest mistake?" Wade asked.

Taking his olive out of his martini to emphasize his point, Joe said, "This olive is beautiful. Notice the uniform color and shape. Now taste it. Doesn't it feel good? I didn't feel good at the UI campus. They've had a dozen or more independent architects, each with his own style and taste and no central theme. They built without a master plan. When we hire our architect we must keep him for the duration; otherwise we'll also end up with a weird conglomeration of buildings."

The men nodded their heads in unison just as the guest speaker, Bill Clayborne, arrived. I hadn't known until that moment that Wade, the modest one, was president of the League. He introduced our speaker to me as we went to the head table. Wade announced that the bar was closed and dinner served. At dessert time he had the secretary call the roll by village and school district. Every time a mayor stood up to answer "present" there was loud applause. Mayor Conti received the strongest ovation. Finally, Wade introduced his fellow trustees, who all received a generous acclamation. The last to be introduced was the college president, who heard a few hands clapping nearby, near nothing in comparison to the reception given to the mayors. Suddenly a united burst of boos came forth from a table in the rear, led by the known adversary, Mayor O'Connor.

I was taken aback, not knowing what to do so I smiled meekly and sat down. Wade whispered, "Herb, ignore it. It's only Mayor O'Connor and his lackeys. The people of River Grove really want this college and they will back you up."

The program chairman proceeded to introduce Bill Clayborne, who spoke for 30 minutes. Some of his highlights were:

1.   Governor Kerner feels that the junior colleges should join the higher education family, rather than continue to be hindered in growth under high school control.

2.   Illinois youth will be denied higher education in the immediate future because the universities are packed and can't take any more students.

3.   We should cease calling these unique institutions junior colleges. A more appropriate name would be Community College or People's College.

4.   These Community Colleges are less expensive for students and taxpayers than any other institution of higher education. The cost per student is about one-third to one-fourth that at the University of Illinois.

5.   These colleges provide specialized training in the occupational and technical areas. In addition, postgraduate training is available on short notice.

6.   For many years parents have endured financial hardship in

order to send their children to expensive prestigious universities. Now that we have discovered that the junior/community colleges *do as well, if not better,* than universities during the freshman and sophomore years, thousands of dollars can be saved. Students who insist on attending all four years at a senior institution are somewhat selfish and show little concern about their parents' finances.

Clayborne reserved the final ten minutes for questions from the audience, and there were many. The younger members of the League seemed highly supportive of Governor Kerner's aim to provide additional facilities for the baby boomers. On the other hand many of the seniors, led by Mayor O'Connor, felt that we were already educating too many college students and no additional financial assistance should be provided.

In closing Assemblyman Clayborne stressed, "The state has a major responsibility to provide higher education for all those who can profit from instruction, and we shall not default from this tenet." Looking directly at me he continued, "If California can do it, so can we. We shall come up with a new Master Plan for Higher Education."

As he ended his remarks strong applause came from Elmwood Park's Mayor Elmer Conti and his contingent, no sounds from O'Connor's sycophants and a mixture of sounds from the remaining municipalities.

Before closing the meeting Wade slowly approached the microphone, adjusted it to his height, looked to the left, then to the right, stared out toward the center and waited for the audience to settle down. As he waited silence eventually came over the hall. The audience listened to their president make his important concluding remarks.

"Fellows, when World War II ended 20 years ago there was fear of great unemployment as the 12 million young military men and women returned to civilian life. It didn't happen. How come? Well, you know what happened! After years of shortages of everything, our factories started to hum, supplying much needed autos, radios and TVs, furniture, clothing and houses. Instead of a depression we had prosperity. In addition, the government wisely invested in our youth by passing the G.I. Bill of Rights. Millions of veterans entered college or trade schools tuition-free, graduated and then earned good salaries in a healthy job market.

"Now, when the sons and daughters of these veterans want to duplicate their proud parents' achievements, there is no room for them in the colleges and universities of Illinois.

"This is not right! The American Dream of improvement of one's status through education must survive. We have recruited Dr. Zeitlin from California to help us build the first community college and technical institute in the state of Illinois. Illinois has the distinction of establishing, in 1902 in Joliet, the first public junior college in the nation. Yet it still operates out of a high school building, and so do all our other 23 public junior colleges.

"This month your college board hopes to select the architect to build our campus, and sometime in March we will ask the people to approve a bond issue. The amount has yet to be determined. A yes vote is needed if we're to keep the American Dream alive in Illinois. I will keep you informed as developments take place."

As Wade sat down I couldn't help but feel that this magnificent man, without any notes, in his low-pitched voice, had pleaded our case directly from the heart. Everyone felt it. A large number of men ran up to him to pledge their support. Bob and I watched in admiration and then slipped away to the River Grove table, where Bob introduced me to his uncle, Mayor O'Connor.

Without even shaking my hand the first thing he said was, "So, you're the young suntanned whippersnapper that's going to change our community. Bob told me all about you. If you want my support you'll have to change the location of the campus. *We don't want it in River Grove!*

"Where should it be, Mayor?" I asked.

"Anywhere except River Grove. Have you considered the Hillside Golf Course? It's a far better site, and everybody knows it."

"Yes we have, but there's a conflict of interest there since that site is owned by trustee Elmore Boeger."

"Gmm. . .Let me tell you this: that rich SOB got on the board deliberately to prevent such a sale. Did you know that?"

"No, I didn't."

"You don't get around much. At least not to the right places. You realize we were only joking when my boys booed you. We did it only to get your attention, and it worked. Let me give you some sound advice."

"Please do, I certainly would appreciate it."

"When you hire an architect make sure he's from Illinois, or else you'll make the people of River Grove very angry. Also, you don't need 40 acres to teach a few hundred delinquents a trade. *Build up, not out!* And what's more, I know of a good architect that can do the job very cheap."

"Please have him send his resume to me ASAP. There's still time for him to be considered."

"I'll do that... You know, Dr. *Zeitland,* you aren't such a bad guy after all. You look something like Ray Milland from *The Lost Weekend.* Have you seen that movie?"

"Yes–who hasn't? It was an excellent story about a man who drank too much."

"Well, I am getting a little worried about Bob. Lately he's been associating with a lot of heavy drinkers and now, Beverly tells me, he insists on having a martini or two every night before dinner. Could you get him to cut down a little? He won't listen to me, but he might hear you since be admires and respects you so much."

"Mayor O'Connor, we're all going to Milwaukee this Saturday to see another architect's creation and I'll make it a point to discuss it with Bob at the luncheon."

With that he gave me a strong and hearty handshake and I left. As I was driving Wade home I asked him to describe Mayor O'Connor.

"Let's keep it all in the family, Herb. I would say he's narrow-minded, ignorant at times, highly emotional, an old bootstrap man but with a heart of gold. He really is the Archie Bunker of River Grove."

When the five trustees and I arrived at the Milwaukee Institute of Technology to tour the campus of over 8,000 students, architect Sommers from Skadberg & Olson greeted us effusively. This was the first technical institute we had visited and we were surprised to learn that more than half the students were enrolled in tuition-free occupational programs.

The school was tuned in to the times, having recently equipped the data processing lab with the best IBM computers. Enrollment in that program had surpassed 400. Mr. Sommers proclaimed that

Milwaukee Tech was the best in the nation. We were fascinated by what we saw, particularly the supermodern continuing education center, still under construction, designed to house the school's educational television station.

After the three-hour tour Mr. Sonimers invited us to lunch at the best restaurant in town. The service was fast, the food was epicurean, the drinks were many and dialogue was positive all the way. By then we assumed that Skadberg & Olson would be the one. After Sommers paid the big bill Wade informed him that the board was scheduled to make a few more visits and he'd get an answer before the end of the month.

As we drove back to Chicago Wade asked each trustee how he felt about hiring Skadberg & Olson. They were all enthusiastic about Tech and its architect, except Joe Farmar, who remained silent and stonefaced.

"What's wrong, Joe?" Wade asked.

He explosively exhaled and sounded off, "Herb, why didn't you tell us about your talk with Mayor O'Connor?"

The fun-loving trustees suddenly became silent, waiting for my response. I felt in the hot seat and my temperature was rising as I sought a satisfactory response. My Guardian Angel said tell them exactly what happened.

"Fellows, the mayor and I had a nice chat and we parted on friendly terms. He made it perfectly clear that he would be very angry if we hired an architect from outside of Illinois."

"Why didn't you tell us this?" Joe asked.

"You know, this is the first time we've been together since the Thursday night dinner. I tried several times on the way up here to tell you about the O'Connor message but couldn't get a word in edgewise since everyone had so much to say."

"Oh come on now, all you had to do was to speak out. The O'Connor threat is very real," Joe said.

"Fellows, let's not be too hard on Herb. I think there's a lesson to be learned here," Wade replied.

"And what's that lesson, Wade?" Joe asked.

"I think whenever a group of us meets with our college president, whether in a formal or informal setting, our chief administrator should be the first to speak"

"I second that motion," was Bob's instant response.

All five trustees nodded in agreement

"Then it's settled as the second informal policy of the board. The college president shall be the first one to give his report at all regular, executive or informal sessions with the board. Tonight when I call Babe and Elmore I'll not only update them on our visit but will tell them about the adoption of our second policy statement."

"You understand, Herb, that in order to win this election we must do nothing to create an opposition group," Joe elaborated. "If Mayor O'Connor opposes the bond election, others will follow, and the election will be doomed. Therefore, I want you to tell our dear mayor that this board is in full agreement with him and the architect will come from the state of Illinois. Also, tell him that the board would welcome another application for the architect's position."

I nodded. As we continued to drive we discussed the strengths and weaknesses of the five remaining architects, none of whom had ever built a community college. I was directed to visit each architect's place of work and evaluate his facilities.

The following week the visits began. First on the docket was Child's & Smith, second in line was Consoer & Morgan, third was Probst, fourth was Shaeffer & Company and last went to Fox & Fox. I decided to visit all firms unannounced, accepting the invitation of "drop in anytime to see us at work." The first three firms had beautiful offices, many architects and draftsmen at work, plus a busy office staff. However, in each case when I asked to see my original contact, he wasn't there. Where he was nobody really knew. Out soliciting– maybe. Could his specialty be public relations? I waited 21 minutes to be received by Child's & Smith, 42 minutes by Consoer & Morgan and 31 minutes by Probst & Company. I was impressed by each company's large and modern facilities, but disturbed that I had to wait so long for them to find me an escort. Frequently the right hand of a large company doesn't know what the left hand is doing.

I had a big surprise entering the office of Shaeffer & Company to find a clerk seated at a small desk and behind her a drafting board, T-square, pencils and paper–that was all. The clerk informed me that Mr.

Shaeffer was not in, and she didn't know when he would return. I remembered Shaeffer as the youngest and his claim that he'd played a major part with several architects working under him in the construction of O'Hare airport. What you hear or imagine is not always what you see. Now that I was in his office I doubted his veracity.

The last office to visit was Fox & Fox, located at 330 South Wells in downtown Chicago. The secretary picked up the phone to announce my arrival and almost immediately John Fox, the president, came out to welcome me. He ushered me into his large private office, where many photos and models of completed projects were on display. He said, "In order to have a successful bond election you have to show the people what they're going to get for their money. This model of Gordon Tech did the trick for the Chicago Catholic Diocese."

"Was Gordon Tech High School the first technical institute you built?"

"Yes, it was and I'm hoping that the next tech project will be your college."

"You know there's a vast difference between a high school and a community college."

"Yes I know, but with your many years of experience at the Phoenix Technical Institute and the California community colleges I'll be able to tap your private resources. Together we can build the first public community college in Illinois. I'm very excited about this possibility."

"How long would it take you to build a miniature model of eight buildings on a 40-acre site?"

"Usually we'd need two to three months. We don't build them. We subcontract them out to the very best model builder in Chicago."

"Two to three months is too long if we're to have a referendum in March. Could you make it in two to three weeks instead?"

"Boy, you really are the speedy one. If you tell me ASAP is what you want, Fox & Fox is noted for doing the impossible. Yes, we can do it if the boys work a ten-hour day, Saturdays and Sundays included."

"Mr. Fox, the board is nearing the end of architect interviewing. As you know your interview is scheduled for next Saturday, and you're the last one. Are you ready?"

"Yes, I am. I've reserved a private room for nine luncheon guests at the Bismarck"

"Will any of your associates be there?"

"No. When you hire Fox & Fox, I, as the president of the company, work solely with the client. I'll see you once or twice a week as my team progresses on your project. Dr. Zeitlin, we will eventually become brothers. I need to know what you're thinking. I will translate your dreams into a beautiful campus. Come along, let me introduce you to my staff."

Outside of his private office was an extra large room subdivided into sections, such as design, structure, heating and air conditioning, electrical, legal, business, etc. John introduced me to Don, Bill and Al, sectional heads, who, surprisingly enough, seemd to know something about the college district. If flattery will get you somewhere, it was working that afternoon. I immediately took a liking to his staff. They did their homework. They knew much about the college and its president, displaying teamwork and welcomed the challenge.

As I left John Fox said to me, "Is it true what they say about being last?"

"What do they say?"

"The best shall be last."

"I really don't know. We'll know more after the Saturday luncheon."

As I was driving home I thought about John's last remark, "The best shall be last." It has worked in my case and the more I thought about it, John was the best man to date. When I got to my office, I called Wade and later the other six trustees to give them verbal reports and urge them to visit Fox & Fox ASAP.

Wade, Roy and Elmore checked out John Fox on Monday, while Babe, Joe and Bob saw him the following day. Fred could not make it on either day, but looked forward to meeting John on Saturday.

The trustees loved these Saturday luncheons. It was always a time to relieve pent-up steam among friends, while enjoying the spirited tonics. Joe, Bob and Fred were on round one when Wade and I arrived at the Bismark at noon. John Fox was busy setting up a slide projector and easel. Then Roy and Elmore arrived, and we waited for Babe. Joe firmly stated that we should not start without the coalition leader. Twenty-five minutes later Babe showed up, breathing heavily and profusely apologizing for his lateness.

As dessert was being served John began his presentation. He projected about two dozen photos of projects completed, pointing out his special construction features. At the easel he sketched out three unique plans displaying how he would place eight buildings on our 40-acre campus. Each plan brought out gasps of excitement from the trustees. None of the previous architects had presented any kind of schematic. But they'd needed "more time to think"

John with an oblique suggestion from the college president, had illustrated some of our dreams on paper. He called the bridges that connected the eight buildings "The Melrose Park Bridges of Learning."

Plan III envisioned a Library-Administration building, Planetarium, Science; Auditorium-Fine Arts, Technology, Liberal Arts & Business, Student Center, Gym & Pool. John and the board seemed to be getting along rather well. I whispered to Wade, "He's the one."

Wade in turn whispered to Babe as Joe and Bob engaged John in dialogue. Wade's very quiet response was, "Babe said maybe. He wants to put it on hold for a short while."

As John started to pack away his projector Wade said, "Mr. Fox, we want to thank you for your splendid presentation. You've given us many things to think about but the board needs more time to deliberate. You'll be hearing from Dr. Zeitlin shortly."

John instantly replied, "Gentlemen, I am ready to start to work for you as soon as we have a signed contract. In the meantime I'll leave these sketches with you so you can mull over whichever one you like the most. Dr. Zeitlin has requested a model of the proposed campus, which I could deliver to you three weeks after the contract is signed."

The group broke up. Babe hastily left, followed by Roy and Elmore. Joe, Bob and Fred went to the bar while Wade and I walked John to his car.

As I drove Wade back to his home I asked, "Why is Babe putting this on hold when John Fox is the one?"

"Don't you know?"

"No, please tell me."

"It's politics. We'll just have to wait."

When Dale Alexison's glowing confidential papers arrived, I immediately called him to arrange an interview. He was everything his papers said he was: brilliant, young and enthusiastic, experienced with computers, well-liked in the community, a happy family man with two pre-schoolers. I liked him and was ready to put him to my final test.

A prospective faculty member may give all the right answers during the interview. But was an interview the best means of getting to know the individual? I always made it a practice to take the candidate out to lunch or dinner before arriving at a decision, so I asked Dale if he could join me for a leisurely dinner away from the office next week. He agreed. A week later Dale arrived returned to my office and we drove to the Homestead Restaurant in my little Skylark. The conversation started with cars. He complimented me on my Buick. One day he hoped to graduate to the same, or maybe an Olds. In the meantime he was very happy with his Falcon wagon.

We checked our coats. In passing I commented about the voluptuous hat check girl, "She is a real cutie. Don't you think so?"

"Oh yes, but wait until you meet my wife. She gets more attractive every day."

Good answer, I thought. He's someone who ignores flirtatious women. A tall, elegantly dressed middle-aged woman took us to our table. A rather robust waitress appeared suddenly and playfully discussed the specials of the day, ending with, "Would you like a drink before dinner?" We both declined.

"You're first, Dale, give the waitress your order."

"Dr. Zeitlin, there's such a variety that I can't make up my mind. What are you going to have?"

"I'll have the small filet mignon, baked potñto, two vegetables, salad and coffee for dessert."

"That sounds good to me. I'll have the same."

When the dinner arrived Dale was served first. He showed restraint, not eating until I, his host, picked up *my* fork. That's good manners.

We exchanged tidbits about our wives, children, sports, books and movies. We both agreed that LBJ was on the right track and hoped his Medicare bill would be passed by Congress. As we were sipping our coffee the waitress reappeared and asked, "Wouldn't you two really want a nice nightcap?"

I looked at Dale. He was expressionless so I said, "Why not?'

Dale ordered crème de menthe and I settled on a B & B. As we enjoyed our cordials I impulsively asked, "Don't you think we're sending too many people to college these days?"

Without blinking an eyelash he responded, "Oh no, Dr. Zeitlin, the only way society will improve is through education. I firmly believe, as I'm sure you do, that vocational education is the only sane, sensible answer for students who are not tuned into academic programs."

"Dale, that's a great answer. Now...I'm prepared to recommend you to the board at its January 13th meeting but first I want you to meet our president, Wade Steel. Can you see him tomorrow at 4:30?"

His enthusiastic response pleased me as I drove him back to his car and said good night. I felt good. He'd passed all my surreptitious tests: he'd showed up on time neatly dressed, ignored signals to flirt (though he was a young, good-looking male with a sparkling personality), expressed concern about the dinner costs before ordering, displayed excellent table manners, chitchatted well and responded excellently to my favorite final question. Above all he had several years of successful business experience and, most importantly, was focused on the future in a world of computers.

Wade called the following day to tell me he'd been very impressed with Dale Alexison and I should move full speed ahead. He had scheduled an executive meeting with the board at 7:00 PM for Wednesday, January 13th so that I could present my recommendation.

I expected the executive meeting to be short and sweet. All the trustees arrived on time, except Babe. Again he was 35 minutes late and apologized for the delay. I then summarized Alex's background and recommended that he start within 30 days.

Dead silence fell. . . . The guys looked at each other and said nothing. Finally Babe said, "Dr. Zeitlin, we don't want to rush things. Let's put him on hold. He's young. He can wait. We want you to interview several others before we reach a decision."

With that Babe hurried out to attend a special meeting with Mayor Richard Daley at City Hall while the other trustees gathered up their things to get to the regular meeting on time.

I was stunned. My first administrative recommendation, who was two years older than Bob Collins, had been rejected. Wade said we would talk about the business manager's position later as he proceeded to call the 13th official meeting of the board to order. It lasted 31 minutes. The salary schedules for the business manager and for the classified staff were approved. Maria got a $10 raise and Don Donahow was given the authority to enter into contract negotiations with the selected architect.

The rejection was reviewed, with no official reason given for the action. We decided to make a recommendation at the next meeting that the board was sure to like. I had interviewed Bill Roetzheim, a PE department chairman at Proviso High School and former U.S. Olympic gold medal winner. He was quite interested in our college and wanted to be its first director of athletics. He was friendly, optimistic, well-liked by all with a superb record of achievement. If hired early be might be able to schedule some sports for intercollegiate competition, as well as develop a strong intramural program.

Dr. Leroy Knoeppel did not want to lose his highly-respected teacher, but felt he was ready for a professional advancement, especially so since he had earned an "A" in Dr. Hoover's graduate course in junior college. Wade felt he would be an inspiration to all our students. We were certain that Babe, the all-American football player, would welcome one of the world's greatest athletes to our college staff. Athletes throughout the state would flock to our campus.

So, prior to the January 18th meeting at a private session of the board, I happily announced I had found a great one for director of athletics. At first it appeared that I had the full support of all the trustees.

Joe laughingly said, "Herb didn't tell us he was going to breed Olympic stars. We know what he's thinking. Get the great one on our campus and he will produce other greats."

The laughter suddenly stopped when Don Dunahow asked me to repeat his name, which I did. All eyes were on the board attorney as he slowly dropped one hand and shook his head "no."

Again silence fell over the group. Who would be the first to speak? With his fingers parted Babe hit his hands together several times before announcing, "There is no end of sports greats who would love this job, so Dr. Zeitlin, keep looking."

Up to that moment I had not known that Don Dunahow, and not

Babe, was the power behind the coalition. Babe had organized the group, but Don Dunahow, attorney for Elmwood Park, private attorney for Elmer Conti and attorney for the college, called the signals. Why had he said no to Bill Roetzheim's appointment, with none of the other trustees saying a word? What deep dark secret was Don withholding from us? My second rejection hit home. I had to talk privately with Wade.

If I struck out again would my job be on the line? No on the business manager, no on the director of athletics. If a no followed my recommendation for John Fox, I'd open the door for negotiations for my termination. I just didn't want to see that happen after only four months on the job.

The next day I had a long lunch with Wade. He assured me that the board liked me and would not want my resignation. I just needed to understand them better. Political trustees felt that their main purpose was to get jobs and contracts for their friends. He didn't know why the great one was passed over but promised me he would find out soon.

"Should I go ahead with John Fox?"

"No, wait until Don completes his investigation."

"How long will that take?

"I don't know but the board wants to know what the contractors have to say about Fox. I'm having lunch with Don tomorrow and maybe I'll have an answer."

On Tuesday night around 11:30, as I was getting ready for bed, Wade phoned. "Sorry to be calling so late, but I have some great news and some sad news for you. I can't tell you over the phone. Can you come over to my house after eight tomorrow night?"

As I hung up I wondered why Wade couldn't tell me over the phone. What was the big secret? The following day went by very fast. I kept wondering what had happened at lunch with Don. At dinner that night Eugenia said, "You have that faraway look again. What's eating you?"

I smiled and said, "Ask me tomorrow morning. I'll be visiting Wade at his home tonight to discuss some new developments."

When I arrived at Wade's home in a modest area of Franklin Park I complimented him on his residence. This was my first time inside his house. Mildred gave me a pleasant welcome and excused herself. Wade took me down to his finished basement bar and offered me a B & B while he had a brandy.

"Herb, I've got to tell you how politics works in this area. Don and I had a few good ones for lunch as he explained the reason for his rejection of Bill Roetzheim. Did you know that Roetzheim is Neil Mehler's brother-in-law? Mrs. Roetzheim is Neil's sister."

"Yes, I knew that. Just prior to the Christmas vacation, at Neil's invitation, I attended a delightful dinner in Maywood at which the Roetzheims, the Mehlers and some Maywood neighbors were present. So what's wrong with this tie-up?"

"Herb, you don't understand Chicago politics. Don and Neil are enemies, for what reason I don't know. But I do know that any friends or relatives of Neil are automatically enemies of Don and vice versa."

"Wade, that isn't fair. Bill Roetzheim or his wife haven't done any harm to Don. So why did Don so adamantly oppose Bill's appointment?"

"Herb, reread *Romeo and Juliet*. Chicago is somewhat like Verona in that families of enemies shall not mix. Any kind of relative or friend of Neil is on Donahow's shit list; therefore you have to withdraw your recommendation for the director of athletics."

"That just isn't fair to Bill Roetzheim."

"Who ever said politics is fair? You have to adjust to our system.... Now, let me tell you about John Fox."

"What did Don find out?"

"Plenty."

"Is it good or bad?"

"Good all the way. First all the contractors that worked with Fox liked him. Fox's blueprints are easy to read and John's friendly relationship with local inspectors makes permit issuing easy."

"Wade, why are you smiling so broadly? What else is there?"

"Lorraine Fox, John's wife, is a dear friend of Mrs. Daley. Every time Richard Daley ran for office, Lorraine hosted many fund-raisers in her big home for His Honor the Mayor. Babe didn't even know that."

"Is that why Babe put John Fox on hold?"

"Yes, Babe isn't tuned into Chicago's high society. He knows everyone in Melrose Park even though his wife Josephine isn't much of an entertainer. Her life is with her children. Daley called Babe on the carpet for holding up John's appointment."

"It seems like Dunahow is a remarkable man in getting vital information so quickly. How does he do it? Are we now ready to proceed with John Fox?"

"Well, not exactly. The picture is not yet complete until I can feel the pulse of the three big political bosses."

"And who may they be?"

"Have you forgotten Mayor O'Connor? He is one nasty scrapper when he's opposed. We can't win if he fights us. On Saturday afternoon I paid a visit to his home and we had a few beers in his basement bar. I told him what a good job his nephew Bob was doing as secretary of the college board and that he should work with Bob and not oppose him. That way, I pointed out, the Bob Collins star would shine and he'd be a shoo-in for mayor of River Grove when O'Connor retired."

"How did he react to your diplomatic remarks?"

"He beamed with delight and said he would support the Chicago Democrat as the architect noted for working well with Republican contractors."

"And who are the other two political bosses?"

"Jim Kirie, head of the Leyden Democrats, is Joe Farmar's political boss. So naturally he wanted to know how Joe was doing as a trustee. I told him he was doing great."

"How did he react to your statement?"

"It pleased him very much. He said he would pass it on to Governor Kerner when the governor requested names for judicial appointments. However, Kirie felt that Joe should serve a year or two as an assistant district attorney, even if it meant a drop in pay."

"Do you think Joe will do it?"

"I don't know. Joe is wrestling with that problem right now. A drop in pay would mean less for Celia and the kids. Maybe he'll find a solution in one of his Manhattans."

"How did Kirie react to John Fox as our architect?"

"He was elated; he felt we would have the best architect in Illinois."

"What about the third big one? Don't tell me, I know who he is. He's the top Republican, who received the most applause at the

Municipal League meeting. He owns a bank in Franklin Park, is the mayor of Elmwood Park and a past state legislator, and Don Dunahow is his attorney. He is a tall, handsome man named Elmer Conti. Did he approve of the Democrat named John Fox?"

"I had dinner with him last night and he was very easy to talk to. He didn't care one way or another whether the architect was a Democrat or a Republican, as long as Bob Collins and Don Dunahow endorsed the appointment. He'd been following the college's development, and is one of your most sincere supporters. He was pumping me for information about you as if you were a candidate for public office. So now all the bases are cleared and we're ready to hire Fox at the January 27th meeting."

As I socked my left hand with joy into my right I suddenly heard a loud rumble. Three cans of coke were bouncing down the stairs. Millie cried out, "I'm sorry to interrupt you boys, but I was about to bring you some refreshments. The cans just slipped out of my hand."

Wade immediately climbed the stair to tell her she should be more careful, and firmly shut the top door. He whispered to me, "Millie always wants to know what's going on. If there's anything wrong she rounds up her brigade and overcomes evil pronto. She's intelligent, kindhearted, a wonderful cook and wife, but I can't keep her down on the farm as my father did with my mother. So, let's talk quietly."

I then realized Millie was eavesdropping as Wade elaborated on her past achievements.

"You must be very proud of her," I commented.

"Yes, I am. She got everyone on this block, plus most of Franklin Park, to vote for me when I ran for college trustee."

"So, what's wrong with that?"

"Nothing, except she now acts without telling me anything. When we were first married, 40 years ago, she wouldn't do anything without consulting me. Today, she tells me what to do without even being asked. She claims that I don't listen to her."

"Is she a dictator?"

"That is an understatement. Just you wait, Herb. When you're married 40 years, things change dramatically; the so-called weaker sex becomes stronger and smarter."

"You know, Wade, as you talked I couldn't help but think of the relationship between Eleanor and Franklin Roosevelt. When those first two joined hands, be was tall, handsome, extroverted and very ambitious. She also was tall, but seen as an ugly duckling, introverted and extremely shy. As the years went by Eleanor carried many messages from her crippled husband in the White House. She grew in intellect, beauty and charm to become the most respected woman in America. *My Day,* her daily newspaper column, was read by millions. She vigorously fought all forms of discrimination against minorities and women. Mainly through her efforts, during World War II FDR signed an executive order ending segregation in the military.

"I'm not worried about women being in control in government and business. But I am concerned about whether the men of this country can accept this change of power. The roles and influence of women are expanding every day, and I'm sure by the end of this century we'll have a woman in the White House."

"Do you consider that good or bad?"

"I think it will be good. Now, Herb, I want you to promise me that when you come to Neoga in the year 2000, when Millie and I are at peace with the world, you'll tell me about how our first woman president is doing."

"Wade, you can count on me. If it happens, I'll tell you all about it."

"I'd like to hear it directly from you though one of Mildred's brigade members will probably arrive at the grave before you. But that's alright, because this time I'll be listening."

16
Strategies in Planning a Bond Election

On January 27th the board, oblivious to the near-zero Chicago temperature, moved quickly on Babe's motion to name John Fox as the college architect. Roy Jones, seated next to Babe, seconded the motion and praised Babe and the other trustees for their diligent search. Fred Knol added that he wanted John Fox because he had experience building a technical institute, Gordon Tech. The other trustees joined in lauding Fox for his expertise in producing buildings at a low cost. The united board approved Fox unanimously. Don stated he needed a couple days to put the finishing touches on the contract and suggested that the board reconvene on Friday night to finalize the papers. They all agreed.

Bob Collins informed the group that according to the school code a trustee election should be scheduled for April 10th. "Should the bond referendum be held on the same date, thus saving the taxpayers the cost of paying the judges twice?" he asked.

Babe strongly opposed that idea, since some new trustee candidates might make the bond election a major issue. "This board is all for the election. Who knows what would happen if we got two new trustees? We should all work together to make sure Jones and Knol are reelected," he said.

Boeger moved and was seconded by Jones that March 13th be the tentative date for the bond election, thus making it earlier and separate from the trustee election.

After adjourning the meeting Wade informed me that Don was meeting with the coalition for a late night snack in a nearby restaurant, and they wanted both of us to be present.

When I arrived 30 minutes later, Joe, Bob and Fred, apparently on their second round, were talking loudly, while Babe, Don and Wade were quietly drinking coffee with their hamburgers. I ordered the same.

Don's first remark was, "Dr. Z, what the hell took you so long? If you're going to be a big shot president, you'll need more horsepower to get here promptly. Wouldn't you rather have a Lincoln or Caddy?"

I smiled, ignored the question and said, "'What's up, Don?"

"March 13th is six weeks away, so we'll need to make two very important decisions tonight."

"And what are they?"

"First, the board must decide on what kind of campaign we should conduct. We can assume that March 13th will be cold, chilly, dreary and dull and the people won't turn out to vote. With a low turnout the precinct workers can gather up enough votes to put the election over the top. Conti, Kirie and I feel it should be done that way, no advance publicity and no speeches. Our sleeper will win."

"What if election day should be sunny, warm and cheerful?"

"It won't be. I checked the *Farmer's Almanac* and it's generally 90 per cent correct."

"But suppose on this occasion it's wrong?"

"We will wait 90 days and try again.

"Wade, what do you think of Don's proposal?"

Wade hesitated before replying. I knew he was wrestling with how to diplomatically modify Don's suggestion. Finally he said, "Don, you're absolutely right. I can recall it happening a few times in the past in one or two smaller communities. But in this case we're asking 14 different cities to voice their feelings. If any one of them erupts with accusations that we're withholding information or are too busy to answer their questions, it would be very damaging to the college's future. We must avoid at all costs doing anything that will create an opposition force. The people said *yes* to the creation of this district and I'm sure they'll say *yes* again if given all the facts. I don't believe a low-level campaign will work. We must, all of us, campaign with vigor."

Looking directly at me he said, "What do you think, Dr. Zeitlin? You've had a lot of experience in school elections. What's the best way to go?"

I rubbed my forehead several times with my right hand, jotted down a few notes with my left and stated rather quietly, "I agree fully with Wade. I don't know Chicagoland like you fellows do, but I do know I'm presently associated with seven very intelligent men, all of whom are good speakers. I need you to go out with me, or without me, to deliver the message to the public. They want to see and hear their elected trustees working with the college president."

Joe Farmar interrupted, "Do you really feel we know enough about community colleges to deliver the message accurately?"

"If you recall, prior to the press conference many of you felt you weren't ready. Then, after the press conference, those smart journalists gave you an "A+." We can and must do it again. The only difference is that instead of 25 writers you'll face audiences of 25 to several hundred at each pitch."

"What groups do you expect us to talk to?" Babe asked.

"I'll get letters out to the presidents of every PTA service club and homeowner association, union leaders, company presidents, etc., requesting 5 to 10 minutes to tell them why a *yes* vote is essential to the community's well-being."

"Do you really think we can do all this within six weeks?"

"Yes, we can. We did it at Southwestern College. We did it at Antelope Valley College and we can do it here. Fortunately, I've retained and will use again and again many of their valuable tools."

Don Dunahow stood up and announced, "Fellows, it's OK with me if you wish to go all out on this election. But haven't you forgotten one important ingredient?"

"I know what it is," Fred said. "What will it cost?"

"Originally the survey team recommended a bond issue of six million to purchase a site, put up buildings and equip them. Do you think that's sufficient, Herb?" Wade asked.

"No, it should be three to four times as much. Please remember that we're not building a college for 1,480 full-time students, as the experts suggested. When the campus is completed, as I see it, we will have over 4,000 full-timers and three to four times as many part-timers."

"Fellows, this is ridiculous," Don said. "I don't know what the good doctor is smoking or drinking but he's leading you astray. His figures will just never happen. The survey team predicted 500 students in two years. Now that we intend to open a year earlier I would assume that 250 will show up. How many students do you expect to be here on opening day in September, Dr. Z?"

"Over 1,000."

"That will never happen. Fellows, stick to the six million mark. Save money and put up butler buildings. A junior college is for students from poor families. Those kids don't expect air-conditioned palaces with golden carpets. I should know. I graduated from Chicago Crane Junior College over 45 years ago and it was OK. Way back when it was white."

"Les, butler buildings are cheap to put up or take down but they are not suitable for student learning. They're hot as hell in the summer and cold and drafty in the winter. When the winds blow, the corrugated steel panels rattle. I know. I saw it happen to a hanger in Amarillo, Texas while serving in the Air Force. They're not safe!"

"Oh, come on now, Dr. Z, steel is strong and safe. Just remember, your car roof is made of steel. I never heard of a roof being blown off by strong winds. If you're worried about heat or cold, just insulate the steel at a slight cost."

Wade ended the discussion. "Fellows, we're not going to settle that question now, so let's get ready for the referendum in six weeks. We need more time to settle on the amount. How about meeting in an executive session this Saturday morning?" Everyone nodded in agreement.

The following morning I arrived early at the office and drafted a letter giving general information about the college and announcing that an election would be held on March 13th. This letter was to be sent to every PTA president and secretary in the district.

I then asked Maria to get Jim Hannum, the county assistant superintendent, on the phone. Jim was surprised to hear from me, greeted me pleasantly and promised to mail me ASAP the names and addresses of every chief PTA officer and principal of every school in the college district.

Next, Maria called Bob Curtis, the local director of the state employment office. Bob agreed to send me the names and addresses of the largest companies, including the name of the president and personnel manager. In addition Bob suggested that I send some flyers or fact sheets about the referendum. When his list of over 60 companies arrived, I was amazed to see the great wealth of the district. Leading the roster was International Harvester Company, with over 6,000 employees and a plant valued at $38 million. In descending order were Automatic Electric, Jewel Tea, Commonwealth Edison, Illinois Bell, Motorola, Zenith Radio & TV, Hillside Shopping Center, etc. All these companies had a thousand or more employees housed in plants in the multi-million dollar bracket. As I reviewed the list I felt confident that if I could just communicate accurately to the big industrial giants the election would be won. A technical institute in their backyard was the answer to their technical personnel needs. Maria, along with Janet La Dere, accepted the challenge to get these letters out within the week.

Later that morning Elmore Boeger invited me to my second luncheon with the Maywood Rotary Club. I accepted. After the meeting I discussed with Elmore "some urgent board matters."

I asked, "What did you think of the last meeting?"

"It was great. We're now on the road to building your great college. Do you agree?"

"Yes, but we're facing some serious procedural problems."

"Such as?"

"Were you aware that Wade had to get the approval of Mayor Richard Daley, Mayor Elmer Conti, Boss Jim Kirie, Babe Serpico and Don Dunahow before I could submit John Fox's name as our architect?"

"No, why did he have to do that?"

"Had any one of these big guys objected to the architect's appointment, he'd have to oppose the election. In the long run, perhaps, it was right. But still, while I'm not really acquainted with Chicago politics, it seems to me all appointments should be based on what the individual can do rather than on whom he knows. Chicago politics is not the right way to run a college."

"What do you want, Herb?"

"I desperately need a business manager and a few deans and I need them now. You've served for several years on the Valparaiso board. Who makes the recommendations for college appointments?"

"Why, the college president. That's the way it's always been and it's the right way."

"I need your help in getting our college board to accept that as our policy."

"What can I do?"

"This Saturday at the executive meeting I'd like to recommend to our board a similar procedure. Would you support such a move?"

In his Gregory Peck style, Elmore waited, gave a sigh and said, "Herb, you know that Bob, Joe, Fred and especially Babe, as experienced politicians, are accustomed to wheeling and dealing. They're neophytes when it comes to knowing the responsibilities of a trustee. We need to educate them. Write out what you want and I'll urge them to accept it. Incidentally, I'll have my secretary drop off tonight the Valparaiso policy on the selection of personnel."

My face lit up. I was relieved at the speed at which I'd found a knowledgeable supporter. I grabbed his right hand, held it hard and thanked him. Upon leaving I called out, "Elmore, I'd like very much to become a member of the Maywood Rotary Club. Could you nominate me?"

"Why, of course. From day one the fellows were after me to get you in. As the chairman of the membership committee I'll induct you into the club in three weeks. And you know I'll look forward to our post-board chats."

The small office at 1829 Broadway was packed on Saturday morning as John Fox and his estimator put figures on the board for the seven trustees, the board attorney and college president to absorb. Dead silence fell over the group when John announced it would cost over six million to build and equip the tech, health careen and business buildings. The estimate for a campus of eleven buildings was well over 26 million. No one said anything for a moment. Everyone was in a state of shock except the college president and the architect.

Finally, Don Dunahow popped up, "This is ludicrous! Dr. Z is planning to build a trade school as if it were a university. It's an impossible dream. Let's get realistic and put up a few butler buildings and see what happens. If the Zeitlin plan were accepted, we'd have no money to buy a site."

Bob and Joe were quietly talking to each other, oblivious to the group, when suddenly Joe took on Don. "Don, this is not an impossible dream. Dr. Zeitlin is a visionary. If it happened in California, it can happen here. Just think of the size of those construction contracts. . . whee, and away we go!" he said, a la Jackie Gleason.

Suddenly the idea developed–let's reduce the project. All seven agreed that the space center would be the first to go, followed by the student center, the library and the fine arts building. All agreed that the tech, health careers, business, science and physical education facilities were essential, when Bob Collins cried out, "Fellows, when the people go to vote, the amount is not the factor, the factor is whether they want a college or not. They said yes when they voted the district in and now I feel they will say yes again when we ask for $26 million. I know my neighbors and I are willing to pay an extra 20 or 25 dollars annually on our tax bills."

"That's all very good, Bob, but the people were told it would cost only six million to build and equip a campus," Wade said. "We can't go back on our word."

Fred added, "Those estimates were made three or four years ago. Everyone knows prices have climbed a lot since then. I think what we have to do is arrive at a middle ground."

Babe stood up, raised both his bands and shouted, "A middle ground would be 13 million, more than twice the original figure. I'm sorry, boys, but I can't buy it. I don't want to be known as a liar and a cheat."

The group settled down a bit after Babe's outburst. Finally Elmore Boeger said, "Let's be reasonable and ask for just a little more. I move that the bond issue be in the amount of nine million." It was immediately seconded by Roy Jones. Many sidebar discussions followed. Slowly and reluctantly seven hands went up.

"I know Dr. Zeitlin and John Fox wanted 26 million, but if all goes well in the future we can try for a second bond issue in three or four years," were Wade's closing remarks.

The exhausted board was about to break up when Elmore asked for the floor. "Fellows, our college president has been snowed with work and it will get worse unless he gets some help. He desperütely needs a business manager and three deans ASAP and we need to help him out"

Babe seemed surprised and asked, "What do you want us to do? There are a couple dozen or more business managers out there. He just has to find one that we like."

"What was wrong with Dale Alexison?"

"He was too young, small townish and computer-focused. We know Dr. Zeitlin likes computers but we've been told by Mayor Daley that many computers break down and then there's hell to pay. Can you imagine what would happen to the city of Chicago if all the payroll checks were put in a computer and the computer broke down?"

Fred broke in with, "Dr. Zeitlin, have you interviewed Bernard Fleener, the dean of students at Proviso East? He seems well-qualified to me."

Roy Jones and Babe Serpico seemed to be getting along very well. Roy announced, "Look no more, Herb. Babe, Fred and I feel that Fleener is our choice."

Joe Farmar put forth his feelings. "Wait a minute, boys. Don't move so fast. I nominate Neil Neuson, the controller at Bekins, for the position. I've known him for years. He's the best purchasing agent Bekins ever had."

Bob Collins appeared stunned at the fast-paced action and spoke out, "How can you fellows pass over Nicholas Paella, the River Grove construction supervisor? Mayor O'Connor feels he'd be great as the college boss of business affairs."

Elmore thanked the boys for their help and directed me to send the three nominees an application and job description and schedule interviews.

"In the future we'll need to spell out our policy on hiring" added Elmore. "At Valparaiso and at other colleges all employees are appointed only upon the recommendation of the college president. I've asked Dr. Zeitlin to put in writing for our next board meeting the procedure he'll follow prior to making a recommendation to the board."

"Please tell us what happens if we reject his recommendation," Joe said.

"It shall be his duty to make another nomination until such time as the board majority accepts his recommendation."

"Suppose we turn down his second or third nomination. Then what happens?"

"He just keeps trying to find an acceptable one."

"Let me get this straight, Elmore. The final decision on who is hired or fired rests with the board. Am I right or am I wrong?" asked Babe.

"You're right. The final decision on hiring and firing always rests with the board majority. I have asked Dr. Zeitlin to mail you his recommended procedures prior to the February 10th meeting so that you'll have ample time to study them."

The meeting broke up after noon. The nominees' sponsors all came up to tell me what a great person each had selected for the business manager. I listened very carefully but felt I'd be in an awkward position if I favored one over the other. I promised to interview each one prior to the next board meeting. This seemed to satisfy the five concerned trustees. Don left in his big car with four of the coalition members. Roy, Wade and Elmore drove off separately. It looked like the coalition had decided to have lunch together, and I had not been invited.

After the trustees left, I called Eugenia to tell her I wouldn't be home for lunch. I intended to grab a snack and work in the office for the rest of the afternoon. Our planned ice skating adventure would have to be postponed until the next day. In front of me were the Valparaiso, the Southwestern and the Flint Community College documents pertaining to the selection of personnel. Taking the best from each college I arrived at a procedure consisting of 14 steps. Using my old Royal typewriter I proceeded to type the following:

It shall be the duty of the president of the college to see that persons nominated for employment shall meet all qualifications established by law and by the Board for the type of position for which nomination is made.

The following steps, whenever feasible, will be followed in the selection of personnel:

1. A detailed job description shall be developed.
2. Employment shall conform to adopted salary schedule.
3. Posting and mailing of general information bulletin.
4. Listing vacancies with placement agencies, including State Employment Office & others.
5. Acknowledging letters of inquiry and forwarding application forms.
6. Classifying individuals from applications.
7. Requesting confidential papers from agencies.
8. Scheduling interviews with deans and chairpersons.
9. Interviewing.
10. Mailing reference check forms.
11. Evaluating reference check forms.

12. Visiting individual at work.
13. Making final telephone checks before recommending.
14. Recommending to Board of Trustees.

The college president is authorized to reimburse candidates considered for faculty appointments for travel expense to Melrose Park Community College campus within the adopted budget allotment.

As darkness fell I finished the typing, xeroxed copies for each trustee and took the envelopes to the post office so the trustees would receive the proposal by Monday, February 1st, giving them 10 days to study and evaluate the document.

Ten days later, the 15th official meeting of the board was called to order at 8:50 PM. Absent were Babe Serpico and Joe Farmar. Wade apologized to an audience of twelve for being late. He informed the group the delay was due to a presentation made by the architect, the trustees and the college president to the North School PTA. The college president reported that seven similar community talks had been given during the first ten days of February, all of them well received. The people were excited about the development of this college.

Under new business I presented the 14 steps and commented about each one. Fred interrupted me with, "Does this mean we lose the right to find jobs for our friends and no longer have clout?"

Dead silence descended over the board. I looked at Elmore; he was patting his fingers against his lips. Wade slowly responded, "Fred, the personnel we'll need are highly educated, skilled, successful and experienced. Lay people do not have the training or know-how to make the right selection. We must leave that to the professionals, such as Dr. Zeitlin, his deans and the department chairs. That's the only way to go."

Bob Collins joined in, "What about clerical and maintenance workers?"

Elmore replied, "These workers have so many different kinds of skills that we must have a job description for each one. And the same can be said for the operational and maintenance employees. Every job is highly specialized. The investigation of employees' past experiences shall be the responsibility of the professional staff. Trustees must not interfere in the selection process."

"Well, this is quite different from the Chicago method," Bob said.

"Bob, the selection of personnel at this college shall be determined by what the person knows rather than whom he knows," I announced.

"Now tell me, what do we do for all those guys that helped us get elected and now want jobs?"

"Tell them to write or call the college. I promise you that all inquiries will be answered promptly and applications sent to those who are judged qualified."

Wade stared at Bob and Fred, looked around for some reaction, and hearing none asked, "Are Dr. Zeitlin's 14 steps acceptable as new board policy?" All five trustees nodded and said "yes." I felt elevated when I realized merit had won over clout. We were on our way to hiring only the best, on our terms. The Chicago system of patronage and clout would not operate at the college.

As we moved along I added that faculty applications were coming in daily and soon I would need space for the deans and clerical help. Approval was immediately given to rent some adjacent apartments on a month-to-month basis.

Continuing with the board agenda, Don Dunahow informed us that the resolution for the bond election was ready but couldn't be approved until the precinct boundaries and polling places were established.

Bob Collins reported on his visit to the Evanston School District and its successful passage of a 14.5 million dollar bond issue. I reviewed the contents of a new booklet entitled, "Give Them a Chance to Learn," issued by the Illinois Board of Higher Education, and urged each trustee to read it, mentioning that some of its contents would be incorporated in our brochure for the bond election. The meeting closed after John Fox presented some new drawings of the proposed campus.

The following day, after our Rotary meeting, I expressed my concerns to Elmore about working with politicians. He assured me that while many people were asking questions about honesty in high places and were gravely disappointed with the answers, the trustees of this college had unimpeachable integrity and all the right answers. He learned something new every time a trustee addressed a community group. He was very proud of them. As Elmore talked his words reminded me of a speech that Paul Harris, the founder of Rotary, made in Chicago on February 23, 1905, at its first meeting. The club would always have members noted for honesty and dependability. As Rotarians, the two of us were going to dig in together to give the college a right sense of direction. I always felt better after talking with Elmore. He tended to alleviate my reservations about the board.

"Our boys may not know the duties of a trustee but last night they showed their willingness to learn. Did you notice how chummy Roy, Fred and Babe have become? The former enemies are now friends. The three are united on Bernie Fleenor for business manager. When do you intend to interview him?"

"Late this afternoon.. Tomorrow morning I'll be seeing Nicholas Pavella and at four o'clock I'll meet with Neil Neuson. Hopefully, on Monday afternoon John Moody from Wellston, Missouri and I will have dinner together."

"Herb, let's hope one of these four will be the right one. In the meantime I'll continue to work on a college name that won't create any objections from the community."

At precisely 4:00 PM a tall, dark man resembling Richard Nixon in a black suit, white shirt and gray tie walked into my office. Bernard Fleenor's first words were, "I like your office, especially the bar. What a way to begin an interview." We both laughed as I extended my welcoming hand, which he shook with vigor. We exchanged pleasantries and discussed family values, education and sports. He had worked his way up to the maximum on the Proviso District administrative salary schedule, which led to his major concern. "What's the salary schedule for this job?"

When I told him, his face dropped. He picked up his coat and headed for the door.

"Dr. Knoeppel told me the salary wouldn't be that great, but I never expected it to be so low. Thanks for your time and good luck with the college, Dr. Zeitlin, but I'd never consider taking a $3,000 cut."

I walked him to his car as he said, "Give my best regards to Roy, Fred and the Babe."

The interview had lasted 15 minutes, not the usual one hour. The nominee with the three sure votes was not interested.

A few minutes before 9:00 AM the next morning a short and peppy young man by the name of Nicholas Favella, in working clothes with paint on his blue jeans and shoes, showed up. He asked Maria for a cup of coffee as I welcomed him. He asked me several questious about John Fox, which I answered.

Finally, I asked, "Why do you want to know so much about him?"

"Well, I assume I'll be working directly under him as the supervisor of construction. At least that's what Bob Collins told me. Am I wrong?"

I explained the duties of a business manager and asked him if he had experience in budget preparation, meeting a payroll, purchasing, keeping books, selling bonds and hiring a classified staff. He answered each question with a loud "no!"

"I guess I'm in the wrong place at the wrong time," he said. I agreed and gave him an application for possible future employment.

When 4:00 PM arrived, I went outside looking for Neil Neuson, guessing that he might be having difficulty finding the office. No sign of him, so I went back to work with Maria. Finally, a few minutes before 5:00 PM, a sad-eyed, shaggy-looking middle-aged man arrived, introduced himself, apologized for being late and asked for a cup of coffee.

I gave him the job description and asked him if he had experience in several areas. His reply was "no" to most of the items. He explained that he was a purchasing agent. He knew little about bonds, payrolls and accounting procedures but felt he could learn on the job. Joe Farmar could teach him. He was looking forward to putting together some good deals with Joe. He stressed that Joe was his sole recommendation and I was not to contact Bekins at any time. He had an antipathy against computers and no intention to learn how to use them, and added that a master's degree was not necessary for the job.

I thought, "Joe Farmar's nominee is not qualified."

On Saturday morning I called the trustees who had made the nominations. Bob accepted my conclusion but wanted me to keep Nick in mind for future assignments. Fred, on the other hand, felt we'd missed the boat with Bernie Fleenor by not having a better salary schedule. Roy agreed fully with Fred. Babe agreed with my conclusion and urged me to keep trying until I found the top guy.

Joe Farmar did not accept my evaluation of Neil Neuson. He urged me to talk to him again, dig deeper until I found the jewel in his background. Not wanting to offend Joe, I agreed to check back with Neil upon receiving his application.

That morning I again reviewed the applications for business manager. Leading the list once more was John L. Moody from Missouri. I got on the phone and set up an appointment for Monday night at 5:00 in my office and dinner afterwards.

It was a case of instant friendship. How come? I noticed his Rotary pin on his lapel and he noticed mine. We clasped hands in a very friendly manner and I asked, "How long have you been a Rotarian?"

"Six years, and you?"

"The same."

We proceeded to make comparisons. John Moody had been president of his small-town Rotary three years earlier, while I'd served as president-elect of the Antelope Valley club in Lancaster, California. We'd both attended the Rotary International conference in Los Angeles. His wife taught sixth grade while Eugenia taught English at the community college. They had one son and two daughters and the Zeitlins had one son and three daughters. I had taught electronics at the Mephan Community College in New York and he taught accounting at the St. Louis Community College on a part-time basis. The match got better as we went along. We were both very ambitious and advanced in the educational world, he as business manager of a high school district and I as a college president. I was three years older, but our wives were the same age. He had attended the IBM executive training program in Poughkeepsie, New York and I in San Jose, California.

John displayed impeccable table manners, even offering to split the tab, as we dined at the Homestead Restaurant. We discussed the philosophy of the community college, curriculum, board and union relations, bond ratings and salaries of administrators. It was quite satisfying to find two administrators with parallel beliefs. He was quite pleased when he learned his entrance salary at our college would be at least $3,000 above his Missouri pay. I asked him to stay overnight so that he could be interviewed the following morning by the president of the college board. He agreed.

The next day Wade called to say, "John Moody is a superior business manager. I particularly liked his background in accounting and finance and how he handled a recent bond sale for his district. Did you know that he sold over $3,000,000 in bonds at an average interest rate of 3.4%? Now, that's darn good. Herb, don't let him get away. Get his name to the board ASAP!'"

"I'm so glad you feel the way I do. I need to make four telephone reference checks before recommending him to the board. If they turn out well, as I suspect they will, his name will be on the agenda for our February 19th meeting."

I asked Maria not to disturb me for the next few hours as I got on the phone to talk to his superintendent, the school board president, the faculty association president and the district governor of Rotary. Each response made his stature grow taller. His boss wanted to know what salary John would receive. When I told him he reacted with surprise and commented, "He'll be making more than I do. Missouri is not noted for big salaries. This is another case of a small city developing a star to be stolen away by the big city."

Later that afternoon I had a snack and returned to the office rejuvenated. Again I asked Maria to hold all calls as I went through all the applications for dean of admissions and guidance. There were 31 candidates, several holding doctorates in psychology. What I was hoping for was a female, preferably someone within one of the district high schools with a doctorate and an administrative credential. Within an hour I selected three applicants to be interviewed, including one female.

I was disappointed with the first two candidates. Both had rich backgrounds with advanced degrees from elite universities, but lacked the understanding of the People's College concept. I baited each one with my favorite departure question, "Don't you think that we are sending too many people to college these days?"

Without hesitation both applicants answered "yes" and then detailed how they would screen out the least qualified. They didn't get it. They felt their major function as the chief admissions officer of the college would be to recruit the better student. One of them actually said, "The unprepared student should be sent back to the high school or a continuation school or somewhere else."

I didn't bother to explain to those candidates that the community college of today was that "somewhere else." Our function was to cater to those who needed a second or third chance, to help the veteran or displaced worker, to encourage the returning woman or new citizen and to help the young adult who may have wasted away his high school years but now really wanted to learn. Hiring brilliant minds who wanted to teach but had no heart for the less fortunate was not the right way to go. These elitist administrators felt college was only for the well-prepared. I graciously thanked them for their so-called pearls of wisdom and was glad to see them go.

My third candidate was John Widergren, director of continuing education at Proviso East High School, who held a B.A. in English from Beloit College, an M.A. from the State University of Iowa and a recent doctorate in Education from the University of Wisconsin. John, age 36, was 6'2", nearly 200 pounds, athletic-looking with a receding hairline, and serious minded. He articulated in a soft but firm, understanding voice. As we went through the job description he listed experience in every area mentioued and expressed excitement about recruiting his own staff.

At dinner he showed remarkable knowledge of the goals of the community college, stressing that a good college must have at least three or more tracks of learning: one for the gifted and talented, another for the average and one for the less-prepared student who should never be sent "somewhere else."

I asked him, "Do you think the quality of students enrolling in college today is better or worse compared to a generation ago?"

"Worse, if you mean according to academic standards."

"How come? Give me some reasons for the deterioration."

"Well, first of all, the preparation in the earlier grades has declined due to a higher student/teacher ratio. Children learn less in a class of 40 than in a class of 20. Secondly, there is less reading and writing and more and more TV watching, and too much social telephoning. Third, when both Mom and Dad are working full-time there is less parental supervision. And forthly, the forced mixing of cultures in one classroom makes it difficult for the teacher to communicate to all."

"How can the community college help?"

"We must open our doors and welcome all who wish to learn. Placement tests in reading, writing, mathematics and science can help determine where a student should begin. Starting at the right place generally puts him on the road to success. Starting at the wrong place leads to dropping out and failure. Experienced counselors will tell you that placement tests are better predictors of success than previous grades. I'm sure you're aware of the studies showing that."

"Yes, I am. I'm also aware that President Kennedy was an atrocious speller who took remedial English courses at Harvard University, as have many other famous people. One should not be ashamed of this but should be proud of the instructors that helped out along the way."

"Dr. Zeitlin, bow many counselors do you expect to hire?"

"Two or three at the beginning. As we grow in enrollment we'll follow the state guidelines of one counselor to every 300 full-time students."

Throughout our two-hour dinner John answered all my questions seriously, without any hemming or hawing. Having recently acquired his doctorate he felt it time to move on and was very excited about being part of the founding of a new college. He had talked it over with his wife and three children and they all thought he would be great at a new college. However, he showed disappointment when I revealed his placement on the dean's schedule to be only $600 above his present salary. I pointed out to him that while our teacher's schedule was the best in the state, the administrative schedule needed improvement. He informed me he had received a better offer from a college in Wisconsin, but the family was reluctant to relocate.

Looking me straight in the eye he said, "Dr. Zeitlin, money is not my primary goal in life. I don't want to relocate, so I'd be very happy to join you in creating a college for all the people if you were to recommend me for the deanship."

I grabbed his hand, shook it and said, "We'd be delighted to have you, but first you must get acquainted with Wade Steel, our board president. Can you make it tomorrow at 8:00 AM in his office at East Leyden High School?"

His "yes" reply made me feel good. At last, in a matter of weeks, a top-notch administrator would be joining me.

The following day Wade called to say, "John Widergren is an excellent choice. I'm scheduling an executive board meeting in my office on February 19th so that you can tell the trustees about your find. I congratulate you in your search for top-quality administrators. I see no problem when you present the two Johns to the board."

Surprisingly, at 7:00 PM on February 19th all the trustees,

including attorney Don Dunahow, were in Wade's office discussing Nixon's decision to bomb North Vietnam. Joe Farmar felt it was absolutely necessary to bomb the hell out of them to get the thing over quickly. Jones, Serpico and Boeger disagreed, feeling that bombing innocent people was wrong. Hitler had tried it on England and failed. When a superpower bombs a small country it's not praised, but condemned. Wade wondered how the college students would react to the bombing. Dunahow laughed and commented, "College students won't give a damn. They're only interested in grades, a good job, the good life and sex."

Finally, Joe Farmar turned to me and said, "Tell us about your recommendations, Mr. President."

I proceeded to discuss John Widergren's background. Several questions followed and my instant replies were accepted. After ten minutes of healthy dialogue, Wade asked, "Is there any objection to Dr. Widergren becoming the first dean of admissions and guidance?"

Hearing no objection Wade announced that Dr. Widergren was in. I made it a point to thank the board for giving me my first administrator. Feeling good, I then enthusiastically presented John Moody's credentials and ended with saying, "He is the most qualified candidate of the six that I interviewed."

Babe said he didn't like narrow-minded people from Missouri.

Bob Collins uttered, "My uncle wouldn't approve of such an appointment."

Fred declared, "The business manager must come from Illinois," while Joe broke in with, "Keep trying, Herb, eventually you'll come up with someone we can accept."

Jones, Boeger and Steel said nothing. We gathered up our things to go to the 16th official meeting of the board. I was upset by my failure to convince the coalition that my candidate was the best, but had little time to mull it over as we hurried over to the Little Theater.

In rapid order the board heard Dunahow report on the need for Chapman & Cutler to approve the bond election; Collins stated he had to purchase election supplies and then store them; and Wade and Roy touched upon the highlights of the American Association of School Administrators convention held in Atlantic City, where they'd learned much.

I thanked the trustees for their splendid cooperation in joining me on my many talks to civic groups, and mentioned that a senior survey would be ready soon. The final item was the unanimous approval of Dr. John Widergren's appointment as the dean of admissions and guidance. Every trustee said something nice about him, showing the avidly attentive press that the college president's appointment was strongly supported by the board. The public knew nothing of the sizzling bubble in my stomach from the coalition's flat rejection of my recommendation for business manager. It hurt so much that I couldn't sleep that night. I'd searched out for the best found it and been turned down by the board. Why?

Immediately after Wade adjourned the meeting, Don Dunahow tapped me on the shoulder and said, "Herb, put some high test in that little putt-putt of yours and join us for a late night snack in 20 minutes at the usual spot."

When I arrived at the restaurant everyone was present except Jones and Boeger. Jim Tarpey had a hamburger and beer waiting for me as the laughing trustees relaxed. Joe and Bob congratulated me on getting the best with Dr. Widergren's appointment.

On a serious note, Don Dunahow said the election date might have to be moved back because Chapman & Cutler was slow in giving its approval. Babe felt it was OK because it would give us more time to talk to more people. He complimented me on inspiring such good teamwork among the trustees in accepting the call to talk, and wanted to know when the brochure would be ready. I stated it was ready now. All we needed was a definite date.

"I have the list of everyone who voted in the election to create the college district," Babe announced. "When the date is settled, we'll need a massive writing party to address the brochures to over 12,000 voters. The question is, where do we find the people to address the brochures? We can't use our office personnel, since they're paid by the taxpayers and it would be illegal for them to work on an election. It has to be volunteers. You fellows have any suggestions?"

Joe Farmar immediately suggested his oldest daughter and wife. Bob felt that Harry and Marilyn Smith would be happy to join in. Each of the other trustees in turn volunteered the services of some family member. I assured them that Eugenia and my son Mark would join the group. Babe insisted that all the addresses be handwritten to communicate a personal touch. None of the writers were to be paid. I was requested to set up the work schedule as soon as the brochures were printed. We would all work from 7-10 every evening until the job was completed. The pain I had received from rejection of the business manager was lessened when I observed the wonderful spirit of cooperation.

I asked Jim Tarpey to do a special feature on Dr. Widergren and include a photo of him for immediate release to all the papers. He replied he'd already written the lead and needed a quote from Dr. Widergren to finish the story.

Wade asked how many of the trustees intended to go to Dallas for the national convention of the American Association of Junior and Community Colleges. Four hands went up and I was asked to make reservations for the Farmars, the Collinses, the Steels and the Zeitlins. I mentioned that while three to four thousand usually attended the convention, this year might be different because some of the colleges were boycotting Dallas after the Kennedy assassination. Joe felt that was stupid, and all of us said the same. The question came up, "Who pays for the wives?" They weren't trustees, and were not entitled to any compensation by law. We agreed that the wives should pay their own way. The rate difference between a single and a double room should be paid by the trustee's partner.

We went home around midnight feeling good, though no further mention had been made of the business manager. Wade said, "Herb, let it rest. For the time being you'll be the business manger."

I thought back to when I was the dean of instruction at Southwestern College, principal of Antelope Valley High School, purchasing agent at the Carter Coal Company, treasurer of the Phi Delta Pi fraternity, chairman of the college dance committee, high school student body president and *Brooklyn Times Union* newspaper boy, all jobs that had required keeping books and staying within the budget. I had done it then and I could do it once more, though I knew it would extend my long hours even further. Oh well, when you give birth to a college, as to a child, whatever is needed, the father must provide, regardless of personal sacrifice.

My mind flashed back to my hardworking father. He never went to college, though his training at the New York Telephone Company gave him the skills of an electrical engineer. In order to provide adequately for a family of nine he held two or more jobs most of his life and never complained. He loved his daytime job as the head installer of telephone equipment in the famous New York Paramount building, 1501 Broadway, where all the VIP's and movie stars gathered to promote their big productions. The family would applaud him when he'd show us the autographed photos he'd received from the big stars, the most famous being Al Jolson, the star of the first talking picture, *The Jazz Singer.* Other photos proudly displayed in his store window included Mae West, Cary Grant, Clara Bow, Rudy Vallee and Douglas Fairbanks and his wife Mary Pickford.

Dad's store, known as the Camera Craft Shop, specialized in photo developing and printing, plus sales and repairs of radios and electrical appliances. The store was located diagonally across the street from our home at 221 Schaeffer Street in Brooklyn, New York. Dad worked every evening from 6:00 to 10:00 and beyond, plus a long day on Saturday and a short day on Sunday. In all he worked over 75 hours per week: 40 hours with the New York Telephone Company and 35 hours plus at the Camera Craft Shop. I can't recall ever seeing my father having dinner with the family, other than on a Sunday night.

Mother, on the other hand, opened the store every morning after sending the kids off to school. At noon she'd return home to prepare hot lunches for the little ones during their recess. Her afternoons were spent in the darkroom at home developing, fixing, printing and finishing photos. At 5:00 PM she'd start to prepare dinner for the eight of us.

My brother Lester attended the early shift at Franklin K. Lane High School, from 7:45 AM until 12:45 PM. At 1:00 he'd reopen the store and stay until Dad's arrival at 6:00. After Lester graduated and got an outside job, Lenny took over the store's management. The sequence continued with Herbert, Arthur and Eddie being forced into an internship at the Camera Craft Shop. Betty and Dorothy were excused from the internship; Dad felt they were not sufficiently mechanically inclined. However, Dad taught all the boys how to load and unload a box camera with film and how to make minor repairs on most failed electrical appliances.

I was very excited to go with my Dad, the master photographer, when on a few occasions he drove all the way to the Bronx to take photographs of buildings condemned to make way for a new structure that later became known as the Triborough Bridge. I felt like the chosen one when Dad selected me over Lester and Lenny to help him out when he installed communications systems in several New York offices on Sundays. The money flew in from Dad's extra jobs. The business prospered so much that we were the only ones on Schaeffer Street to own a car, a seven-passenger Studebaker that could carry nine or ten when Grandpa or Anna Marie, our tenant's daughter, came along with us.

Sunday afternoons in the summer meant a day in Coney Island, Luna Park, Brighton Beach or Hollis Woods, or a trip to Bellerose, Long Island, where Uncle Charlie and Aunt Ann lived. Mother would pack lunch, usually two dozen hardboiled eggs plus a variety of sandwiches. Our neighbors often said the Zeitlins were the hardest working, noisiest and happiest family on the street. I hadn't realized it then, but in retrospect I agree. Our father firmly instilled the work ethic in all of us. Each brother tried to outdo the other in work production. Competition was keen and encouraged by our grandfathers, who left Bismarck's Germany to avoid the draft and seek a better life in democratic America.

Returning to the present, I accepted the fact that I'd be spending less time with the family. I was about to follow in my father's path, giving less time to the wife and kids in order to succeed on the job. Eugenia and I talked it over and reluctantly she accepted the new mode of living. I wondered if I were making the right decision.

17
The Gravy Train:
An Invitation to Graft

T he day after the board gave me my first dean Don Dunahow called to insist on taking me to lunch at the newly opened Golden Steer Restaurant. He arrived promptly at 12:30 in his big black Buick During the ride over to the restaurant he asked me to explain in detail exactly what Dr. Widergren was to do, so he could draw up a contract. He was taken aback when I explained to him that it wouldn't be necessary, since we'd be using a standard contract form for all the administrators. The duties were spelled out in the job description the administrator received before being interviewed.

Don stopped talking, thought a few minutes and then said, "That's not a good idea. It's too mechanical. I write a special contract to give the new employee a personal connection with his boss. Don't you think that's a good idea?"

"Well, Don, it maybe helpful for political appointments, but not for college and university staffing. Everyone holding an office at our college will know well in advance what his major duties are to be. And to capture any unforeseen duties you'll note that all the job descriptions at this college will include the catch-all line: *Performs a variety of other duties as may be assigned by the president.*"

Don said nothing until we arrived at our destination. As we left the car he pulled me over toward the rear of his car and said, "Dr. Zeitlin, as a chief executive officer, you are not very smart. At least you don't know much about the Chicago method of helping each other. I've handled hundreds of contracts to the satisfaction of the big bosses. Do you know why they're so pleased with me?"

"I guess it's because you protect their interests. Is that right?"

"Yes, but more important, every time I write a contract the CEO gets a gratuity from me."

"What's the gratuity?"

"Wake up, Dr. Zeitlin, and get on the gravy train. For every contract written by me I give the CEO a white envelope with a US greenback of Benny Franklin enclosed. If you cooperate with me, by the end of the year the gravy will so accumulate that you'll change from your little putt-putt to a Roadmaster. And what's more, nobody will know how it happened."

I nervously cut short this dialogue as I made him hurry along to the beautiful new epicurean restaurant. He automatically ordered Manhattans for both of us as I placed an order for the prime rib special. I got him to talk about his early beginnings. His parents were poor and worked very hard to send him to college. After obtaining his law degree he joined the Republican Party to make the right money connections. It had helped him a lot. In due time his practice as a lawyer grew and he married, but the coming of children brought much pain. His daughter was stricken with polio. With his new wealth he purchased a big boat, which gave him much pleasure during the summer months. He invited me to go fishing and promised me that with the bait he used I'd catch a big one. I declined his invitation. He'd thought of retiring but Elmer Conti, his boss, insisted that he continue because Elmwood Park could not get along without him. To top it off the big political Democratic boss of the Proviso Township, Ralph Serpico, had insisted that he be the college attorney. As we enjoyed our meal he loosened up and cracked some jokes.

"Do you want to hear the latest one on lawyers?"

"Yes, please tell me."

"Why do you bury a lawyer 12 feet deep in the ground?"

"I have no idea."

"Because deep down they are all good. Now, do you mind if I test your architectural knowledge?"

"Try me."

"What's the tallest building in the nation?"

"That's easy, the Empire State Building in New York, with 102 stories."

"Well, well, Mr. College President, you are wrong. It's the public library, since it has over thousand stories."

"Ugh, you've got some unusual ones." We left the restaurant and drove back to 1829 Broadway. A thick wet snow had fallen, coating the roads with slush. Les cursed out a driver who'd skidded towards him.

After recovering from his outburst he asked, "What's the weather like in San Diego this time of the year?"

"In February it's sunny and in the high seventies, and if we're lucky we might get an inch or two of rain."

"It looks like we're in for a big one today. Tonight this slush will turn to ice and we'll have a few hundred auto accidents unless the salt boys melt it down first. This is the month I'd like very much to be in Florida. Have you and your family adjusted to the Chicago climate?"

"We're trying, but to be frank with you, I've been out every night with the board these past two weeks and my major concentration has been on winning the election. I haven't been too concerned about climatic changes."

"Do your kids like the snow and ice?"

"They were awed when they first saw snowflakes and as yet they haven't discovered the negatives of ice. However, they immensely enjoyed ice skating at the Ridgeway Commons."

As I opened the door to leave Don's car he cried out, "Do you have a secretary for Dr. Widergren yet? My wife has a church friend who's interested. What should I tell her?"

"Tell her to pick up a job application ASAP, since Dr. Widergren should be on the job in two weeks. He'll have the final say. What's her name?"

"Virginia Sybilla. I heartily recommend her." We waved good-bye to each other.

The rest of the afternoon I concentrated on reviewing the many applications for dean of instruction. Toward early evening I finally found what I was looking for, someone with a high academic background: Dr. G. Robert Dames, age 49, dean of Olney Junior College in the small community of Olney, Illinois. He had a doctorate from the University of Oklahoma, an M.A. in Music from the University of Denver and a B.A. from Kansas State University. I immediately got on the phone and scheduled him for an evening interview upon my return from Dallas.

The following day an attractive, well-dressed, middle-aged lady named Virginia Sybilla was waiting for me as I arrived in the office. We chatted briefly. She was presently the secretary to an elementary school principal in Forest Park. Her job was getting boring and she wanted a new challenge. She'd read about the college in the newspaper, and her principal had encouraged her to apply, especially since she was good friends with the Dunahows. I gave her an application form and requested that she return it promptly. She left. Ten minutes later I heard a tap on the door.

"Here is my application. Maria allowed me to use her typewriter. Any questions?"

I was amazed. It was letter perfect, and done so fast. I thanked her and gave her a copy of the salary schedule, which she accepted with joy, especially so when I placed her on an advanced level.

"This I like," she said. "I want to be part of your college." As she left I told her Dr. Widergren should be contacting her within two weeks.

18
Trouble on the Homefront

On Saturday morning I was having a leisurely late breakfast alone when Eugenia popped in and defiantly asked for the keys to the car. "What's up, dear?" I asked.

"I need to get to the dress shop to have Ann's uniform shortened and Joyce's lengthened."

"What are you talking about? My daughters are not in the military. What's this all about?"

"I wanted to talk to you about Ann's plight last night but you were so busy I couldn't get a word to your ear. It's getting to be too much for me to do it alone. I need to talk to somebody."

"What's this about Ann's plight? Is she sick?"

"Yes, she is, sick and tired of Chicagoland and its horrible weather. Is it ever going to get warm again? Thursday at noon, while you were having a delightful luncheon with the college attorney, I had to deal with Ann's outburst."

"What was the outburst all about?"

"She had to walk through three blocks of slush. Her feet were all wet and her shoes were ruined. As she neared Cortland Parkway a big truck turned the corner and she got splashed in the face with dirty ice water. I couldn't control her crying, and to make matters worse Clare cried with her. Your five- and six-year-old daughters begged me to get you to go back to California."

"Well, what did you say to get them to quiet down?"

"I promised them something new. Fortunately, after Sunday's church service I got acquainted with Joann Hicks and her two daughters, Ellen and Mary Jo, who are the same ages as Joyce and Ann. Her kids go to St. Vincent Ferrer School and they don't have to come home for lunch. So, starting Monday Ann and Joyce are looking forward to going to an all-girls private school. I have to get moving so that they'll look their best on their first day."

"Hey, wait a minute. Am I correct in assuming our kids will be taught by the Sisters of some Order?"

"Yes, every day starts with a morning prayer, with emphasis on religion, family values and rigid academic standards."

"That may sound good to you but I don't like the idea of my kids going to a private school. Can you understand the embarrassing situation you've put me in? Here I am, an advocate for the public schools and community colleges, and I send my own kids to a private school. People will consider me a real hypocrite."

"Not if they understand our difficult situation. I can't understand why the Illinois public schools are so old-fashioned. All the schools you and I worked in had lunch rooms so the kids weren't forced to go home to eat. You know there's an underlying message here."

"What's that, Eugenia?"

"Can't you see? They don't want mothers to go to work or have a career other than motherhood. They want to lock us in as homebodies with their trite thinking: Wife and mother is the noblest career a woman can achieve. Well, my dear, women of today want something more than that. Is your community college going to help us realize our maximum potential?"

"You can rest assured this new college will open its doors wide for women to take any program they wish and at any time. Today, two out of every three college students are male. I sincerely hope that within ten years we'll have reversed that ratio."

"I'm willing to accept all these inconveniences because I believe in you and know you can accomplish anything you set out to do. But please, I need a little help."

"How can I help?"

"First, try to be home every night for dinner on time. Last night you were in such a rush to get in and out that you didn't even notice Mark's swollen fist."

"What happened to him?"

"He was in a fight, It seems an attractive girl started to talk to him about California while he was in the cafeteria line. When he brought over a glass to her table, her boyfriend got up, a few blows were exchanged and it was over in a matter of seconds. He was warned to stay away from girls that were already taken."

"My God, I should have noticed. He didn't say a word last night."

"The whole school knew about it except his Dad. His father is so involved in his own agenda that he doesn't notice the little things that count. Mark needs some attention from his Dad."

"What would you suggest I do?"

"His light clothing and blond hair are not in keeping with his fellow students. He doesn't want to be seen shopping with his mother. So can you take him to Sears to buy some dark trousers, shirts and socks?"

"I'll do it as soon as you get back with the car."

"And that's another thing. I'm cooped up here all week and all I have is Clare to talk to and she's very angry. She misses her school and we can't go anywhere. *I need a car!*"

"Tomorrow after church, Mark and Joyce can watch the kids while you and I look for your wheels. We can't afford a new car right now. It has to be a used one."

Eugenia seemed a little relieved. She had let out some pent-up feelings. Later I spoke to Mark about his fight as I looked at the reduced swelling. His opponent had been a tall, heavyset, popular football player. Mark had returned his blow with a left-handed swing that hit his opponent's metal belt buckle. A faculty member who was supervising the cafeteria broke it up fast. Everyone but Mark had known that gorgeous Nancy was taken, making her forbidden fruit. The kids had grown up so fast that I wasn't aware Mark had "discovered girls." I assured him his future with women was bright because he was tall, thin, good-looking and blond. For the first time in his life he asked me rather personal questions about when I first met Eugenia, what happened on our first date and when I discovered I was in love. It was delightful observing Mark carefully listening to my every word. His motivation was high since he'd fallen in love with Nancy, the beautiful cheerleader. I told him about my first love at age 12 with Anna Marie, our tenant's daughter, who embarrassed me tremendously when she showed my love letter to members of my family. When Lenny and Arthur joked with me about it my hurt was compounded greatly. I gave up on women for several years after that incident. I felt women couldn't keep a secret.

When Eugenia came back with the car, Mark and I drove off to Sears, continuing our serious dialogue. He discovered he had a father who could relate to his concerns, and I discovered the delight of helping a member of the family. After several hours of shopping my son had the right clothing and he was immensely pleased.

The following Sunday afternoon Eugenia and I flew out to Dallas with the Steels, followed by the Collinses and the Farmars. Joe Farmar told me that after registering at the convention center he'd reserved a table for eight that night at one of the best restaurants in the city. By the time the headwaiter showed the Steels and Zeitlins to the Farmar table the party had already begun, with martinis and manhattans waiting for us. With her golden earrings and sparkling diamonds Cecil Farmar looked like a very successful movie actress, while Millie, Beverly and Eugenia were glad just to be part of the happy entourage. The men talked, walked and acted with vigor. It was great to be away for a few days from cold Chicago.

The next day we had a fast breakfast at the hotel so we wouldn't miss the opening remarks from the governor, the mayor of Dallas and other VIP's. The most impressive speaker was the president of the American Association of Community & Junior Colleges, Dr. Edmund Gleazer. He inspired us all with his spirit of optimism in facing the challenge of America's greatest social invention, the junior college. He stressed that the day had come when the junior/community college would provide equal opportunity to all ethnic, racial, social and national groups.

We had expected the convention hall to be filled with thousands, but there were only hundreds. The Kennedy assassination had kept the rest away. It had indeed been a sad day for Dallas. The number one tourist attraction, visited by all the women's groups, was the site of the tragedy. The men did not visit the sordid area because they were too busy attending the many workshops for trustees, college presidents, faculty and student body presidents.

On Wednesday afternoon we all took the same plane back to Chicago, filled with new hope and much information to be used in meeting the challenges to come. There was no tension within our little group; we all enjoyed each other's company. Eugenia and I were happy to be part of a new family.

When I returned to the office on Thursday morning, waiting for me was a Mrs. Ellen Atkinson with a letter from one of Mayor Daley's top aides. The letter described Ellen as a loyal Democratic precinct worker with over 40 years' secretarial experience who was willing to start work at the college immediately. I gave her an application and asked her to fill it out on Maria's IBM typewriter. She studied the machine and abruptly stated, "I never used this kind of machine before. Is it electric?"

I replied in the affirmative and said we would accept a printed handwritten application if she didn't have a typewriter. With a slight gasp and an annoyed look on her face she uttered, "1 can't read this fine print and I didn't know that an application was required."

I started to review the form when she interrupted me with, "I didn't graduate from high school, but I know so much more than these young kids." I smiled and asked her to estimate her typing and shorthand speed. Her instant response was, 'I don't know my typing speed and I don't know shorthand."

"Can you give us three references of persons you've worked for and their phone numbers?"

"I have to think about that. Isn't this letter from the Mayor's office enough?"

"No, we need references of individuals who know the kind of work you do."

My remark disturbed her. She folded the application and put it into her handbag. She gave Maria a phone number, asked her to have a taxi pick her up, and angrily left. As soon as she closed the door Maria looked me directly in the eye and loudly sounded off, "Ellen was very bossy when she first came in and wanted to rearrange the desks so the vacant one would be closer to the window, giving her more light. She was very inquisitive and asked me many personal questions about you."

"What did you tell her?"

"I told her you were a slave driver: no coffee breaks, no personal calls, no vacations and no hospitalization benefits!"

"You couldn't get her to leave?"

"No, it didn't work, but if you dare hire her Janet and I will quit."

"Don't worry. She wouldn't be hired even if she were Richard

Daley's mother. And, of course, I appreciate your humor in handling this delicate situation."

Maria was greatly relieved when she realized that even Mayor Daley's influence wouldn't work. She gave me over a dozen messages, ending with, "Joe Pulitano, president of Melrose Park Furniture Company, has invited you to lunch with him tomorrow at the Millionaire's Club. What shall I tell him?"

"Thank him and tell him that I can't get away." I got on the phone to follow up on the messages. By 6:00 PM I had completed all the urgent tasks and was about to leave, when Dr. Widergren called to say that he'd be reporting on Monday morning. No sooner had I hung up than Don Dunahow sounded off over the phone.

"What's the matter with you, Dr. Zeitlin? Are you crazy? You still don't understand the Chicago way of doing things. When the Mayor's office sends you someone, you hire them with no questions asked. Why didn't you put Ellen Atkinson to work?"

"Don, she is not qualified. We can't afford to have dead weight on the payroll. She should have retired years ago."

"She's 63 and intends to retire when she reaches 65. So what if she can't type or take shorthand? It's your job to find out what she can do. You can put her in the backroom and have her stamp and seal envelopes."

"Don, we have no backroom and I can't create jobs for incompetents."

"As you well know I've been a leading Republican for many years, but when Daley's Democratic aides call, I listen. They are in control and I cooperate. You've got to hire Ellen Atkinson. I wouldn't dare say no."

"Mayor Daley is not running this college. We will not hire incompetents."

"That's bullshit. You're going to be very sorry from this day on."

His remarks disturbed me. My stomach juices began to boil. Fortunately, I got home on time, and Eugenia had prepared my favorite dish, filet mignon with mushrooms, mashed potatoes with gravy, creamed cauliflower and Coors Lite on the side. The kids were laughing and talking loudly. Mark had made friends with his former opponent, Vincent Pulizzi, the star football player, who urged him to go out for the team next semester. Joyce and Ann loved their new school, particularly since they walked home with their new friends, Ellen and Mary Jo Hicks. They'd visited the Hickses' home, four houses down the street from our own, and been fascinated by the stuffed animals Dr. Hicks had brought back from his African safari. Little Clare was happy for the first time in many weeks. Eugenia had registered her for the fall semester at the Martin Enger School for the handicapped in Franklin Park. Clare and Eugenia had toured the facility with her teacher and loved everything about it.

Clare took me by the hand to the calendar posted in the kitchen and said, "Five months, Daddy, then I go to school." Eugenia had crossed out day 151 and day 150 and said to Clare the remaining 149 days would go by very fast.

As I ate I couldn't believe the spirit of my family had changed so much within two weeks, from gloom to optimism. How? Buying a Ford Falcon station wagon had given Eugenia freedom. The four-day interlude in Dallas had been an added tonic. (Eugenia enjoyed showing off her newly-acquired tan.) Mark couldn't wait to get on the football team, Joyce and Ann were enjoying their newfound friends, and Clare was counting the days to her new life at the Martin Enger School.

As usual after dinner Ann cleared the table, Mark washed the dishes, Joyce dried them and Clare set the table for the next day. Our house rule for TV was rigid. No TV for the kids on school nights; that time was reserved for homework

Later that evening, as Eugenia and I watched TV in the den, she told me how delighted she was with her Falcon wagon and volunteered to exchange cars with me if I needed the wagon to carry the model of the campus to my talks. I gave her my schedule, which required switching cars four to five days per week. She was considering visiting a few colleges where she wanted to get on the substitute list for teaching English courses. She felt that way she could retain her teaching skills. Besides, we could use the extra money.

19
No Go With the Pimp

Monday, March 1st, was cloudy, cold and windy on the outside, but at 1809 Broadway it was warm and bright. Why? My first administrator arrived, in the person of Dr. John Widergren, 6' 2", age 36. I gave him a hearty welcome, went out to his car and helped him unload his boxes in a nearby apartment that had a desk, three four-drawer files, four chairs and a phone.

I reviewed with John the agenda for the week The selection of his secretary was the most urgent need. I gave him a folder of applications. Next was getting the copy of the *Survey of Educational Needs* to the printer before Friday. I asked him, a former English teacher, to edit the text so that it would really communicate. Our strategy was to release the survey to all high school seniors two weeks before the election. In that way the dinner conversation between the senior and his parents would be on college, and hopefully the parents would have the wisdom to vote the right way at election time. Third, I asked him to join me on Thursday for a noon luncheon as Babe and I pitched the election to the Kiwanis Club. Fourth, I gave John a folder of 22 applications for counselor and asked him to find one good one from among the local high schools and one from an Illinois university.

I reminded him that under no circumstances was anyone to be recommended for hiring until I had interviewed the individual. We discussed the 14 steps the board had approved for the selection of all personnel. We took a solemn pledge that there was to be no exception to this policy. We would follow it to the letter.

Foremost in my mind, and for the board, was a willingness to do anything and everything that would produce a successful election. I told John never to turn down any requests to talk to a group. At noon I pulled him away from his work to join me for lunch at the Melrose Park

Rotary Club, where I was given five minutes to deliver my pitch. However, this time it was a little different. Thanks to Eugenia I had borrowed her wagon and brought along the model of the proposed campus. After the meeting a dozen or more Rotarians gathered around the model. I heard a mixture of comments. Some marveled at the possibility of having such a beautiful campus in the community, while a few jokingly said it would never happen and called me a snake charmer. I retorted with, "If you are willing to pay an extra five or ten dollars on your tax bill, *it will happen!*. That's what this bond election is all about."

As I drove back to the office John said that Abe LoBuno, president of the Melrose Park Bank, had told him that the Proviso Municipal League would not support the election. The people felt that they'd already voted one tax increase when the district was formed, and they were not going to vote a second. The Republican leaders called it double taxation and openly opposed the bond issue. I told John that Mayor O'Connor, Bob Collins's uncle, had led a contingent of boos when I was first introduced at the Leyden Municipal League. His uncle believed we were educating too many people and soon would have no one to do the community's dirty work. Fortunately, Bob had locked horns with his uncle on this issue. Bob believed the real people of River Grove would support him even though the city council opposed a tax increase.

"We're indeed lucky that Bob is on the board," I said. "When his uncle retires he'll take the throne because the people like his ideas."

Before leaving that evening John dropped into my office to announce that he'd found an experienced counselor from one of the local high schools and would be interviewing her late Wednesday afternoon.

"What's her background?" I asked.

"She's 40, has a B.A. from Hanover College and an M.S. in guidance from Indiana University. What's more, Dr. David Byrne, principal of East Leyden, has praised her highly for her counseling skills."

"That sounds good to me, John. What's her name?"

"Gertrude Wilson. I once heard her give a talk at a state guidance meeting. She's attractive, mature and has class."

"If she's the one, John, I want you to make a telephone check on her to her department chairperson, her principal and the faculty association president before presenting her to me for final approval."

"Consider it done. I'll include what I hear in her personnel folder. Can I assume that you'll determine her placement on the salary schedule?"

"Yes, I'll do it subject to the board's approval. Now, how are you doing with your search for a secretary?"

"I'll be interviewing two women tomorrow night and may make a recommendation on Wednesday."

As I drove home I felt good. At last I had an associate to share some of the responsibilities. John might have a counselor and secretary on board soon and I was looking forward to my interview with Dr. Robert Darnes on Friday night. These folks would need furniture. Maybe Joe Pulitano could help us out when we talked the following morning.

The next morning Maria was all smiles as she introduced me to Joe Pulitano, who had presented her with a beautiful bouquet of roses and laughingly said, "Any relative of Babe is an instant friend of mine." He fondly looked at Maria as she giggled. "Particularly so when she's as beautiful as Maria."

As we went into my office he told me that he'd known Babe and his family since high school days, and he was one prince of a guy. Babe had told him I'd be needing a lot of student furniture, and he was just the person to equip the college. I told him we'd probably be using a high school next year and would not be needing much until we occupied the new campus. His smile disappeared and his face showed disappointment. I then told him that within the next few weeks we'd be needing desks, chairs and four drawer files for several incoming administrators and secretaries. His face brightened slightly as he reached out for his catalog, saying, "What kind would you like?"

I tapped my hand first on my desk, then on the chair, and then got up and walked to the file cabinets and said, "They have to be Shaw Walker, just like these. All metal, beautifully constructed and built to last a lifetime. I ordered my first Shaw Walker desk over 25 years ago while I was working in New York. When I went back recently to my old office, it was still in use by one of my replacements."

"Dr. Zeitlin, we don't have any Shaw Walker desks or files in our warehouse. It would therefore take four to five weeks instead of two or three weeks to deliver. Is that OK?"

"That's OK, but before placing the order with you I must have your price in writing. Can you sharpen your pencil for the sake of our students and get a low bid to Maria by tomorrow afternoon?"

"Why of course. I'm looking forward to working with you. You'll find it well worth your while to do business with my company. We reward our special clients, and I know you'll benefit from it."

I passed over it at the time but later I wondered what he meant when he said, "We reward our special clients."

The following day Maria opened the bid. We compared it to the previous Discount Furniture bill. We were shocked! Joe Pulitano was quoting a price of $399 for the same desk that we'd purchased four months before for $199. The retail price for the desk was $299. Discount Furniture had given us a third off, while Melrose Park Furniture was double Discount's price! If we were to purchase 100 desks, Joe Pulitano would be getting $20,000 more than his nearest competitor.

How should I handle this situation? What would Babe do when I rejected his best friend? I could feel the steam coming out of my head. Finally I got Babe on the phone and explained the situation. I waited a dreadful two minutes for him to respond as he worked his calculator, all the time fearing a Don Dunahow type of reaction. I was dumbfounded when finally Babe shouted over the phone, "Tell that son-of-a-bitch to go to hell. He's a gonif. Put him on your shit list."

I was so relieved. Babe's stock went up tremendously. He wasn't going to permit a political business big shot to fleece the college. Maria overheard my talk with the Babe and said, "My brother-in-law is a very good person. He's always helping people. It hurts me when they say bad things about him. By the way, Tony was very upset when I came home last night with a bouquet of roses."

"Why?"

"Tony said men don't give gifts to women unless they get something in return."

"Well, it seems rather simple to me. He wanted you to help him get his bid accepted."

"It goes deeper than that, Dr. Zeitlin. At Tony's inistence I called Gloria Biazzo, who had graduated with me and was immediately hired by Joe Pulitano as his secretary."

"What did she tell you about him?"

"She said a mouthful. I'm almost ashamed to tell you. It's men talk, but I will. When she arrived for her first day of work, he welcomed her with a dozen long-stemmed roses, which she felt made him an exceptionally nice man."

"What happened next?"

"Nothing much. Gloria spent the day typing invoices, answering the phone, opening the mail and scheduling appointments for her new boss. However, on her second day, she agreed to work overtime to type out an out-of-town buyer's selection. When she finished the last page around seven o'clock, the client invited her out to dinner. She immediately declined and left in a hurry, feeling they had nothing in common. He was so old, at least three or four times her age. At 18 she was beginning to feel like a mature woman but was still a little scared about sex, fearing it would conflict her moral values."

Maria told me the whole story. The next day when Gloria arrived for work Joe Pulitano was waiting for her with anger on his face. He said, "Gloria, I'm disappointed with you. Mr. Trimarco is a fine gentleman with a wife and four grown children in Canton, Illinois. He just didn't want to eat alone. At his age, well over 60, he's harmless. Can't you understand that it's my job to provide dinner partners for out-of-town customers? I was very lucky that Lucy, my former secretary was available. She had a great dinner with him and everything worked out OK."

Feeling bad, Gloria apologized. She explained that she had not been aware that having dinner with a customer after hours was part of her job. That was something they hadn't taught her in school. She agreed to help out the next time around. During the following week, just before quitting time, Joe would approach her from the rear and gently massage her neck muscles before she left. At first Gloria resisted, but by the third time she really started to enjoy it. However, during the third massage he complimented her on her figure, adding that she gave glamour to the office. He suggested that she wear a cocktail dress the next day since he had reserved a table for four at the Millionaire's Club.

She was to be a dinner partner for Nick Caccamo, an insurance broker, while Lucy and he would be the other couple.

Gloria was immensely pleased the following day when Nick arrived in the late afternoon. He was tall, dark, handsome, mid-thirties, with a beautiful smile, and he had *no* ring on his third finger, left hand. They promptly got to work reviewing the company's inventory for the purpose of increasing its fire insurance. After several hours of intense, backbreaking work Nick asked, "Are you tired?"

"A little, but we're almost finished," she replied.

"Joe tells me you enjoy neck massages. When you finish typing the last page you'll be in for a special treat. I was a physical therapist while serving in the military and gave hundreds of back rubs, so hurry up for a real pick-me-up."

That line excited Gloria and she finished fast. Nick had her remove her sweater and seated her on a stool nearby. He slowly massaged her upper back, digging deeply into her skin for several minutes. With her permission he extended his penetrating hands to her seat just as Lucy and Joe arrived.

"That's a good way of getting acquainted," Joe smirked. "Let's all have a drink."

As Gloria sipped a rum and coke she chatted with Lucy, a tall, very young buxom redhead who giggled at everything that Joe said. Lucy gave Nick a big kiss and hug as she was introduced to him. He returned the hug and kiss with two slaps on her fanny and the party began with much laughter and joking. At the Millionaire's Club they had a great meal, the best in the house, and finished it off with two cordials each. It was a tipsy quartet that glided their way to Joe's Cadillac. Joe, still having some sense, had a cup of black coffee before driving. Lucy turned on the car radio and started to sing a song with sexy lyrics. Nick put his arm around Gloria as they relaxed in the back seat.

As the car approached the Forest Preserve on First Avenue Joe found a very dark spot in the section known as Lover's Lane, parked the car and turned off the lights. In seconds he slipped down behind the wheel. A zip was heard as Lucy bent over him. Nick started to kiss Gloria on the mouth as Joe, breathing hard, let out moans and groans. Gloria tried to stop Nick as he fondled one of her breasts with one hand while starting to stroke her vital spot with the other. She fought as he tried to remove her panties. He continued with vigor. She tried to scream as he covered her mouth with kisses. Unsuccessful in removing her panties, he got on top of her and relieved himself. Almost at the same time Joe cried out "Eureka!" A few seconds later Lucy lowered the window and spit out a substance. It happened so fast that Gloria couldn't talk. Nick, his breathing slowing down somewhat, continued to kiss her gently on the neck. Finally she pushed him off of her, adjusted her bra, inspected her dress and hose and snapped out, "You've ruined my dress with your gummy stuff."

She folded her arms in defiance and retreated to the far end of the seat. Nick laughed, "You were good at times but not good enough."

Joe drove Gloria to her car. His parting words were, "Get home safely, Gloria. You were a lot of fun. See you tomorrow."

Gloria thought and thought. How could she have been so wrong in judging men? They were both sex fiends and Lucy nothing but a call girl. Joe would call her and she'd enjoy performing. And at what price? Finally Gloria figured it out why Joe had such a large turnover of secretaries. If they pleased his clients, they were in. If not, they were out.

Gloria made up her mind. She would quit, but she had to return to the office to pick up some personal items. Upon returning the following morning she noticed a large envelope addressed to her on her desk. As she opened it Joe came out to say, "There's a $100 bill to replace the soiled dress. Nick liked you but was unhappy you didn't go all the way. Did you know that Lucy makes twice as much for an evening of fun as a secretary makes in a whole week? Gloria, you've got to grow up and learn to use your assets wisely. You have a great body, two beauts, pearl white teeth and kissable red lips. Men don't like brainy women. They like passionate women who laugh and have bodies that smell good. Join our club, have some fun and get rich."

Gloria said nothing, just stared at Joe in disgust, picked up her things, including the $100 bill, clasped her hand on her crucifix and left.

Upon hearing the story from Maria Tony had been outraged. "Joe Pulitano is not only a gonif but a pimp. He manages to get so many orders from his clients by procuring young call girls for them. Maria, goddamn it, you stay away from him. Fuck those flowers!"

Maria had thrown the roses on the floor, broken the vase and stamped out the blossoms, saying, "How could I have been so stupid?" as she'd started to sob.

I was amazed she had the gumption to relate the story to me. She was young, perhaps a little gullible at times, but she definitely knew right from wrong. A special thanks to her parents for her high moral standards. Tony, a few years her senior, was more sophisticated. As I observed their relationship I could tell she would learn much from him. I was sure this was a marriage that would last.

I tried to console Maria. I said Joe Pulitano should be avoided. If he called back she should put him through to me immediately. One of these days, I assured her, Pulitano would be caught and charged with procuring. I said it to relieve her of her pent-up feelings, but I wasn't too sure it would happen. I realized that some companies used call girls frequently to achieve their goals.

John Widergren and I went to the Kiwanis meeting on a day, Thursday, March 3rd, that had started on a sad note in the morning but turned out to be delightful in the afternoon. John and I never expected such a splendid reception from the Kiwanis Club of Melrose Park. Babe introduced us as two doctors with medicine that would help the residents of Melrose Park live a healthier and better life. And, what I didn't know at the time, was that John and I were the day's program. Surprisingly, the Kiwanians didn't even quiz us. Instead they focused on ways we could win the election. Each Kiwanian stood up and told us how he intended to help. I was amazed to find such a team of supporters. Even Rotary couldn't duplicate this atmosphere. Babe had done a superb job of building rapport with this hardworking group. I knew then that Melrose Park would give us an overwhelming yes vote. If there were only facsimiles of Babe in the other eleven communities, the vote would go over the top.

Before leaving I asked Babe whatever happened to his high school buddy Joe Pulitano.

"I told you to put him on your shit list," he said. "And that means he smells bad, stay away from him. He's another case of a good man gone wrong, for what reason I don't know. Maybe he's obsessed with the opposite sex. He should get married to a nice Catholic girl instead of putting his stick into every dame that comes along."

As we left John commented, "I've heard lots of stories about Ralph

Serpico, some good, some bad. I don't know what to believe, but he really is the Godfather of Melrose Park. I just wonder how many votes he can produce."

Late that afternoon, at Dr. Widergren's request, I interviewed Trudy Wilson. She was soft-spoken, attractive, intelligent, well-informed about community colleges and highly praised by her colleagues and students. I knew we'd have a winner if she joined our staff. She was quite pleased with her salary placement and prepared to work within four weeks. I told her that her name would go to the board on March 10th.

That afternoon John brought over Virginia Sybilla's folder and said, "I don't know where you found her but she would be great as my secretary."

"What did you like about her?"

"She has superior secretarial skills. She can type a letter as I dictate. No shorthand needed. I never saw that in a person before. Her principal will let her go, reluctantly. She'd be an excellent addition, mature, in her 40's and a possible mother figure to the students. Please get her to the board ASAP."

"John, she came highly recommended to us from Don Dunahow, the attorney for the board, who sometimes feels he *is* the board. Mrs. Sybilla is a dear friend of his wife. I'm sure she'll turn out OK."

I then discussed with him the awkward position we were put in when a trustee recommended someone. "We've been lucky so far. On my first day of work Babe recommended Maria as my secretary, and you can see she's doing great. Shortly after that Bob Collins pushed for Jim Tarpey as our part-time public relations specialist. It was Jim who wrote the glowing news story about you. He sets a good tone with the audience prior to every board meeting. A problem is sure to develop if we reject a trustee's candidate. The good rapport we had with the trustee will be endangered and we don't want to see that happen!"

"So what can you do about it, Dr. Zeitlin?"

"We're going to have an executive session this Saturday to clarify some important items. I'll bring it up at that time. We need a board policy that would prevent each trustee from outdoing the other in finding jobs for his friends. I like the idea of a trustee having his friends apply for a job on his own, without using a trustee for a reference."

"Do you think a politically-elected board would accept something like that?"

"If I can get the endorsement of the board president and secretary it may. Oh, by the way, John, I've scheduled an interview with Dr. G. Robert Darnes, the dean at Olney Community College, for this Friday night at the Homestead Restaurant. Would you be able to join us at 6:00? Right now he's in the lead position for dean of instruction."

John agreed to join us and added, "Wouldn't it have been better to find a dean from a larger college?"

"John, we had 29 applications, mostly from the midwest, but very few with doctorates and experience in community college administration. Dr. Darnes has what I'm looking for, several years of successful experience directly in an Illinois community college. The size does not really matter. He knows Illinois college administrators and he can help me get acquainted with the leaders."

We both felt we had a whole evening to find out as much as we could about the real Dr. Darnes. I would concentrate on asking him questions relating to his educational background and professional experience, while John would focus on his family, cars, clothing, food, sports and political beliefs. Together we made a list of questions that needed right answers. What method should we use in getting responses? We decided on a nonchalant, easy-going approach with frequent by-the-way questions.

Just before she left on Friday evening, Maria announced, "Dr. Darnes is here." I met a short Barry Goldwater look-alike with dark, horn-rimmed glasses, impeccably dressed and fidgeting around. The first thing he said was, "Dr. Zeitlin, I have an emergency!"

Having had the same feelings many times in the past, I responded instantly, "Here's the bathroom!"

A few minutes later we laughed and exchanged pleasantries. He discussed his speedy trip north at mostly 70 miles per hour in his new Buick Electra. As he spotted the organizational chart on the easel behind my desk he blurted out, "I like that. It tells everyone where they stand and who's who. Where am I?"

"You're between the dean of technology and the dean of admissions. All the academic chairpersons report to you while all the deans take their direction from the college president."

"I like what I see. This is the first college in Illinois to have a dean of tech. At Olney I tried to convince my superintendent and his board that we should offer some voc-tech courses, but it fell upon deaf ears."

"Why was that?"

"Everyone felt their kids should become doctors, dentists, lawyers, engineers, stockbrokers, business executives, professors, CPA's, actors or musicians – but under no circumstances farmers, skilled tradesmen or technicians."

"How do you feel about that?"

"I feel they're dead wrong. That's why I'm here. I want to be part of the first technical community college in the state. Please tell me, what kind of a board do you have? Will they support you in the furthering of voc-tech?"

"Yes, I feel indeed fortunate that this board is unanimous in upholding the technical part of the college. As I'm sure you know, a technical education is not complete unless the student receives a third or half of his education in the liberal arts and sciences. That aspect of education will be the principal responsibility of the dean of instruction. Are you up to it?"

"I wouldn't be here if I didn't believe in you and your goals."

"Dr. Darnes, a decision will not be made tonight, as I'm committed to interviewing two other candidates. You're the first, and it's a delight to find someone in so much agreement with our philosophy and goals. Now, I want you to meet our newly-hired dean of admissions, with whom you'll be working with very closely if you're hired."

After the long and the short shook hands I soon realized height was not the only difference between Widergren, 6' 2", and Darnes, 5' 6", almost a head apart. Widergren spoke slowly and softly in an accent-free English while Darnes, age 49, roared out rapidly in a nasal Oklahoma twang. Different they were. The major question was, could these two men so different in style get along together? Would the common goal unite them?

When we arrived at the Homestead, Dr. Darnes was the first to check his coat. The hat check girl, young, pretty, vivacious and flirtatious, helped him off with his coat, He in return responded in equally suggestive remarks for several minutes while John and I waited impatiently. The first question he asked me after receiving the menu from a tall, stately, mature waitress was, "Who's paying for this? You or the college?"

I told him the board had granted me an expense account to be used in the recruitment of personnel. His eyes lit up. He clapped his hands and said, "That's great. I'll order what I like," and proceeded to select one of the most expensive meals. John and I ordered the more reasonable restaurant special. As we sipped drinks Dr. Darnes opened up without any prodding. "Dr. Zeitlin, after serving more than nine years as chairman of the department of fine arts at the Oklahoma College for Women, I know how to get the most from the ladies."

"Pray tell, what is your secret?"

"You know, when a man goes out for dinner he showers, shaves and dresses within minutes, while a woman takes two to three hours to get ready. I always make it a point upon meeting a lady for the first time to focus my eyes on her hair, lips, make-up or dress and compliment her."

"So you believe that flattery will get you somewhere."

"It sure does, if done correctly. By that I mean, show sincerity. Don't be automatic with your remarks. Find something about her that deserves praise."

"Bob is right," John interrupted. "That's how I won over my wife many years ago."

"If a woman comes on to you in a flirtatious way, whether she's sweet or a sour Sarah, respond positively. Her day will be ruined if you ignore or reject her completely. Always appear somewhat interested but don't forget to inform her that you're a married man. If she doesn't step back slightly with that remark, you make it a point to back up with a smile. Remember and remember well that women always like to feel they have sex appeal, regardless of how old they are."

John and I laughed and thanked Bob for his words of wisdom, though he confessed later that his first wife had divorced him. As the dinner progressed Bob continued to talk, at times nonstop. He seemed to anticipate most of our concerns and talked openly about them. With great pride he informed us he'd been chosen the most outstanding young man in the state of Kansas eleven years earlier, having won numerous state, regional and national awards while serving as the director of the Garden City Band. He slowed down a bit when he discussed the Garden City farmer and his family–whom he'd known well–whose massacre had been the subject of Truman Capote's best seller, *In Cold Blood.*

After Dr. Darnes left to return to his motel, I asked John for his frank opinion of our candidate for dean of instruction.

"He's sharp, alert, knowledgeable and a real doer, but a bit garrulous."

"Don't you think that's a bit of an understatement? Wouldn't you say he's something of a windbag?"

"No, a windbag just lets out air. When Darnes talks, you listen, because you know he's well-informed, shrewd and insightful into human behavior. I learned something from his monologue on how to treat a woman."

"And what did you learn?"

"Women are just as playful as men. For most of my life I've felt they were more restrained. I think I'd enjoy having Bob on our team."

I smiled, thanked John for his counsel and returned to the office to prepare for Saturday's executive meeting with the board.

On Saturday, March 6th, the executive meeting started promptly at 10 AM, with all the trustees present except Joe Farmar. Bob Collins and Don Dunahow informed us that the election date had to be moved back since final approval of the 45 precincts was not expected until the following week. All of us were relieved since it would give us two additional weeks to campaign. At Dunahow's suggestion the bond amount was changed from $9,000,000 to $8,900,000. All agreed.

I then presented the proof of the election brochure. "It worked at Southwestern College," I commented, "so let's hope it will succeed again."

After the trustees inspected the proof and made a few suggestions, I said, "I'll give this copy to the printer this afternoon. He promised me that 30,000 copies would be ready by Wednesday. I'm now passing around a sign-up sheet for volunteers to help address these brochures to all those who voted a year ago to create this district. Thanks to Babe we have the names and addresses of over 12,000 voters."

Without any hesitation each trustee wrote in the name of his spouse, a member of his family or a friend. All 60 spots were filled in for 10 nights of addressing. I put down Eugenia and Mark for one night each. Bob Collins wrote in Cell Farmer, Beverly, Jim Tarpey and Marilyn Smith. The brochures were scheduled to be mailed first-class one week prior to the election date. With pride I held up the roster and thanked the board for its splendid cooperation.

Still having the floor, I distributed to the board the 16-page proof of the *General Information & Survey of Educational Needs,* which they studied very carefully for 20 minutes. Many questions were raised but not a single word was changed, and that made me feel good. Finally Wade asked, "How many are you going to have printed?"

"One for every graduating senior in the district. That's over 2,800, plus around 1,200 for any other citizens that may wish to take courses."

"Was the origin of this species also at Southwestern College?"

"Yes, but with many modifications."

"Dr. Zeitlin, you've described here 39 different occupational programs. Now surely you don't intend to offer that many on opening day, do you?"

"Not on opening day, but eventually when we get on our new campus, I expect a lot more than 39."

"This is ridiculous," laughed Don Dunahow, "It will never happen. Please don't inhale Dr. Zeitlin's exhaust. It's far-fetched."

"Don, if 15 years ago Phoenix, Arizona, with a population of 94,000, could support a technical school with over 30 programs, we, with a population twice as large, surely will do much better. As a matter of fact I'm positive students from all over the state will be attracted to our college, as the first public technical community college in Illinois— just like it happened in Phoenix."

The fellows looked at each other and waited for someone to say something. This really was a test to see whether the group would accept either the brilliant attorney's opinion or the vision of their college president. Finally, Bob Collins stood up quietly and said, "Did you fellows know that 40 per cent of those employed in our district are in manufacturing, and their company managers are calling for technicians of all kinds? I think we should inhale deeply and show our support to Dr. Zeitlin. No offense to you, Don, but we hired Dr. Zeitlin because of his vast experience in working with industry and we're right behind him."

It took courage for Bob to stand up and take a stand against the college attorney. I felt at that moment he was really acting like a good brother, and later I thanked him for his stand.

As the men were standing up, ready to leave, Wade stopped them with, "Hold on a minute, fellows. There's one more item to discuss."

"What is it?" asked Babe Serpico.

"Herb has been getting calls and drop-ins from individuals claiming that this or that trustee had told them there was a job waiting for them at the college."

"So what's wrong with that?" Babe indignantly asked. "If we're going to have thousands of students, as Dr. Zeitlin proclaimed, surely we'll need hundreds of workers. Am I right or am I right?"

"You're right in your thinking but wrong in your procedure. As a specific job opens, it will be announced by the college and only then should an applicant apply. Recently an applicant burst into the president's office and stated he was a dear friend of a trustee and wanted to take over the purchasing of all our furniture. Later on he submitted a bid for some desks that was outrageous."

"Well, how can we prevent this from happening again?"

"Trustees should not recommend friends for jobs or contracts. We need a rule or policy preventing this from happening. There's a conflict of interest when a trustee recommends someone and then solicits votes from the board to accept his recommendation."

"What kind of rule would you suggest?"

"The rule or policy should say that trustees are not permitted to recommend anyone for a job or contract."

"Oh, come on now. Our friends expect us to return favors."

Wade replied firmly, "They're counting on you first of all to help them get a good job that they can handle, based on merit. At a college you just don't dish out jobs to anyone who comes along. The applicant must be fully qualified, as judged by the professionals, our administrators."

"If we can get them to accept that, it would be a big load off our backs."

"Babe, you must get them to accept that procedure, or else the good relationship that we have among our trustees will deteriorate. Think also of how the public will react if inefficiency becomes the mode at the college. The people are waiting anxiously to judge us and we must make a great effort to receive a good evaluation."

"If Dr. Zeitlin feels it is necessary, then let's give it a try," Babe reluctantly replied.

"The rule shall be simple: Trustees are not permitted to write letters of recommendation.

Bob Collins ended the session. "Let's give it a try. We can always change it if it doesn't work. I wouldn't mind if we got out of the act entirely." The group left for lunch at Tom's Steak House.

A group of sophisticated politicians agreeing not to push for jobs for their friends was a relief greatly welcomed. The new rule would not have happened if I hadn't received strong and instant verbal support from the board president and secretary. I expressed my deep thanks to them both at the luncheon.

For 11 consecutive nights, starting on Thursday, March 11th, the trustees' wives, relatives and friends hand-addressed the election brochures to some 14,000 individuals who had voted a year before. Such teamwork was a sight to behold as the group worked diligently from 7 to 10 PM every night, including Saturday and Sunday. Each evening a different team member brought in cookies, coke, popcorn or candy for the 8:30 PM break time, which gave us a chance to become better acquainted as we discussed our important mission. John or I supplied the coffee and pizza. Finally, on Sunday, March 21st, the task was completed, brochures were stamped and packaged for delivery to the post office the following morning.

Marilyn Smith, who had given up a Saturday and Sunday night for the writing session, wished me well. She said her husband Harry predicted success by a slight margin, provided Mayor O'Connor's message was not heard by too many. I belatedly thanked her for the envelope she'd given me on Thanksgiving night after dinner at Bob Collins's house.

What had been in it? A newspaper reprint that stressed *14 Nuggets of Knowledge*, a guide for better living. I told her Eugenia and I were using it on our kids. They now knew:

1. The best day is always *today.*
2. The greatest handicap is *fear.*

3. The easiest thing to do is t*o find a fault with someone.*
4. The most disagreeable person is *the complainer.*

She stopped me on number 4 and said, "I'm not complaining, but on the two nights I worked there were only women writing–no men. How come?"

"Marilyn, all the trustees were out with either John or me talking to civic groups and showing off this model of the new campus."

"Did any man volunteer to write?"

"No, I volunteered my son Mark and Bob volunteered his friend, Jim Tarpey. All the other writers were women."

"Doesn't that tell you something?"

"Yes, it does. We have a big job in front of us in changing sexual stereotypes. I promise you in the world ahead we'll have more female lawyers, doctors, professors, business executives, police and fire officers. And in return we'll try to get more men to enter nursing, secretarial work–and addressing election brochures."

We both laughed as Harry arrived to pick her up.

At the March 10th official meeting of the board, attended by all the trustees and ten visitors, action was taken on:

1. Election date changed to March 27th.
2. Instructor's standard contract form to be reviewed by board attorney.
3. Trudy Wilson and Virginia Sybilla hired.
4. Printing of election brochure and senior survey approved.
5. Bills to be paid.

I reported that during the first part of February, 88 professional applications had been received. None had come in for nursing, library science or women's physical education.

The meeting was short, snappy, positive and over within the hour. Later on everyone except Jones and Boeger gathered together for a snack and tonic flow at the Red Steer, for additional planning. The men promised to distribute the brochures to friends, neighbors and company employees. We were determined to do everything possible to prevent the election from failing.

Farmer eloquently stated, "People don't plan to fail. They fail to plan." So we kept on planning. . . .

The following day I confirmed appointment dates for the instructional dean. The first contact was with Dr. Alfred Livingston, coordinator of the community college program at San Diego State University, who had sent me several well-qualified instructors at Southwestern College. I was disappointed when he told me that for two reasons he was dropping out. His wife disliked the weather in Chicago and he felt that the dean of instruction, like the deans at Southwestern and Mesa Colleges, should be the top dean. His decision left me with one more choice.

Her name was Dr. Eleanor Hoffner, a coordinator of instruction at a Michigan junior college. She was scheduled for a dinner appointment with me Friday night. She arrived on time, conservatively dressed, soft-spoken and very polite. Her main accomplishment had been promoting a successful developmental reading program in Michigan. She had applied twice for a dean's opening at her college, but had not been accepted. I wondered why. As I asked her questions, she would wait several minutes before replying. She was not sure of herself, the exact opposite of Dr. Darnes. I wondered what it would take to get her to speak out without waiting so long. I thanked her for coming and we parted.

I thought more about Dr. Darnes and called his superintendent, who described him as an unhappy fireball. I asked him what would happen if Darnes teamed up with a happy fireball. His immediate reply was, "You two working together would light up the universe."

I liked what he said. I needed such an ally and perhaps Darnes was the one. His boss said Darnes needed a challenge and probably would work out well in a metropolitan rather than a rural area. After further discussion with Dr. Widergren we decided to go with Bob Darnes.

When I informed Darnes I was recommending him to the board at the March 19th meeting, he was very pleased and said he was prepared to join us within 30 days. His parting words were, "Dr. Zeitlin, I'm very excited about joining your staff and I want to assure you that I won't be seeking a presidency for at least three years."

"And I want to assume you if you do a good job I'd be most happy to recommend you for a presidency...elsewhere!"

On March 19th the trustees enthusiastically accepted Dr. Darnes. Acting chairman Joe Farmar said, "Wait until the public hears about this appointment. The first administrator we hired had a doctorate from Stanford. The second received his doctorate from the University of Wyoming, and now we have a third chief who received his third degree from the University of Oklahoma. You are flying high, Dr. Zeitlin. Imagine how the public will react when they read about a technical institute starting out with three doctors. Three top-rate doctors at the helm will heal and find remedies for everything."

It was nice to hear such flattery from Joe, but I wondered if he really meant it. At this point Bob injected, "I think the public will be very pleased. Dr. Zeitlin wants to start out the same way Stanford did over 80 years ago."

Bob had read my mind. I added, "Dr. Darnes will start work within 30 days. One of his major responsibilities will be to recruit the university-transfer faculty. And sometime in April I hope to submit to you the names for the dean of technology, business manager and coordinator of student activities."

"Do you have any candidates from Notre Dame?" Joe asked.

"Yes, an experienced mathematics teacher is waiting to be interviewed by our new dean."

"How many teacher applications have you received thus far?"

"Over 250 applications from all over the nation. We are rejecting all beginners. When the college opens, the students will be facing the most successful, experienced and enthusiastic teachers that money can buy. They'll be mostly in their 30's, 40's and 50's."

"How are your talks going?" Joe inquired.

"During these past 30 days I've addressed 23 different organizations, reaching an audience of over 2,800. Several additional groups will be visited prior to election day. On the whole the people are very excited about having a community college in their backyard this September. I was interviewed by the Chicago Sun Times last week and they'll write an editorial urging a Yes vote."

"That sounds good to me. I'm working my dogs off trying to change people's opinion in Elmwood Park from the last election. You know, Dr. Zeitlin, I'm glad you selected my town of Elmwood Park for your home, because together we can change the outcome. Did you know that over 1,000 voters said No in the last referendum?"

"Yes, I heard about that from Clem Lowe and Ray Libner when I addressed their high school PTA several weeks ago. Their audience showed great excitement when I displayed the model of the college campus. I told them that while we may start out in a high school in the late afternoon or evening, if the bond election is successful we'll be on our own campus within two or three years. I'm also happy to say I received the same positive response when I talked to the Elm School, the Elmwood School and the John Mills School PTAs. If my radar is accurate, this time Elmwood Park will go our way. Thanks to the support of Lowe, Libner and Mayor Conti."

Moving along on the agenda my recommendation to hire Jack Simpson & Company to clean our offices every night between the hours of 8 and 10PM on a contract basis was approved.

Not on the agenda was a surprise resolution presented by Fred Knol and seconded by Bob Collins to pay attorney Smith for all his services 1/2 of 1 per cent from the sale of the bonds. With hardly any discussion it was unanimously approved. After the board ended the meeting a trip to Horwath's Restaurant followed for food, fun and frolic with fair friends. The spirit was high in anticipation of victory next Saturday.

Because Roy Jones was without a car he asked me to take him to the post-session at Horwath's. As we drove along I asked him, "Isn't it a little unusual for a board attorney to also act as bond salesman? Isn't there a conflict of interest here? In all the districts where I've been employed school bonds are sold through the business manager's office to the lowest bidder."

"Well, Dr. Zeitlin, you don't have a business manager and Dunahow's fee of 1/2 of 1 per cent is a good one. Merrill Lynch, Dean Witter or Paine Webber usually charges 1 to 2 per cent to purchase bonds from a school district and their sales executives reel in another 1 to 2 per cent when they sell the bonds. Banks and bond companies can earn as much as 4 per cent for handling a bond issue. In our case 4 per cent multiplied by $8,900,000 amounts to $356,000 – that's the way to go. In my next life I'm going to be a banker or stockbroker. Now don't you forget, Dunahow is only charging us $44,500. He's a bargain!"

"What if the bond issue is not successful? How will Dunahow be paid?"

"I'm surprised at you for even thinking such a thing could happen. If the election fails we would revert to our original contract with Dunahow. Pay would be on an hourly basis with a minimum rate as specified by the Chicago Bar Association."

I originally felt uncomfortable with the decision made by the board, but was relieved when Jones convinced me that we were getting a bargain.

On Monday, March 22nd, I called all five high school principals and requested a return of the senior survey forms. Two days later I was disappointed to learn that out of 2,800 forms delivered to the schools, less than 400 had been returned. Instead of receiving the anticipated one-third to one-half, we received less than one-seventh. That was not a good sign. It was somewhat disheartening to count the following results: zero returns from West Proviso; 48 from East Proviso; 37 from Elmwood Park; 147 from East Leyden; and 203 from West Leyden.

I could not understand the wide variation among the schools. I decided to call Dr. Ed Stubbs, principal of West Proviso High School, the school with the most seniors and with zero returns.

With indignation Dr. Stubbs said, "I informed all the seniors over the public address system that if they were interested in attending the new junior college they should pick up a survey form in my office. A dozen or two came by but none of them returned the forms. I'll put out a reminder in the school bulletin next week"

"Ed, I can't understand why I haven't received any returns from your school. Can you explain it?"

"Why of course! First of all, it was silly of you to put out the survey in late March. It should have been done in October or November; that's when the decisions are made by the students and their families. Secondly, the junior colleges in Illinois lack status. Good students, and that's all we have at our school, just don't go in that direction. However, you'll find rejects from the university and a few misfits opting for the junior college."

I thanked him for his candid opinion. It was pointless to continue a discussion with such a biased principal. He lacked knowledge about community colleges and was no friend of the movement. Before hanging up I asked, "Dr. Stubbs, what did you think of the survey form?"

"Dr. Zeitlin, I've been so busy that I just didn't have time to read it. I'll get after a few of our incorrigibles and try to talk them into taking some vocational courses at your school."

My gastric juices were sizzling after talking to Ed Stubbs so I got up to join Maria in a coffee break. "Maria, since you spent four years at East Proviso, how would you describe your principal, Hugh Pitt?"

"Middle-aged, a little on the heavy side, very smart but a tendency to lecture a little too long when he addressed us at the assemblies. I was never in his office since I never broke any rules. My girlfriend, Gloria, was caught smoking once and she ended up in his office. She said he was very nice and enjoyed his lecture on the evils of smoking, which convinced her to stop."

"How about renewing your friendship with your old principal and getting him on the phone for me?"

For the next few minutes I heard Maria exchanging East Proviso moments of glory with her friend, the principal. They talked as if he were a lifelong friend until she said, "Let me put Dr. Zeitlin on the line."

His first line was, "What do you think of our secretarial graduate?"

"Wonderful, send us more such students. Now tell me, what did you think of the senior survey I sent you last week?"

"It was a bit long but one of the best I'd seen in a long time. Our counselors have given them to all interested students. You can expect a large number of students from Maywood. This Friday I will forward additional returns."

I received a similar response from Ray Libner, principal of the Elmwood Park High School. When I got to Dr. David Byrne, principal of East Leyden, he informed me that since Trudy Wilson was leaving for my college he would put her in charge of the senior survey. All 111 returns came from her counselees. What a remarkable feat from one busy counselor! I felt so good that everything Dr. Widergren said about her had come true. She was a terrific worker. Dr. Byrne said that additional forms would be forthcoming from the other counselors.

My last call was to Dr. George Cox, principal of West Leyden High

School. I told him that with 203 returns he led the four high schools and asked, "How did you do it?"

"Well, Dr. Zeitlin, I felt your request was urgent and very important. Therefore, I didn't delegate it to anyone else. With the teachers' approval I went into every senior class and discussed the advantages of going to a community college. I helped each student who was interested in going to fill out the survey sheet. About half of the seniors did so. The interest was high and I hope these returns will give you some clues on what to offer."

I thanked him and reflected on what he had done. A busy high school principal had actually taken the time to help the college get organized. His stature grew with me.

20
Will the Door Be Opened or Closed?

S aturday the 27th of March turned out sunny and crisp, but anxious, as the trustees started to appear in the office. Bob Collins, Joe Farmar and Jim Tarpey arrived first and announced that the judges of all 45 precincts were present and accounted for. Sunny weather usually meant a large turnout. This day, however, might be an exception. There hadn't been much action since the polls opened.

Jim Tarpey wrote down on my chalkboard all the precincts by community, starting with Forest Park, precincts 1 to 4. In the last election the Forest Parkers had voted 457 to 398 for creation of the college district. With the exception of Don Dunahow, everyone felt sure they would do better the second time around. Westchester, the community with many new homes, had defeated the referendum last year with by 1,125 to 1,025. I thought back to the February 22nd meeting of the Westchester Home Improvement Association, when Fred Knol and I had fielded many questions from the group and left with some reservations. Had we done well or badly? Tonight would tell. Fred's comment was, "My people are not against the college; they just don't want any new taxes."

As Jim listed all the communities within the district, Babe arrived breathing hard, carrying two black loose-leaf books and a dozen or more legal sheets. He said, "Dr. Zeitlin, I have lots of calls to make. May I use your two phones?"

I cleared my desk and Babe took over. He called the many names in his black books, plus those listed on the legal-sized pages. As he connected to his calls, I was amazed at his remarkable memory of previous events. He greeted each contact by first name, recalled his last contact with the individual and asked the person about his father, mother, sister or brother. He'd end up with, "I need a favor from you."

"Whatever it is, you know the answer is yes," was the usual response.

"Get out and vote and get all your family and neighbors to do the same."

As Babe continued nonstop in his calling, Wade dropped in to pick up the voter sheets for Northlake, Franklin Park and Schiller Park and commented, "Babe is doing it alone. In my office and the nearby offices Mildred has assembled her brigade. They're working like mad to get the voters out."

I thanked Wade for having such a terrific wife and marveled at Babe's enduring vigor. As 7:00 PM approached, Babe left to monitor his precincts, without eating his dinner.

Shortly after the polls closed, the other six trustees with their wives assembled in the 1829 offices. Eugenia had baked some cookies and purchased a large pizza. She greeted everyone. We all waited with great anxiety for the results.

A chorus of "Oh no" went up as Tarpey marked Forest Park on the chalkboard with 258 no's to 89 yes's. Smith said with a smirk, "Forest Parkers felt it was double taxation. Next time you'll listen to me. You fellows just stirred up the no vote."

Further pain erupted as the Westchester return showed 520 no's to 377 yes's. Crestfallen, Fred Knol muttered, "I can't understand how so-called smart people can do such stupid things."

I felt crushed as my eyes stayed focused on these first two cities, who had voted "no" with a vengeance. Eugenia consoled me. "This is only the beginning. Wait until Melrose Park and Franklin Park come in."

I had never worked so hard in my life. Laboring up to 15 hours daily on the college's future, I'd deprived my kids of a father for over six weeks. Yes, despite their many strategy sessions, it looked like the best plans of the politically active trustees had failed. Who was to blame? I closed my eyes and covered my face, and thought. As the executive officer of the board and chief administrator of the college, I was to blame! I had insisted on an all-out campaign, and gotten it, and now it looked like I had stirred up a big no vote. Could it be that Smith had been right in recommending a quiet and lethargic campaign?

Jim Tarpey smiled and waved to me as he posted the results from the third city, a winner! Hillside, the residence of Boeger and Jones, gave us 164 yes to 109 no. Berkley followed next with a nick and tuck race of 104 yes to 103 no. The totals for the first eleven precincts were 897 no to 734 yes.

Fifteen minutes later precinct number 12 reported yes 146 and no 100. We stilled trailed by 117 votes. For the next 35 minutes there were no reports, so the trustees and I feared the worst. Around 9:00 PM Babe called in from the Mt. Carmel School and asked for the results. His reaction was, "Don't worry. We got one terrific turnout here, so we'll be late in responding."

It was so easy for him to say, "Don't worry," while pessimism was in all our hearts. The cardiac beater started to pound faster as Tarpey posted 584 yes to 168 no for the city of Northlake, site of George Cox's high school. Cox's strategy and sincerity with the seniors and their parents had paid off. I couldn't help but reflect on Cox's positive qualities as I wondered what the score might have been had the other principals done the same. Cheers went up for the first time as we soared with 1,464 yes to 1,165 no. A few minutes later Bellmore's final count came in: 307 yes to 276 no, a narrow win but another winner. Our spirits picked up.

The next hour a euphoric atmosphere developed as the remaining communities voted yes. Wade was patted on the back and Mildred received a few kisses when Franklin Park proudly displayed 1,035 yes to 257 no, the biggest lead to date. Maywood surprised us with a 476 yes to 187 no. We never expected such a large turnout from that city.

The group congratulated Bob Collins as the River Grove final count was 533 yes to 324 no. Bob had taken on his uncle and won. He was sure to be the next mayor. Elmwood Park, which had given a large no at the last election, reversed itself with a 444 yes to a 204 no. Joe and I found each other, shook hands and spontaneously shouted, "We did it!"

A few minutes past ten o'clocl a thunderous roar went up as Babe's town of Melrose Park, the last to report, delivered the knockout blow of 1,663 yes to 297 no. Almost unbelievable, but true. Babe had delivered as promised. No question about it, Melrose Park was his town and he was the Godfather. No one else would even come close if he decided to run for mayor there.

Eugenia grabbed me and gave me a big kiss as the others cheered. The final count was 6,387 yes to 3,022 no, a victory of more than 2 to I. The door was now open to higher education for the 14 suburban communities of Chicago. Joe Farmar took the floor and loudly announced, "Now hear this," in the tone of a commanding Navy officer. "All yee hard workers, let us celebrate this great victory with fun and frolic at Kirie's restaurant. See you all there in 15 minutes."

Neil Mehler, the owner and editor of the *Franklin Parker,* congratulated Wade and me as he hurriedly wrote down the results. He said, "Now all you have to do is sell the bonds, buy the land and build a college campus. When will you be on your new campus?"

"By September 1967, if things go according to schedule," I replied as we parted. The Steels and the Zeitlins were the last to arrive at Kirie's, as a happy and noisy party of 18 took over the restaurant, near closing time. Joe introduced me to his political boss, the head of the Leyden Township Democratic Party. He informed us that he usually closed around that time, but for this special celebration he'd stay open until the party was over.

Everyone seemed to be talking at the same time until Fred Knol raised his glass and said, "Here's to our politicians, the college's best friends, for whenever you find four politicians together, you're sure to find a fifth." The men all laughed and later the ladies joined in after the husbands explained the significance of the fifth.

Joe stood up and toasted, "To the hardest worker in Melrose Park, the man who got us the largest number of yes votes, 1,663 to be exact. My dear friend and the college's closest friend, Ralph Serpico."

The audience started to cry out, "Speech, speech, speech. We want the Babe."

Josephine pushed her husband up and he slowly expressed himself. "I owe a lot to Mayor Richard Daley, since he taught me how to get out the vote. Now, don't you folks forget for a moment the great effort that our board president Wade Steel and his wife Mildred made. Together they're a wonderful team. They awakened the sleepy village of Franklin Park and got out a big vote."

"Steel, Steel, Steel, we want Wade," the chorus echoed.

Wade put down his drink as Millie whispered a few words to him and then said, "Mildred reminded me that there are eight ladies here who played a major part in this campaign. You know who you are. Stand up, if you please, and take a bow. We love you all."

I had to poke Eugenia to get her up and the seven trustees had to force their mates to take the bow. They were embarrassed when they received a standing ovation.

Bob came over to my table, stood behind me with both hands on my shoulders and said, "Don't forget this guy from California. He's one of us now. Our dreams and his are the same, and together we'll build the finest community college in Illinois."

I replied, "Thank you, Bob. I salute you and definitely feel that you'll be the next mayor of River Grove. We will make it happen." Everyone applauded as Bob smiled and waved to us.

Roy Jones, seated next to the Babe, made his toast. "Thank you, my colleagues on the board, for the splendid work you've done and will continue to do. It's a real pleasure to be part of this team."

Boeger, last to speak, elegantly said, "There is one word that accounts for our success today, and that is *teamwork.* May it be a continuing practice for this hardworking board."

Boeger's toast was short and sweet. He received much applause from everyone – except for Dunahow, who was stoic much of the evening.

The drinks continued to flow and laughter accelerated. The adulation for everyone was excessive as a midnight snack was ordered. Never had Eugenia or I seen such a fun-loving, friendly and constructive team. It was great to be an accepted part of it.

As the party came to an end, I was somewhat surprised when the waitress gave me the bill. I informed her that it should go to Joe Farmar, the host who had invited us. A few minutes later she came back and asked me if I was the president of the college. I said "yes," and she replied that Mr. Farmar had told her it was the president's party and that I would handle the bill.

I excused myself and went to my car for the college checkbook. I added up all the entries and found the total to be $444, not the amount requested, $554, a $110 overcharge. I quietly reviewed this with the waitress and she firmly informed me that all checks were added upon a machine by Mrs. Kirie. A few minutes later she returned with a corrected total. I paid the bill and wondered if the overcharge had been deliberate. While several party members were stoned, I had remained sober throughout the affair. Had the machine really made the mistake?

Driving home Eugenia and I reviewed the wonderful evening, and looked forward to the sale of the 8.9 million dollar bond issue.

21
Warning Signals

On Tuesday, March 30th, the adjourned meeting of the previous week was reopened with all trustees present except Farmar and Knol. The major purpose was to canvass the votes of Saturday's election.

What is a canvass? Not to be confused with a canvas, a strong coarse cloth, a canvass with a double "s" is a procedure in which the precincts' election envelopes are opened in the presence of the trustees and officially inspected and then recorded. Prior to the canvass the head judges telephone the results to the secretary of the board. Does the call-in count differ much from the official canvass?

If the judges are experienced and alert the count should be the same. However, in this case, due to the inaccurate marking of some ballots, the final result was four fewer yes votes.

I asked Bob, "Wouldn't it be faster, easier and more accurate to have each precinct use a voting machine, like they do in New York and other eastern states?"

His instant reply was, "No, it wouldn't. The machines are expensive and quite often break down. Illinois politicians believe that paper ballots, used for generations in the state, are the best. People like to feel the paper, and the political parties provide them with sample ballots showing them how to vote."

Although I disagreed with him I said nothing, feeling he was so set in his ways that I couldn't change his opinion. I thought about it. Could it be that this procedure provided an easy way to stuff the ballot box? Was that why they wouldn't give up the box?

Richard Nixon, when he lost to Kennedy, noticed that Chicago led the herd in sending in late returns. Why the delay in reporting? The precinct captains needed the extra time while waiting for instructions from Mayor Richard Daley. The mayor told the captains the number needed and the captains always had extra ballots on hand to pack the boxes. It was downright fraud, but for Chicago it was a way of life. Nixon, fearing he would be labeled a sore loser, never asked for a recount.

The canvass was long and boring. After the official count was approved a motion to pay the 135 politically appointed judges for the March 27th election, and reappoint them to the forthcoming trustee election of April 10th, was made and approved. Fred Knol and Roy Jones, who were up for reelection, said nothing.

For the past several months Jones had been in complete harmony with the rest of the board, so it was assumed that both men would be reelected. However, it was strange that no one seemed to know anything about the other candidates running against Fred and Roy. Strange indeed. I doubted it.

After adjourning, Roy and Fred came up to Wade and me and insisted that we go to the Illinois School Board Association meeting the following night at the Sherman House to hear the best school attorney in the state of Illinois, Louis Ancel.

The next day when we arrived at the Sherman House the room was packed. Farmar, Collins, Knol, Steel and Zeitlin had to stand to hear the master lawyer. His topic was *Firing the Incompetent Teacher.* He stressed the importance of documenting the evidence in writing before starting dismissal procedures. In rapid order he answered many tough questions. He concluded with saying he only took cases he knew he would win. To date, he had never lost a case.

Joe Farmar, upon leaving, said, "He is one helluva an attorney. I certainly wouldn't want to lock horns with him. If ever we have to dismiss a chief administrator, Louis Ancel would be the one to do it."

Joe smiled, patted me on the back and added, "Of course, this would never happen to you. We like you and you like us." Was he subtly trying to tell me something? I thought about the rejection of Neil Neuson, Bekins's purchasing agent. Was Joe holding that against me?

Although the sun never came out and it drizzled the entire day, Saturday, April 10th, trustee election day, will long be remembered for its surprising turns.

Jim Tarpey, followed by Collins and Farmar, were first to drop into the office. After Jim listed the precincts by community on the chalkboard the three men left to monitor the results.

Around eleven o'clock Roy Jones came in, banged the door hard and, filled with violent anger, furiously sounded off, "That fat son-of-a-bitch, Babe, double-crossed me. Look at this sample ballot one of my friends gave me. There is no 'X' in front of my name. He's endorsed Knol and his dear neighbor, Nick. I had a weird feeling this was going to happen when Babe told me not to spend any money on the campaign since I was a sure winner."

I didn't know what to say to the rejected trustee, whose eyes continued to water as he spoke. He was more than angry, he was frightened and sick at heart. Finally I said, "Why don't you call Wade Steel?"

He did and within 20 minutes Wade arrived and took control.

"Roy, it isn't over yet. We have eight hours to go. Why don't you have your wife contact the local president of the American Association of University Women? Ruth has been a longtime member and the AAUW is always highly interested in all educational causes. Get your son, daughters and your minister to call everyone they know and ask for help. You've lived for years in this community and you may be surprised at what your neighbors will do for you. Surely your elementary school trustees and the PTA's need to know the college would face a severe crisis if you lost your board seat. In the meantime I'll have Mildred call the president of the League of Women Voters. I know for sure she'll round up her brigade and they'll go into action. Roy, we need you on the board more than anyone else. So don't you dare quit. I'll have Leroy Knoeppel, Clem Lowe and David Byrne call every PTA in our district to get out the good voting public."

Could Wade rescue a drowning man? He gave Roy a double shot of adrenaline and so re-energized him that he left with a determination to fight up to the last minute.

Shortly before 5:00 PM, Babe quit campaigning, came into the office with confidence and introduced me to Nick, who he proclaimed was my new trustee. Babe assured me that Jones, the pipsqueak, was out and the board from then on would have smooth sailing.

"Dr. Zeitlin, had that stupid bastard remained on the board we'd never get the college built. I say good riddance to bad rubbish. Anytime a serious question came up he wanted a committee to resolve it. The people voted us in as a committee of seven, also known as the board, and we'll handle all the problems as they come up."

I said nothing. I rather liked Roy and felt we were losing the most capable and experienced trustee. At that moment Bob Collins popped in with Jim Tarpey and congratulated Nick, saying, "You're in! Don't worry about this guy Jones. He has no political backing. He doesn't have a ghost of a chance. The coalition is behind you and we always produce a winner."

Bob went to the bar and prepared five scotch and sodas to toast Nick. Nick was a nice, gray-haired, well-dressed elderly gentleman in his mid-sixties. We waited for him to react to the enthusiastic toast. Finally, with an Italian accent, he spoke. "Thank you very much, but I don't know what to say. I know nothing about being a trustee. Babe asked me to run. Now that I'm in. I will always look to Babe for help."

Babe smiled and announced, "Nick will make a wonderful trustee. You know this election has had a low turnout so the final count will be in around 8 or 9 at the latest. After that we'll all have a victory party at Tom's restaurant. It's on me. Herb. You and your wife are invited."

I thanked Babe as I left for dinner with my family, feeling sad. Roy was an honest man and it hurt me to see him rejected. To celebrate his defeat would only lower my spirits. When Eugenia told me she had a slight cold and couldn't attend the party, I immediately called Babe. He wasn't surprised and said, "It must be the beginning of the flu season since Millie Steel, Phyllis Boeger and my own Josephine are also not up to attending. So I guess we'll have a smaller party."

When I returned to the office around 7:00 PM, Ruth and Roy Jones were staring at the chalkboard while the other six trustees were discussing Joe Namath's new contract of $400,000, the largest ever given to a rookie. Suddenly a big cheer went up when the Mt. Carmel School, the first to report, showed Nick leading Jones by almost 4 to 1. A few minutes later the three precincts from River Grove gave Nick a 3 to 1 lead. Smith, Serpico and Collins smiled while Joe Farmar smugly said, "It's over. The coalition has won again. Let's party."

"You fellows can go now," Wade said, "but I'm going to wait. Two cities out of 14 do not speak for all."

Thirty minutes later Forest Park came in just about even-steven between Jones and Nick. Franklin Park followed and surprised all, giving Jones a 2 to 1 lead. In rapid fire order the remaining 10 cities reported. Jim Tarpey declared Knol a winner, but held off on Jones and Nick until he ran the figures twice by his computer.

Finally, with a lump in his throat, he declared Jones the winner by a narrow margin. Babe Serpico and Bob Collins, in a state of shock, couldn't believe it. They kept their calculators going. On the other hand Roy and Ruth, with arms around each other like newlyweds, walked over to Wade. Ruth gave Wade a kiss, saying, "We will never forget this day, Wade, and we owe it all to you. You are the quiet and brilliant one!"

In eight hours Wade's strategy, with Millie's brigade helping a lot, had turned a sure defeat into a narrow victory.

The coalition members meekly congratulated Jones as they left, not to party, but to commiserate over their loss. In a strong voice Wade offered them some parting words: "It was one helluva tough fight but if this college is going to be built we must bury the hatchets of yesterday. Tomorrow is the beginning of a reinforced board team."

They all nodded in unison, smiled and departed.

On Monday morning I got a call from Bob. "Herb, can you meet Babe and me for dinner tonight at the Golden Horns? We gotta talk."

I agreed.

When I arrived at the restaurant, they were both seated at a table, Babe sipping a coke and Bob with a martini. I joined them and ordered a Manhattan. In a laughing manner Bob asked me, "I know you're a smart guy, but can you tell me, why does a skeleton refuse to cross the road?"

"This is a new one. I don't know why the skeleton refuses to cross the road."

"Because it has no guts."

Babe injected, "Talking of guts, Roy Jones certainly fooled all of us. Here we thought he was gutless, but with a little help from Wade his guts overtook us. Bob and I underestimated him. We were told he was harmless, with very few friends. Bob, you gave me incorrect information. Now we know he's as good a politician as any one of us.

What it adds up to is that we have him for another three years."

Bob's face turned sour. He uttered an "ugh," projected his lower teeth forward and replied, "I don't like it, but if we must, we must. We quit too soon. If we'd worked another hour or two, Jones would have lost. Now tell me, Babe, did you use your Dead Men's Squadron?"

"No."

"Why not?"

"I thought we could win without their help. Besides that they've grown too efficient and too expensive.

"Excuse me," I interrupted, "I'm missing something here. What is the Dead Men's Squadron?"

"Gee, Herb, you are rather naive. A better name for this group would be the obituary boys. They're retirees who read the obituary column every day and take on the dead person's name for voting purposes. Most of them earn a buck or more every time they vote as directed by the party."

Babe declared with a broad smile, "My boys vote at least four times in each precinct and sometimes they cover four to five precincts. They're better trained than the Republican obituarians."

"That may be true but we never get caught."

"So what? When our boys get caught, we take care of our team members."

"How many of these men do you have working for you?" I asked.

"I can't tell you but the number is getting larger each day. As more people die our squadron gets larger."

I couldn't believe what I was hearing. Could it be true? Were these two well-established politicians exchanging tidbits of fraud and proudly boasting about it? I still didn't understand Chicago corruption. Surely my two trustees were exaggerating just to impress me with their so-called wisdom.

Bob asked, "Tell the truth now, who was really responsible for Kennedy's election?"

"Mayor Daley has been given most of the credit because he was in the command post, but I was the one who called in the precinct that put Kennedy over the top."

"Speaking of command post, who calls the signals at the college?" Bob asked.

"The board calls the signals and the college president carries them out in accordance with board policy," I replied.

"That sounds OK with me, but in the packet you sent us Friday night one of the five faculty members you submitted was not acceptable to Joe Farmar."

"Who was that?"

"Robert Dale for business manager. You know Joe wants Neil Neuson, the purchasing agent at Bekins, for the job. You interviewed him several weeks ago and haven't answered him. What happened?"

"He wasn't a strong candidate, and I haven't answered him since he never filed an application. I didn't think he was really interested. Our policy calls for 14 steps to follow before recommending anyone to the board. I assume you want me to follow the established policy."

Babe, looking straight at Bob as the commander in chief, said loudly, "Get Neil to file an official application. The president can't make any recommendation without one. Is that clear?"

"Yes, it is. I will tell Joe that he has to get Neil to go by the rules," Bob replied.

It was refreshing to hear the top boss support me in front of Bob, especially since Babe was emphasizing playing by the rules. As we started to eat I noticed Babe's huge plate: an extra large New York Steak with mushrooms and onions, and on the side mashed potatoes covered with gravy. His portion was large enough for two, while Bob and I each had a small fillet with boiled potatoes and a vegetable. I wondered if his heart could take it. I knew he wasn't concerned about the evils of red meat. He loved it. To finish off his meal he ordered a big piece of cheesecake and coffee with four lumps of sugar. I bypassed the dessert while Bob ordered Baileys Irish Cream for his cordial.

While we were all in a relaxed state Babe announced, "Mayor Daley wants me to quit the board. He feels it's taking me away from more important matters in the assessor's office. I can't keep up with all the material the college president keeps sending me. I never was much of a reader and it takes hours for me to digest his material. I spoke to Wade about resigning but he feels I should continue until my term is up, even if it means missing some of the meetings."

Bob and I were surprised at Babe's announcement and urged him to continue. He reluctantly agreed and then started to elaborate on what a privilege it was to work for the finest mayor in the nation, Richard Daley. He never would have gotten his job at the tax assessor's office if it hadn't been for his boss's influence. Turning to me he asked, "Now tell me about the five faculty jobs you're recommending to the board Wednesday night. Who is this Bob Dale?"

"Robert Dale is everything I've been looking for in a business manager. He holds a B.S. from Western Illinois and an M.S. in business management from Northern Illinois University, and is presently working for an advanced certificate in computer science. His experience as business manager at a Du Page school district is excellent, having sold several million in bonds at a low interest rate. He is married, has two school-age children, is highly personable and well versed in areas of school business management."

"Dr. Zeitlin, are you still set on computers?"

"Yes, definitely. Every record in the future will be on the computer. We have to keep up with the times and I want people who are willing to accept changes."

"I see you've finally come up with someone for the dean of technology. Where did you find Gordon Simonsen?"

"As a matter of fact he spotted us when he saw our announcement in the American Vocational Education Journal and applied for the position. Simonsen holds a B.S. and M.S. in Industrial Education from Bradley University and is presently the Director of Adult and Vocational Education in the Aurora High School district. Like Widergren, he's married with three children. He's a specialist in vocational education and will bring much federal and state money to our district. In addition he's a former faculty association president who negotiated salary issues with his board."

"Briefly, tell me about the other three."

"Dr. Victor Dye, the fourth doctorate to join us, comes to us with experience in counseling and guidance from Northwestern University.

"Bernard Verweil holds a B.A. and M.A. from Loyola University with experience as a journalism teacher at Loop College and a California community college. He'll be the advisor to the college newspaper.

"And finally, I'm recommending Tom McCabe, an experienced mathematics instructor with degrees from Northern Illinois University and Notre Dame University. I'm sure Joe Farmar will be pleased when a fellow alumnus joins us."

"Let me see now. So far you have on staff Drs. Widergren and Darnes, plus Miss Wilson, and now you're recommending five more men. That's seven men and one woman. I don't like the ratio. Can't you find more women and minorities?"

"Yes, we can, and will. Foremost in my mind is that we recruit well-qualified and experienced faculty. This we have done, and when school begins, our students will be welcomed by the best teachers anywhere. On the docket, waiting to be interviewed by Dr. Darnes, are several women and two black science instructors. While we want to hire minorities, we will not do so unless they are fully qualified as judged by the deans and me."

"Herb, our college will be a huge success if the student body and staff become a great mixing bowl. Now, I'm going to support all your recommendations Wednesday night provided you promise me that you'll add more women."

"I surely will," I said as I left the dinner meeting. I felt good, since I had received the top man's support. I also felt a little wiser having learned about the Dead Men's Squadron. I wondered about the integrity of the 45 judges appointed by Bob Collins and his political allies.

As I stepped into my office the following morning Maria informed me that Don Dunahow was waiting on the phone.

"What's up?" I asked.

"Herb, are you aware that Accurate Springs, a small manufacturing company, has completed a factory on a small segment of the Carey farm? Two and a half acres are gone, and month by month other segments will be sold until there will be nothing left for the college. Do you want that to happen?"

"Heavens no! What can we do to prevent it?"

"Can you use their new building for one of your shops?"

"Why, of course – with some modifications, that is."

"Good, I'll talk it over with the rest of the boys and if they agree, I'll file a condemnation suit next week. I'll show their attorney they can't sell the property while we're in the middle of negotiating. That SOB will be sorry he turned down my offer." He hung up.

At lunch time I decided to visit Accurate Springs again. The building of over 100,000 square feet, located in the far end of Palmer Street, looked good. It was clean and neat, light and bright, had a high voltage system, plenty of parking and ample space for faculty offices. I only wished Dean Simonsen would get on the job fast so we could decide what shop or shops would be in the building. How lucky could I get? Here was a shop built by others and ready to be used for the college upon the opening of school. Would it happen? Don assured me it was a sure thing. I knew if we went to court it would take a long time. All Don had to do was get a cash settlement. Could he do it? We would wait and see.

WANTED: A Name For New Suburban College

Know if a good name for a college?

The members of he Junior College District 300 (hardly a proper name) are looking for a good one.

The junior college, expected to be constructed within the next two years, will serve graduates of Elmwood Park, Leyden and Proviso Township High Schools in liberal arts, commercial and technical instruction for two years. It will offer many courses for adult education in the evenings.

It has already aquired its president, a distinguisher California educator, Dr. Herbert Zeitlin, who has assumed duties in the board's temporary offices at 1829 Broadway, Melrose Park.

"A good name means a lot to a college," Dr. Zeitlin told The Peacock Newspapers Monday. "I'm sure it will help us in establishing this facility for the North West Suburban area.

Termed provisionally the Community College and Technical Institute (another tongue-twister, according to board chairman Wade Steele and Zeitlin) the college is in need of a good monicker.

Suggestions So Far

Already suggested to Zeitlin and board members have been:

DR. KEITLIN

North College, Cook County College, John F. Kennedy College, North West College (too similar to Northwestern).

Name droppers for the new college are asked to send their suggestions to Dr. Herbert Zeitlin at 1829 Broadway, Melrose Park.

There's no big cash giveaway, but the winning entry will give itts author an immense sense of satisfaction and (and this doesn't happen everyday of the week) a chance to brag to his friends: "See that college? I named it."

Village Firemen

286

22
College Named at 21st Meeting

When I arrived at the 21st official meeting of the board on Wednesday, April 14th, to my surprise the room was filled with many strangers, plus several reporters. Something big was about to happen, I thought. I was correct when Jim Tarpey showed me the sign-in sheet. There in bold black ink was the signature of Louis Ancel, the most powerful school attorney in Illinois, followed by a dozen other signatures representing Accurate Springs.

Wade called the meeting to order at 8:05 PM, with all trustees present. In an instant the short man with a most dynamic voice stood up and said, "Mr. Chairman, may I have the floor? I promise not to be long. This concerns the college's future and the future of my client." Wade, departing from the agenda, acknowledged his request.

"This morning I agreed to represent the Accurate Springs Company when they heard that your attorney was going to file a condemnation proceeding against them."

He stared at Don Dunahow with contempt, waited a few seconds like a good actor, and continued. "I have three words of advice for you. 'DON'T DO IT!' Should you proceed you'll be very sorry. You'll force me to tie up the college in a long and expensive litigation suit. Building your campus will be delayed many years. If you want that to happen, do the stupid thing."

He then introduced Mr. Gillis, the company treasurer, who told the board that his company had invested a lot of money in the plant, feeling it would be an asset to the community. A delay in the start-up, scheduled for the following month, would be very costly.

Wade thanked the 12 men and women from Accurate Springs for coming and promised a reply very soon. With anger on their faces they left, clearing out the front row.

After a few moments of deep, silent stares at each other by the trustees, Wade called the meeting to order again. Fred moved that the minutes of the two previous meetings be accepted. It was seconded and carried.

Of major concern was the long-delayed decision on the naming of the college. Bob Collins displayed a folder, over two inches thick, containing suggestions for a name made by several thousand people over a period of a year. No clear majority was in favor of any particular name. The board was frustrated! They'd declared a name would be selected after the election. That day had arrived, and still nothing seemed to click.

I looked through my folder of college names as I prepared to answer any questions that might come up. Among the famous, John F. Kennedy led the list with over 400 votes, followed by Eisenhower, Hoover and Mayor Richard Daley. Next in popularity, with over 100 votes each, were West Suburban, Futura, Proviso-Leyden, Crescent, Bataan, North, Des Plaines and Rotary.

My eyes focused on Rotary, my first choice. How great it would be if Rotary College became a reality. Millions could be tapped from the Rotary Foundation. Scholars from throughout the world would stop over on our campus. Eventually we'd construct the Paul Harris International Building to house our foreign visitors and students.

My dream bubble burst badly when Sister Candida, President of Rosary College, wrote us stating, "...I hope you will not consider it an intrusion for me to say that the choice of such a name might cause confusion for both colleges...."

Later when I spoke to her on the phone she emphatically emphasized, forcefully stressed and accentuated the point to avoid the name Rotary College. After reviewing the issue with Wade we acquiesced to her wishes.

Other names submitted included:

Abysis	Denwood-Vista	Lincoln
Allright	Dave Everette	Martin Luther King
Aux Plaine	Douglas MacArthur	Mary McCloud Bethune
Barbara Lynn Gracious	Elmwood Heights	Olympic
Choice	Eureka Heights	Orbit
Claude La Framboise	Founders	Oxford
Cordell Hull	John Glenn	Pioneer
Crescent	Leonard Koos	Ponce de Leon
	Leyden-Vista	Pro- ley

Prodent	Tom Dooley
Providence	Tri-West
Reno Heights	West Cook
Sir Isaac Newton	West Towns
Thatcher Woods	Yonders
Three Oaks	Zenith

While I was waiting for something to happen, I recalled Roy Jones once suggesting at a closed executive session, with great sincerity, that the college be named after one of its creators. When they'd tried the idea out for size it hadn't exactly clicked. For instance: Steel College, heaven forbid, might be known as Steal College. Lowe College would turn into Low College and the football team become the low ballers. And as for Knoeppel College, the students might shorten it to Nipple College and the football team be called the Milking Boys. For several minutes each one had tried to outdo the other with wisecracks.

Wade had called a halt. "Let's stop this nonsense. I assure you that none of us ever expected to have a college named after him, so let's quit cold."

"Wade, at the right time," Joe Farmar had said, "We'll name the science building after you."

That was a pleasant flashback. Now, here we were at the 21st meeting of the board and we still couldn't reach a decision on a college name. When we'd first launched the campaign to have the community decide, we thought it would be short and simple. It wasn't! Thousands had participated, hundreds of names had come forth, but no name had an acceptable ring.

The audience waited for the trustees to say something. Finally Elmore Boeger, in his Gregory Peck manner, recommended the name *Triton*, explaining that Tri represented the three school districts that made up the college area. Secondly, he recalled that the name "Princeton" was an abbreviation of "Princetown." So, Tri-towns would become Triton. He also pointed out that Triton was a Greek sea god who used a three-pronged weapon known as the trident to control the seas.

Silence fell over the group. Someone in the audience called out, "How about John F. Kennedy College?"

Immediately we heard, "I like Eisenhower College," followed by "We should honor the greatest mayor in the nation by naming the college the Richard J. Daley Community College."

All of a sudden several sharp-tongued persons penetrated the trustee area with their favorite names. Wade called for order. After a lengthy discussion in which other names were considered, it became the general consensus that Triton Community College and Technical Institute would be most appropriate.

Elmore Boeger made the motion, seconded by Fred Knol and unanimously carried. Strangely enough, no further backlash developed.

Under new business I recommended the hiring of Janet LaDere and Rose Bernhart as part-time office personnel. It was approved without questions.

Next I discussed in detail the five faculty appointments under schedule 4. To my surprise the trustees complimented me on finding such well-qualified instructors but I was taken aback when Joe Farmar made the motion to accept schedule 4 with the exception of the business manager and the dean of technology. He said he needed more time to study the folders of these two administrators. Bob Collins almost immediately echoed the remark. Looking for support, I caught Babe's eye. He smiled and then turned his eyes to Farmar. Wade was staring straight ahead. Fred Knol seconded the motion and it was unanimously carried.

I was hurting on the inside when it came to me that by saying no to the tech dean and possibly to future administrative posts, Joe was punishing me for not recommending Neil Neuson. I wanted to object but could not; Wade was moving rapidly along with the agenda.

Approval was given to the president to rent additional office space, apartment #11, and also to have William Gurrie prepare the following year's college budget.

The question of a temporary facility for the operation of the college in the fall came forth. Elmore Boeger reported that the Leyden School Board was receptive to the college's using West Leyden High School after 4:00 PM. Final details would be worked out ASAP.

Dean Widergren stated that over 500 students had returned their senior survey forms. This was vital in planning the curriculum of the college. A college calendar similar to West Leyden's was accepted without any comments.

A long discussion started with my recommendation for awarding the printing of the college catalog to the lowest bidder. As the acting business manager for the past eight months, I had followed standard business procedure in advertising for bids, using the same specifications I'd used the previous year at Southwestern College. Four written bids had come in, with a wide variation in prices. The highest bid, more than twice the lowest, had come from a local printer. Babe couldn't understand the great difference in price and felt we'd receive inferior workmanship if the contract went to the North State Press in Hammond, Indiana. Boeger felt that to maintain good will with local vendors, preference should be given to them, but only if their quotes were competitive. In this case the local printer was way out of line and had to be rejected.

Joe Farmar motioned to accept the lowest bid. It was seconded by Fred Knol and carried 6 to 0. In a sulky mood, Babe decided not to vote, since the highest bidder was one of his fellow Kiwanians and voting against him would be considered a betrayal. He accepted his friend's loss of the contract and said, "I have to tell Alex the results. He has to be more competitive, but next year he can try again."

I remembered Alex well from when John and I had spoken to the Melrose Park Kiwanis Club. He'd been exceptionally nice to us, but being supportive of the college movement did not guarantee special privileges to a vendor. I remembered very well serving as the purchasing agent for the Carter Coal Company in Radio City, New York many years before. The nicest and smoothest sales agents, relying on their personalities to guarantee an order, had generally been the least competitive.

The next item for discussion was the North Central accreditation. I reviewed the long, drawn-out procedure and examination that usually followed and stressed the urgency of developing a board policy book and a faculty handbook. Wade then appointed himself, Joseph Farmar, Robert Collins and Roy Jones to act as a committee to formulate board policies, rules and regulations.

Continuing with my report I mentioned the talk I had with architect Fox and the State Superintendent's representative Robert Birkheimer. Since there'd never been a community college built in the state of Illinois, he recommended that we visit the state where the best and most were, California. It was moved, seconded and carried by Boeger and Serpico that the architect, college president, and trustees be authorized to visit colleges in California.

While I was upset about not having my deans, I was surprised and pleased that finally the board and I would see the best in the western area. Fast, unanimous approval was given without discussion; no one even mentioned the expense. I felt, regardless of the cost, that it was essential the eyes of the board be opened to the state where the community college was not the last choice, but the first preference, of students.

Secretary Collins then read the final item, the bills to be paid. A big wow went up from several persons in the audience when Bob called out the Kirie's restaurant bill of $444. Instantly Neil Mehler stood up, representing himself and a few other reporters, and asked, "What was that for?"

No one answered. He'd caught us by surprise. I said nothing. Finally Wade said, "The success of the bond election was due to many volunteers working long hours to promote the cause. The board decided to award them by giving them a late dinner for their work."

"That's not what I heard," Neil retorted. "I heard there was a wild and drunken ball for the trustees and their wives. Now, Wade, is that the proper use of taxpayers' money?"

"We thought it was, since we pay our election judges for their dinner and these individuals worked just as hard, if not harder, than the judges."

With that Wade adjourned the meeting and all of the trustees disappeared from the scene in a hurry.

The next morning Joe got me on the phone and yelled, "Herb, how in the hell could you do such a stupid thing as to put the Kirie bill on the bills to be paid?"

"It's the standard procedure we've been following for many meetings."

"That's no excuse. Fuck standard procedure – use common sense. For God's sake, get smart! Put it on your expense account so that it will be covered up. The trustees expect you to pay for all luncheons and dinners with us, and there will be plenty. I'll talk to Wade about giving you a special account of $2,000 for dinners and entertainment. It's the usual practice for all college presidents in Illinois. Now, damn it, don't you ever embarrass the trustees like that again." He banged down the phone.

For the first time in our eight-month relationship Joe had yelled at me nonstop. He was more than upset, he was sizzling. He demanded that I follow his orders, and didn't want any dialogue. My gastric juices were once again boiling over, so I skipped lunch and drove to Wade's office for direction.

Wade informed me that it was perfectly legal to use taxpayers' money for lunches or dinners with trustees, as long as the purpose was to discuss school matters. It was standard practice in the state of Illinois; he'd been doing it for many years. Instead of giving me an annual grant he proposed that the cost of the luncheons be added to my regular expenses and submitted to the board monthly. I agreed.

23
World Built on Tips and Favors

When I returned to the office, Attorney Dunahow was on the line. "Herb, I want to pick you up for lunch at the Golden Horns tomorrow at 1:00 PM. Is that OK?" I agreed.

As we were driving along North Avenue the next day, Dunahow declared, "The boys asked me to talk to you about city politics. Do you know why you were hired?"

"Yes, I thought I was the most qualified. Isn't that correct?"

"Yes, it is, but you were put over the top when you said you could work with politicians. To tell the truth, you're not working well with us."

"With a few exceptions, I thought we were getting along fine."

"Those few exceptions are very important. For instance, Wednesday night you made two big blunders. First, you publicly rejected Alex's bid for the printing contract, knowing he was a dear friend of Babe's. If you'd called Babe in advance, Alex would have submitted a revised bid."

"But that's not following the state rules on awarding contracts."

"Oh come on, now. Rules are broken every day. My job is to find the ways and means of breaking rules, and I'm damned good at it. Secondly, why didn't you ask me how to cover up the $444 bill from Farmar's party? I would have given you several alternatives. Thus far, you have two strikes against you. I just don't want to see you strike out, and you're close to it now."

I said nothing as we got out of the car. But I was greatly disturbed and decided to listen and learn more about his methods of deception. He ordered a martini and an elaborate luncheon, while I had a ham sandwich with iced coffee. He discussed the Watts riots in Los Angeles. I felt very sad that the racial issue had exploded, and stressed the need for better understanding. He, on the other hand, felt the best solution was to ship all those niggers back to Africa. I mourned the passing of Winston Churchill, while he was happy over his death. He said that Churchill was overrated and had tricked FDR into getting us into the war. I was 46 years old and Don was 66. We were more than 20 years apart in thinking. As he continued talking I realized that we lived in two different worlds, one believing in greed, the other believing in fairness.

As I tried paying the check he grabbed it away from me, saying, "This is my party, don't insult me."

While driving back Don mentioned that the boys hadn't liked my rejecting Ellen Atkinson. It was an insult to Mayor Daley's office.

"Please tell me, has the coalition liked any of my appointments?"

"Babe was elated when you hired his sister-in-law as your secretary. Bob Collins's spirits were overwhelmed when you put Jim Tarpey to work, and my stock went up with my wife many points when Dr. Widergren hired my wife's girlfriend, Virginia Sybilla."

"Don, please keep in mind these individuals were hired not because of connections but because of their proven ability."

"That's easy for you to say, but without these connections they never would have entered the front door. Now tell me, how are they doing?"

"They're doing fine. As a matter of fact they're all superior workers."

"We want you to hire one more superior worker. His name is Neil Neuson. Why are you fighting this?"

"Neil does not appear to be interested in the job. He hates computers and has never filed an application."

"He doesn't need an application, since Joe knows him well. Between the two of them they'll run the business office. May I impress upon you, your job is to keep your nose out of that office. You've already proven you don't know how to handle contracts. Need I say more?"

The car had reached our office. Don turned off the ignition and we stared at each other in dead silence. "Dr. Zeitlin, if you cooperate with us you'll be a wealthy man when you retire. Haven't you noticed that when those big university presidents retire, they're always granted great annuity packages by their boards? The bigger the annuity the more completely they'd cooperated with the politicians. Your main function is to talk like an educator, act like an educator, pretend to love humanity, build the curriculum and always remember to stay out of the business office."

"Why is that so important?"

"Politicians need to have a little gravy."

"How much is a little gravy?"

"Good politicians deserve a tip of at least 10% to 20% on most deals. That's the same rate you generally give a waitress."

"If that's so, how do you explain Joe Pulitano, Babe's dear friend, who tried sell us some office furniture? His bid was $400 for desks that we eventually obtained for $200."

"Babe explained that he's a gonif and was kicked out of our circle."

"What if I insist upon Robert Dale as the business manager?"

"Your days will be numbered. You'll be out fast. We don't want to see anything bad happen to you."

"What do you mean? What can happen to me?"

"I mean you'll never get a recommendation for a future job. The board will think of some way to dismiss you and you can expect it to be ugly. However, we don't want to see that happen. Wise up, play ball with us and we'll make you a hero."

I said nothing, rubbed my head and was about to leave when Don stopped me and said, "You know, Dr. Zeitlin, if you read between the lines in the Bible, you'll discover that when Jesus was born the three wise men – who were nothing but business traders – brought gifts to Mary and Joseph. And for what purpose? They were tipping the Lord's parents because they expected favors in the future. The world is built upon tips and favors and the sooner you know that the better it will be for all of us. All people in positions of influence are constantly receiving tips. The bigger the tip, the larger the favor requested. As a lifelong Republican I've given many tips and have received just as many. And that is the way of the world. Do you get it?"

I returned to the office, somewhat stultified by the conversation. Maria had just gotten off the phone. When she saw me, she started to cry. I tried to console her, touched her shoulder and asked, "Is there some death in your family?"

"No, no," as the tears burst out all over.

"Is somebody ill?" She grabbed her handkerchief and stopped sobbing.

"No, no."

"Did you have a fight with Tony?"

She looked at me, mascara streaming down her cheeks, and quietly said, "I'm worried about you. What's going to happen to you?"

"What do you mean? I'm happy, have some ups and downs but I'm in good health."

"I heard you had some differences with the board. You're a wonderful person, filled with such vitality, and you have such a great family. I don't want to see any harm come to you."

"Oh come on, now. Nothing is going to happen. We'll talk over our differences and we'll work it out."

She pulled herself together and continued to type as I closed the door to my office and started to analyze her remarks. I knew she was very close to her brother-in-law, Babe, and kept him informed of all my activities. That was OK. I had told all the trustees to drop in anytime and I would post them on my daily activities. Bob and Joe took me at my word and dropped in two or three times a week; Babe, Fred and Roy less frequently. So now, what was the coalition planning? I had no idea. I would have to wait and see.

At 10:00 AM the following day, Saturday, April 14th, I got a clue as the board gathered to canvass the recent trustee election. They were not their usual jolly selves. While Steel and Jones greeted me pleasantly, the others said nothing. The coalition boys next to us were unsocial, and I was ignored. Joe's first comment as he looked directly at Wade and me was, "Let's get this damned canvass over with quickly. I have things to do this afternoon."

An hour and a half later the canvass was completed. Secretary Collins read a resolution validating the results. The resolution was moved, seconded and carried by Boeger and Collins. The annual organization meeting was scheduled for noon. We had 30 minutes to kill.

As Roy, Wade and I sipped some coffee on the stage of the Little Theater the three attorneys, led by Joe Farmar, had a sidebar conference nearby with the other coalition boys.

"What are they hatching up now?" Roy asked.

"I don't know. It's a toss-up – will Bob or Joe be the new board president?" Wade whispered. "Who do you think it will be, Roy?"

"It would be damned stupid if they didn't elect you president again, and those boys are not noted for doing stupid things."

"I wouldn't be too sure of that. They know your strong support from Franklin Park came from Millie's brigade. Their revenge will not be sweet for me."

"Could they be discussing the business manager's position? Bob and Joe had plenty of time to study Dale's dossier. They're just stalling for time so that their lackey will get it. Are you going to let that happen, Dr. Zeitlin?"

"I'm trying desperately to prevent it."

At exactly noon Wade called the 23rd official meeting to order and had Don Dunahow administer the oath of office to the newly reelected trustees, Fred Knol and Roy Jones. In very swift order Wade was unanimously reelected president of the board after Joe Farmar nominated him.

The board secretary's salary was increased to $100 monthly and then Bob Collins was reelected.

Smith was reappointed board attorney.

Meetings were to be scheduled twice a month.

I was surprised when the short meeting adjourned without any comments and the coalition members disappeared fast.

Wade and I wondered, why such a short meeting? Roy said, "Fred told me that Joe had called for a luncheon meeting at Kirie's at 12:30. We were not invited. Why not?"

I told Wade and Roy about my luncheon with Smith and his urgent message that I recommend Neil Neuson or else. "The *or else* bothers me. Should I drop the best candidate, Robert Dale, and recommend Neil Neuson, the incompetent, to satisfy Joe?"

Wade suggested that I withdraw Dale's name and continue to serve as the acting business manager. He complimented me on obtaining such a good printing contract. He felt it was the only way to go. By continuing as business manager I would retain control of the money. Roy, on the other hand, urged me to push for Dale's and Simonsen's appointments. I left the two in a quandary.

My world had changed so much in two weeks. I walked on air when the bond issue had passed due to the efforts of a united board. Now the board was divided, and, as I discovered, corrupt. What was I to do? I felt betrayed by Bob Collins. He was no brother but a tool of the coaltion.

Late that night, after the kids had gone to bed, I reviewed my options with Eugenia. She was greatly surprised and amazed at what I told her. She ruled out completely the thought of working with a corrupt board and said, "You must resign. We'll go back to California."

"My dear, there is no going back. I can't get my old job back. They've hired someone new. I intend to serve out my three-year term regardless of how stormy it may become.

"If worse comes to worse you stay home and look after the kids and I'll get a teaching or counseling job." We continued to speculate on other options into the night.

On Monday morning I called Dr. Leroy Knoeppel, who had freely offered to help me if the going got tough. In September he told me that the coalition was a bunch of crooks. I hadn't believed him at the time. Now that I knew the truth, did Dr. Knoeppel have the wisdom to tell me how to deal with crooks?

After lunch with him in the faculty dining room, we adjourned to his office. His first question was, "How are you doing?"

"Two weeks ago, after the success of the bond issue, I felt I was doing great. Today I'm frustrated."

"Why?"

I proceeded to tell him about the Dunahow dialogue and ended up saying, "What you told me seven months ago was true. I am now dealing with a coalition of thieves. My question to you is, can I work with them?"

"You know, Herb, I've been following your progress very closely. Your news items were good, your personal contacts have been many and your election techniques were superior. But you have one serious fault."

I was taken aback by his sincerity. "And what is that one fault?"

He smiled. "You are too nice to everyone. You want to be liked and try to please all. Continue to do that and you'll end up pleasing no one. Do you know what happens to nice guys?"

"No, please tell me."

"They always finish last and then fade away. Do you want that to happen to you?"

"Of course not. What do you suggest I do?"

"Toughen up. Roy told me about your disappointment when your recommendations for business mñnager were rejected. Don't let it happen to Robert Dale. He's a good man. Our office is presently using his manual on accounting procedures."

"Exactly what do you propose I do?"

"Start sounding off at the board meetings. Keeping it inside will get you sick. You know you're neglecting your strongest ally."

"And who is that?"

"The general public that created the college. Don't hesitate to challenge any trustee when you know you're right. And when you correct him look at the audience, and particularly the press. They're listening to every word you say and will always stick by you if they know you're for clean government."

"I've always been reluctant to correct a trustee at a public board meeting. I don't want to embarrass them or appear to be a smart-ass."

"Wake up, Herb, the journalists are with you. They're suspicious of the political coalition. They generally have contempt for politicians and love to expose misbehavior. I'm surprised the press didn't pick up on Babe's disappointment at his friend's not getting the printing contract. Serpico exposed his leaning when he refused to vote for the lowest bidder. Give the coalition a little more rope and they may hang themselves."

"Dr. Knoeppel, I don't want to see any trustee in a hanging state. If they're on the wrong track, I'll try to get them back on the right one. That's my job as the executive officer of the board."

"If you bend to their wish on the business manager's position, it won't be the last time. You'll be bending regularly."

"No, it shall not happen. I am determined this time to stand firm on Bob Dale as the boss of the business office, regardless of the consequences. His name will again be on the board agenda next week."

"Good luck, Herb. My office will support you."

As I drove back to the office I thought about the differences in style between Wade Steel and Leroy Knoeppel. Wade was soft-spoken, a great listener, and geared to resolving differences through mediation. Leroy was a dynamic speaker, quick on the draw, with no room for compromise on the vital issues. While their styles were quite different both were highly successful chief administrators. When I got home that night, I told Eugenia how much I'd learned from Wade and Leroy. I'd recently received invitations to their retirement dinners, a week apart. We were both looking forward to the events.

The following evening, just as I was about to leave for home, Bob called. "Herb, we gotta talk. Can you meet Joe and me in your office at 9:00 tonight?" Even though it was rather late I agreed, knowing that the clean-up crew usually finished around 8:45.

At last, after the two-week silent treatment, Bob was speaking to me again. I had high hopes that our differences would be settled and we would get on with staffing the college.

24
Ferocious Farmer Fight Foiled

A s I walked into the office Joe turned around and slammed the door shut. He was sizzling and cried out loudly, "You're going to hire Neil Neuson or else you'll become another crippled son-of-a-bitch."

He seemed out of control as he advanced toward me with his bloodshot eyes. You could smell the booze emanating from his body. He wanted to fight. He shoved me against the wall. I didn't feel like putting up my dukes. Would it be a fair match? A 6' 2" drinker weighing in at around 260 pounds versus a 5' 9" athlete of 145 pounds? Could a lightweight father of four defeat an intoxicated father of six? Not likely, but possible.

A flashback came to my mind. Stupid Herbie, at age 12, had taken on Willie Furley, age 15, the bully that threatened the kids on Schaeffer Street. Willie had just grabbed Herbie's baked potato, which he'd nurtured in the street bonfire. Herbie ran after Willie, caught him and hit him with his bonfire stick. With ease Willie punched Herbie in the nose, drawing blood. As Herbie fell down Willie broke the stick in half and laughed. An infuriated Herbie stood up, the blood gushing, and tackled Willie. They both fell to the ground. As the combatants got up Willie threatened to make Herbie into a meatball in minutes, and began pursuing him.

Suddenly, Willie felt two fists hitting his back. Lo and behold, Lenny, Herbie's big brother, age 14, joined in with a swinging attack He denounced Willie. "You damn bully, why don't you fight someone your own size? Leave my kid brother alone."

Lenny changed positions and landed a hard right and left to Willie's solar plexus, causing him to bend over. Seeing his opportunity, little Herbie tucked in his head and with the speed of a cannonball hit Willie in the vital spot between his legs. Willie collapsed in pain. Crying out, "You hurt me," he picked up his cap and retreated to his family's flat down the street. A cheer went up from the bystanders. Bobby Doolittle shouted, "Hurrah for the Zeitlins for getting rid of the bastard of Schaeffer Street."

Now, 33 years later, I faced another bully in a small office in Melrose Park, with nobody to help me. As Joe advanced toward me, breathing hard, I knew he wanted me to strike the first blow. Then he would have a real excuse to clobber me, and Bob would be his witness that I hit him first. I said nothing.

Joe yelled out, "Dr. Zeitlin, we've given you everything you wanted. Now it's your turn to give us something."

Oh, how I wished my brother Lenny were there to rescue me again. If I hit Joe, I could duck and dance away as he tried to connect. During my junior high school days I was considered one of the best fighters on campus, but I still didn't want to hit the intoxicated lawyer from Notre Dame. It could lead to a horrible ending.

I turned to Bob Collins in a desperate plea for help. He quietly said, "Herb, Joe doesn't want to hurt you, but you just have to cooperate with us."

"And that cooperation must begin right now. So what do you say, Mr. President?" Joe added.

"What do you want me to do?"

"Damn it. You know what you're supposed to do. Just recommend Neil as your new business manager to the board Wednesday night. Praise him and Bob and I will follow up with additional complimentary remarks. You've got to convince the trustees and the general public that after an exhaustive search he was your number one choice."

"I'm sorry, I just can't do it."

"Why not?"

"Because Neil Neuson is not qualified. He has no college experience, lacks a master's degree, dislikes working with computers and has no professional references. All he told me was that he's been the purchasing agent for Bekins for the last few years and that he would like working with you."

"And what's wrong with that? Mayor Daley has dozens of his

friends working for him who don't have master's degrees. Most of them learn on the job, and look at what a great city Chicago is."

"It doesn't work that way in higher education. This college has great potential, but it will never achieve it if we hire inexperienced personnel. Besides that, I can't lie to the general public – or to myself."

"Oh, yes, you will, or you won't walk out of this office tonight."

With that remark Bob turned to the front door and threw the top latch. I now knew where I stood with brother Bob. The two of them must have planned this showdown prior to coming to the office. They'd needed the extra booze to carry it out. I was scared. What were they going to do to me? Why hadn't I listened to Waddie Deddah and the others when I was in California? I wondered if I would ever see Eugenia or my four kids again. Fear overtook me. I once read that the Mafia's first warning was a broken leg or arm. The second warning was a bomb that went off when you started up your car. Or they would arrange a fatal auto accident for you. The final treatment: a resting place in Lake Michigan in a large oil drum filled with concrete. My throat became very tight and dry. I couldn't speak as I sat down in a chair next to the conference table.

Bob sat down in the adjacent chair. Joe put on his black fur-lined gloves. With fire in his eyes he advanced towards me.

"Please, may I have a cup of coffee?" I uttered.

"Surely, let me get it for you, Herb," Bob immediately responded. "Do you want cream and sugar with it?"

"Cream only, no sugar." Biting his tongue, Joe showed great annoyance. He wanted to get it over with.

Bob noticed Joe's impatience. "Joe, you just wait. It's better for all concerned that we have no violence."

As I sipped my coffee I realized that I'd be at their mercy if I didn't agree to hire Neal. I put my coffee down, dropped my head and covered my eyes with both hands.

Bob interpreted my body language as surrender. He said, "Here, take another sip. Things will be all right now that you've agreed."

At that I spit out the coffee over my white shirt and started coughing. As I made a slight turn toward Bob my coffee spilled into his lap. He jumped up immediately and ran toward the bathroom. I ran to the door, unlatched the lock and got out. It happened so fast that it left

Joe in a paralytic state.

My little Skylark started instantly. I backed up with haste and headed toward the Eisenhower Expressway, keeping a steady eye on all mirrors. If there were to be a chase I d give them a run like they never had before. After I hit 75 on the expressway my rational mind returned. I slowed down, feeling those two white collar crooks were too drunk to follow. But they weren't too intoxicated to contact some henchmen. I needed time to think, so I stopped at the Palmer House and had some tea.

Should I call the police? The threat on my life had occurred in Melrose Park, where Babe Serpico was the Godfather and the police took their orders from him. So that wouldn't work. I was a resident of Elmwood Park, so was Joe Farmar, and he had the police and mayor in his pocket. So, Herb, don't even try!

Was River Grove, the future home of the college, a possibility? Mayor O'Connor, Bob's uncle, had told me to take my cotton-picking hands off the River Grove site. He'd be delighted to have me locked up on any excuse. My last resort was the city police of Chicago. I could ask for protection but would they be likely to give it to me? It would be my word against Collins's and attorney Farmar's, and they'd deny that anything had happened. After all, a shove against the wall might not be considered significant. A broken nose or black eye would have helped the case.

They scared the hell out of me and that may have been their purpose. It would have worked had I agreed, but since I hadn't, they would try another method of persuasion. I would talk this out with Wade tomorrow.

I slowly drove back to Elmwood Park with my head on a swivel, noticing everything. As I approached my Cortland Parkway home I was surprised to see that the streetlight directly opposite my house was out, making my driveway very dark. Could Joe or Bob have a hood in waiting to attack me? It was possible. What should I do? My doctorate from Stanford hadn't prepared me for this. As I drove away I kept repeating to myself, "Use common sense, use common sense."

If a hood were waiting to attack me how would he get away? There were no car parked on my side of Cortland Parkway, so he must have had an accomplice drop him off and waiting nearby to pick him up. Or was he planning to take my car after knocking me out? I drove to North Avenue, parked under a bright light, opened my trunk, took out a ball peen hammer and a heavy open end wrench. If all else failed my industrial arts tools would be my protection.

I drove back to Cortland Parkway and parked over a block away with my lights off and doors locked. I kept my eyes focused on 7919 and waited. Within the hour three cars drove by, but none of them slowed down or stopped. Around one o'clock in the morning I decided to move and drove into the driveway, flashing my upper and lower beams. I blew my horn twice, hoping to scare away the hidden menace. My inside coat pocket held the open end wrench while the hammer was hidden under my sleeve. I opened the garage door, parked the car and quickly entered my home from the back porch, without incident. I immediately double-bolted the locks, breathed a sigh of relief and thanked God for helping me.

I went upstairs, where a small hall light was on. Eugenia had dozed off, like the sleeping beauty she was, with a book beside her. Mark was snoring. Joyce was smiling in her sleep. Ann Victoria had a worried look on her face while Clare had the covers, which I removed, over hers. My eyes grew misty as I thought about the night's adventures, which I could not yet share with the family. The fear of not seeing them again had been the worst nightmare of my life.

"I can't believe Joe or Bob meant you any harm," Wade said with a puzzled look after I described the previous night's frightening experience. "Joe, an officer in the U.S. Navy, and from a fine family background, just doesn't fit the stereotype of a hood."

"If I hadn't run out when I did, there would have been blood spilled, and mostly mine. Joe said if I didn't cooperate I'd leave the office a crippled son-of-a-bitch. Wade, please be honest with me, are these two men members of the Mafia?"

"Herb, I really don't know. . .Bob's mentor is Elmer Conti, and I suspect Elmer is. I've seen Conti talking, or rather directing, two strange heavies prior to a meeting of the Leyden Municipal League. And, as everyone knows, Joe takes his orders from Jim Kirie, the River Grove restaurant owner and head of the Leyden Democratic Party. Jim's restaurant has never been bombed, and he's told me it never will

be since he knows how to work with the mob. And Babe has told me
he likes playing poker with Tony Accardo, who's helped River Forest
Catholic churches with financial aid to their schools. Accardo's not
interested in such a small fry thing as a local community college."

"You're joking about Babe playing cards with Tony Accardo,
aren't you?"

"I don't think so. At the mention of Tony's name people show
Babe more respect."

"My God, what have I got myself into? I don't think I can carry on."

"Herb, if you live in Chicagoland any length of time you'll find that
anyone of any importance has had some contact with the Mafia or
friends of the mob. They enjoy boasting about it. I've been with the
Leyden district for over 30 years but I don't ever recall making any
school deals with those guys. The mob goes where the big money is –
booze, dice, vice, dope, labor and the big building contracts. You must
remember the Mafia boys have large families and they want the best
schools and parks for their kids just like anyone else. They have no
intention of exploiting the schools."

"Are you sure?"

"Only time will tell. You carry on with what has to be done and I'll
support you. Please don't leave us now. I admire how you've begun.
You're very creative and imaginative and we need you."

Wade's complimentary remarks lifted my spirits. I drove to 1829
Broadway. When I arrived, Maria and Virginia Sybilla were talking
quietly. As I opened the door the conversation suddenly stopped.
Virginia stared at me, looked me over from head to foot and left. It
seemed like she expected to see an injured president. I didn't know
if she was disappointed or not. Maria told me that Bob Dale had called
and hoped I could get back to him immediately.

Dale informed me that he'd received another offer and had to give
them an answer within a week. We talked for about ten minutes as I
tried to explain the reason for the delay. I promised him that his name
would be submitted again to the board and, hopefully, fully approved
this time. By this point I was determined to have Dale join us, regardless
of the consequences. I was ready to negotiate my exit should the board
suggest another delay.

As I hung up Maria came in smiling and offered me a hot cup of coffee with cookies. "Did you bake these?" I asked.

"No, Virginia baked them last night. They're real good. Here, take a handful. She felt you'd need them today."

I thanked Maria as she left. Suddenly a horrible thought entered my head. Could those two be plotting my destruction? That their chatter had turned to silence when I arrived was not a good sign, particularly since Virginia had stared at me, amazed that I wasn't injured. I thought and thought. A few days ago Maria had cried and expressed concern about "What will happen to the president?" She might have overheard Babe giving orders to Bob and Joe to rough me up a little. Smith had given me a warning. I knew something was coming, but I never expected Joe to reach that ferocious state. I smelled the cookies and coffee. They smelled good, but I decided not to eat or drink, remembering the days of ancient Rome when the Emperor would be disposed of with poisoned wine or grapes. Virginia was a dear friend of the Smiths, but was she also a mob plant?

An hour later Maria came in and had me sign some letters. She was surprised that I hadn't touched any of the goodies and asked, "They're so good. May I take one?"

"Why, of course." She proceeded to gobble one down with gusto. I wondered if she was reading my mind when she said, "Don't worry, nothing is going to happen to you. Please try one."

I took a small one, put it in my mouth and started to chew. Maria smiled and left. I refused to let her know I was suspicious. I spit out the contents into my handkerchief. If only I could find a microbiologist to examine under the microscope what I had tasted.

Around one o'clock I went home for lunch with Eugenia while the kids were in school. She asked me how it had gone with Farmar and Collins the night before. I knew if I blurted out the details she'd insist on my resigning. After Wade's encouraging remarks I didn't want to quit, so I said, "Well, we have some differences on hiring procedures but I'm sure we can work it out eventually."

I placed the dirty dishes in the sink and she started to vacuum the house. Left alone in the kitchen, I hunted for an empty jar and finally found the one I was looking for, an empty Maxwell House coffee jar. I emptied the contents from my handkerchief into it, stored it on a rear shelf in the garage and left.

Upon returning to the office I found Maria and Virginia on their knees near my desk scrubbing away the coffee stains left on the floor. The three of us lifted my desk a few feet away from the usual spot so that a thorough job of stain removal could be done. To my surprise, Virginia cried out, "Hey, what is this big black spot?"

I bent down to inspect it and said, "It's probably some spilled burgundy."

"No, I don't think so," Maria replied. "It's dried-out blood."

"Maybe so," Virginia said. "Les has told me that in the past this office was frequently used to persuade incorrigibles to cooperate."

The minute I heard "persuade incorrigibles to cooperate" I considered Virginia part of the Leslie Smith contingent. I decided to play the stupid one and said, "Forget it, girls. The desk was moved over here to cover the blemish. It's wine or grape juice and let's leave it at that."

What I said might have been true, but in my heart I knew it wasn't. My job at that moment was to act not scared even though I was.

Virginia lightened up and said, "It may be grape juice, but then again maybe it isn't. Let's be thankful it didn't come from Dr. Zeitlin's head."

We all laughed and then suddenly stopped, realizing it really wasn't a laughing matter. I felt they knew of last night's attack on me by ferocious Farmar and Collins. How could I continue to work in such an environment? Anyone from the outside would ask, "What do you expect when you hire the coalition leader's sister-in-law and the board attorney's dear neighbor?"

Were they loyal to the college president or to those who got them the job? This was another case of "Only time will tell."

Well, if Jim Kirie could work with friends of the mob, I guess I could manage it with their wives and girlfriends.

Broadview Rotary Provides Scholarship to Triton

BROADVIEW ROTARY Club will provide a scholarship to Triton College for a full time student who lives in Broadview. The scholarship provides tuition only for one academic year and will be given to either a freshman or sophomore student. Broadview Rotary club president Harry B. Behrmann (right), presents check to G. Robert Darnes (left), dean of instruction at Triton College. The scholarship is based on need and previous academic scholarship as determined by the admissions and guidance committee of the college.

25
Showdown With the Coalition

I asked myself many times, who are my friends and who are my enemies? Wade Steel and Roy Jones were the only two trustees who were with me for an honest administration. That left the coalition of five. If only I could reduce it to four or three, I might still have a chance. Where should I start?

I decided to visit Elmore Boeger at his office before going to Rotary. He set aside an hour for me to talk about the college's major concerns. He showed much empathy for me with my challenges. How could I open a college for 1,000 within four and a half months with only two administrators and three faculty members hired so far? He listened attentively and expressed great surprise when I related to him, without going into detail, the pressures put upon me to hire an incompetent business manager. It was urgent that at the next board meeting Robert Dale and Gordon Simonsen be hired. If the board rejected my recommendation for business head for the third time I was prepared to negotiate a departure without any animosity, provided there was a fair salary settlement. He was adamantly opposed to such an idea and promised me that he would talk it over with the boys. I left feeling much better.

He called the following day. "The boys want you to interview Neil Neuson again. They felt you didn't give Neil a fair shake. Try again."

"I can't until he gives me a written application."

"The fellows didn't tell me that. If Neil doesn't comply with the proper procedures, then I'll support you in your effort to get Bob Dale."

"Even if it means a split with the coalition?"

"Yes, I don't want you to leave. Maybe you should postpone this issue for a little while."

"Elmore, I can't wait any longer. It's been an issue now for several months. Will you help me?"

"Yes, you can count on me. I'm a Rotarian and we Rotarians must stick together for good clean government."

"Thanks."

Later that afternoon I called Roy Jones. We decided to meet in my office after 6:00. He was not surprised as I summarized the last few days' events.

"Those boys are going to ruin this college. We've got to get them out!" Roy said.

"Is there any possible chance they may change?"

"You're dreaming, Herb. Once a crook, always a crook!"

"They all come from good families. What's making them go off on the wrong end?"

"I'm not too sure of your first conclusion, but to answer your question, money is their god."

"What can we do?"

"I don't know yet, but I'll be working on it."

Before sending out the agenda I thought I'd have another talk with Wade, so he agreed to meet with me in his office. I told him that Elmore would break with the coalition over this issue. "That's good, Herb. We now have a 3 to 4 vote. We're getting closer. If only I can find someone else to go with us."

"Who will it be?"

"I don't know yet. I'll talk with Jim Kirie and Mayor O'Connor. If Farmar and Collins won't listen to us, maybe they'll listen to their political bosses."

Late that evening Wade called me. "Herb, Kirie and O'Connor are strongly supporting their protégés. They will fight us all the way. I suggest you postpone your recommendation for the time being."

"Wade, I've already waited too long. We have to bring this to a head. I hope you'll be on my side when they ask for my resignation." I thought about the possibility of shortening my three-year contract.

"Don't talk that way, Herb. You won't go out easy. Their aim will be to ruin you. We must keep that from happening. If you're fired it will be extremely difficult for you to get a job anywhere."

"Wade, I want to stay, but I just can't be the chief administrator to a dishonest board. Everything Eugenia and I stand for is at stake. Just pray that we can find a fourth vote for my recommendation."

Later that evening, after the kids had gone to bed, Eugenia and I talked it out. What would I do if I were dismissed? I wanted to stay in college administration, but if I were fired other boards would be reluctant to hire me. So, what do I do? What do I do, I kept repeating. First of all, we would all stay put in Elmwood Park. The kids were beginning to enjoy their school and teachers. Mark was going to try out for the football team. Joyce and Ann were getting straight A's in all their subjects. Clare was looking forward to going to the Martin Enger School in Franklin Park in September. We just couldn't ask them to make three changes within one year.

I studied the "Help Wanted" sections in the *Chicago Tribune* and *Sun Times*. There were many openings for machinists, so I got out my micrometer and tried it out. It worked, and all my old measuring skills returned. As I continued to read the classifieds I discovered many other possibilities: car salesman, radio technician or sales, purchasing agent, personnel specialist, insurance, real estate sales, etc., all areas in which I or one of my brothers had some experience. My fears for the future disappeared as I read of the many opportunities in Chicagoland.

It was a delight talking to my kid brother Eddie, who owned an auto supply store in Miami. He offered me a partnership if I wished to join him. For his part, brother Arthur, who owned a sales and service TV store in Huntington, Long Island, felt that I could eventually become the top TV salesman on the island. My two younger brothers made me feel welcome and wanted me on their team. Lester, my oldest brother, a real estate broker, was down in the dumps since his car had been stolen twice near his office in Jamaica, New York, and he was planning to leave real estate. He had no suggestions for me. I tried to reach my buddy brother Lenny several times, without success. His wife Elaine told me he was very busy handling some big deals in upstate New York. I didn't bother to talk to my mother or sisters, feeling they would become too emotional about the bad turn of events. In their case silence was golden.

Eugenia, right from the beginning, wanted me to quit regardless of the outcome of the business manager impasse. She felt confident she could get a job as a seventh or eighth grade English teacher, a high school or junior college teacher of English or high school or junior college counselor. She'd successfully held all those jobs in the past. She would work full-time while I became a house husband, a new title that really didn't appeal to me.

We went to bed that night hoping God would hear our request: "Please give us four yes votes for Dale and Simonsen."

I arrived with Wade at the April 22nd board meeting early and was surprised to see a larger than usual crowd. What did it mean? Was it a good or bad sign? Jim Tarpey distributed the agendas and welcomed all the newcomers, who were rather quiet. Farmar and Collins arrived next and greeted me pleasantly, as if nothing at all had happened a few nights before. I thought, what great actors those two are. Well, I could also act. I shook their hands and said, "Nice to see you guys again." I really didn't like my lines but felt it was necessary to carry on with the job. Within minutes Knol and Jones arrived, said nothing and sat down quietly. When the Babe showed up, they all stood and gave him a hearty welcome. There was no question about it, he was the boss of the coalition. The last trustee to arrive, at 7:05 PM, was Elmore Boeger. He had a blank look on his face as he slowly sat down. Could I count on his being the third yes vote? This was beyond the Four Way test program and I took Elmore at his word. If a fourth yes were coming I felt it would be Serpico or Knol, and that was wishful thinking.

Wade called the meeting to order as scheduled and then a strange thing happened. A tall, middle-aged man with a crew-cut distributed to each trustee a white legal-sized envelope, marked OPEN IMMEDIATELY in bold print. This surprised everyone. I didn't know what was in the envelope. Silence fell over the board table as each trustee read with wonderment. They stared at each other, not knowing what to do, until Babe said, "Let's take a few minutes out. Please excuse us." The five coalition members left their seats to go backstage.

Wade said nothing as Smith, who had just arrived, left the table to join the quintet. While we could not hear them, we could see the six of them all talking at the same time in very low voices. Babe was reprimanding Joe as he pointed to the bottom of the page. Joe got red in the face. It wasn't liquor this time. He was put on the defensive by

Babe. Oh, how I wanted to see that letter! Roy and Wade had their own sidebar discussion. I was left out from both quietly talking groups.

Elmore appeared to be the silent one as the coalition generated steam. Finally they all turned to Boeger to tap his wisdom. They listened carefully as he spoke, gesturing with his hands. Within minutes, a decision reached, they all returned to the board table.

Joe raised his hand and said, "Mr. Chairman, we have some old business from our last meeting that I think should be handled now."

"What is that business, Mr. Farmar?"

"I've studied the folders of Mr. Simonsen and Mr. Dale and I hereby recommend that they be placed on the dean's salary schedule as listed on schedule 4."

Roy Jones seconded the motion; no discussion, no roll call vote: it was unanimous.

I couldn't believe it. It had happened so fast! All my plans to force the issue on the board had turned out to be time wasted. I spend sleepless nights planning and speculating on how to break the gridlock and along comes a stranger with a letter, and my foremost wishes are fulfilled. Who was this stranger? Was he really a stranger, or an angel in disguise?

There was little time to think further as Wade moved swiftly on the agenda. Elmore gave a detailed report on the use of the West Leyden High School for instructional classes and the purchasing of buildings for urgently needed office space.

Fred interrupted Boeger's report with, "I want Dr. Zeitlin to tell us what this additional space will be used for."

I proceeded to outline how the buildings would be used. "We will need at least two classroom sizes for each of the following: library, student store, student center, faculty center, clerical pool and admissions and guidance office. In addition, we must have separate offices for five administrators."

It was moved, seconded and carried authorizing the administration to obtain appraisals on the property needed.

Fred then gave a lengthy review of life insurance and hospital plans as a fringe benefit for all employees. He requested more time before a recommendation could be made.

Don Dunahow stated he had met with Amos Watts, Chapman and

Cutler's bond consultant, who recommended that $2,000,000 in bonds be sold in order to pay for land acquisition. The trustees authorized Dunahow to obtain appraisals of the sites before selling any bonds. Don ended his report inviting the trustees, president and architect to the School Construction Conference on May 11th as guests of the Inland Steel Company.

During my presentation I endorsed the Illinois School Board's Code of Ethics and urgently requested the trustees to adopt it or revise it as they saw fit before the close of the school year. I also recommended that the board policy committee meet as soon as possible and start adopting policy. Before adjournment I reviewed the itinerary to visit California community colleges, which included the College of San Mateo, Cabrillo College, Foothill College and the City College of San Francisco *(to see its Food and Hotel Management program in action).*

As the meeting ended all the trustees but Wade, Roy and Elmore quickly disappeared. Jim Tarpey came up to us with a puzzled look. "Who the hell is Jack Rossetter?"

"Please, Wade, let me see the letter," I insisted. He gave it to me and I read with great amazement:

april 22, 1965

open letter to
triton community junior college board of education,

one never knows the validity of rumors – until he goes directly to the people involved, but rumor DOES have it that certain members of the present community college board are showing reluctance to approve the recommended personnel for major education positions – personnel whose background and qualifications have been thoroughly investigated and approved, and their recommendation for employment MADE by the superintendent.

as one who has been in educational circles for the past 30 years, may I vehemently protest such a stand by ANY board of education, should such exist.

in educational circles, if any single premise is accepted it is that the HIRING and choice of STAFF is the sole responsibility of the ADMINISTRATION, the superintendent-

– and in NO sense the province of the board, in fact, should it ever be necessary TO reject a recommendation made by the superintendent, it would be a prima facie case of showing lack of faith IN the superintendent (or president) and time to get a new one.

i HOPE there is no foundation to this rumor, as applied to our present triton college board, for any new board needs public confidence – and there would be no quicker way to lose same than to have the public feel that the hiring of professional personnel was to be in the hands of NON-professional, lay members of the board.

if there is effort in the direction of a "board infringement upon the province of the president", not only i but a large segment of the interested public will protest, fight, and take the question to the general public in every way available to us, including the local press.

very truly yours,

jack c. rossetter
1811 n 74th ave.
elmwood park 35 ILL.

I just couldn't believe what I was reading. What a remarkable man this Mr. Rossetter must be. How did he know so much about the Triton board? Who was supplying him with his information, all so true? I didn't really care. His message had hit the board between the eyes: *"Give the college president his legal right, the right to search out and find the most qualified faculty without any interference from individual trustees, or else let them be exposed to the public."* Amen!

Before the meeting I thought it might be my last, because I was going to insist upon Dale's and Simonsen's appointments. The coalition had immense power and they were going to use it in dismissing a president who refused to hire an incompetent.

Rossetter's letter had changed all that; on one eloquent page he had scared the board into backing down from their infringement on the president's responsible duties.

After the audience left, remaining on stage were Steel, Jones, Boeger and Tarpey. I repeated Jim Tarpey's question, "Who is Jack Rossetter?"

"He's a math teacher from Oak Park High School," Wade

responded. "Seated next to Mr. Rossetter was his wife, the president of the League of Women Voters, and her entourage."

"How did he know about my predicament?"

"I have no idea," Wade flatly asserted. The others joined in denying any knowledge of Jack Rossetter. I decided not to push the question but felt deeply thankful for the power above that had sent him to our meeting.

Roy wanted to know if anyone was accepting the invitation from the president of Inland Steel. Wade was taken aback by the question and replied, "I can't understand why Don wants us to go when the board stated months ago that they would not build a campus with butler buildings."

"Oh, come on now, Wade, you and I know why."

"Why?" I asked.

Boeger, silent up to now, said, "Could it be that Dunahow wants to get on the gravy train with Inland Steel?"

Jones jumped in, "You can rest assured that anything that Dunahow suggests is in the best interest of Dunahow and not the college students. I heard he's brownnosing the company president, hoping to become their attorney."

"Oh, you're just guessing," Boeger said.

"No, I am not. I heard it from a reliable authority. If the college negotiates a good contract with Inland Steel to build a campus of butler buildings, then Dunahow becomes the company lawyer."

"What do you think, Wade?" I asked.

"Triton College will never build with butlers. I'm not accepting the invitation to the conference."

Jim Tarpey was listening attentively, writing down some of the comments. I wondered if he was with me or with Bob Collins. After Tarpey left Roy asked, "How's he doing as our public relations specialist?"

"Very well," I replied. "He's gone home to write the minutes, as well as a news release on this meeting. I edit all his news articles before they're released. He's liked very much, tells good stories and is very cooperative. I would miss him should he decide to leave."

"Don't worry, he won't leave. He's Bob Collins's secret weapon. He stayed behind after our meeting so he could give Bobby-boy the scoop about Rossetter. I don't trust him," Jones said.

"I'll continue to trust him. After all, he works for the college, not for Mr. Collins."

"Dr. Zeitlin, you're so naive. You live in one of our better suburbs. But if you live anywhere in Cook County, Chicago corruption is part of the system. And in our system trust is rare."

I thanked Roy for his advice but felt he was wrong to condemn the masses instead of a few rotten eggs. Wade and I were a team that believed good would always overcome evil. I left for home at a rather early hour for a board meeting night.

Eugenia's first words were, "What happened? Are you coming or are you going to be a house husband?"

"I'm coming full speed ahead. I never would have predicted tonight's outcome. We owe it all to a Mr. Jack Rossetter."

I proceeded to review the remarkable meeting. "I got everything I asked for and the board has at last accepted me as the chief administrator. I never could have done it without Mr. Rossetter's help."

We went to bed very happy that night. Eugenia dropped her drive to get a teaching job and promised to continue to play the part of housewife and mother. The following morning after the kids left for school we were having a leisurely breakfast when all of a sudden we heard a pounding on the door, followed by the bell chime. Since the breakfast nook is quite a distance from the front door it took me a few seconds to get there. I opened the door and no one was there. As I closed the door I noticed a legal-sized envelope, addressed to Dr. Herbert Zeitlin, scotch taped above the knob. I opened it and read:

april 22, 1965

dear dr. zeitlin,

you have dramatic talents I should never have imagined! you are terrific! some day let us do macbeth together !"why, suh, whoever heard TELL of this here new board even dropping the tiniest HINT that it might choose someone from its own hind pocket: unheard of, suh!"

but from the scrambling that went on two minutes before the meeting, with my letter being rushed out into the "cloak-room" with the major interests, I sort of imagine there was some mind-changin went on right fast like.

and i'm such a NICE-seeming guy when y'first meet me! (I have a tigerrrrrrr in my tank.)

I am Nobody's hatchet man -- ever! know that! but if anyone you know cares to let me know of wisps of smoke that look sorta suspicious, ever, i'll investigate and have a fire department in reserve. I am pretty close to the situation, having done all the publicity in all local press, including the brochure etc. for the formation of the jr. college district up UNTIL it was officially voted in.

it might amuse you to know that I had five MINUTES in which to write tonite's letter – and even then used words your good secretary couldn't pronounce. give me 24 hours and i'll really dish you up a job!

don't answer this, ever – but we cleared the air tonite, as you well know – and certain things just won't develop again, of course something else always will, but know whose side i'm on – until YOU start cuttin some corners – and then POW – play no faves.

stay in there; there's just the CHANCE that we might have a real top notch college with MOST of the money getting into education!

rossetter

p.s. my wife (and her league of women voters) spread the alarm – but they didn't quite know how to handle the situation; there's where I got drafted! the gals are busybodies, but pretty good sorts!!

I had to read the letter twice before saying a word. Then Eugenia took it from me. I said, "Wow!" and closed the front door.

"He is one wonderful man," Eugenia said. "I'm going to telephone him and thank him for his courageous letter." She left to look him up in the phone book.

"Hold on a minute, sweetie pie. It's true, he saved the day for me. But what about the days to follow? I'm going to accept his advice and not contact him. I can't get secretly involved with someone I don't know. Put down the phone and let's analyze this letter. Do you see anything unusual about it?"

"It's all in lower case, no caps, with some slang expressions. Why is he writing to you?"

"I don't know. He does strange things. He wants to be noticed as someone who's different. Notice his comments about being close to the situation, having done all the publicity for the formation of the college. And yet none of the trustees have heard about him. He has a big ego, judging from his statement that it only took five minutes to compose the letter."

"What did he mean by you two doing Macbeth?"

"He thinks I was performing as if in a play. To him, all of us on the stage are playing a part. As a matter of fact, I wasn't performing. I was in dead earnest with the board. I wanted them to get off the dime, adopt a code of ethics and authorize me to hire a faculty ASAP, without any interference from any trustee."

"With all the delays, do you still have enough time to open the college after Labor Day?"

"We have four months. With a business manager and a dean of technology joining us shortly, we'll stretch the working hours and days in order to open as scheduled."

"Do you think the board will cooperate with you now?"

"They're all smart, college-educated men. Not cooperating would get them exposed by Jack Rossetter as trustees not to be trusted."

"You may have some reservations about Rossetter but I like him very much. I hope he sticks around."

"So do I."

administration

With so many Warriors around the campus, the administrators have many important duties; without the administration Triton College could not carry on. Thus, to become better acquainted with how your college operates, it is a good idea to get to know who these administrators are.

president

DR. HERBERT ZEITLIN The President of Triton Junior College District 504 is responsible for all of the functions of the college. With the aid of his staff, he supervises all on and off campus activities and may be contacted in Room 258.

dean of instruction

DR. G. ROBERT DARNES The Dean of Instruction, whose office is in Room 257, directs the college transfer program of Triton. Information concerning academic and instructional procedures may be obtained here.

dean of technology

DEAN GORDON K. SIMONSEN The technological programs of the college are administered by the Dean of Technology. Students interested in any one of the colleges eighteen occupational or vocational programs may find the Dean in Room 257.

dean of admissions and guidance

DR. JOHN WIDERGREN The Dean of Admissions and Guidance directs the college policies on admissions, records, and attendance from his office which is located in Room 254.

dean of business management

DEAN ROBERT T. DALE The dollars and cents end of the college is under the direction of the Dean of Business Management. The Dean, located in Room 256, works with his staff to keep college and student finances in order.

26
Productive Concilliation

April 28 was so different from a month before in Chicagoland. Spring had arrived, the lawns turned green and the trees showed a new life cycle. Continuing in this spirit, all the trustees arrived early with zip and zing for the 25th official meeting of the Triton board. Could they have received a shot of adrenaline? I didn't know and I didn't care. It was great to see them laughing again, showing each other respect and listening attentively as each expounded on his summer plans.

As the executive officer of the board I could not have asked for more as we waited for 8:00 PM to arrive. The mood had changed 180 degrees. The president was no longer resisted; we were a team again. Ferocious Farmar had been tamed into a sagacious attorney. Bob Collins, with much effort and kind words, tried to reestablish rapport with brother Herb. Babe complimented the college president on recruiting such a fine administration. I guessed that at a clandestine meeting of the coalition Babe had issued the order to cooperate, and cooperate they did.

Fred told the group that he and Betty were going up to Wade's cabin that summer in the wilds of Wisconsin near Cornicupo. If he returned safely, then the rest of us could follow next summer. Roy, his wife Ruth and daughter would be spending the summer at Fish Creek, Wisconsin. He was looking into buying a home there for retirement. Elmore had not yet arrived so we didn't know of his plans. Don Dunahow was planning a fishing party on his cabin cruiser with Bob and Joe.

He turned to me, saying, "Dr. Zeitlin, I gave you a written invitation in December. I cleared my book and set the July 4th weekend for the Triton cruise. Well, are you going to join us?"

"Gee, I'm glad you asked me because Eugenia wanted to know more about the cruise. She's never taken such a trip. She wanted to know if she should bring anything such as food or liquor, and how long the cruise is."

"This is a fishing trip. Women don't like the smell of fish so they haven't been invited. It's just for us men. We'll anchor in the middle of Lake Michigan. I'll supply you with some great bait that's sure to hook in the big ones. So what do you say?"

"I'd love to go with you guys but I don't know if I'll have the time to get away."

Wade got into the agenda. Much discussion followed as Frank Cullen, business manager of the Leyden High School District, discussed the rental terms of the West Leyden campus. With the exception of the administrative offices and some of the athletic facilities the whole campus would be ours from 3:30 PM to midnight. By Cullen's formula there would be a basic fee, plus an additional amount if the Triton ADA (Average Daily Attendance) exceeded 500 students. I was very pleased when the trustees agreed to finalize the contract at the next meeting of the respective boards. It meant we at last had a place to teach our students.

All that remained was to find a place for the faculty and administrative offices, including a library. I reviewed my talk with Mr. Paul Shlensky, president of Modern Space Facilities, who estimated we'd need 8,000 square feet at a cost of $120,000, with a buyback clause after three years, giving us an actual cost of $80,000. It didn't sound bad but the board decided to hold, to consider other options.

Don Dunahow reported that he hadn't heard from the appraiser John Davies and recommended that we hire another appraiser, which the board approved. Unresolved was when to sell the bonds and in what amount. If we sold the total issue of $8,900,000 and used only one-fourth or one-third for land purchase, the balance could be put into the bank and earn interest for the benefit of the college. Everyone liked that idea and Don was complimented for brilliantly revealing another source of income for the college.

Don then highlighted our discussion with Edward Benjamin, a noted bond consultant. If Triton were to become his client he would have the bonds rated by Moody's or Standard & Poor's. A Triple-A rating, the highest and safest, would sell the bonds fastest and cost the taxpayers the least. The AAA's were currently going out at 3.1 to 3.2 per cent. On the other hand, an unrated general obligation bond would sell one to two points higher, giving the buyer a greater return at the expense of the taxpayer. He strongly urged having the bonds rated.

For this to be done he would have to provide the rating agencies with much financial data, about the twelve cities within the Triton district. The data collected would be put into a prospectus, expediting a favorable sale. The prospectus would then be mailed out to 200 or more buyers throughout the nation, in order to solicit many bids.

Babe interrupted Don with, "How long would this take and how much would it cost Triton?"

"It would take from two to three months. Benjamin's company would charge us 2½ per cent, or around $50,000, for a sale of two million bonds."

"That's too long and too much. Why don't you and Dr. Zeitlin continue to interview more bond consultants before the board arrives at a decision?"

All the trustees nodded their heads in unison as Don and I agreed to do so.

Someone in the audience yelled out, "You tell them, Babe, that bond consultant is overrated."

Wade called for order as Fred Knol gave his report on medical plans. Knol stressed the need for such a plan for all employees, but no action was taken due to Elmore Boeger's absence. I presented a proposed classified salary schedule, which was readily accepted with the exception of the clause covering vacation and sick leave benefits. Bob Collins felt he needed more time to consider those provisions.

In the packet of material sent to the board I stressed the need to adopt a policy on controversial issues and asked Bob, as the secretary of the board, to read the policy. He did it slowly and well and to my surprise all the trustees commented positively on it.

"We'd never really be a college of any worth if only one side of an issue were to be given," Joe Farmar said. "The right to speak out on any issue is a right the board should give, in a controlled environment, to all individuals and the student press."

The college fully endorsed the policy on the search for the truth at all costs. Freedom of speech was guaranteed. It was moved, seconded by Jones and Knol and carried unanimously.

The trustees adjourned two hours later; the next meeting scheduled for Wednesday, May 12 at 8:00 PM in the Little Theater of East Leyden High School.

I felt particularly good since almost everything I requested had been approved and I received the pleasant invitation from Don Dunhaow to join him with Farmar and Collins on a fishing trip. Everyone leaving the meeting was in a positive mood and I wanted foremost to forget the unpleasantries of the past. I reminded Boeger, Collins, Farmar and Steel not to eat breakfast Friday morning since we were flying first class out to San Francisco. A fabulous breakfast would be served once we were aloft. Never having traveled first class before, I was looking forward to the occasion.

One of the nicest times in married life is the quiet period after the kids have gone to bed, when you can talk with your beloved without interruption. So the minute I returned home Eugenia stopped reading and said, "I can see it on your face. You had a good meeting. Am I right?"

"Yes, my dear. You're right! The classes will be held at the West Leyden High School. We passed the controversial policy and adopted a classified salary schedule. We'll hire a new appraiser and hopefully will have on board a bond consultant to get our bonds sold. The trustees are talking pleasantly to each other and to me. Teamwork is apparent. And to top it off I was invited to go fishing with the boys on Don Dunahow's cabin cruiser to the middle of Lake Michigan."

"You're not going, are you?"

"Why not?"

"They're a wild drinking group and something can happen to you. I don't like the idea of no wives being there."

"Oh, come on now. What could happen to me?"

"Plenty." We prepared for bed.

"Tell me, what's going on in your head?" I later asked.

"A fish could pull you into the water. What you caught in Mexico was a small bass, weighing less than two pounds."

"On these big boats, the fisherman is strapped into his seat so no big fish can pull him into the water."

"Maybe so, maybe not, but have you considered these great trustees might be up to some foul play? I know you're a great swimmer but if you're pushed overboard, you may not be able to swim to shore, particularly if you've had a couple of drinks."

I didn't answer Eugenia right away as we lay in bed. I turned over on my side and thought. Could she be right? I never did tell her about Collins's and Farmar's planned attack on me when they were loaded. Could they be planning something similar? The more I thought about it, the more convinced I was that Eugenia had more insight than I. Before reaching slumberland my final words to her were, "My dear, you may be right. Besides that, I don't think I can spare any time away from the office. So I'll decline Don's invitation."

"Thank God for listening to me. I feared another sleepless night if you didn't change your mind." She snoozed off. The music she emitted, low-pitched and rhythmic, was pleasant. I knew she was happy as she slipped away with a smile on her face.

The plane took off from O'Hare as the sun started to rise on the horizon. All of us were a little sleepy but were pleasantly stirred when a hostess came down the aisle and asked, "Champagne?"

She received a "Why, of course," from the Triton sextet. So this is first class, I thought. Big roomy seats, cloth napkins, choice of cereals, eggs with bacon, ham, steak or chicken, plus potatoes, tomatoes, choice of juices, bread, rolls or bagels with lox.

Breakfast fit for a king, fast service by a most attractive hostess. Somehow or another I felt a little guilty traveling first class as a public servant, so I asked Wade, "Is this the usual mode of travel for college trustees?"

Wade smiled and said nothing. A few minutes later he answered, "It's OK if there's money in the budget. However, except for the governor's party or high administrative officials, most public servants travel economy class for short trips."

"Are we considered high administrative officials?"

"Joe Farmar feels that since we're responsible for a budget in the millions, it's OK. Aside from that, trustees serve without pay and are entitled to such fringe benefits."

"I don't feel comfortable without a written policy on travel."

"Farmar feels that the less policy we have the better off we are. Too much policy puts us in a straightjacket. He hopes the committee will see it his way."

"Perhaps we can get Joe to attend the next meeting of the Illinois School Board Association. Other trustees may enlighten him."

"That's fine. Let's insist that he attend."

When we landed at the airport we turned our watches back two hours to 9:30 AM, giving us one hour to keep our appointment with President Julio Bortolazzo of the College of San Mateo.. Having no luggage, we immediately went to the Avis counter for our reserved station wagon. The weather was warm and sunny, and Bob was the driver.

In the college's parking lot our eyes popped as we stared at the buildings, a striking blend of glass, white concrete and colonnades. Could this be Rome under Caesar? It might have been, if you replaced the parked cars with chariots. John Fox madly snapped away with his Minolta. Joe turned to me and said, "This can't be a junior college. It's larger and more beautiful than most of the universities in the midwest. It must have cost a fortune to build this campus."

"Let's ask Dr. Bortolano."

We entered his large and beautiful boardroom. Joe's first question was, "We love your campus, but please tell us, what did it cost? And what's your tax rate?"

"This 153-acre campus, which includes all the buildings, grounds and equipment, is valued today at over 19 million. Our tax rate is less than 50 cents per $100 of assessed valuation. The city of San Mateo has a population of 85,000 and the total college enrollment is 19,000," Bortolano automatically responded.

"That's amazing," Joe whispered to me. "I can't believe that San Mateo, with a population less than half of Triton's, could finance such a project."

"Everything you see here today, Joe, we can duplicate or do better. We have about the same assessed valuation with half the income, but we can do it by tapping several other sources of income. And of course we'd have to be more efficient."

Dr. Bortolazzo continued his remarks. "Many of our students come from neighboring districts, plus hundreds are from out-of-state and from 35 different foreign countries. We're happy to have many faiths and many races here, and I believe they're all happy to be part of us."

Bortolazzo turned the meeting over to his public relations man, who led the tour. First stop was a large, light and bright impressive building in the center of the campus – the library. This facility had a seating capacity of over 750, an audio section with over 200 stations, more than 50,000 books, 600 periodicals, five full-time librarians, an FM station and a TV studio. We were very impressed with the large number of well-behaved students quietly coming-and-going.

In rapid order we visited the labs for science, engineering, nursing and foreign languages. Walks to the shops, physical education and athletic fields followed. Our tour director had to yank the trustees away from the cosmetology students. They were fascinated by the various means the students used to keep their clients young and beautiful. We ended up at the student center, which included the bookstore, the recreational rooms, student government offices and the cafeteria. While waiting in line at the cafeteria we decided we'd all eat at different tables so we could talk to as many students as possible.

We each asked five questions of the student seated opposite:

1. What is your major?
2. Why are you taking this major?
3. How do you like your teachers and the classes?
4. What do you like most at the College of San Mateo?
5. What do you dislike about this college?

I was amazed as I looked around at the trustees and the architect. They were absolutely wonderful in establishing rapport with their respective talking mates. After lunch we sped away to Foothill College in the Los Altos Hills, 40 miles south of San Francisco.

The boys had been rather sleepy when we'd arrived at O'Hare, but now, nine hours later, they were filled with zip and zest with Zeit. Why? They loved what they saw. My dreams of a great Triton College had been readily transferred to them. They all wanted to say something.

Joe started off. "My boy was a star football player in high school who turned down a scholarship to Berkeley because he wanted to continue to play. His high school coach had advised him to go to the junior college for two years, then two years to Berkeley, and play continuously. Not a bad idea. I wished I'd done that myself."

Bob added, "My pretty young lady was not much of a scholar in high school and barely got through. However, now that she's in a beauty school she's happy because she's making others happy. And the tips keep coming in, something she'd never expected. What she likes most are the many handsome men and unlimited dating. With help from her Dad or the chosen man in her life she hopes to open her own beauty shop."

Wade interrupted, "I spoke with three students, one with a major in teaching, the second one in engineering and a third in political science. They all intend to transfer to a university two years from now, thus saving their parents thousands of dollars."

Elmore was next to speak. "My shy little lad was afraid he'd be lost in a large university. Here at San Mateo he's enrolled in psychology, which he feels is helping him to understand himself better. Whenever he has a problem, his counselor is always available."

John Fox joined in. "In a nutshell we can say all these students love their college and teachers. The only complaints I heard were: parking is very tight in the evening, registration takes too long and it's disappointing when a needed class is closed."

The boys turned to me and asked, "Well, Dr. Zeitlin, what happened to you?"

I smiled. "I asked Mark what he liked the most about this college. He replied instantly, 'Girls, especially the beautiful ones. On Monday, Wednesday and Friday I take general psychology, where the ratio is four women to one male. And on Tuesday and Thursday I play volleyball in a coed class, where I'm in demand teaching the fair sex how to serve the ball. I only wish they had a major called girls.' "

The stories continued all the way to Foothill College, until Joe burst out with, "Do you really feel Triton could become as good as San Mateo? Could we possibly afford it?"

"The answer is yes to both questions. Our assessed valuation is slightly more, and it will grow with annexations. We won't be as good, however—we'll be better. All we need is the money to make it happen."

"But we don't have the money."

"We'll have over 10 million to start up with when the college opens, about 9 million for a site and construction and almost 2 million for educational purposes. I'm blessed with a board that collected tax money before classes started and a governor who stands for more financial help to the community colleges. To me, that's a bright future."

"If you think so, make it happen! To be better than San Mateo would be a miracle. Now, tell us something about Foothill College."

"Their 122-acre campus has won national awards for architectural and landscape beauty. The construction is a unique blend of old brick, redwood, massive concrete piers and hipped shake roofs that reflect the rural character of the region. It's presently considered the most expensive community college in the nation."

"What did it cost?"

"Over 16 million, which includes the planetarium, the observatory/ meteorological station, theater, 23 science labs, olympic-sized pool and FM station."

"What should we look for during our visit?"

"First, I want you to meet one of the finest presidents in the nation, Dr. Calvin Flint. Make note of all the special features on this campus, see the space program, visit the athletic facilities, and, John, take some pictures of the landscaping. Perhaps we can duplicate their best creations."

As we got out of our station wagon Dr. Flint was there to welcome us. He led us into his sedate office, large enough for all six of us to be seated around his desk. Wade asked, "We are very impressed with the beauty of your campus. How in the world were you able to pass such a large bond issue?"

"It wasn't easy, but fortunately I have a wonderful board and faculty, and an intelligent public led by the president of the Chamber of Commerce. Incidentally, he was also the president of the local Rotary Club."

"Can you be more specific? What did you tell the voters?"

"I told them the truth. I firmly believe that through education one's life is improved tremendously. They were told a beautiful campus would be most conducive to improved learning and their kids shouldn't object to spending two more years living at home before leaving for an out-of-town university. Those kids specializing in the vocational areas would have a job waiting for them after one or two years of training."

"Did it really work?"

"Ask our students. Fortunately the president of the local realty board is a part-time faculty member. He stressed that home values would go up if the voters invested their money in their college."

"And did home values increase?"

"You're darn right they did. The homeowner is now paying an extra $50 to $100 in taxes for a home that's increased in value in the thousands. Plus the parents are saving thousands while their most loved ones live at home for another two years."

"Do you have any regrets?"

"A few. We should have provided more parking facilities and built a larger auditorium. Our attendance at lectures, forums, space center and musicals have exceeded all projections. The mass of people just love to come on campus for any excuse. We're working on some expansion plans. Come on, let me show you the latest."

It was nice to be escorted around the campus by its president. His words were music to my ears and I noticed how the trustees were digesting his comments. Being surrounded by flowers, shrubs and flowers heightened our intake of oxygen and made the tour a healthy delight. Before we left, Dr. Flint told us how the success of Foothill College had had an impact on the city of San Jose.

"How's that?" Joe asked.

"Many of their students prefer Foothill over San Jose City College, resulting in our having an extra large out-of-district enrollment. I'm sure the city fathers of San Jose will awaken to updating their old college campus."

We all thanked Dr. Flint for being such a gracious host. I was directed to send a bouquet of flowers to his wife, thanking her for her husband's time away from home.

As we got into our wagon Joe asked, "Do you think Triton College will have much effect on the Chicago city colleges?"

"Not much while we're in temporary facilities, but on a new campus the Chicago kids will be no different from the San Jose students. Kids are smart enough to know the difference and will prefer the new over the old."

It was 6:30 PM California time when we arrived at Rickey's restaurant and hotel in Palo Alto to check in. The trustees were exhilarated by the visits, talking loudly and praising me for planning such a splendid day. Fox was not tired. He was euphoric, stimulated by new ideas. I was thrilled to see my plan was working.

"What's on the docket for tomorrow and Sunday?" Elmore asked.

"Tomorrow it's San Francisco City College in the morning and Cabrillo College in the afternoon. In the evening we fly to San Diego. On Sunday we visit Mesa College in the morning and Southwestern College in the afternoon."

As usual the men ordered a round of drinks before even looking at the menu. What surprised me most was that Joe and Bob hadn't had a drink since we'd left the airport in the morning.. Here it was, nine hours later, and they were still walking, talking and acting intelligently. What did that prove? In a low voice, Wade whispered in my ear, "Our boys may be heavy drinkers, but they are not alcoholics. An alcoholic cannot last nine hours without a drink Our boys did, so they're OK."

Although the restaurant was crowded this Saturday night the service was fast, the food was superb and the conversation was filled with optimism. John was considering revising our site plan so that the library would be in the center of the campus, with colorful terrain between the buildings. Flatlands were unimaginable. He would engage a landscape architect to design mounds of beauty between the buildings. Having seen a short presentation at the planetarium at Foothill the men informally supported my desire for one at Triton. Before the meal was over I received full endorsements for a beauty school, programs in auto mechanics, electronics, refrigeration, printing and food services, and a swimming pool and athletic facilities.

The next morning, after an early breakfast, we arrived at the City College to see a food preparation class in full swing. The director took us through the kitchen, where we saw large ovens, stoves, huge refrigerators, big cutting boards with chefs cutting away, and kettles for preparing soup, potatoes and vegetables. The students were preparing dinners to be served to over 500 later that night at a large hotel. We were pleased to hear that many of the hotels and restaurants within a 100-mile area had employed their graduates. In the director's office there were a few dozen plaques and letters proclaiming the San

Francisco City College program the best in the nation.

Bob Collins poked me in the side and asked, "Will Triton ever be able to achieve anything like this?"

Without any hesitation I said, "Yes, we can. All I have to do is find a creative and talented director. His clients will he our students, faculty and staff. The program will be located in the student center, where a fast-food counter, a cafeteria and a deluxe dining room will attract the epicurean personnel."

"I'll give you a medal if you can make it happen," Bob said with a laugh.

Cabrillo College, 90 miles south of San Francisco, was rather different from the previous college. Everything was much smaller. Total enrollment was 2,843, library seating 386, total volumes 20,211, periodicals 252 and three full-time librarians. Dr. Robert Swenson, however, was much taller than most college presidents – as well as patient and well-informed on construction procedures. John Fox enjoyed being briefed on how Dr. Swenson had handled difficult engineering problems. The campus was being built in phases, with completion expected within two years.

Because it was Saturday afternoon, there were no faculty members present or classes to visit. As we walked along the dusty roads it was interesting to see some buildings almost completed, some half-completed and others just starting. Before we left, Dr. Swenson complimented us on our wisdom in visiting Foothill and San Mateo, which he considered the two best colleges in the nation. Due to limited resources, very few colleges even came close to their greatness.

Bob drove with fury to get us to the airport for an evening flight to San Diego. He asked, "What's Triton going to be, a Cabrillo or a San Mateo?"

I was delighted to hear the sextet sound off instantly, "San Mateo!"

"And let me say this once more to you, Herb," Bob added. "If you can make Triton as great as San Mateo, the board will give you a medal."

One and a half hours later we continued on the merry-go-round as we landed in San Diego and took a cab to the El Cortez hotel, the temperature a balmy 70. On this Saturday night the hotel was humming with activity. A happy party banged into us as we took a swift ride upon the glass elevator. Fifteen minutes later, as we zoomed down, we caught a gorgeous view of the city of San Diego fully lit up.

"I like this city. I love California. Why wasn't I born here?" Joe said as he led us to the restaurant and ordered drinks for all of us.

"How does Ceil feel about California?" Wade asked.

"She loves it but our kids have their roots in Illinois and we can't think of leaving until they're all grown up, not for another ten years or so. Herb, how in the hell could you leave this paradise?"

"It wasn't easy," I replied with hesitation. "I guess I decided to try for the presidency after reading the blue copy of your survey."

"I still haven't read the damn thing. I started to but found it rather boring."

"To laymen, most educational surveys are. What I liked most about the survey was its use of superior research techniques. The only thing I disliked was the conclusion."

"That's interesting. Tell me, how did your conclusion differ from the highly paid researchers'?"

"Well, for one thing, they predicted a start-up enrollment of 500, given two years of planning. I'm gearing up for an enrollment of over 1,000 even though we have only eleven months to prepare."

"Be honest with me. Do you really think you can solicit 1,000 students?"

"Yes."

"Well, if it doesn't happen, be prepared to return to Chula Vista."

Bob, overhearing our conversation, added, "Joe is only kidding. Herb, could you really get your old job back?"

"No, I don't think so. Tomorrow morning you'll meet my old boss. He'll introduce us to his new dean of instruction."

The evening went by fast. Elmore, Wade and I retired after the long day while Joe, Bob and John Fox had a nightcap or two, or maybe three.

The next morning the sextet was reduced to a quartet as Farmar and Steel overslept. We were informed they would join us for lunch as we headed for Southwestern College in Chula Vista.

After giving my friend and former colleague Chet DeVore, the president, a hearty embrace, I asked, "Where is your dean of instruction?"

"You're looking at him right now! Since you left I've been serving both as the dean of instruction and president. But in two months I'll have some relief when the new dean arrives."

"Gee, I'm sorry my leaving created so much extra work for you."

"You can say that again. My four kids see little of me these days and Helen is annoyed because I'm constantly late for dinner. You are the one responsible for making so many changes in my home life."

"I can guess how Helen feels since Eugenia reacts in the same way. How's your enrollment doing?"

"As you know the enrollment increased quite a bit when we moved to the new campus. This fall we're planning for a 4,000 total."

After President DeVore was introduced to the trustees and the architect, we drove around the newly landscaped 158-acre campus, stopping to explore the planetarium, the little theater, library, science and numerous control facilities. To me Chet seemed a little thinner and I wondered if my departure was a contributing factor. However, the ex-marine colonel, now college president, was his usual affable self, joking incessantly as he led the quartet. Upon leaving, the boys graciously thanked Chet for releasing me from my contract to go to Triton and wished him well with his new dean of instruction.

When we returned to the El Cortez Wade and Joe were enjoying a leisurely breakfast, so the quartet ordered coffee and sandwiches. We prepared to squeeze two other colleges into the itinerary. Bob managed to race us to the new campuses of San Diego Mesa College and Grossmont College in the desert town of El Cajon. It was rush, rush, rush as we viewed the delightful new grounds.

We climbed over 40 steps from the exceptionally large Mesa parking lot to the inner quad of the campus. While it tired all of us, Joe made it a point to cry out, "This is crazy. I think I'm about to have a heart attack"

We all disliked the climb and felt it was unreasonable to expect adult students to do it every day to get to class. Elmore remarked, "Why didn't they remove half the dirt from the mesa to the parking lot and create a level site?"

"It could have been done but it would have cost more than a ton," Wade replied.

On the flight back to Chicago there was a bar in the rear of the plane, which we all enjoyed as we conversed tonic high. The trip was viewed as a success, as a vision of a new Triton unfolded.

Upon my return home Eugenia's first words were, "How did the trustees like California?"

"They liked almost everything. It was a great success. Bob and Joe were exceptionally cordial to all of us and I now have no further fears for the future. Together we'll build a college filled with the latest innovations."

The following day I called Don Dunahow from the office. "How are you coming along with the search for a bond consultant?"

"We're getting close to finding one. Tomorrow I'm having lunch with Elmer Conti and a bond consultant he's recommending."

"Please keep me informed."

"I'll do that!"

May turned out to be an exceptionally good month for me. Not only was spring bursting out all over but the arrival of Bob Dale as business manager and Gordon Simonsen as dean of technology gave Triton two additional stars. I welcomed them into my office the day they arrived and said, "You two are the best I could find anywhere, and it's great to see you here. We have less than four months to open. There's a tremendous amount of work to be done and so little time to do it."

"Don't worry, Dr. Zeitlin. We know the spot you're in and are prepared to work long hours – and that includes Saturday and Sunday if necessary," Gordon proudly proclaimed.

"I have a lot of confidence in you two. You'll be given much freedom to do your job. I'm not one to meddle in another one's work. All I ask is that you keep me informed about your activities."

I stressed the necessity of meeting regularly with the two other deans, being firm on the hiring policy and keeping an open door to each other. Their immediate concern was finding a secretary. I gave them the folder on office applications and again stressed that we only hire those who'd been successful elsewhere, which had to be verified in writing or by phone call.

The two May board meetings were good, with the following accomplished:

1.   Rental terms for the West Leyden High School facilities were approved, including the additional office space. Principal George Cox, who was monitoring the construction, was looking forward to working with me.

2.   The move to West Leyden was scheduled for June 15th.

3.   Smith was authorized to offer 80 cents per square foot to the owners of the Carey Farm.

4.   Insurance and medical plans for all employees were on the verge of being approved.

5.   The college catalog was presented, contents approved and special commendation given to Dean Widergren and his assistant for a job well done. The photos were taken from last year's Southwestern catalog. The total faculty as of May was 18.

6.   Dean Widergren surprised everyone when he announced that 300 students had already registered.

7.   All recommendations for additional faculty and office personnel were approved, with a special commendation to me for recruiting such a highly qualified staff.

8.   I received additional recognition for getting an article and picture of the coming Triton campus into the national publication of the American Association of Junior and Community Colleges.

9.   A few staff members were approved to attend the library buildings conference in Detroit and the National Defense Educational Administration conference in Springfield.

What was nice about the May meetings was the warmth and depth of understanding displayed by the trustees as each item was thoroughly discussed and then approved. It felt great to be the executive officer of such an intelligent board. I felt we were about to make history.

The day after the May 27th meeting I called Don Dunahow. "We missed you at last night's session. What's happening in your search for a bond consultant?"

"I apologize for Babe and me missing the meeting but we had dinner with Mayor Conti last night."

"Well, what happened?"

"Don't worry any more, Dr. Zeitlin. I have the top guns of each party working for Triton. Babe and Conti met for the first time and they're in complete agreement on the Carey site and my choice of a bond consultant."

"That sounds good to me, but did Carey's attorney accept your offer?"

"It wasn't presented. I can't do so until the offer is put into a formal resolution, which I've prepared for the next board meeting."

"When do I get to meet your recommendation for bond consultant?"

"You'll have to wait. He's leaving this Friday night for vacation and won't be back until around the middle of June."

Later that day I called Wade to review my dialogue with Don. Wade felt the prospectus should include the full sale of the $8.9 million rather than separate sales in smaller amounts. He stated proudly, "At an interest rate of 5% the 8.9 million would earn us $445,000 per year. How does that sound to you, Herb?"

"It sounds great, but I can't understand why the college has to get the approval of the Democratic and Republican chiefs before proceeding."

"You just don't understand Chicago politics yet. But in time you will."

True to his word, at the June 9th session Don Dunahow read a resolution entitled, "Resolution authorizing attorney to make an offer to the Carey Estate," which was passed by the board unanimously. Don was directed to hire three appraisers to make sure the price was right.

Also on the agenda:

I explained to the trustees the possibility of the college receiving much financial help if we made an application for funds to the National Defense Educational Administration in the areas of foreign language, mathematics, English and reading, science, history and vocationalltechnical education. The idea was enthusiastically approved, as well as the statement on Civil Rights.

Dr. Darnes presented a proposal for the purchase of library furniture, which was referred to the library committee for immediate action.

Robert Dale, as the business manager, stressed the immediate need for liability and workmen's compensation for all employees. It was referred to the insurance committee, also for prompt action.

Continuing, Dean Widergren gave an optimistic report on the enrollment and announced that the Broadview Jaycees had given Triton its first scholarship, in the amount of $150.

The last item on the agenda was the approval to hire subject area consultants to assist the administration and architect in the campus planning.

We left the 28th official meeting of the board with unusual zip and zest and optimistically looked forward to the June 23rd meeting, scheduled to be held at the West Leyden High School.

The following morning as I arrived in the office I was greeted by Neil Mehler, editor and publisher of the *Franklin Parker.*

"Nice to see you, Neil. How can I help you?"

"You can help me by telling me the truth. Have your bonds been sold?"

"Absolutely not. What makes you ask?"

"There's a rumor going around in the bond circles that they've been sold at a rather high interest rate."

"Oh come on now, Neil, you're too smart a guy to believe in rumors. Some people just start them for fun, out of boredom. If you track it down, you'll find it to be false. Who did you hear it from?"

"From a reliable banker source whose name I can't reveal. I'm suspicious of your attorney and his cohorts. Are you sure some secret deal hasn't been made?"

"Absolutely. The bonds have not been sold but they will be as soon as we hire a consultant to prepare a prospectus."

"And when will that be?"

"Probably at the next trustee meeting, which is scheduled for Wednesday, June 23rd."

"Good, I'll be there."

Traditionally in the U.S.A., May and June are noted for graduations. Proud parents watch their most beloved young ones receive diplomas and degrees. Equally important, but not given as much attention, are the farewell banquets in which faculties honor and give accolades to their retirees.

In this frenzied world Eugenia and I welcomed the invitation to share pleasant moments with the Leyden and Proviso families. The special events were scheduled a week apart. The program sheet given to us at the Leyden affair was entitled, "Will Rocha Steel?" Strange title. What did it mean? Later it was explained to us. George Will and Enrique Rocha, teachers at Leyden High School, were to be honored concurrently with Wade Steel, the district superintendent. As the program unfolded it was a delight to see a rendition similar to "This Is Your Life" featuring all three recipients. The accolades would have made a lobster blush. I marveled at the creativeness of the planning committee headed by Trudy Wilson, now Triton's first hired counselor. Her administrative talent for detail was remarkable. I wondered if in the future she'd be our first female administrator.

Wade's successor, Dr. David Bryne, proudly introduced me to the group, ending with, "Let's give Dr. Zeitlin a hearty welcome and best wishes for success as he prepares to open a college in our community." Eugenia and I, reflecting on other farewells we'd attended, ranked Leyden's the best. After the formal program ended I made it a point to chat with many faculty members and their families as good wishes for the new college continued to flow in. Before we left, Clem Lowe, superintendent of the Elmwood Park High School District, informed me that his best business teacher had filed a teaching application at Triton, and one of his finest counselors was thinking of doing the same. Kindly, he said, "Herb, let's understand each other. This is your limit from my school for this year."

"I understand, Clem. What's the teacher's name?"

"Vernon Magnesen, the only male secretary that gives the board instant playback."

"How's that?"

"He's secretary to our board and also a teacher of shorthand."

"Thanks for letting me know. I'll tell the new dean of technology to keep his eyes open for the application."

As we headed toward our car a tall, handsome young man stopped us to introduce himself. "My name is Malcolm Berd and I teach history at East Leyden. Ever since I heard you talk at Dr. Hoover's junior college class I've been seriously thinking about making a shift from high school to the junior college. Do you need a history or political science teacher?"

"Yes, we'll need several. The first step is to file an application with Dr. Robert Darnes, the dean of instruction, as soon as possible."

As we were talking Wade and Millie joyfully joined us. After Berd left, Wade whispered, "I know Malcolm wants to join the Triton faculty."

"You guessed right. Is he a good teacher?"

"One of the better, if not the best. He's very knowledgeable and a dynamic speaker. He stirs up the students. My reservations about him before he was hired did not come true."

"What were your concerns?"

"He came from a rather affluent family and holds a degree from Harvard. I wondered how well he'd fit in teaching the children of industrial workers."

"Well, what happened?"

"He exceeded all expectations. Not only was he a superior teacher but he was a warm-hearted counselor to those students who had serious problems. The adage about Harvard graduates just didn't apply."

"What's that?"

"*You can always tell a Harvard graduate. . .but you can't tell him much!* As a matter of fact he sought my advice prior to getting married. His parents refused to attend the ceremony because he was marrying out of his religion. Millie and I attended the wedding."

"How is the marriage holding up?"

"They both appear to be extremely happy even if their folks aren't."

"I'll ask Dr. Darnes to be on the lookout for his application. I'm sure Triton would be enriched by having a Harvard man on the faculty."

A week later we attended Leroy Knoeppel's farewell party, which did not follow the usual pattern. The capacity ballroom crowd waited with great anticipation to see the recent child bride of the retiring superintendent. She wasn't exactly a child bride, though she was about 35 years younger than her husband. Dr. Knoeppel proudly introduced the new Mrs. Knoeppel to his colleagues, who joyfully wished them much happiness. Strangely, none of the male faculty members kissed the beautiful bride even though they may have wanted to do so. The groom, looking more like her father, moved them along rapidly during the procession.

The formal part of the program started with glowing remarks about Leroy from his board president. The faculty association president followed with not so glowing praise of Knoeppel as an uncompromising administrator who was always right. The speaker for the classified personnel stressed what a tight ship the boss had run, but always for the benefit of the students. Finally, the student body president enthusiastically thanked the retiree for employing great teachers who gave them the finest education in the nation.

Tremendous applause followed as Knoeppel stood up and smiled. He slowly walked up to the podium, adjusted the microphone and waited for absolute silence. In a strong, vibrant voice he sounded off, looking at each individual as he recalled events of many years before. His memory was remarkable. He'd point to someone at each table and with precision describe an incident otherwise long forgotten. He concluded 50 minutes later stating that America was the place where opportunities never end. The greatest opportunity he'd received was serving his community, and he'd continue to do so.

Before our leaving, Dr. Widergren introduced me to Arthur Shearburn, the director of student activities at West Proviso High School, who asked me, "How is my old football buddy Ralph Serpico doing?"

"He's doing fine. I'll tell him you asked."

"As a matter of fact, he wasn't my buddy but my opponent. When I was a freshman at the University of Illinois I served as practice material for the varsity squad. I'll never forget the first time he tackled me and knocked the wind out of me. No one wanted to take him on. Twenty years ago he was the greatest, and made all-American."

"Thanks for letting me know. I'll get Jim Tarpey to write a story about our trustee, the former all-American player."

As Arthur left John asked me, "How do you think he'd do as our coordinator of student activities?"

"I can't tell until I see his papers."

"You will. I'm recommending him for the position. You'll have his papers the first thing on Monday morning."

We all departed from the glorious farewell.

Bond Sale Jars College Board

$8.9 Million Dispute Rages

Watchdog Group for Triton

By FRANK CORRADO

CHARGES of neglect of the public interest and backroom deals have jarred the Triton Junior college school board in the wake of last week's sale of $8.9 million in bonds for the new Junior college.

The bonds were sold to the firm of McDougal & Condon at 3.6996 per cent interest.

BANKING and bond officials questioned by The TIMES all observed that the McDougal & Condon bid was not necessarily high but that competitive bidding might have produced a lower bid, lower by about as much as one-half per cent.

"This is going to cost the taxpayers $200,000," said school board member Roy C. Jones, who was joined by board President Wade Steel in opposing the sale.

A meeting was set for Monday by Mrs. Robert Johnson, president of the Elmwood Park League of Women Voters, and other citizens interested in setting up a watchdog group.

(Continued on Page 2)

"CITIZENS for Triton College resolution, passed 4-2 a week ago, authorizing the sale of $8.9 million in bonds against the judgment of legal counsel and without seeking competitive bids.

If the request is not honored, the CPTC, which has taken steps to incorporate itself as a non-profit organization, may institute a taxpayers' suit against the board and seek an injunction to prohibit sale of the bonds. As a non-profit organization, the CPTC then could not be held liable in any counter-suit by the board if the bond sale were held up.

A GROUP of about 30 persons, many of them community leaders who took part in the formation of the Triton school district gathered at the home of Mrs. Robert Johnson, president of the Elmwood

(Continued on Page 2)

lege," a watchdog group formed Monday night in the aftermath of the college bond sale, will attempt to speak before the Triton board Wednesday night.

The CPTC hopes to ask the the board tonight to rescind its

Published Weekly

HARLEM-IRVING TIMES

A Lerner Newspaper

SERVING NORTHWEST SUBURBS:

Norridge, Schiller Park, Franklin Park, Elmwood Park, River Grove and Rosemont

CHICAGO, WEDNESDAY, JUNE 30, 1965

Office
7235 W. Irving Park
Chicago, Illinois 60634

Suburban
4104 N. Harlem
Norridge, Illinois

10c Per Copy

News Phone: 763-7300
Advertising Phone
City   625-3100
Suburbs GL 6-6600

THE FRANKLIN PARKER

VOL. 2, NO. 8   NEWSSTAND PRICE 10¢ PHONE: GL5-8873   JULY 1, 1965

Banker Says-- They'll Never Know if Price is Right

$8.9-MILLION IN TRITON BONDS LET WITHOUT COMPETITIVE BIDS

By NEIL MEHLER

The Triton College board by a 4-2 vote has approved a resolution to issue $8.9-million in bonds by negotiated sale rather than by advertising for bids.

The bonds, authorized by Leyden and Proviso Township voters at a special election March 27, are for purchase of a campus site and construction of a physical plant for the new college.

Issuance of bonds in an amount this great without bids is considered unusual, questionable and unwise, The Franklin Parker has been told by several bankers, edu-

bonds and inquired of a board member about the situation. He was told there had been some discussion about such a sale, but

ally different," he said. This official also commented that the school board should have waited to see what the Illinois Legislature would do to the Junior College Master Plan then pending in Springfield. The plan is expected to contain a provision for the reimbursement of up to 75 per cent of construction costs for a junior college.

A third banker contacted by this

intendent, and also has been a teacher, Roy Jones, a supervisor for Commonwealth Edison Co., has been a school board member for 14 years. Currently he is on the board of District 87 (Hillside, Bellwood and other suburban grade schools) and is a director of the Illinois Assn. of School Boards.

The four trustees who voted for the non-competitive bond sale have no previous school board

employee of Lindberg Steel Treating Co. in Melrose Park, says he has had some "sleepless nights" since the June 23 meeting.

"I know we're going to get criticized and roughly," he said this week.

"I voted to sell the bonds this way because I think the need is urgent. This thing could have been kicked around several more months. The boys (other board

Triton's President Speaks Out

Board Tables Security Move

Sept 23, 1965

By ROBERT NEWMAN

In a dramatic confrontation at last Thursday's Triton College board meeting, College President Dr. Herbert Zeitlin accused the Board of "making exception to employment policy and assuming administrative responsibilities" when the Board attempted to hire Louis Case as "security officer" of the College without consulting the administration.

The showdown came when board members Robert Col-

HERBERT ZEITLIN

Worries about accreditation

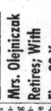

officer at a salary of $10,000 a year. The board had authorized Smith to write the contract on September 8, despite the fact that no job description existed for the post.

After Board President Wade Steel questioned the move, asking, "How can a man proceed without knowledge of his duties," Zeitlin reported on an interview, arranged by him, that he had held with Case on September 13. The Triton president reported that Case had neglected to bring a copy of his contract with him for the interview, had professed not to know the normal procedure of hiring, and was unsure of his new duties. Zeitlin announced the unanimous recommendation by Business Manager Robert Dale, the three college deans, and himself that Case not be hired. Zeitlin also warned that the employment "would have a detrimental effect on Triton's accreditation."

Case is a retired captain of detectives in the Oak Park police force and has been developing a security system for the Ford City shopping

action by saying that the present security officer is "inadequate," emphasizing that the students must be properly protected. Board member Ralph Serpico asserted that Zeitlin only has hiring authority over "professional" people. Serpico also said that he had seen someone on the campus with a blackjack, implying that Triton's temporary campus was an unsafe place at night without a security officer.

Steel and Board member Roy Jones objected strenuously to the hiring, stressing that "we have to have confidence in the administrative staff's ability." Elmore Boeger asked his colleagues "not to do anything which would damage our accreditation."

Finally, on Steel's urging, Collins read the contract under discussion. Included were provisions that Case "is answerable to no one except the Board," "should take an inventory of all college equipment," and "should conduct security checks on all teaching and non-teaching personnel." These provisions drew an audible exclamation of shock from several observ-

public relations and in future Board - administration relationship. Case got up and asked that "in the interests of avoiding controversy, for the sake of the school and the students," the matter be shelved until further discussion could be held. Thus spared the necessity of an embarrassing vote, the Board unanimously approved a motion by Fred Knol to table the motion to ratify the contract.

Mrs. Olejniczak Retires; With Firm 22 Years

Mr. Anna Olejniczak, 305 S. 46th ave., Northlake, has retired after 22 years at Automatic Electric Company.

A machine operator, Mrs. Olejniczak has worked in the miscellaneous machines department throughout her career with the telephone and electronics equipment manufacturing company.

Raised on a farm in Thorpe, Wis., Mrs. Olejniczak, a widow, plans to re-

KIWANIS UNIFORM OF THE DAY—paper hats and red ponchos—here worn by Kiwanis Kids' Day Peanut Sales Chairman, Bob Sinn, will brighten street corners throughout Illinois, Eastern Iowa and Northern Indiana on Friday, September 24, as 10,000 Kiwanians become humble peanut vendors to raise $300,000 for the benefit of handicapped and underprivileged children. Al Anderson, owner of Anderson Florist, 2601 N. Harlem avenue, and

27
Bonds Sold Without Bids

Something seemed a little strange as Wade called the meeting to order ten minutes after the hour. What was so different? The usually laughing coalition trustees arrived a few minutes apart, pokerfaced and silent. They opened their folders as Don Dunahow asked for the floor.

"Gentlemen, I've been informed that House Bill 1710 will be passed and signed by the governor next week."

"Why is this so important?" Joe Farmar asked.

"It means that all junior colleges in Illinois will be governed by a state board instead of a local board. Local autonomy will disappear and a whole new set of rules will be developed as the state bureaucracy grows."

"I don't see it that way," responded Roy Jones. "I've read the bill thoroughly and talked with several legislators. We all agree the benefits will open higher education doors to our students. Just think, the state will provide 75% of all building costs and reimburse us for 50% of the cost of educating a student. We couldn't ask for a better deal."

"It just isn't that simple, Mr. Jones," replied Dunahow. "After the bill is signed, it will take months before the state trustees are appointed, followed by months to search for an executive director of the board. And this director will need a staff, and who knows how long that will take?"

"What do you suggest we do?" Joe asked in exasperation.

"I think we have to get off the rear of our anatomy and sell the bonds fast forward before the rates go up, which they're sure to do. I have an offer from McDougal & Condon to buy 8.9 million at an average rate of 3.6998%. What should I tell them?"

Babe stopped whispering to Bob and said, "Let me look at that offer."

The two studied the paper and then showed it to Fred and Joe. It ended up in the hands of Roy and Wade. There was a deep silence for a few minutes until Babe quietly said, "I move that we accept this offer." It was seconded by Joe.

In the discussion that followed Roy strongly objected, stating it was wrong to sell without competitive bids. Wade supported Roy's objection and commented, "We don't know if 3.6998% is good or bad. The only way to find out is to solicit bids in the bond market nationwide."

Roy stood up and shouted out with defiance, "I move that this motion be tabled." It was immediately seconded by Wade and defeated 4 to 2. Seconds later Joe called for a vote and the coalition showed its unity by loudly crying out yes four times to Roy's and Wade's no.

In a conciliatory manner Bob looked at Roy and Wade and said, "I respect you gentlemen very much and know in normal times competitive bids would be the way to go. But these are not normal times. If we don't get some money soon the River Grove site will be sold from under us."

Neil Mehler, who had arrived at the meeting early, was trying to take down every word. I, on the other hand, was excluded from the dialogue. I sensed the coalition trustees had been late due to a prior meeting where their plan of action had been approved by Babe. I wondered how Neil would treat the story. The rumor he described to me had turned out to be true. Since Dunahow had the leading part I assumed he'd written the scenario.

Shortly after the vote was taken Dunahow read a well-worded resolution approving the sale, which passed by a 5 to 1 vote. I couldn't understand why Wade, who disapproved of the sale, voted yes for the resolution. I would talk to him at another time.

In his customary fashion, Wade returned to the agenda and to my surprise all items I presented were approved without comment. It was OK to instruct the architect to plan for a 3,000 student campus and approval was given to purchase library furniture and the Croft books on board policy. To my surprise all faculty appointments were accepted without discussion. Ed Sexton was appointed the bookstore manager and Janet LaDere was promoted from clerk-typist to accounting clerk.

As soon as Wade adjourned the meeting the coalition boys speedily disappeared with Don Dunahow. I looked for Jim Tarpey but he couldn't be found. I joined Wade and Roy, who were busily responding to questions from two angry men, Neil Mehler and Jack Rossetter.

Looking at me in disgust Neil blurted out, "Wake up, Mr. College President. You don't know what's going on."

I said nothing. Neil was right. His rumor was correct. I had been misled by our college attorney. Looking at the three of us, Jack Rossetter erupted with, "You haven't heard the last of this. You have a corrupt board and unless you do something about it, I'll organize a crusade to get rid of those crooks."

Wade unsuccessfully tried to soothe him as he left, talking with Neil Mehler.

"Herb, I think you should stay out of this board conflict. Refer any calls that come in about this matter to me," Wade ordered as he left with Roy.

The following morning I met with my administrators, updated them on the latest happening and requested they not get involved. Concerned about the dark clouds that would fall on Triton if the public were informed, they agreed with reluctance. Bob Dale assured me that 3.7% was way too high. Had the bonds been rated they would probably go out at 3.1 or 3.2%. You couldn't withhold this from the public. Knowledge of it would reflect badly on the business office. John Widergren wondered how this news would affect the enrollment, while Dr. Darnes felt that unless the board rescinded the sale, Triton's accreditation would be delayed.

"Tomorrow I'm meeting with some manufacturing presidents. What should I tell them if they ask about the bonds?" Dean Simonsen asked.

"What do you know about them?"

"Not much. Only that they sold at 3.6998%."

"That's what you'll tell them. Please don't elaborate or interpret. In the meantime I'll work with Wade and Roy in trying to get the board to rescind their vote." We departed, very concerned.

Since nothing appeared in the news on Thursday, Friday, Saturday or Sunday, I began to feel that perhaps I was overreacting. My eating habits returned to normal. However, on Monday morning as I was having breakfast with Eugenia she placed in front of me the morning news and announced, "Well, well, you made the front page of the *Chicago Sun Times.*"

I gasped as I read the headline, "WATCHDOG GROUP FOR JUNIOR COLLEGE FORMED." The article was by a reporter named Germanski. His lead described the necessity for creating a watchdog because the Triton board did not arrange for competitive bids to sell their bonds. Jack Rossetter was quoted in the article; I assumed he was the reporter's source.

My immediate reaction was one of embarrassment. That a watchdog group had been organized to observe my trustees meant the trustees were not to be trusted! I felt fortunate that my name was not mentioned, but as the executive officer of the board I was somewhat responsible for the public's negative reaction. Why hadn't I recommended the hiring of Mr. Benjamin two months before? I recalled Babe saying that a $50,000 fee was too high. Now we had to pay a higher fee – the loss of the public confidence in Triton College we had sought so hard to gain.

When I arrived at the office, Maria told me that reporters from four newspapers had called and it was urgent that I call them back. My fifth returned call was to Mr. Benjamin. I got him on the phone instantly.

"Dr. Zeitlin, is it correct that all your bonds have been sold?"

"Yes, last night the board accepted a bid of 3.6998% from McDougal & Condon. Is that good or bad?"

"Recently I sold three million at 3.156%. Rates are slowing creeping up. Today the going rate for rated general obligation bonds is around 3.2; that's a half a point less than what you paid."

"As a specialist in the bond market, can you tell me how much are we overpaying the first year?"

"One half of a percentage point multiplied by $8,900,000 amounts to $44,500, but that's only part of the story."

"What's the rest?"

"I can't tell you until I see the retirement schedule. Thirty years of interest payments of $44,500 amounts to $1,335,000; 20 years of interest would cost you $890,000. However, most school districts retire their bonds in small increments in the early years and larger increments in the later years."

"Why do they do that?"

"Long-term bonds are more attractive to buyers because they earn higher interest for a longer period. Do you have any idea how much Dunahow has made on this deal?"

"Yes, our contract with him calls for 1/2 of 1% of the bond sale, which amounts to $44,500."

"Dr. Zeitlin, you're so naive! The $44,500 represents his commission from the seller, Triton College. On the other band he also represents the buyer, McDougal, and his commission from them is 2%, or $178,000."

"Are you telling me that Dunahow earned over $222,000 on this single transaction?"

"Yes, and what's more that son-of-a-bitch of an attorney screwed me royally. He led me to believe that I would be Triton's consultant, so I gave him valuable information."

"He also led me into believing he was shopping for a consultant at a rate lower than yours."

"He lied to both of us and as a result Triton's reputation will be ruined if you go ahead with the sale. Please remember I can still deliver at a lower rate if Triton cancels the sale."

"I'll get back to you. I need to talk to the other trustees." I hung up.

I tried to reach Wade several times but his private line was busy, so I got into my car and drove over to East Leyden. When I arrived he was on the phone with Dr. Knoeppel. After hanging up he said, "Herb, let's get out of here. My phone has been ringing all morning. All hell is breaking loose. We've got to talk."

Fifty minutes later we arrived at a quiet restaurant in a remote area of Du Page County. Wade ordered a double martini and I had a Manhattan.

"Herb, we're facing a major crisis! Clem Lowe and Knoeppel are not buying the Dunahow story, nor are a group of prominent citizens. They want the coalition to rescind the sale and open the bonds to competitive bids, or else."

"Just what does 'or else' mean?"

"It means that the citizens will organize, and get thousands of signatures to recall the coalition trustees."

"My God, do you really think they'll do that? My stomach is churning. What a helluva way to start a college. Isn't there a simple, satisfactory solution to this crisis?"

"Yes, cancel the sale. But the coalition won't buy that. However, I'm going to get busy and contact the power structure in this community, starting with Mayor O'Connor. Maybe I can get him to change his nephew's vote. Next I'll talk to Jim Olson, Bob's boss at the telephone company. I'm sure he wouldn't want his protégé to be labeled a corrupt trustee. It would also give the phone company a bad name. Both these men want to see Bob become mayor of River Grove. If that fails, I'll have a heart-to-heart talk with Bob. He's a good clean kid being influenced by the wrong people."

"Any chance of getting Joe to change his vote?"

"Joe will change only if Jim Kirie tells him to do so. I have to convince Kirie that Joe will never become a judge if be's dishonored as a trustee."

"What can I do?"

"Try to reach Elmore Boeger in Michigan and feel him out. If my intuition is correct, he would not have voted with the boys. In the meantime Roy and I will try to cool down the outraged citizens."

"Has Neil Mehler called you?"

"I was on the phone with him for almost an hour. I'm afraid he's going to put out a special edition on Triton. I shudder to think about it."

"Do you think Mayor Daley is involved?"

"I don't know, but you never can tell. Why don't you see Babe at City Hall and try to find out?"

"OK, next week I'll be visiting Babe at City Hall, Elmore Boeger at Rotary and Jim Hannum at the Cook County School Superintendent's office."

"Herb, may I remind you that I won't be at the June 30th meeting. It will be in capable hands if our vice president Roy Jones conducts it. I have to be in Cornucopia to open my cabin and get my boat out of drydock. I'm preparing for a lot of visitors this summer, including the Fred Knol family."

I arrived at my office on Wednesday, June 30th to find six different newspapers spread out on my desk. They'd been given to Maria by the various administrators, who all lived in different communities. I was shocked when I read such headlines as:

Birth in the Twilight Zone
Split Triton Board OK's Bond Sale
Watchdog Group for Triton Formed
Bond Sale Jars College Board – Dispute Rages
Scores Bond Sales
Citizens Ask Triton Board to Solicit Bids

There was no doubt about it. The Triton community and the nearby areas were aroused, angry and laced out against the politicians on the board. I called Roy Jones and asked him if he'd seen any of the articles.

"Yes I have, and so have hundreds if not thousands of other upset citizens who thought they'd elected an honest board. Be prepared for a long and fiery meeting. Since Wade is out, I'll try to control the irate crowd that's sure to be there. And as the chairman I'll grant permission to anyone who wishes to address us. Maybe when those rogues hear the people speak out they'll change their vote."

"Roy, I certainly hope so."

In anticipation of a large audience I asked Maria to run off 50 agendas instead of the usual 25. Jim Tarpcy called to say he had read some of the hot articles. His reaction was, "Wow, there will be a big show tonight, and I'm ready!"

Returning a dozen calls I assured the parties that their questions would be answered that night. I re-read Robert Newman's article in the *Proviso Herald* and thought he was right on the mark. I would read it to the board, but that wouldn't be enough. I needed some facts from reliable sources. I asked Maria to hold all calls as I made contact with those who would know. My first contact was with Dr. Lyman Glenny, Executive Secretary of the Board of Higher Education; second was James Hannum, Assistant County Superintendent, and third was Professor Dr. Lichty, who represented the State Superintendent of Schools and was the author of House Bill 1710.

And last I managed to get on the line Professor Richard Browne, the former Executive Secretary of the Board of Higher Education. My suspicions were confirmed by the four foremost authorities in the state. What surprised me most was that after I announced myself as the president of Triton College, the secretaries put me through to their bosses immediately. Now I knew there was no need to rush the sale of the bonds. The new community college board would not control the local tax rate or sale of bonds. Governor Kerner would sign the bill soon and machinery be put in motion to appoint the new trustees, who would shortly select an executive secretary. They all more or less implied that Dunahow's reason for instant action was invalid. That was all I needed to make a strong pitch to cancel the sale.

I arrived at the meeting place ten minutes before the hour. The room was packed and obviously in violation of the fire laws. Dr. George Cox came over and suggested we shift to the cafeteria, which we did.

Before the meeting started Jim Tarpey showed me the signatures of 95 attendees, including six press representatives, who officially signed in. Many more came in *without signing*. The air was filled with tension as the up-front crowd crossed their arms defiantly and waited. Roy Jones apologized for the inconveniences but before he could deliver his message, Fred Knol moved that Joe Farmar be appointed president pro tern in the absence of Wade Steel. It was seconded by Babe Serpico and carried. Roy did not vote.

Standing tall, dressed meticulously in a dark blue suit, Joe Farmar in a firm and loud voice called the meeting to order and asked me to present the faculty handbook as the first item on the agenda. I stressed the necessity of having a book that outlined to the faculty the rules, regulations and legal requirements to follow in the operation of the college. Without any hesitation it was unanimously accepted.

Suddenly a voice from the rear yelled out, "Tell us about the bond sale!"

Joe ignored the question and called upon Fred Knol and Bob Dale to present the hospital and medical care plans. After a lengthy discussion it was moved, seconded and carried to accept the proposal from the lowest bidder, Kemper Insurance, as submitted.

A second voice from the audience rang out, "Hurray, that's the honest way to go. Why didn't you do it that way with the bonds?"

Joe said nothing. You could feel the tension. A tall lady in the front row stood up and declared, "You can't ignore us. We are the taxpayers that created this college and we demand some answers now!"

Before she sat down she acknowledged a tremendous burst of

applause.

A second lady in the middle row shouted, "We are not going home until you explain why the big rush to sell those bonds?" More applause and a few whistles followed.

Joe nervously looked at his fellow trustees, hoping someone else would respond. But no one did. In a low sarcastic voice he said, "My dear lady, I don't mean to be disrespectful but that item is not on the agenda and we can't discuss it tonight."

Immediately a chorus of protests followed, with many boos and several cries of "Why not?"

Joe's response had added another log to the fire. The audience continued to talk aloud to show their disapproval. Joe issued a call for order, which the group ignored.

Sensing the feeling of the audience, Roy Jones took the floor and announced, "I can't speak for the rest of the board but at the end of this meeting I will remain and will be very happy to answer any and all questions. Which of you fellows care to join me?" He looked and hoped for some companionship.

Bob, Fred and Elmore raised their hands slowly, indicating a yes, while Babe, Don and Joe looked at each other and said nothing. Joe continued with the agenda and received unanimous approval for awarding the general liability insurance contract to the Reliance Insurance Company. When the Code of Ethics for school board members came up, a lengthy discussion followed, with many assuring remarks on how necessary it was for it to be followed.

Laughter broke out when Bob Collins read, "To remember at all times that as an individual I have no legal authority outside of the board . . . ."

"Are you listening, Serpico and Dunahow? If you had it to do over again would you still sell the bonds without bids?" a voice from the rear shouted.

Babe, aroused, shouted back, "I would do it again if I had to. Don Dunahow and I brought forth a good offer because time was running out."

The laughter turned into a roar when Bob read Item V, "To resist every temptation and outside pressure to use my position as a school board member to benefit either myself or any other individual. . . ."

"The unanswered question is, how much are these politicians benefiting from their secret deal?" was a roaring whisper.

After the code was unanimously accepted a Tarzan-like character stood up and announced, "This is good stuff, but will these crooked so-called trustees ever follow it?"

Several anonymous speakers followed, venting their feelings with, "Throw these dirty politicians out. Impeach the SOBs"

Joe was sizzling as the board came under fire and the meeting turned into a donnybrook. I studied him carefully. He was red all over. I feared he might have a heart attack if the free-for-all continued. In an effort to calm down the audience I suggested to Joe that he put Bob Dale on to present his purchasing manual, and not respond to any of the wild remarks.

With dignity and in a low voice Dale discussed the highlights of the manual. The audience heard and saw a new face and listened attentively as Roy Jones asked several questions. Action was deferred until the next meeting.

Next Dunahow informed the trustees that the offer of 80 cents per square foot was not likely to be accepted and recommended that three independent appraisals be made of the various parcels. Roll call vote was all ayes.

My recommendations for faculty and classified appointments were accepted without comment. The last item on the agenda was the correspondence. Bob Collins read a letter from Dr. Richard Whalen, President of Black Hawk College, in whieh he invited our board and administration to a conference in August for the purpose of discussing the formation of a Class I Junior College Association.

I was directed to notify Dr. Whalen that a meeting during the month of September would be more advantageous to the Triton board. At this point Bob Collins made a motion to adjourn the meeting. I interrupted him with, "Hold on, please. There are several other letters to be read."

Reluctantly he read a letter from the Citizens for Triton College, in which they asked the board to rescind the bond sale. No comments from any trustee. Bob called again for adjournment when Roy Jones insisted that he read the letters from Jack Rossetter and Dr. Leroy Knoeppel. Both letters criticized the board's action on the bonds, saying the rate of interest was too high and there had been no bids. Roy requested that the board talk it out now.

To this Joe replied, "Mr. Jones, I'm faced with a motion to adjourn by Mr. Collins, seconded by Mr. Knol. We can't discuss the bond issue until we get more information, so I am adjourning this meeting."

I immediately interrupted Joe and said, "Don't you do that! Today HB 1710 was explained to me by one of its authors and three other highly knowledgeable individuals in the state of Illinois. Dr. Lyman Glenny, who helped draft the bill and who is also the Executive Secretary of the Board of Higher Education, told me that the legislators hoped that all junior colleges in Illinois would eventually become Class I colleges."

"What's behind this push for Class I status?"

"Two major factors. First, higher state aid for every student enrolled and second, up to 75 per cent reimbursement for capital costs in building new facilities."

"And how long will we have to wait for this newfound money?"

"Not long, since the state legislature has already earmarked over 20 million for junior college construction and, in addition, 8 million in federal funds will become available. How does that sound to you, Mr. Farmar?"

"Too good to be true. But what did Dr. Glenny recommend we do about our bonds?"

"Sell a smaller portion of them through competitive bidding and make application to become one of the first Class I colleges in the state."

"Thank you, Dr. Zeitlin. The board will consider it at a later date. Let's end this meeting."

"Hold off, Joe. First, I want to read a letter I received from Robert Newman, student editor of the Elmwood Park High School newspaper, who has written on behalf of the entire student body."

In his letter Newman stressed how hard his and many other parents had worked for the creation of Triton College. Now that the college was about to be born the motives of the political trustees were under suspicion. He urged the trustees, in order to regain the confidence of the public, to cancel the previous vote.

I added, "Joe, this young man is on the right track. I fully support him and hope that you will too. As the editor of a school newspaper he has much influence, having close contact with our other four public high schools. In the past we welcomed student participation and support. If we lose that support now, our potential enrollment will shrink. You don't want that to happen, do you? Therefore, I implore you to cancel last week's vote and open the bonds for competitive bidding."

I was interrupted by applause and cheers by the donnybrook crowd. Looking straight at Babe and Dunahow I continued, "I know your intentions were honorable and the interests of the students were foremost in your mind, but you were misled and misinformed by some uninformed individuals."

More cheers followed.

"Triton was created for the benefit of the students. Through me they've delivered a loud, clear and intelligent message that I support and hope you will too."

At this point Farmar succeeded in adjourning the meeting over the strong objection of Jones. With an informal meeting open to comments from the public, Jack Rossetter spoke:

"I personally hold nothing against this board for not having heard me during the official meeting as originally requested. They are operating strictly within the law, which is their prerogative. There's such a thing as the letter of the law and the spirit of the law, but they are within their rights."

Rossetter continued. "There was not a single person in the CFT who agreed with the Serpico-Dunahow action. I realize that when you talk in small percentages it seems trivial, but the interest rate on these bonds runs into real money. We are also concerned about your attorney's fees. The fee of $45,000 is extremely high in proportion to the services rendered. It's about $30,000 above the recommended charge."

Several others spoke out against the bond sale. The meeting ended with an agreement between Farmer and Rossetter to discuss the matter more fully the following week at the Citizens for Triton meeting at the Little Theater of East Leyden.

As the crowd dispersed Bob, Joe and Don looked at me with disgusted, dirty looks and left fast.

Roy said, "Let them go. The people have spoken and if they have an ounce of intelligence, they'll veto the sale."

"Are you sure of that?"

"With these guys you can't be sure of anything. However, I was very proud of you. At last we know where you stand, and don't worry about being fired. The people are behind you. Those crooks won't go against the people, now that they know the facts."

As I left with Roy he asked Boeger, "If you'd been at last week's meeting would you have voted for the bond sale without bids?"

Boeger hesitated for a minute, shook his head and said, "I don't think I would have gone along with the boys. What they did is contrary to good business practice, and as a Rotarian and attorney I would have voted against it."

"Hurrah for you, Elmore. Now, Dr. Zeitlin, all we need is one more vote and we can regain the public's confidence. Why don't you work on one of those boys. I know it might seem like an impossible task but you must never give up."

"I'll try," I said as I left, feeling there was still a possibility the coalition might change its direction. I missed not having Wade to talk to and wondered how he was making out with the big political bosses. When I got home, Eugenia and the kids were sleeping, so I helped myself to a big glass of milk with cookies and thought about the night's drama. I had never seen such an angry crowd, with reporters picking up every word. Joe had been wrong in not letting the people speak. The dirty looks of Bob, Joe, Babe and Don disturbed me, but I had to let it out: "You were misled and misinformed by someone uninformed."

For months I tried to please the board at every turn, but tonight I'd pleased myself by speaking the truth from the head. I even surprised myself. I fell asleep thinking about what I had done, and the possible consequences to me personally.

By speaking out I forced Bob to read the letter from the Citizens for Triton College. I insisted that he allow Roy Jones to read the letters from Dr. Knoeppel and Jack Rossetter. The fourth letter, addressed to the board and me, I read loudly and slowly, looking directly at Joe and members of the press. Robert Newman, student editor of the Elmwood Park High School newspaper, had pleaded eloquently with the board to operate with integrity. As read Newman's letter, Joe displayed fire in his eyes, sneering at me. I knew him to be violent; I worried about how I would deal with him in the future. Roy Jones's assurance that I wouldn't get fired actually made me think more in those terms.

Were those boys now secretly meeting to plan my fast exit? Yes, I was sure they were, but in my heart I didn't want to leave. My goal was to reform the coalition, by appealing to the sublime in each of them,

28
Board Under Fire

The following morning, while Eugenia and I were eating breakfast, the front doorbell rang. No one was there but an envelope was taped to the door. I immediately knew its origin. In lower case letters the envelope read, *dr. herb zeitlin*. I opened it and read:

dear herb,   july 1, 1965

you looked damned GOOD last nite, man, and I think you know it. but in case you are "insecure" enuf that you aren't SURE you registered, lemme underline the fact that not i alone, but others who have already called me (by 9 o'clock this morn) were VERY impressed by your guts and forthrightness, in a situation where it TOOK these qualities.

I am VERY pleased with the meeting and am sure in my own mind that the board lost inESTiMably by NOT acceding to our request for a hearing DURING the meeting; they merely put themselves on open RECORD to the public AND (thank god) the PRESS, so their efforts were sadly backfiring.

again, tho, for your courageous and intelligent stand, thanx. this has (knock on wood) been a magnificent "democratic uprising" and gives heart to those who would say, "yeah, but what can y'DOOOOOO about it?"

and as always, rest assured I understand the tightrope walking necessary; i expect NO answers, ever, to these notes! i've been around; i ain't no fool! and, by the way, i know when i'm good without bein told, so there!
                                                    Jack
the enclosed is just a politic way of bein sure a special meeting isn't run without our knowing, just in case they still haven't seen the light!!!!!

"Darling, call Jack at once and thank him for his encouragement," Eugenia pleaded.

"No, I can't," I sympathetically responded. "He's right about the tightrope I'm walking."

We were interrupted by a phone call from Gordon Simonsen. "Herb, have you seen today's copy of the West Cook County Press?"

"No, what does it say?"

"Plenty. The front page headline reads, in their largest bold type, 'TRITON COLLEGE BOARD UNDER FIRE, WATCHDOG GROUP FORMED.' A subhead reads, 'Citizens Committee Objects to Bond Selling Procedure.' Reporter Patrick Butler goes into detail about last night's donnybrook meeting. You know I have an occupational advisory committee meeting at 4:00 PM today. How should I answer the questions I'm sure to be asked?"

"Gordon, contact the deans immediately and tell them we'll meet at noon to discuss strategies."

I put down the phone, kissed Eugenia and drove off to work.

At the office Maria had spread out on my desk four other newspapers with similar front-page headlines:

Franklin Parker–$8.9 MILLION IN TRITON BONDS LET WITHOUT COMPETITIVE BIDS. BANKER SAYS – THEY'LL NEVER KNOW IF PRICE IS RIGHT.

Proviso Herald–DISSENT FROM BOARD MEMBERS, CITIZENS. TRITON BOARD GIVES BONDS TO CHICAGO FIRM.

Maywood Herald–CITIZENS GROUP PROTESTS TRITON BOARD DECISION.

Suburban Life–TRITON COLLEGE MAY SELL BONDS WITHOUT BIDS.

The stories were highly damaging to the board's reputation. Leading the group was Neil Mehler's article in the *Franklin Parker* quoting each trustee, as well as three big bankers. (One banker said, "This board had a lot of gall and opened themselves to a taxpayer's suit.") Also in the *Franklin Parker* was an in-depth article on the formation of a citizens group to watch the board. An editorial entitled, "Seems Like Old Times" compared the Triton board's actions with the worst Chicago corruption of the past.

As I read each story I was shocked beyond belief. Every reporter attacked the trustees mercilessly. In the past, aware of the tremendous power of the press, I always tried to get on its good side by speaking to it openly. Our fate as individuals is more dependent than we realize on the integrity and ethics of journalists. Truth and news are not necessarily the same; some stories tell us more about the reporters' cynicism and contempt for politics than about the character of the people they write. I felt very sorry for the wives and children of the trustees. I wondered how they would be treated by neighbors and friends. Some of the kids would not want to face their teachers and fellow students.

When I met with the deans, it was decided that they would try not to get involved in the board controversy or show any leanings one way or another. If questioned they would respond with, "On June23 the board voted to sell the bonds without bids, but as of today they are considering other options." The goal was to make it short and express no opinion.

After returning several calls, I tried to reach Joe and Bob, but neither was available. When I spoke to Roy Jones, he enthusiastically said, "I've seen all the stories. They're wonderful! Thank God we have an intelligent press. Have you talked to Babe yet?"

"No, he's next on my list to call."

"If you can convince him to change his vote, the others will follow without question."

Later that evening Babe returned my call and agreed to meet me in his office on Friday at 2:00 PM. The first thing he said when we met was, "Dr. Zeitlin, you are in deep trouble. You're supposed to support your board, not challenge them. You'll be on your way if you don't change."

I tried to explain to him that the going rate was 3.2%, not 3.7%, but he didn't want to listen, saying, "Get this straight, Dr. Zeitlin, the bonds are going to be sold as presented and nothing you say will make us change our minds."

"Excuse me, but does Mayor Daley feel the same way?"

"He has nothing to do with this deal. Yesterday he was the first one to show me all those outrageous and distorted articles and shouted at me, 'Get off the Triton board. You're hurting my office. You have better things to do.' "

"What did you tell him?"

"I'll be out as soon as my term is up."

During our conversation we were interrupted several times by telephone calls. Suddenly he started to straighten out the papers on his desk and quickly said, "Don't leave now, my boss will be here in a few minutes. I want you to meet him."

How nice, I thought. At last I was about to meet Chicago's greatest mayor, Richard Daley. Maybe if I could have a few words with him I could get him to change Babe's mind.

Two minutes later a heavyset elderly man burst in, gave Babe a piece of paper and said, "Tom Jenkins is a precinct captain in the fifth ward. His uncle feels his property taxes should be lowered due to a recent sale. Get on this right away, Babe, and see how you can help him out."

As he started to leave Babe introduced me to his office boss, P. J. Cullerton, the Cook County Tax Assessor. I extended my hand to shake his. He abruptly stepped back, looked me in the eye distastefully, said nothing and left.

I asked Babe, "What's wrong with him?"

"Don't you know by now? Your actions Wednesday night have put you in the doghouse. You don't understand Chicago politics. Come follow me and let me show you how we make adjustments."

As I followed him to a large rear file I thought about Babe's many bosses: his wife, Josephine; his Democratic Party boss Mayor Daley; the Triton boss, Wade Steel, and finally his office boss, P. J. Cullerton. Four power bosses all trying to direct him, and he trying to please all. He must have had a strong constitution to withstand those diverse forces.

Babe opened a large file, pulled out the record of Jenkins's uncle, noted the address and the assessed valuation and remarked, "Now, I have to look up the most recent sales in his area and match the square footages, known as the comps."

He continued to work the comps on his calculator. Finally he announced, "Property values are dropping in that area so I'm reassessing his property. Jenkins will receive a $531 tax reduction."

I thanked Babe for the short lesson on appraising property. I'd learned two important things from my visit. First, that the coalition would not change its vote. And second, that if you had the right connection in the Assessor's Office your property could be adjusted quickly by Babe Serpico. Money and power were in his hands.

What I didn't know was whether there were tips involved. If, as Don Dunahow had assured me some time ago, there were, where, when and how were they given? Was Babe the principal beneficiary or were there others involved?

As I started to leave Babe's secretary brought in an extra large pizza and asked, "Mr. Serpico, I need some money to pay the man." Without any hesitation Ralph pulled out a big wad of bills and tossed her two tens. While Babe's salary was about half the mayor's, the extra benefits may have made his income much higher. By how much, I didn't know. But now I was beginning to know more about Chicago politics.

When I returned to the office, a little sadder, I returned a call to Mabel Oberg. "Dr. Zeitlin, I have good news for you. Due to a cancellation my cabin at Bonner's Lake is available from Friday, July 17th until Sunday, August 1st. How does that sound to you?"

"That's great. I'll take it!" I drove home that evening, my spirits lifted remembering my year-and-a-half stay in Madison, Wisconsin during World War II. Living in Wisconsin in the summer was great for summer sports. I knew Eugenia and the kids would love swimming in the clear water of Bonner's Lake. When I broke the news at the dinner table, the kids became excited and looked forward to 16 days of vacation. Eugenia was annoyed when I said I couldn't get away for the full 16 days, only for the weekends. She was also upset when the TV news announced that General Westmoreland needed 125,000 more American troops in Vietnam. Added to her worries was LBJ's executive order to double the draft call.

She cried out, "You know, Herbert, this so-called police action in the Far East could develop into a big war. Mark could be called up."

"Eugenia, you worry too much. LBJ is a doer, and with the additional troops he'll get, it over with within a few months or a year. So relax and enjoy the July 4th weekend."

On Saturday night Eugenia and I saw the movie, *Dr. Zhivago,* which we enjoyed very much. After seeing the many scenes set in frigid

Russia, it was refreshing to leave the theater and feel the warm Chicago air. On Sunday, however, it was hot, so we all left for the Ridgewood Swimming Pool in Oak Park. Mark and Joyce showed promise swimming the crawl, while Ann spent most of her time horsing around at the low end. I was unsuccessful in teaching her the side stroke or crawl. Clare was happy just kicking her feet at the side. In the evening we celebrated Independence Day by having dinner at Eugenia's favorite restaurant, the *Homestead* in Melrose Park

The following day, Monday, July 5th, a declared holiday, Mark and Joyce took off to see a baseball game while Eugenia and the two little ones stayed home to watch TV. During lunch I received a call from Bob Darnes.

"Herb, could you interview two teachers this afternoon? They're both from out-of-state and I feel would be great additions."

I said okay and hustled down to the office to see Deans Simonsen and Darnes discussing the applicants they'd interviewed. Here it was a holiday and both men were working to complete the college staffing. With two months to go before opening day I knew we'd make it, observing these two super-efficient administrators working so well together. After completing the interviews I realized what Darnes had said was correct. We were about to hire two superior instructors. The names would be on the board agenda for July 14th.

As evening approached Roy Jones called me, "Dr. Zeitlin, is Wade back yet?"

"No, he isn't. As you know there's no telephone in his cabin. I'll call Millie at their Franklin Park home."

"Please do that and remind all the trustees that we're scheduled to attend the Citizens for Triton meeting tomorrow night. It's most important that we all attend if we're to regain the citizens' confidence."

My first call was to Boeger. "It's on my calendar. I'll be there."

The second was to Bob Collins. Beverly answered, "Bob will not miss this one."

Next was Joe Farmar. Ceil took the message and said, "I'll tell Joe."

When I called Fred Knol, he replied, "They're out for blood. I'm not looking forward to this meeting but I guess I'll show."

Babe was annoyed when I called him and shouted at me, "I don't want anything to do with that bunch of do-gooders. They won't listen to reason and they can kiss my ass," and banged down the phone.

Millie called back, "I'll be there but Wade won't. He told me he'll be back for the July 14th meeting."

The following night, when I arrived at the Little Theater, seated at the table on the stage were Boeger, Jones, Knol, Rossetter and three of his officers. After waiting until 15 minutes after the hour Rossetter opened the meeting.

"It's nice to see three Triton trustees here, but where are the others who promised to talk it out tonight?"

Nobody said anything. Rossetter sarcastically continued, "Oh,! know when the heat's on they find a place to cool off."

Knol, as part of the coalition that had voted without bids, was under fire. He coolly stated that he was there to listen and would do "some soul-searching" on the matter. Rossetter made the following requests:

1. Would the board rescind its previous vote?
2. Would the board now advertise for bids?
3. Would the board reduce the amount requested?
4. Would the board reexamine the fee paid to the attorney?
5. Would the board make a firm policy to advertise for bids on all large contracts?

Although no definite answers were given to the audience of over 70 people, they left with the feeling was that some positive action would take place at the official meeting of the Triton board, July 14th. That date was fixed in everyone's mind as the time of decision for the Triton trustees.

On Tuesday, July 13th Wade showed up in the office just before lunch time. Again, we decided to drive out to our hideaway restaurant in Du Page County to update each other. He'd been floored when Millie showed him copies of the various newspapers. He commented to me, "If I'd been at the June 30th meeting I would have permitted the citizens to speak out. Joe has put the trustees in a bad light and the impression was multiplied on July 6th when Knol appeared as the spokesman for the coalition."

"What can we do to correct a bad situation?"

"At the July 14th meeting I'll give anyone who wants to talk plenty of time to sound off. We must work hard to regain the public's confidence. In the meantime I'll try to contact McDougal & Condon to see if the college can get out of the deal. Just remember the resolution to sell the bonds has not been signed by Bob or me, and I don't intend to do so. I've got to convince the politicians in this town and my fellow trustees that it would be crazy to sell those bonds after the public's display of such big disapproval."

"How did your talks go with Conti, Kirie and O'Connor?"

"Not well at all. They're all supporting the coalition."

"Why?"

"I managed to talk to several bankers who were approached by Dunahow. It was hard to get them to say anything since they didn't want to talk about Dunahow's devious methods."

"What did you get out of them?"

"Dunahow demanded a $100,000 contribution to the local Democratic and Republican Parties or else there would be no deal. He claimed it was the normal way to do business in Chicago. They didn't buy it. Now everyone knows that McDougal & Condon did."

"Wade, this is all new to me. I always thought the Democrats and Republicans were fighting each other. Now it appears that when it comes to sleazy business they can work together. Is that correct?"

"Yes, at last you're beginning to understand Chicago politics. And that's only half the story."

"I can't believe this. What else is left?"

"Smith presented himself as the agent for both the seller and the buyer. As in real estate, he was to receive a double commission."

"How much would he be getting?"

"Most companies pay a 1% to 2% commission to the seller or the buyer of the total sale. However, since Dunahow was representing the buyer and the seller he was willing to cut his commission of 4% to 3% to make the deal, which would amount to $267,000."

"Is there any more?"

"Oh yes, there are a few more details."

"Such as?"

"In addition to the commission from McDougal & Condon, Dunahow will receive a fee of $44,500 from Triton College."

"Now, are you telling me his total earnings for this transaction would be $311,500?"

"Yes, provided it goes through. He's agreed to share his commission with the boys who made it happen. I've been told that Collins, Farmar, Knol and Serpico each will receive $50,000, for a total of $200,000. The leftover balance of $111,500 will go to Dunahow for masterminding the deal."

"I can't believe this. It's ugly, and the taxpayers are being cheated. Now that I know the truth it hurts. We really are dealing with a bunch of crooks. Roy told me this several times, and I didn't believe him. How could I have been so stupid?"

"Listen, Herb. Don't blame yourself. There are millions of taxpayers taken for a ride every day and they don't know it. The little guys pay for it with more taxes while the big earners buy tax-free bonds with high interest returns. It's another example of the poor getting poorer with the rich continuing to get richer."

"Can we prevent this from happening?"

"Yes, I think so. As long as we have people like Jack Rossetter around to help we can clean up these dirty deals. He knows the score and will not let it happen. We'll be faced with some rough days but Roy, Elmore, and I will try to prevent it from happening. Incidentally, Kirie and Conti want me to fire you. I told them if I were to do that the public would have a double outrage. Firing you would ultimately lead to their own destruction. The public likes you so you do what you must do. As long as I'm president of the board you'll be our college president."

Later that evening before retiring I gave Eugenia the cold facts. "We have three trustees, the college president and the general public opposing the sale, while four trustees and three big political bosses support it. The impasse may be broken tomorrow night when the coalition faces the fury of the public."

"Do you think the coalition will back down on the sale?"

"They're unpredictable. Right now I imagine Dunahow is brain storming the boys with some new twists or angles to justify the sale."

"I would love to attend that meeting to watch those big boys sweat. May I go?"

"No, my dear. You stay out of it. I don't want you to join Millie's brigade, at least not right now."

"I find it hard to understand how a company can contribute $100,000 each to the two major political parties. Just what does the company stand for, politically, I mean?"

"In Chicago the so-called battle between the Republicans and the Democrats is just window dressing. It's a joke! When in power they unite to fleece the public if they can get away with it. In this case the coalition's corruption will cost the taxpayers over half a million."

"I'm now beginning to understand Chicago politics. Does this kind of stuff happen in all big cities, such as New York, Los Angeles or Miami?"

"It happens whenever the taxpayers are sleeping. But it will not happen at Triton, because the journalists caught it in the early stages. Their continuing attacks will make it difficult for the politicians to perform in the usual fashion. As long as we have people like Wade, Roy, Elmore and Jack Rossetter we'll stop it."

I then showed Eugenia eight additional articles that had appeared within the last week. With avidity she read the *Chicago Tribune's* July 8th story entitled, "Triton College Holds Up Sale of Bonds" and the *Suburban Life* featured article, "Debate College Bonds Tomorrow," which I felt would guarantee us a full house for the next day's meeting.

On the morning of July 14th I called Jim Tarpey and asked him to prepare for an extra large crowd. He said he would be there early, as Maria ran off 150 agendas.

Around six o'clock I called all the trustees, except Fred Knol, who was on vacation, to inform them that the meeting would be held in the cafeteria and that they should expect a large crowd as a result of the latest attacking articles. When I arrived a few minutes before the hour, my expectations were proven correct. The room was packed with reporters, teachers, special organizations and a large group from the Citizens for Triton. Wade, Roy and Elmore were seen at the stage table talking freely with a variety of citizens. Eight o'clock arrived, and no Smith, Serpico, Collins, Farmar or Jim Tarpey. Eight-ten – no sign of the missing trustees or their attorney.

At 8:20 PM Wade announced, "No quorum, no meeting. However, we three trustees along with the college president will remain to answer any of your questions."

A loud voice rang out, "When the heat's on, they're gone."

Another brazen voice shouted, "Impeach the sons of bitches."

A third party said, "Fire the crooked attorney," as a dozen more side remarks were heard.

Wade pounded his mallet several times, calling for order, and finally stood up and announced, "We must have an orderly meeting or no meeting at all. I will not be part of another donnybrook session."

Jones and Boeger stood up as if to leave. Wade asked the two trustees to wait as the crowd settled down and order was restored.

Rossetter was the first to speak. "If anything, the absence of these trustees and their attorney proves that they're guilty as hell of unethical procedures, and who knows what else? It's obvious the coalition was afraid to face this hundred or more accusers."

There was a long pause, everyone waiting for Wade to reply. Wade looked at Roy, Elmore and me, hoping we would field the question. With nothing coming forth, in a low voice Wade said, "I apologize for the absent trustees. I don't know why they're not here. They're all family men, well-educated, respected members of the community who were elected by you. Maligning them publicly without any solid facts is not fair. I beg of you to be patient. We'll hear from them at the next meeting, which is scheduled for July 28th."

Rossetter responded, "We're not here to attack the coalition. We're here to make sure the taxpayers get a fair break As our name implies, we are citizens for Triton. We want to be sure that the patronage system does not become a part of this college. We want the college president to have full authority to run a first-class college without interference from any trustee or combination of such."

A couple of "Hear Ye! Hear Ye!" shouts came from a now subdued audience as the questions started to flow freely, most of the concerns focused on the bond issue or the attorney. The three trustees vowed they would work together to stop the bond sale. Before leaving Rossetter had a few ones for the college president.

"Dr. Zeitlin, I want to know if the negative publicity about Triton that appeared in 22 news articles and was also heard on all the radio stations has had any effect on faculty or student recruitment. I know it's a hot one but how would you answer it?"

"Yes, it has. How much we can't tell at this moment. Dean Darnes and Dean Simonsen have told me several scheduled faculty interviews were cancelled by the teachers, and Dean Widergren reported that over two dozen students have officially withdrawn from the college. It follows, a good college reputation attracts students while a tainted reputation discourages enrollments."

"How many students do you expect on opening day?"

"Presently several hundred are enrolled. On Tuesday, September 7th we expect to greet over 1,000 new scholars."

"Huh, that's an optimistic Californian's pipe dream. How many teachers have been hired and where are they coming from?"

"As of today we have 21 full-time faculty and 51 part-timers. At a later date I'll give a more detailed report to the board."

As the long meeting broke up in a peaceful mood Wade handed me a large brown envelope that he'd received in the mail from McDougal & Condon, and commented, "Read it tonight. I think you'll find it interesting."

Before going to bed, even though I was rather tired, I was re-awakened as I read President J.P. Condon's letter and the ten-page resolution. Signed on June 18, 1965, it referred to a mutual agreement of June 1st. That this agreement had been kept secret from Wade, Roy and Elmore proved that Dunahow had lied to us and that Neil Mehler's so-called rumor was well-founded. Wade had warned me in the past never to confront Don Dunahow with his lies; just give him enough rope and he would hang himself. Included in the letter was the following paragraph:

"In the event the above-described bonds are not delivered to us by July 30, 1965, we reserve the privilege after this date to continue our commitment hereunder, or withdraw from our undertaking at our option upon written notice to you."

As I reread the paragraph it seemed to me the door was open for us to get out of the deal if President Joe Condon agreed. All three trustees present at the meeting that night had vowed they would try to do just that. I fell asleep feeling that would happen. It was a real good feeling.

29
Harassing the College President

Before I left for work the following morning Eugenia reminded me that we would be off for our vacation at Bonner's Lake the following afternoon. She insisted that I get a short haircut so I could swim better.

After lunch, when I arrived at Nick's barbershop in Melrose Park, he was not his usual smiling and joking self.

He said nothing as he motioned me to his chair so I said, "Is something wrong? Some bad news?"

"No, no, I was just thinking." He started to trim the sides.

"Does your wife like being one of the Triton judges at Mt. Carmel School?" I asked.

"Oh yes. She enjoys working with Babe. He's done so much to help us. Remember he sent you to us, so we want to help him."

"It is wonderful to have such a good friend."

"You know, when he first met you he liked you very much."

"Yes, I've been told that before. Are you telling me he doesn't like me anymore?" I queried as he started sharpening his long razor on the side leather.

Nick didn't answer me as he moved the sharp razor up and down my neck. A sudden fear hit me when Nick softly said, "Babe told me yesterday that if you don't cooperate you'll go to the dogs."

He looked me directly in the eyes and asked, "What's wrong with you? You don't know a good friend when you have one. Take my advice and learn how to work with Babe. He'll always help you out if you do what you're told."

"Thanks for the tip, Nick."

I realized news traveled fast in Melrose Park. "Don't worry, my friend, Babe and I will work well together. We have some slight differences but we'll find a solution soon."

I said good-bye. Suspecting that his razor might slip if I didn't conform to Babe's wishes, I realized that this was a final so-long to Nick.

When I returned to the office Maria complimented me on the short haircut and wished me well for the coming weekend.

"Where is Bonner's Lake?" she asked. Deep in the woods, I explained, and almost impossible to find!

I left the office at 3:30. Eugenia was waiting with Joyce and Clare in her packed station wagon. Mark and Ann jumped into my little Skylark and away we drove to Wisconsin in a two-car caravan. When we eventually arrived at our cabin, we quickly changed into our bathing suits and had a delightful dip just before dinner. After Joyce and Mark took care of the dishes we cleaned the kitchen table for a hot game of canasta.

Saturday morning we visited the small public library in Burlington, where everyone found something interesting to read. Later on we shopped in a general store, enjoyed hot dogs for lunch and then returned to the lake for extended swimming and sunning.

Sunday morning was church, exploring the lake area, lunch and back into the crystal clear water. After racing Mark and Joyce to the far-out raft I heard a familiar voice call out, "Dr. Zeitlin, we're here."

I couldn't believe it! On the shoreline stood Maria, Tony and little Joseph. "May we join you for a swim?" Maria asked.

"By all means." I led them up to the cabin, where they quickly changed into their suits. We had one great afternoon chatting, swimming and sunning. Clare and Ann with little Joseph started to collect different kind of rocks. As dinner time approached Maria ran up to their car, pulled out a large pot of spaghetti with Italian meat sauce and heated it up. We all ate with gusto.

After they left Eugenia said, "What a wonderful secretary, wife and mother Maria is. It's amazing they found us in this wilderness."

"Yes, it is. Maria told me that Babe drew her a map. I wonder how he knew where we were located."

"Does it matter?"

"Yes, it does." I racked my brain many times over how he might have known where we were headed.

Before retiring that night I appointed my 15-year-old, 6-foot son,

Mark, the man in charge of home security. I showed him what doors to lock and the shortcut through the woods to a public telephone. He promised to call me every evening at the office to let me know everything was OK.

Monday morning I was up at six and left before seven to be in the office before nine. Dean Widergren and Trudy Wilson were busy registering students while Deans Simonsen and Darnes were interviewing teachers. In mid-morning Wade called me. "Herb, have you seen today's issues of the *Proviso Herald* and the *Mont Clare Herald*?"

I told him no, but I would pick them up on the way to a Rotary meeting at lunch time.

"We have two more blistering attacks. The bold front page headlines read in one, 'Lingering Twilight' and in the other 'When the Heat's On, Triton Board Is Gone.' Babe called this morning to tell me that Mayor Daley is furious about the attacks and wants them stopped."

"What did he suggest?"

"He apologized for the absent trustees last Wednesday night and suggested, and I agreed, to meet in executive session this Wednesday evening to work some things out. He promised all the boys would be there."

"Should I make up an agenda?"

"No, Dunahow wants to present some new approaches, but please take notes and make any suggestions that will improve the Triton image."

As I was about to leave Maria stopped me. "Dr. Zeitlin, have you noticed the police car that's been parked in our lot most of the morning? The officer, an old-timer, seems to have his eyes focused on your car – or is it mine?"

I told Maria not to worry, Bob Dale probably called him for a protective escort to the bank. The police were hired to serve and protect, and thank goodness they were doing just that. A few minutes before noon I left for the lively Melrose Park Rotary Club. One of the Rotarians, vice president and general manager of the Melrose Park Bank, told me that he had many buyers waiting for Triton's 3.7% bonds and wanted to know when Mr. Condon was going to put them on the market.

He commented, "It's an exceptionally high rate and will be sold within a week or two even if they're sold above par."

He was taken aback when I told him the board was now considering rescinding the sale. The ears of other Rotarians were tuned in as I spoke, and a wide variety of comments flowed out. After the meeting I drove south on Broadway heading toward Lake to buy some newspapers when all of a sudden I heard a siren and saw flashing red lights in my rear view mirror.

I looked at my speedometer and it showed 30 miles per hour. The officer that stopped me turned out to be the old-timer who'd been parked in the West Leyden parking lot. Had he been waiting for me to do something wrong? Yes, and he'd finally caught me.

"What's your hurry?" he asked. "Let me see your license and registration." Before writing he checked my bumpers and lights and then wrote the ticket.

"So you're Dr. Zeitlin," he said. "I don't give a damn who you are. You were racing 40 miles per hour in a 20-mile zone. Now you can pay the fine, go to jail or tell it to the judge."

The following evening, July 21st, as all the boys assembled in my office Babe announced, "You know we have a speedy weedy president. When he's behind the wheel, he becomes a driving maniac."

Looking directly at me he added, "You know, Dr. Zeitlin, if you receive two more speeding tickets you lose your driving license. The state of Illinois is going after speed demons and you are one of them."

"I'm aware of that and I don't intend to receive any more speeding tickets."

Babe responded, "1 can take care of it if you want me to."

"No, that's not necessary. I'll pay the fine tomorrow."

I was then convinced that I had been set up by someone in the coalition. How did I arrive at that conclusion? Quite simple! The officer had referred to me as Dr. Zeitlin, even though my license and registration read only "Herbert Zeitlin," no doctor. What I wanted to know was, who had directed the officer to get me?

Babe opened the meeting sounding off on the horrible news stories and asked how we could get even with the press. He told us that Mayor Daley insisted we do whatever it took to stop the press from fueling the fire.

Dunahow immediately responded, "Let's knock the wind out of their sails until it hurts."

"Please explain that," Farmar said.

"You mean we should slash the reporters' tires," Bob said.

"No, Don didn't mean that." Joe, in deep thought, continued. "We can get them to shut their mouths by suing each paper for a few million."

"No, I didn't mean that. What I would like to do is ruin them financially."

"Just how would you do that?"

"Every paper is dependent upon advertising. Without it they would collapse. I would contact every advertiser personally and persuade them to withdraw their ads."

"Do you think it would work?"

"Yes, definitely, and I would like to start with that SOB Neil Mehler's *Franklin Parker.*"

"Fellows, we're on the wrong track. Such a procedure would backfire on us and make matters worse, so let's stop seeking revenge," Wade loudly interrupted.

"What would you suggest we do, Wade?" Babe asked. "How can we regain the public's confidence?"

Everyone looked at Wade. He said nothing and then slowly responded, "First we must rescind the bond sale. We now know the press, the Citizens for Triton and masses of others want us to do it. If we don't, you can be assured the movement for our recall will begin. We'll be continually assassinated with every bad name in the book."

"OK, we'll do it if Joe Condon lets us out of the contract.". Bob, Joe and Les opened their mouths in shock, and shook their heads but said nothing as their leader spoke. By the look on their faces I could see they were opposed to losing the $50,000 gratuity from Condon.

Babe continued, "Is there anything else we should do?"

"The public senses there's a conflict between the college president and the board. We must make an effort to eliminate that feeling."

"How the hell do we do that?"

"By accepting his recommendations and occasionally complimenting him to show that there are no hard feelings left."

"So tell me, Dr. Zeitlin," Babe asked. "What needs to be passed at the July 28th meeting?"

Even though Bob, Joe and Les had angry looks on their faces I was pleased to hear Babe's encouraging words. As the leader of the coalition the boys would have to follow his direction whether they liked it or not. I then stressed that with only five weeks to go before the college opened it was urgent that the following items be approved ASAP:

1. *BIDDING ON PURCHASES.* Since the public outcry over the sale of bonds without bids was so great the board should readily accept Bob Dale's recommended policy on purchasing. *"No purchase shall be made over $1,500 without securing three or more bids."*

2. *ADDRESSING THE BOARD.* Any citizen shall have the right to address the board by putting in writing 48 hours prior to the board meeting such a request to the college president.

3. *AWARD TO LOWEST BIDDER.* Approval of the contract with Olson Office Company of Forest Park for the purchase of urgently needed furniture in the amount of $8,784.

4. *INSTRUCTOR'S CONTRACT.* Approval of the form submitted by the college president.

5. *APPROVAL OF ALL FACULTY AND CLASSIFIED APPOINT-MENTS.*

6. *DEVRY ELECTRONICS LAB.* Approval of contract in the amount of $13,056 for courses in electronics.

7. *STUDENT ACTIVITY FUND.* Approval needed to purchase office equipment and supplies, and to finance college lecture and forum series.

8. *APPOINT BOARD COMMITTEE* to meet with Joseph Condon to obtain release from purchasing bonds.

I couldn't believe it! This was a 180-degree shift in direction with the board. No one objected to any of my requests. The July 21st executive meeting was a good rehearsal for the official one scheduled for July 28th. Was this executive meeting legal? Wade said it was because all decisions were related to personnel matters. I felt that was stretching it a little.

Minutes before adjourning Don handed a fistful of photos to Fred Knol. "See what you missed by not joining our fishing trip this weekend?"

Fred quietly let out, "Wow!. They're all well-endowed with beautiful equipment." Don directed Fred to pass them on to me. What I saw amazed me. Don was sipping drinks with three barechested women with see-through aprons in a variety of poses, laughing along the way. As I looked at the last photo Bob grabbed them from me, his face red all over, and quietly said, "Damn it, Don, this is not the time or place to display that stuff."

"Tear those fuckin' pictures up," Joe said quietly, so as not to disturb the others. Hearing this, Don ran over to Bob, pulled the pictures from him and put them into his inside coat pocket.

This whole incident took only a minute or two. Since Babe, Roy and Elmore were having a side conversation with Wade on the pending meeting with Condon, they only saw Dunahow taking the photos away from Bob.

Wade, noting the distraction, asked, "What's going on here?"

"Believe me, it's of no significance to you," Joe remarked. "However, I want you to count me in whenever you meet with Condon."

Joe Farmar's passing off the incident as being of no significance was utterly false. It was of major importance, since it established that Dunahow used sex and call girls to get his way. Since Bob's face had gotten red and Joe had issued the command to "tear the fuckin' photos up" I knew those two were aboard the ship with Don and the three naked women. I thanked my lucky stars that I had the good sense to reject Don's invite to go fishing.

If my imagination projected an accurate picture it had been Don's plan to get me aboard for a supposed fishing trip with Bob and Joe. Once the little speedboat dropped me off at Don's yacht I'd be greeted by a charming hostess – anchors away and the wild party would begin. In Don Dunahow's secret files there were now probably several pictures of Bob and Joe "frolicking" away with naked women, which Don could use to blackmail them. If you have something on somebody you can force him to do almost thing to avoid being exposed. I was just lucky in not falling for Don's scheme.

When the meeting broke up Bob pulled me over to the side of the stage to show me something. "Herb, I want you to read these letters I received recently from three prominent precinct workers."

Read them I did, though I didn't know any of the individuals. One writer called the college president a jumping jackass who'd shoot off his mouth over nothing and should be dismissed pronto. The second writer called me rude, disrespectful, disloyal, lacking in professionalism and deserving of termination. The last writer nominated Clem Lowe as my replacement since he was calm, dignified, mature and displayed loyalty to his board.

"So, Herb, do you want me to read these letters aloud at the July 28th board meeting?"

"Bob, you do whatever you think is right."

"Oh come on, now. You don't really want me to do it. I can see the newspaper headlines the following day: PROMINENT CITIZENS WANT ZEITLIN TO QUIT, CLEM LOWE MAY BE NEW PRESIDENT. You know we, too, know how to make big headlines."

I swallowed a little and said nothing. "The big boys feel you should be fired since we have the votes and we can do it next Wednesday night – but we won't. We'll give you everything you want at the 28th meeting to show you we're cooperating. Now, can you learn to cooperate with us as well?"

"I certainly will try. We must work together if we're to open Triton on September 7th." We shook hands and parted with a new understanding.

One of my surprises from the letters was that copies had been sent to each one's respective boss, which included Mayor Richard Daley, legislator Jim Kirie and Mayor Elmer Conti. Wade had previously told me that the big bosses wanted me fired. Now I wondered if the boys were willing to give up on their $50,000 bonuses.

As I was walking to my car with Wade and Roy they asked me, "What did Don pull from Bob's hands?"

"Oh, there were several pictures of Don having fun with three naked ladies on his boat."

"You mean call girls, don't you? It doesn't surprise me," Roy remarked. "I've been told he has a string of highly paid beauties at his beck and call. It is one damn shame how he's corrupting Bob at such an early age."

"Was Joe in any of the photos?" asked Wade.

"I didn't see any of him or Bob, but Bob's face got flushed when Don distributed the pictures."

"If you ask me," Roy continued, "Joe's main love is the bottle. He's married to one of the most beautiful ladies in the community and doesn't appreciate her. He probably went on Don's boat trip just to think up other ways to fleece the public and fill his own pocket."

Wade added, "Fellows, please try to forget that last incident. We had one helluva productive meeting. At last the board is beginning to work again as a team. Don't you feel that way, Herb?"

"Yes, I do." I left feeling good that my seven items had been approved and lucky that I had declined Don's invitation. Now I knew that Don was someone to be avoided.

That night as I brushed my teeth before retiring I rehashed the day's events. I was sorry I couldn't share the good news with Eugenia, whom I missed very much. The house was strangely quiet and produced an eerie feeling in the pit of my stomach. I became somewhat relieved as I had a large glass of milk with crackers. Finally around 1:00 AM I hit the sack very tired and fell into a deep sleep.

I was suddenly awakened by the phone ringing. Who the hell was calling me at 2:15 in the morning? My God, something was wrong at Bonner's Lake. I got up and ran to the phone. "Hello, hello, hello." No answer. Probably a wrong number, back to bed.

At 2:45 the phone rang again. This time I could hear deep breathing. It continued as if the person were nearing a sexual climax. I waited a few seconds. The deep breathing increased in tempo, then a loud "Geronimo." Someone was playing a joke on me, so I hung up.

Thirty minutes later, the same thing. I hung up and then left the phone off the hook so I could get some sleep.

Despite the three annoying calls, the following morning I was up bright and early, shaved, showered and dressed. I picked up my copy of the Chicago Tribune on the front lawn and noticed an Elmwood Park police car with two officers parked a block away. A little unusual for so early in the morning; perhaps they were taking a coffee or cigarette break. I dismissed their presence from my mind, had breakfast, read the paper and left for the office around 8:10.

As I backed out the driveway I again became disturbed. The police had been there for over one hour. Some coffee break! The thought hit me, maybe they could tell me what to do about the three upsetting calls I'd received. On second thought I dismissed that idea and did some speculation. Could it be possible that they were the culprits who'd called me last night? Quite possibly – after all, the police chief of

Elmwood Park reported to Mayor Conti and Conti was the one pushing for my dismissal. I was sure Conti would blame me if the $100,000 contribution to the Republican Party fell through.

I decided to feel out the officers. I slowly drove up to the police car, stopped, rolled down my window and asked, "What's up, fellows?"

They both smiled, said nothing for a while and looked at each other. Finally the driver responded, "Can't tell you. It's a military secret."

"Oh, I understand. Keep up the good work and have a pleasant day." I drove away, not to the office but down to North Avenue and back to my home within two minutes. The police car was gone. Since they'd left shortly after me I was now sure they were stalking me.

When I arrived at the office Maria greeted me with a big smile and happily asked, "How did things work out last night?"

At that moment I felt she had received some advance information and just wanted to confirm it, so I said, "Just fine. All my recommendations were accepted, thanks to Babe's help."

She responded, "Last weekend I showed Babe all those critical news articles and he said it had to stop. I told him it would only stop when the board rescinded the bond vote. He said he'd work on it with the boys."

"He did a fine job. The coalition has agreed to contact Condon to see if they can get out of the contract."

"That just goes to show you that my brother-in-law is a good person. He's done so much to help the people of Melrose Park that I think one day they'll elect him mayor. It's the greed of the others that got Triton into today's mess. It wasn't Babe's fault, as so many people claim."

"I also heard the same things, Maria, but basically Babe is a good man. And I want to thank you for helping me out during these critical days." She cheerfully returned to her typing.

Since Dean Simonsen was in Springfield, my scheduled executive meeting was changed from Thursday morning to Friday. Shortly before noon I left for the Maywood Rotary meeting and sat with Elmore Boeger. He was very optimistic about the future and felt the bond fracas would fade away as time passed. I hoped that would be the case, but it didn't seem likely. Dean Widergren had reported that registration had slowed down a bit. Some parents felt that Triton was becoming a clout college since the politicians were running the school. Elmore disputed that conclusion, saying, "Herb, you're the chief administrator and you run the college. At the next meeting all your recommendations will be accepted. I guarantee it."

It was always a delight to talk with Elmore because of his positive point of view. He was always the optimist, like many Rotarians. It even seemed to me that the food at the club tasted better due to the pleasant fellowship of its members. Going to Rotary was always stimulating for me.

Back at the office Maria had left the folders of three candidates to be interviewed. Pleasant juices started to flow as I read the credentials of the teachers who were strongly recommended by Darnes and Dale.

John C. Vaughn, B.S. from Southern Illinois, M.S. from Northwestern, was an industrial chemist, part-time university teacher and very active in the Maywood community, serving as chairman of the Cotillion Ball and Maywood Scholarship Committee.

Equally impressive were the credentials of Alex Lane. B.S. from Johnson Smith College, M.S. from the University of Illinois and doctoral candidate at the University of Chicago. His specialty was zoology and anatomy. A superior high school teacher, he was hoping to move to the community college.

The third candidate was Carole Jean Widiger, for assistant librarian. B.S. from Western Michigan, M.S. in library science from the University of Wisconsin with a transcript of mostly A's and a few B's, and glowing recommendations from all her professors. Dean Darnes wrote, "I know you told us not to recommend any beginners, which I've followed to the letter. However, in this case I think we should make an exception. She's highly qualified, very intelligent and exceptionally attractive, and the students and faculty will love her."

It was a pleasant experience interviewing the three candidates, each so enthusiastic about joining Triton. I called Bob to thank him for recruiting three superior faculty members and told him they would all be on the board agenda for July 28th. What the board did not know and what would please them very much was that Vaughn and Lane were black.

I remembered well Joe Farmar saying, during the early stages of my interview with the trustees, "We want this college to have a faculty and student body that is multiracial, multiethnic, multireligious and multisex."

Babe had added, "That means we want to see black, brown, red, yellow and white students and faculty on this campus as long as they are qualified. Do you get the picture? Make it happen, Mr. President."

I wondered then how many boards preached that to the public but surreptitiously avoided carrying it out. I sincerely believed that the Triton board would practice what it preached.

At 5:30 PM Mark, as scheduled, called me to say that everything was OK. Swimming was great, no rain, a little cloudy but warm. The family had liked its visit to Lake Geneva.

"What time can we expect you?" he asked. Early, I said, so that we could swim out to the raft together with Joyce.

I left the office at 7:00 PM, drove home, stared at the house before entering it and said to myself, pretty house, but it's nothing without Eugenia and the kids. I missed the noise and the excitement. After eating a TV dinner I watched the news, prepared my suitcase for the weekend in Wisconsin and hit the sack.

At exactly 1:00 AM I was suddenly awakened by a phone call. The voice, loud and clear, said, "Dr. Zeitlin, let me give you some good advice. You are not one of us so pack your bags and go back to California."

"Who's speaking?"

"It doesn't matter! If you continue to be a do-gooder, you'll be sorry." He hung up.

After hearing that I couldn't sleep so I turned on all the lights, went down to the kitchen and sat at the table thinking. Who made the call? I knew what he wanted. Obviously he wanted me to leave town. Finally I drank some milk to help settle down the sizzling juices. I paced the floor trying to think out the meaning of "You'll be sorry."

The phone rang again. "I'm glad you're up and thinking it out. If you leave without giving us any trouble you'll receive a good settlement. If you don't depart with grace, you'll end up at the bottom of Lake Michigan in a barrel of concrete. It's your decision," he loudly proclaimed, not waiting for any response.

It was impossible to sleep after that threat. I took the phone off the hook, turned off all the lights, returned to bed and stared up at the ceiling. If the purpose of the caller was to scare me, he succeeded! I got up and checked all the doors and windows to be sure they were locked. The only window I left open was in the rear second story, to my bedroom. It was obvious to me that the caller or his cohort was watching the house. What should I do? I asked myself the question several times. I got up and found a baseball bat in Mark's room and took it to bed with me.

I couldn't call the local police since they may have been involved in the threat.

Could it be one of the coalition members or one of the big politicians? *Possibly.*

Could it be one of the three letter writers? *Possibly.*

Could the threatening caller be someone unknown to me? *Quite possibly.*

Was I overreacting? Maybe, but doubtful. I had to admit it. I was damn scared! Who could help me?

Suddenly, I recalled my interview with Harry Behrman, a retired FBI agent with a degree from Notre Dame University who had been hired to head up our police science program and supervise the Triton security force. I remembered his parting words, "Chicagoland is different from all other cities, so if you ever need some help don't hesitate to call me."

Before leaving for work the following morning I managed to get Harry at his home. He was delighted to hear from me and agreed to have lunch at a quiet restaurant in Elmhurst.

Upon arriving at the office I asked Maria to be sure I wasn't disturbed while I met with the executive committee. The fellows asked, "Well, what's happening?"

I wanted very much to tell them about the threatening calls but didn't, fearing that they too might get scared. We had a college to open in five weeks and I didn't want to throw any roadblocks in the way. So I accented all the positives.

"The board has agreed to cancel the bond sale provided Condon releases them without any penalties. We had a wonderful executive meeting. They agreed to accept all eight of my recommendations. I hope the July 28th board meeting will result in a turn around with the press. At least it will display the college president and board working well together. Now, Gordon, tell us what happened at your meeting with the State Director of Vocational Education."

"Plenty," he said. "The chief laughed at me when I told him we intend to offer 17 different occupational programs when we open September 7th."

"I don't see anything laughable about that. Please explain."

"He looked at the Triton catalog and said it's padded. He claimed that most junior colleges start with one or two occupational programs; to start with 17 is ridiculous! No other college in the state has that many. We'd never make it."

"Why did he say that? That's very discouraging."

"He doesn't believe junior colleges offering vocational education will ever succeed. He's a believer in area vocational schools and feels the colleges can't mix vocational training with university transfer programs. The elitist faculty would not permit it."

"Boy, he is really a dyed-in-the-wool vocationist."

Dean Darnes interrupted us. "You know, Gordon, when I was at Olney College I tried to add electronics and automobile mechanics to our curriculum but the faculty council said no. I didn't want to give up so I tried to get the board of trustees to overrule them."

"What happened?" I asked.

"The board straightened me out when they said concentrate on the academic; they didn't want Olney to be a trade school. Some time later I had a talk with Dean Ernest Clements at Wright Junior College and he had the same problem. The faculty senate emphatically said no-go on vocational education at Wright."

"Well, Bob, if you and Gordon continue to work well together we'll prove to the elitist educators in Illinois that the vocational and academic people need each other if we're going to improve society. Did the state director have anything good to say about us?"

"Yes, he did. He congratulated us on becoming the first public technical junior college in the state. I told him that Triton will succeed because the tech dean and academic dean are of equal status and on the same salary schedule. He laughed again and said, 'How long do you expect that to last? You know darn well it won't last because the academic elite runs the college senate and the senate president directs the college president.' I told him about my own president's career as industrial arts teacher, then as counselor at the Phoenix Technical School, and later as the first academic dean with a vocational background at Southwestern College in Chula Vista. He was impressed."

"Did he have any good news for us?"

"Oh, yes. He gave provisional approval to our programs in data processing, electronics and both drafting courses of study. And the clincher is we may get up to 75% total reimbursement for these programs."

"That's wonderful news. With that kind of reimbursement the occupational lab courses can be limited to 16 or 20 and will cost far less than a full academic course."

"There's more! The state vocational board will give to any school district that constructs a building exclusively for vocational education a grant equal to the construction costs for the purchasing of equipment and supplies."

"Gordon, this is simply wonderful. I want you to give a full report to the board on this development Wednesday night."

We were all very happy hearing Gordon's report. Dean Widergren, however, was not smiling. He feared that the slowdown in enrollments would surely result in fewer than 1,000 on opening day. Discussion followed on how we could increase the number. All agreed that the bond sale controversy was like a kick in the stomach. We were all hoping that with the announcement from the board on July 28th that the bond sale may be cancelled, the good image of the college would be restored. The press would surely treat the trustees much better.

Darnes responded, "Don't count on that. When the press is after someone they just won't let up."

After much brainstorming it was decided to distribute copies of the schedule of classes in late August to every library and school within the district, as well as to banks, food markets and other business establishments with the approval of their managers. I was determined to reach our goal of over 1,000 enrollment.

Bob Dale, realizing the urgency of getting furniture and equipment in place before school opened, requested additional classified help. He was quite pleased when I informed him his request would be granted as soon as I could interview his candidates. The board, subject to its later approval, had granted me permission to hire whomever was needed in order to have a successful opening. I also asked Bob to present his policy on purchasing to the trustees on July 28th and to give additional copies to all members of the press. I wanted everyone to know that whenever feasible, Triton would obtain three or more bids for every purchase over $1,500.

After the meeting I couldn't help but reflect on what hardworking, visionary, knowledgeable administrators I had recruited. They accepted and were meeting the challenges I had put before them. I was so proud of them.

Before I left the office for lunch with Harry Behrman I told Maria I would return in the late afternoon. I usually told her where I was going and with whom but this time I didn't want her to know I was having lunch with a former FBI agent, fearing that the secret meeting might be communicated to Babe.

The restaurant that Harry selected was off the main highway and had a small bar with six stools and 12 dining tables, each with seating for 4 to 6 diners. The restaurant was half filled, with only one tall, well-dressed gentleman seated at the bar sipping beer. As soon as we placed our order the man at the bar got up and carried his beer to a table where we'd be in his view all the time, and susceptible to eavesdropping. Aware of this, we talked about the weather, sports, President Johnson and everything except my major concern.

Having sized up the situation Harry made it a point to conceal his face with a newspaper and whispered, "This is not a good place to talk. Let's hurry with the lunch and talk in my car."

I focused on the character at the near table. The gentleman had had three Bud's but no food when we left.

In the car Harry asked, "Did you tell anyone where you were meeting me?"

"No, I told no one, not even Maria or any of the deans."

"Well, that settles it for me. Your phone is being tapped."

"By whom?"

"Don't you know?"

"Bob Collins?"

"Yes, of course. He's the wizard master of secret electronic devices. As Peck's bad little boy for Jim Olson, he does all kind of good things for him. Your stalker is a rogue ex-policeman from Oak Park by the name of Herman Furlong."

"How did you know that?"

"The FBI keeps records on all sleazebags. Herman was dropped from the Oak Park police for bashing a gay. He used to boast about how he dished out punishment to homos, blacks, Latinos, Jews and other so-called inferiors. At first we didn't believe him. Later on when I saw some of his victims I knew he wasn't lying. As you've probably heard, some Chicago suburbs had active American Bund chapters and Herman was a member of one of them. Here it is 20 years after the war and these Hitlerites still practice Nazism when the opportunity presents itself."

"How can that be?"

"It happens. Try as we may we just can't eliminate hate groups. All the FBI can do is to keep our eyes on them and pick them up when we have evidence against them. Now tell me, who hates you?"

"I wish I knew." I told him about the past night's threatening calls and the trouble I was having with the board. I liked Harry because he was so knowledgeable and didn't interrupt me once.

Finally I asked him, "Is my life in danger? What should I do?"

Harry put his hand over his mouth, slowly removed it and said, "Your life may or may not be in danger. It's obvious that the coalition is trying to scare you in the usual Chicago ways. You just don't know the local tactics. If you leave the area, their scare methods will have worked and it will end right there."

"What will happen if I don't leave?"

"I can't tell you whether they'll carry out their threats or not. All I can say is be careful."

"Any special precautions I should take?"

"Yes, there are several. First, don't ever park your car on the street overnight. I noticed you have a little Skylark whose hood anyone can open. Get a car with a hood that opens only from the inside. Gangland has a group of goons that are readily available to attach sticks of dynamite to a starter. Learn fast the many ways to check your car before you put the key into the ignition. Tell your wife and kids to never, ever, let a stranger into your house. And please remember, if you receive a call to meet one of the coalition members or any stranger, don't meet him alone. Confide in one of your administrators; always let him know where you're going, or better still, take him along with you."

"Is there anything positive you can tell me?"

"Yes, I'll enter a record of our conversation into the FBI files today in the event anything should happen to you. However, I really don't think anything will happen because, thanks to the press, everyone knows that you and the coalition are at odds. They would be immediate suspects if you disappeared or if your brakes didn't hold while driving down a hill."

"Thanks so much for your advice, Harry. I will follow it. Now the challenge in front of you is to develop a topnotch police science training program at Triton. I'm here to help you, having organized such programs at two colleges. It's no easy assignment. My files have every course of study from those schools if you wish to borrow them."

"Thanks a lot. I'll borrow them next week. You can rest assured, Dr. Zeitlin, that once we have the program under way a new day in police services for this area will begin. The staff we hire is very important because they'll be taught how to screen out potential rogue cops."

When I returned to the office, Maria had prepared all the board material with its many exhibits ready to be delivered to the trustees that evening. She took out Babe's packet since she was having dinner with the Serpicos that evening and would personally deliver it to him.

Later, as I was driving up to Bonner's Lake, I thought about the past few days' events. Maybe those threatening calls were from some nut in the community and the coalition had nothing to do with it. A wishful thought; if only it were true, my fears would evaporate. I decided not to tell Eugenia for fear she would start packing and take the kids with her. I hit my head a few times and said, "How the hell did I ever get into this jam? Why didn't I listen to Waddie Deddah?" Eventually I came to the conclusion that I had to act the part of a happy husband and father despite the pain within. I was determined to show no fear and enjoy fully the weekend with my family. A year before I got married, my mother, after seeing me perform in the North Merrick PTA play with Eugenia, advised me to stick to teaching and not consider acting as a career. However, I always recalled Shakespeare's famous line picturing life as a stage, a tale told by an idiot, full of sound and fury, signifying nothing. The pain within me was something real. but I hoped it would dissipate when I appeared on a different stage.

As soon as I arrived at the lake Joyce and Mark were ready to race me to the raft. This time Mark won, Joyce came in second and Dad was a close third. At dinner time Eugenia surprised me when she proudly announced that her brother Eddie, his wife Helen and their kids were arriving the next day and staying over for a week at the lake and another week at our home in Elmwood Park while Ed attended a University of Chicago workshop on reading.

"Are you sure Eddie will be able to find this hideaway place?"

"No problem. I slowly went over with him every checkpoint along the way. Eddie is a good listener. He wrote down everything I said and read it back to me accurately. We can expect him around noon so I'll be busy preparing for five guests."

"Is there anything I can do?"

"Yes, tomorrow morning you can take Mark, Ann and Clare to Burlington and do all the shopping while Joyce and I get ready for them. Here's the list."

The next day, shortly after breakfast the kids and I got out of Eugenia's hair and had much fun shopping and eating frozen yogurt. Upon returning to the cabin I was amazed to see Eddie, his family and their big trailer parked a few hundred feet away.

I greeted him enthusiastically. "It's great to see you. How in the heck did you find us?"

"It was easy. I always learned to listen to my big sister carefully. She said turn left about 300 feet after I spotted the little red school house and bingo, I was here."

Since the Pawliks and the Zeitlins hadn't seen each other for over three years there was incessant dialogue most of the weekend.

Early Monday morning Eugenia prepared a breakfast of juice, ham and eggs, toast and coffee while the gang was sleeping. Before leaving I remarked how great it was to have the two families together and asked why she had taken so long in telling me about their visit.

"It was iffy a few weeks ago when I first spoke to Eddie. When his grant check came in last week, he wrote saying be was coming. I only received his letter Friday."

"How long will the workshop last?"

"Five days. It starts on Monday, August 2nd, and ends on Friday, August 6th. I assume it will be OK for him to park his trailer in our driveway."

"No problem, darling. I hope you and Helen will take the kids to the Oak Park pool, the Riverside Zoo and the Melrose Park Kiddieland. The kids will enjoy the rides."

I re-thought the parking situation as I drove back to the office. It would be OK for Ed to park his big trailer in our driveway, but would the other three cars fit in behind? The answer was no. It would take Eddie's and Eugenia's cars, and that was all. My car would have to be parked on the street, and Harry Behrman had warned me not to do that. If I opened the hood every morning to check for dynamite sticks, neighbors might ask me some embarrassing questions. What should I do to protect myself? I went into deep thought but couldn't come up with a satisfactory answer.

Although I'd succeeded in getting my mind off those threatening calls while I was at the lake, some of the missing parts came together. Maria had received directions to the lake from Babe. How had Babe known where we were located when I'd never told him? But Eugenia did tell Eddie Pawlik over the phone how to get to our cabin. Harry Behrman had said he felt my phone was tapped. Now, I knew it was so.

I flashed back to the day the phone was installed by Bob Collins. I had complimented him on the instant playback he received when he gave me my new number, 456-4525, a full house, three 5's and two 4's. I hadn't realized the full house was really the playback house for the coalition.

At the office Maria informed me that she had scheduled three interviews one hour apart for office positions. First to arrive was Elizabeth Wardle, an old acquaintance of Bob Dale and recommended to be his secretary ASAP. Mrs. Wardle, a little on the quiet side, had excellent references, was well-dressed and in her mid-thirties, typed flawlessly and answered all my questions with brief replies. I welcomed her aboard and expressed my delight when she told she was ready to start within the week

Before I interviewed the second applicant, Dorothy Beckman, John Widergren phoned. "Dr. Zeitlin, I want you to know that Dottie has served as my part-time secretary at Proviso for the past year. Now that she's graduated I would like to have her full time. On several occasions Bob Darnes has worked with Virginia Sybilla and would be pleased if she could be transferred to his office if it meets with your approval."

"Sounds good to me. I'll move it along fast."

The references in Dorothy's folder were glowing, and there were almost all A's on her transcript. She appeared a little nervous when I first spoke to her but as time went on she became more relaxed. Even though she would be the youngest secretary at the age of 18, I felt she would be a fine addition.

At 4:00 PM Maria told me that Eve Adams, the third applicant, was phoning to request that her appointment be changed from 5:30 to 6:00. I agreed.

Maria left at 5:00, so I was alone in the office waiting for Eve. Finally, shortly after six, a tall, buxom bleached blond burst into the office, grabbed both my hands as I stood up and apologized all over the place. The perfume on her was overwhelming and the dress showed off a lot of cleavage. Her constant hitting me on the knee as we faced each other in the office chairs kept me wondering what she was really after. Triton needed a clerk typist and not an over-solicitous hostess. Her application was incomplete and I wondered why Maria had scheduled her with me.

As she got up to leave she said, "I'm hungry. Where is a good place to eat?"

I suggested the Homestead on North Avenue, to which she replied, "Thank you so much. You're so nice. Would you care to join me?"

I declined graciously and walked her to the door, wondering what she was really trying to sell and who had sent her.

At home I ate a TV dinner, watched the news for a while and retired around 11:00, wondering if the late calls would resume. To protect myself I put Eugenia's pillow over the phone. Once again at 1:00 AM the phone did ring; this time the sound was rather subdued, thanks to the pillow. It rang again one hour later but I didn't answer. Although I heard it in my dreams I continued to sleep. The big problem was solved.

What took me so long to learn? The solution was so easy, just ignore the caller.

The first thing I asked Maria on Tuesday was, "How come you scheduled Eve Adams for an interview when her application was incomplete?"

"When Mr. Dunahow brought in the application yesterday morning, I told him that you don't interview anyone unless we have a complete file on the person."

"What did he say to that?"

"He said there were exceptions to all rules and this was one rule Dr. Zeitlin would enjoy breaking. 'Eve Adams is so charming I'm sure she'll get the job. Just trust me!'"

I laughed, shook my head, opened my eyes wide and looked deeply into Maria's until she finally spoke. "Dr. Zeitlin, don't tell me, I know. Evie was no exception and is unacceptable. I should not have let Mr. Smith twist my arm. It won't happen again. Besides that, I didn't find her as charming as most men would, looking at her *zaftig* shape."

At noon on Wednesday, July 28th I had a pizza with Wade as we met in his office to review the agenda. Wade thought we should prepare for a large crowd that evening since the tension between the press and the coalition continued to build. I agreed to run off over 100 agendas and get Jim Tarpey there early to distribute them. Both June meetings had been bad and the July 12th session a confession of guilt by the coalition, which hadn't appeared after promising to be there. I suggested that Wade make a few remarks informally before opening the official meeting to assure the public and the press that all their major concerns would be handled that evening. He agreed.

When I arrived ten minutes before eight, the cafeteria was packed. Jim was distributing the agendas and signing people in. Neil Mehler and four other representative reporters had the table directly facing the trustees. All the trustees arrived early and looked good in their dark suits and white shirts. Don Dunahow, looking like a senior judge, gazed over the heads of the audience.

Wade, true to his word, with empathy reviewed the agenda and stated that anyone who wished to speak would be given that opportunity after breaktime, which was scheduled for 9:30.

The meeting came to order at exactly 8:10 PM with the approval of the June 23rd and June 30th minutes. The audience was dead silent when Bob Dale presented the policy on purchasing. A few cheers came from the rear when he said, "No purchase of over $1,500 shall be made without securing three or more bids."

I was amazed at the way the trustees handled each item. They asked no end of questions, showing that they were well-informed and concerned. I gave them all A's for effort. The break at 9:30 allowed a reaction from the well-behaved audience and press. They seemed rather pleased with the integrity and intelligence of the board. The trustees listened attentively as Jack Rossetter discussed the sale of bonds, relating it to House Bill 1710. He also read letters from N.E. Hudson, legal adviser to the state superintendent, and from Dr. Lyman Glenny, executive secretary of the Board of Higher Education. The letters were good news because they implied more money to the community colleges upon passage of HB 1710.

The policy on addressing the board was quickly passed without any dissent. Joe Farmar looked at me in an apologetic manner and said, "Too bad this policy wasn't presented to us sooner."

I ignored his statement, remembering he had been the strongest opponent of such a policy. It's interesting how politicians change their positions to please whatever audience is listening.

After months of delay my one-page contract for instructors was finally approved. Roy Jones commented, "I want to commend Dr. Zeitlin for using economic methods in saving the district much money. We'll save thousands of dollars by using this one-page contract for all instructors, instead of having our attorney interview each one before drawing up a separate contract."

A few hands applauded Roy's remarks as I presented Schedules 4.17 and 4.18, a long list of faculty to be hired. Serpico, Farmar, Knol and Jones asked many questions about the backgrounds of the various candidates.

Bob Collins ended by saying, "I am very much impressed with the recruiting done by the administration. It's wonderful to have these experienced teachers with degrees from so many elite universities. Now, Dr. Zeitlin, how many faculty have been employed thus far?"

"As of July 14 we've hired 21 full and 51 part-timers. A profile and photo of every instructor hired will be given to the press soon. This is just another way of whetting the student's appetite for Triton and promoting the college's greatest asset, the faculty."

I continued by announcing that the fall schedule of classes was at the printers and when finished a copy would be bulk mailed to every household in the district. Dean Simonsen stated that the first meeting of the electronics advisory committee would beheld on August 10th. As time went on an advisory committee for each of the 14 occupational programs would be established. Over 100 leaders from business and industry would be called upon to help the college organize the courses of study. Hopefully some of these advisors could be trained to become part-time teachers.

The trustees were astonished when Simonsen told them that the state vocational board would reimburse Triton up to 75% of the cost of every approved program.

"I can't believe this," Joe Farmar remarked. "I wonder why Notre Dame never offered vocational/technical programs."

I explained, "Notre Dame University is one of the finest institutions in the nation, offering a rigid program in the liberal arts and sciences. But the thought of having voc/tech training is a big no-no."

"Why is that such a no-no?"

"The people in the Archdiocese don't make the decisions on the university programs. They're made by the academic senate, and like at a thousand other academic senates throughout the nation, the mere mention of voc/tech at the university is taboo."

"What's to prevent the Triton senate in the future from stamping out these programs if what you say is true?"

"It won't happen here at Triton as long as we continue to have board support and administrative and faculty understanding of the value of job training vs. status-seeking programs. It's sad indeed for the greatest democracy in the world that its universities each year graduate thousands with degrees in writing, journalism, theater arts and psychology, with no job prospects. However, we're most fortunate at Triton to have superior administrators who understand, appreciate and endorse vocational/tech education. They're a unique and rare part of a new educational movement."

For the first time in a long moon the trustees showed much optimism and supported all the proposals made by each administrator. When

Bob Dale read a resolution creating a student activity fund it was heartily applauded by everyone.

Elmore Boeger expressed the general feeling: "I think it's a great idea. The students will have their own bank account to be used for sports, travel and a great lecture and forum series. The series should bring to the Triton campus renowned figures in the arts, athletics, business, education, government, sciences and the theater. I'm very proud to be part of this board. Our boys have much insight into the future. I believe with this movement Triton will become the prime center of cultural and intellectual activities in this community."

It was nice to hear Elmore, one of the most respected members of the community, voice confidence in his board. The press representatives were actively writing and I hoped their articles would paint a better picture of the coalition. Even though Rossetter and the press were critical of Dunahow's past actions they listened without any interruption as he gave a detailed report on the Carey farm offer, the appraisals, the bond sale and contracts for professional help. Collins made a motion that Dunahow should direct the appraisers to come up with a fair market value of two parcels with and without the buildings. Boeger seconded the motion and it was carried unanimously.

Without any discussion it was moved, seconded and carried that the college president, two of the deans and the coordinator of business attend the fall conference of the Illinois Association of School Administrators to be held in Peoria in October.

Before adjourning Wade announced that the board was working hard to rescind the bond sale. Suddenly there came a loud outburst from the rear, "Thatta boy, Wade. Keep the boys honest."

Roy Jones moved that Steel, Farmar and Boeger serve as a committee of three to meet with Joseph Condon in an effort to cancel the bond transaction. The motion was seconded by Boeger and carried with much enthusiasm.

Another shout was heard: "At last the board has listened to us and they're going the right way."

The long meeting adjourned at 11:10 PM and everyone seemed happy with the actions taken.

Before leaving Jack Rossetter said to Steel, Boeger and me, "I'm sure that if Joseph Condon is as smart as I think he is, he'll agree to cancel the sale."

It had been one of the longest and most productive sessions held by the trustees. It showed to all who attended that if the board had made some mistakes in the past, they'd corrected them tonight. I envisioned the newspaper headlines in the days to follow:

"TRITON COLLEGE TO CANCEL BOND SALE; NO CONTRACTS WITHOUT THREE BIDS; BOARD AND COLLEGE PRESIDENT WORKING WELL TOGETHER; ROSSETTER SOUNDS OFF"; etc. Several other possible headlines flashed across my mind, all with good images.

I went home feeling good, parked the car in the garage, ate some cookies with milk and went to bed around 12:30 AM. Once again around 1:00 the muffled phone rang several times. I ignored it and continued to snooze.

The following morning before breakfast I opened the front door to pick up the *Chicago Tribune* and the *Chicago Sun Times,* hoping to read about last night's Triton board meeting. Nothing in either paper. Oh well, I guess it was too late for the reporter's deadline. It should be in tomorrow. Suddenly my eye caught a small headline on the right-hand side of the *Sun Times,* "Restaurant Owner Dies From Injuries Caused by Car Blowup." How horrible! I prayed that the next headline would not be about a college president.

As I was about to close the front door I noticed an Elmwood Park police car pull up about a block away. I walked down the street a bit to see who was in the car. Surprise of surprises, the same Joes of last week. I waved to them but they ignored the greeting. I was disturbed. Were they monitoring me again? Were they responsible for the early morning phone calls? I didn't know but felt every uneasy. I liked the sign on their car, "To Serve and Protect," but in reality they were not serving John Public. They were serving special interests by harassing the college president. What should I do? I called Wade and asked to meet him on his football field within the hour. He agreed.

I opened up, telling him about the meeting with Harry Behrman and Herman Furlong observing us. He also had heard about Furlong and his hatred of gays and minorities and urged me to be very careful. Furlong was definitely a rogue cop. Wade felt there was a relationship between the late night calls and the Elmwood Park police. Mayor

Conti had been seen on several occasions talking to discharged police officers. Perhaps Conti or Dunahow had set the watchdogs on me. This was a matter not to be joked about!

"Wade, how do I protect myself?"

"Get yourself a bigger car with a hood that opens from the driver's seat."

"My car will be parked on the street all of next week. How will I know if the bad boys have planted something during the night?"

"Don't get your car washed. Throw some dirt over the windshield, doors and hood and place a small piece of scotch tape over the opening of the hood. If the tape is broken or the dirt is disturbed you'll know someone has been near the car, and it may spell serious trouble."

"And what if I discover the tape is broken?"

"Call me. Don't dare try to start it. Call me and I'll get you some help."

It was pleasant talking to Wade but I was more worried than ever. What should I do? Who was trying to get me? I knew why but had never expected the coalition to use violence against me. Was Dunahow the culprit or was it someone else?

Before I left Wade informed me that Farmar, Boeger and he would be meeting with Joe Condon the next morning. If things went well, the tension between the board and press would be relieved. He agreed to meet me at the West Leyden Field House in the afternoon to tell me the result.

I arrived at the office feeling sad but was cheered by the peppy voices of the deans as they gathered in my office.

"What's up, fellows?" I asked.

"Several thousand of the printed *Invitations to Learn* have arrived," reported John Widergren as he happily gave a large packet to each of us.

The *Invitations* were the Fall 1965 Schedule of Classes. In the middle of the front panel was the following message: *"Here is your invitation to learning. Since the number of these booklets is limited, will you please share this copy with your friends?"*

The schedules looked mighty good – maroon ink on light tan paper with a sketch of the proposed new campus on the front panel.

Bob Darnes remarked, "I wonder how many of these 175 classes will go."

"Right now, with over 500 students enrolled, I would predict that if we're lucky about 50 per cent will meet the minimum requirement of 12 students per class. Do you agree, Gordon?" Widergren asked.

"I think we can do better than that. If we get these schedules to the libraries, banks, churches, service clubs and shopping centers we should pick up a few hundred additional students."

With vigor I added, "I agree with Gordon, so starting today and if necessary continuing all day Monday, let's get these schedules into the community ASAP."

Within minutes the deans and I loaded our cars to make deliveries. As I left the bulk mailed schedules in the post office I seriously began to wonder what would happen to me if only 500 students showed up on opening day. Would the board fire me? Given my past conflicts with them they probably would try to do so on the grounds I had painted a false picture of the future. Babe had predicted only 500 would enroll based on the survey team's analysis. Yet I, as the chief administrator of the district, had led the board into believing over 1,000 would arrive on the first day of school. An error of 50 per cent would be sufficient grounds to terminate my contract. I once faced a similar situation at Southwestern College while serving as the dean of instruction and won by recruiting through bulk mail. With four and a half weeks to go before the opening date I relied heavily on the deans to recruit as planned. By Labor Day we would know.

30
Soft Money Counts

At 1:00 PM I met Wade at the Field House. We sauntered slowly around, his eyes focused on the ground; I knew the meeting with Joseph Condon had not gone well. Wade said, "It's no go with Condon."

"Why not?"

"He claims he has buyers for all of the bonds right now, even though the bonds haven't been delivered to him."

"Do you believe him?"

"Yes, I do. While other school bonds are selling at a 3.2 per cent return, the Triton bonds will go out at an average of 3.7, a fabulous return for those rich investors. He complimented Don Dunahow on his great job in jointly representing the seller (Triton) and the buyer (McDougal & Condon). He felt Dunahow well deserved his 3 per cent commission."

"Did he mention anything about the deal with the political parties?"

"Indirectly yes, when he said there's 200 grand available in soft money."

"Just what is soft money?"

"That's the term used in Chicago for vast but unregulated contributions to political parties."

"How will Conti and Kirie each use their 100 grand?"

"In any way they wish, while pocketing a little on the side. So I'll assume Conti's Republican Party will contribute to Collins's and Knol's reelection and Kirie's Dems will do the same for Serpico and Farmar."

"So that's how the politicians keep getting reelected."

"Yes, plus money flows into their hands whenever they help party members achieve some secret deal. Dunahow will pay for the cooperation he received from the four members of the coalition."

"Do you really think our boys will each receive $50,000 from Smith?"

"Oh yes, particularly when Farmar urged me to change my vote and make a public statement supporting the coalition's position."

"What did you say to Farmar?"

"I said I would think about it, but it wasn't likely. To which he said if I agreed to join them he'd give me two free round trips to Hawaii, all expenses paid, to be used anytime within a year."

"Isn't that a bribe?"

"Yes, it sure is. Joe claimed the tickets were given to him by a friend he did a favor for a long time ago. He just didn't want the tickets to go to waste."

Although I was better informed about Chicago politics, I was still very leery of the future. Later that afternoon I pushed the right button as I drove up to Bonner's Lake to spend a frolicking weekend with family and guests.

Hitting the cool waters is a wonderful way to clear your mind of evil images. Once again the therapy worked. As we raced to the raft Eddie came in first, Mark second, Joyce third and Dad last. My 6' 2" brother-in-law, weighing in at 230 pounds, was puffing hard at the finish line. While he was the same height as Joe Farmar, his frame was more athletic. Joe served as a navy officer in World War II while Eddie was a highly decorated machine gunner in the Korean conflict. In high school Eddie was the Saturday football hero. I liked walking next to him because he was a good conversationalist and his frame would serve as my bodyguard. I wondered if I should tell him about the problems with the board. I decided not to since it would leak to Eugenia.

Saturday we toured Lake Geneva, ate a pizza, had frozen yogurt and later took a boat ride. Sunday after church we packed the cars and returned home from a great vacation.

Eddie carefully back-parked his trailer into our driveway. Eugenia's Falcon and then Eddie's car followed. I parked my dusty, dirty Skylark on the street. After dinner, feeling rather tired, we retired early for a good solid night's sleep without any phone calls.

Monday morning Eddie and I had an early breakfast. As we picked up the newspapers the same old Joes from the Elmwood Park police arrived and parked a lot closer to our house. This time Ed and I walked up to the driver.

In a low but hardsounding voice Eddie asked, "How can we help you fellows?"

The driver studied Eddie's big frame and slowly replied, "We heard there was a problem up here. We don't see or hear nothin' so we're gone." They drove away.

As an all-star football player Babe had had the speed of a bullet. When he tackled someone they long remembered the earth-pounding fall. Eddie, on the other hand, never made the all-star team, but those who survived his tackie remember him as the cannonball express. So I figured the two police officers didn't want to challenge Eddie. It felt good being in Ed's presence.

Before starting up the Skylark I checked the dust, dirt and tape and was relieved to see that nothing was disturbed. Upon arriving at the office I reviewed what I wanted in the first issue of the school newspaper to be printed by the newly hired journalism teacher, Bernard Verweil.

He wrote down everything I expected in the first issue, including: a big welcome to the first students, pictures of them registering, pictures and stories on the three men mainly responsible for the creation of the district, a progress report on the building plans, the history of Triton to date, an announcement of the first college dance, profiles on faculty and anything else he felt would be appropriate.

"Bernie, can you have the first issue out on or before September 7th? We have 30 days to go before the opening date."

"I'm sure I can, provided I have the full cooperation of your staff and an adequate budget."

"Let's get the budget question settled today. Take the dollar amount needed for this first issue, multiply it by 10, and add on the cost of office supplies and equipment and the cost of photography, traveling and mailing of copies to a selected audience. Submit the total to the business office by tomorrow and I assure you it will be approved. Now, how is that for cooperation?"

"I can't believe it. Never have I seen an administrator act so fast.

You're a rare one."

"We're under great pressure to open a first-class college on schedule and it calls for fast decisions. You have the background to produce the best college newspaper in the state and I'm here to help you make it happen. Have you decided on a name for the paper?"

"Yes, I have. I would like to call it *The Trident* since Triton and Trident are interrelated. Triton was a sea god in Greek mythology, the son of Neptune and Amphitrite, who lived at the bottom of the sea. He carried a three-pronged spear, a symbol of his power over the waters. He also stirred up or calmed the waves by blowing a trumpet made of a large twisted sea shell. Since the trident has three prongs I think it's a good symbol for the three high school districts that make up the college area."

"Mr. Verweil, you're very creative. Please include that Greek mythology bit in the first issue. It's not my intention to dictate what should or shouldn't be in the publication, with one exception. After the first issue I won't interfere with your first amendment rights. I hope you'll include many human interest stories on the students, faculty and staff."

"What is that one exception, Dr. Zeitlin?"

"Don't you know? I'm sure you've heard the expression, 'Don't bite the hand that feeds you.'"

Verweil thought and suddenly emerged with, "Oh, I know now. It's the board of trustees. Am I right?"

"Right you are, and if you're as wise as I think you are, you'll never write, or cause to be written, any article attacking the trustees. And please remember, when the trustee elections are held *The Trident* must never favor one candidate over another. Doing so would endanger your own future. Should you not support a trustee, and he wins the election, he'd be after me to find a way to get you out. That's the usual scenario, and I don't want to be part of it. Is that clear?"

"Yes, it's perfectly clear. I'll make it one of the ground rules of the journalism class that we never take sides on board elections. By the way, Dr. Zeitlin, several of the teachers I've spoken to feel that you should be called Dr. Triton, since you emerged from the troubled waters with your trident to poke those misbehaving trustees."

"Please, Bernie, don't let your creativeness add fire to the conflicts.

Your job and mine have similar goals. We must create the impression that the students this semester will be greeted by the best faculty that money can buy. I'm confident you'll prove it to be true. And I'm hopeful that over time our trustees will prove to the public that they're honorable, honest and hardworking people. If they've made any mistakes in the past they corrected them at the July 28th board meeting."

"I haven't read anything about that meeting."

"Neither have I. The journalists chose not to write about it even though six reporters attended the session. You know, you journalists have tremendous power, and it's not always used wisely. If you like what you hear, you'll print it and if you don't, you'll ignore it. You have the power to shape images in the minds of the public. Isn't that so?"

"Well, not exactly. It all depends on the background of the writer. My job as an instructor will be to teach students always to give both sides of an issue and not to speculate or plant seeds of unknown possibilities."

"I like what you say but several of us feel that the fate of this college, and the nation, is highly dependent on the quality of our writers. Do you agree that journalism is history written in a hurry?"

"Yes, I do, and that's why I teach students to report only the facts, the truth, and not hearsay, rumors or gossip. No article will begin with the statement: It has been rumored that. . . ."

"Remember, our goal: to make *The Trident* the best community college newspaper in the state of Illinois. You don't need an appointment to see me. Just drop in anytime you need an answer to an important question. I'm counting on you to present a good picture of the college. Speaking of pictures, please take as many as you can to tell your story. Now, let me take you on a tour of our new air-conditioned facilities."

We moved rapidly through the debris and roadblocks. Mr. Verweil got an early view of where the bookstore, library, faculty and administrative offices would be. Those facilities were scheduled to he ready one day before the opening of school.

Scratching his head, he said, "Dr. Zeitlin, you have to be an extreme optimist to believe this area will be ready in 30 days. No way. As far as I can see it's not possible."

"I am an optimist. It will be ready. We have to vacate our offices so they can be converted back to classrooms and move our stuff and staff to the new area. All this work will be done on the Sunday and Monday prior to opening day. Dr. Cox has assured me that his staff and the Triton staff will be working overtime to make it happen!"

"Well, I guess Sunday and Labor Day will be extraordinarily long days of labor for all your administrators, secretaries and crew."

"Everyone has been requested to wear their working clothes, bring their own lunches and not to leave until the move is completed."

"How did the staff react to your directive?"

"Surprisingly quite well. Everyone wants the child of our dreams, Triton College, to have a successful birth and everyone will be proud to aid in that blessed event."

The following day I met with Arthur Shearburn, the newly appointed coordinator of student activities, in his office. After he hung up a busy phone he asked, "How is my old friend Babe Serpico making out?"

"I didn't know he was an old friend of yours. Be careful how you use that word 'old.' Remember, you're both about the same age and I always thought we hired a young man to direct the student activity program."

"I can't believe it but 20 years ago I was on the freshman football squad at Ul when Babe knocked the wind out of me with his thundering tackle. It didn't surprise me one bit when he made all-American. What surprised me most was his phenomenal rise in Chicago politics from precinct worker to Tax Collector for Cook County in such a short time. How did he do it?"

"His precinct was small, but it grew and grew as he pushed for registering many voters into the Democratic Party. Mayor Daley liked it so much that Babe was awarded with rapid promotions."

"I only wish I could grow as fast at Triton as Babe did in Cook County."

"Are you telling me you want to follow in his footsteps?"

"No, no, I didn't mean that. Babe's pockets are loaded with the illegal money he collects regularly for fixing traffic tickets. It's pretty well known in this area that Babe fixes at a price."

"What is that price?"

"He fixes minor violations for 50 bucks and major ones at $100 or more."

"How do you know that?"

"My friend paid him off last week with 10 ten-dollar bills and was surprised when he saw Babe pull out a big wad of soft money. Babe seemed to be proud of what he's doing."

"Tell me, Art, what's the difference between soft money and hard money?"

"Soft money is given to some VIP when you expect him to do a favor for you. Politicians openly accept it. Hard money is generally sought by people who are desperate and will pay exorbitant interest rates to obtain cash. Most of the time such cash comes from gangland ties or borderline lenders."

"Babe is a mixture of good and bad traits. One day the bad will overcome the good. He's just too boastful of his big deals. Would you like to be in Babe's position today?"

"Heavens, no! I left a dean's position at Proviso High School to become a coordinator at Triton, a step below, with the thought that eventually I would catch up. I believe great things are going to happen at Triton despite your battle with the board. Will I ever become a dean?"

"Don't worry, you will. You're on the ground floor now and next year you'll be one higher. Now, how are you doing with the lecture and forum series?"

"Quite well. We've booked Commander Eugene Cernan, one of the astronauts scheduled to go to the moon, as one of our first speakers. Others include the real Maria von Trapp from *The Sound of Music*, Dr. Robert Havighurst, world-famous sociologist, Tom Ewell, star of stage, screen and television, and Roger Ray, musical humorist. I'm still working on getting more famous people to come to Triton."

"It sounds good to me. Have you anyone lined up as athletic director?"

"Yes, I have. His name is John Swalec. He's presently the director of athletics at a nearby high school and holds a B.S. and M.S. from Illinois State University. He's scheduled to be interviewed by the deans this afternoon and with you after four o'clock today.

"Good! I'm happy to hear that, because this director will have a difficult job ahead of him until we have our own athletic facilities. For now I've received clearance from Dr. Cox to use the West Leyden PE equipment and facilities from 10 PM to midnight. In reality we cannot enter into interscholastic competition until we move to our own campus. Until then we hope the athletic director can develop a strong intramural program from ten to midnight."

"Don't worry, if John Swalec is hired, I know he's just the man to do it."

"Art, I know you're working hard on the college activity programs but you may need a little help. So I'm giving you a copy of the Southwestern College Student Handbook, which will provide you with material on clubs, duties of officers, constitutions, organizational charts, etc. In the near future I want you to develop with student leaders a similar handbook for Triton. We want this campus humming with student programs as our students learn how to work with many different racial and ethnic groups through planned activities with each other. It's been said many a time that more is learned and remembered through student activities than organized course work. Do you believe that?"

"Yes, I do. Our community consists mainly of hardworking people with an unusual mix of cultures. Some of them may not get along well with each other today, but here at Triton everyone will be treated equally, welcomed and appreciated. When I start to appoint committees I'll instill in everyone the idea that we want input from all ethnic groups, and I'll try to get more women to participate. By the way, will you and your wife be at our first college dance on September 17th?"

"Absolutely, and so will all the deans with their spouses and a few trustees. You can count on all of us being there."

On Friday, August 6th I drove over to Wade's office to discuss the August 11th agenda. He led me to his conference room to show me the following news articles spread out across the long table:

TRITON COLLEGE BOARD AND CITIZENS GROUP MEET TWICE
JUNE 30 – NO RESULTS   JULY 6TH – SAME STORY
THE WATCHDOG BARKS   SMITH HITS WATCHDOGS

HEAR WATCHDOG PROTESTS   ROSSETTER WRITES
WHEN THE HEAT IS ON, TRITON BOARD IS GONE
LINGERING TWILIGHT
THE ROAD BACK (EDITORIAL)

"Herb, these stories are selling newspapers but they are not selling Triton. Every article is a blow to the stomach. If this continues we'll be knocked out before the college opens. Everywhere I go someone stops me to offer advice, sympathize with me or condemn me or one or more trustees. We're the press's best copy in years and the papers will not let up. Any suggestions on how we can stop the slaughter?"

"Wade, we have to stand firm even if Condon doesn't release us from the bond sale. The press won't let up until the sale is withdrawn. All we need is one more vote to make it happen. Were you able to get any help from Dunahow? How did the luncheon go?"

"The meal was good but it's impossible to obtain any help from Dunahow. He really is the mastermind of the deal. He told me that the $50,000 earmarked for each one of the boys is already spent by them. Joe needs it to pay off some bills and to send his oldest daughter to an out-of-state university. Bob and Fred intend to pay off their home mortgages. Babe is the only one financially fixed but he won't go against Kirie or Conti. Those two big boys definitely want their $100,000 each. Dunahow claims that if they don't get it, someone will get hurt."

"What did he mean by that?"

"I don't know exactly, but he assured me it wouldn't be me. He went on to tell me how hard he's worked all his life, how he deserves every penny he gets. Joe Condon thinks he's the greatest and is glad to pay him the double commission of $267,000 he worked so hard to earn. Dunahow supports his boys, who've stood fast and repelled the flack from the press. He can't understand why I haven't joined the coalition and has offered to cut me in with a five-way split of the $200,000 if I change my vote on the bond issue."

"How did you answer him?"

"I strongly opposed his offer, and let him know that politicians' taking school money for tips is like taking money from children. He ignored my remark and went on to say he was happy to reward all his boys with $50,000 each. Later he confessed his personal take would be well over $100,000, which he feels he rightfully deserves since he engineered the project. Dunahow feels one is stupid to have power and not use it."

"How does someone use his power?"

"In Dunahow's world money is power, money is his God. So he takes it while he can. Accepting little tips along the way is the expected mode of the politician. He believes all high-ranking officials have always had their handout from the gravy train. He claims the do-gooders, meaning the Citizens for Triton, are angry with him because they don't have the opportunity to get aboard the train."

"Wade, if anything is certain, it's that Dunahow will not give up his push for the bond sale. He's not only the mastermind of the deal, but the master of chicanery."

"You can say that again, Herb! You know, as we were leaving the restaurant, both a little tipsy, he put his hand over my shoulder and asked, 'Wade, how would you like to make a thousand dollars for 15 minutes of work?' 'I've never made that much in 15 minutes. What would you want me to do?' 'I need a respected citizen to testify in court that the strippers at the big Cicero's nightclub are not prostitutes. Could you join me this Saturday night to see the show? It will be a lot of fun and the easiest thousand you ever earned. What do you say?'"

"Well, what did you say?"

"I told him I'll think about it."

"Think no more about it. Reject it completely. Wade, you'd be leaving yourself wide open to all kinds of trickery of Les's invention. I can see a photographer taking a picture of you with one or more strippers on your lap or hugging you. The next day it would appear in the papers with the caption, 'Triton College Board President Has Fun at Cicero's Hot Nightclub.' Wade, don't you dare go!"

"Herb, relax, I've already turned Smith down. By the way, he thinks you're misleading the board with your prediction of 1,000 students on opening day. If it doesn't happen the coalition may negotiate a settlement with you. He suggested that Clem Lowe be appointed acting president when your contract is terminated."

"How did you answer him?"

"I told him we're very fortunate to have a Californian with such vision and the board would be big losers if you were to leave. Now, Herb, don't you dare think of leaving."

"Wade, to date we've enrolled almost 700 students. With the bulk mailing and the help of the deans I'm sure we'll reach our goal of 1,000 despite bad news coverage. Had there been positive articles we would have already reached our goal. I was quite surprised to find that many students from Chicago and Elmhurst have also enrolled, even though we did no soliciting. There's an unknown enrollment potential for students from out-of-state and out-of-district areas. Any of our 14 unique occupational programs, offered nowhere else, will attract these future students. There's a good possibility that those negative forecasts will be proven wrong."

"I hope so. Dunahow has made so many ugly statements. He has no ethics. He says that Chicago politicians are expected to receive little tips or bribes along the way and are crazy when they refrain from getting on the gravy train. Now, let's stop talking about Smith and get into the agenda for the August 11th meeting," which we did, for over an hour.

On August 11, 1965 the 32nd official meeting of the Triton board was held at West Leyden High School, with five members of the press and an audience of 53. The once laughing, jolly and happy board was gone. The trustees arrived quietly, in a somber mood, not talking to each other or to anyone else. After waiting, to no avail, until ten minutes past the hour for Babe Serpico to arrive, Wade called the meeting to order.

First order of business was Dean Dale's recommendation for an improved salary schedule for the classified. With hardly any discussion at all it was tabled with one comment, "Can we afford it now?" Surprisingly, though, Dale's decision to upgrade and reclassify Sandra Horton, Maria Provenzano and Virginia Sybilla was endorsed with positive remarks. How come? It turned out that, unknown to many, Sandra Horton was Roy Jones's oldest daughter. Almost everyone already knew that Maria Provenzano, my secretary, was Babe's sister-in-law, while Virginia Sybilla, Dean Darnes's secretary, was known as a dear friend of Leslie Smith's wife. The administration was praised for recognizing and retaining these very talented individuals.

Next on the agenda, Bob Collins read a letter addressed to Don Dunahow, who was absent, from architect John Fox on test boring on the site. Basically, the borings had a mixture of "acceptable" and "not good" values. The site was not acceptable for a high-rise, but Fox felt that by going seven feet below grade level a good bearing value for spread footings could be obtained. The high water level meant no go on basement construction.

From the rear a voice shouted out, "Get a new site."

Bob angrily responded, "There isn't any other. Either we build on this site or we don't build at all." The rumblings stopped.

Joe Farmar firmly added, "I've spoken to John Fox and he said he could build on it but no more than three stories. We have faith in John's engineering so we'll go with it." All the trustees nodded approval after hearing Joe's and Bob's remarks.

Continuing, Bob informed the trustees that appraisers Harry Shlaes, Richard Leyden and James Felton had been requested to proceed as rapidly as possible.

Dead silence fell over the room as Wade announced that the bond committee had met with Joseph Condon. Several "oh, no's" were heard as he reported that McDougal & Condon expected Triton to abide by its contract. He stressed that Condon would seek legal damages if the board rescinded the agreement.

Irving Nuger, representing the Citizens for Triton, stood up and asked to be recognized. Speaking loudly, clearly and with much sincerity, he said, "We feel the board made a drastic mistake when they approved of the bond sale at such a high interest rate without soliciting any bids. You said you would try to rescind your mistake and we expect you to do so. The public is watching and the unrest will continue until the board learns to follow good business procedures, which up to this point you have not done."

A few cheers and a little applause followed. One loud voice sounded off, "Right on, Irv. Give them hell."

Looking at the loud one Irving continued, "The Citizens for Triton are not at war with you. However, we are united in our efforts to develop a college with high ethical values, starting with the board. We want to work with you, not against you, in reaching that goal. We felt our efforts were rewarded when the board passed the new policy on purchasing. It's a good beginning. May you continue to do the right thing."

All the trustees were stonefaced. If the public ever learned of the secret Dunahow deal I wondered what would happen. As I looked at Wade I felt he was thinking the same thing. If the secret deal were not completed very soon it was sure to leak out, since the circle of persons that knew about it was enlarging. While the CFT suspected some wrongdoing, they had no real evidence. Their suspects included the four coalition members, attorney Smith and the officers of McDougal & Condon. The longer it took to complete the deal, the greater the danger that some of the leaks would lead to full exposure. The wives of the principals were not known for their discretion. For that reason Dunahow, in his wisdom, was pushing for a fast sale.

Next on the agenda was the request to add more faculty and classified. I was surprised and pleased when the board cooperated by approving all my recommendations without comment. Referring to the Faculty Bulletin, Volume I, No. 6, I reported that to date we had hired 81 instructors, 21 full-time and 60 part-time. The incoming faculty had been trained in 24 different states and one foreign country. Of the 711 students enrolled, approximately half were part-time. As Bob Collins read the program for the first faculty workshop, scheduled to begin on Monday morning, August 30th, all of the trustees indicated they would attend for a short while.

In rapid order the board approved purchasing a station wagon, invoices to be paid and conferences for faculty to attend.

The last item on the agenda was the reading of the resignations of Loretto Lescher and Irma Stallery, who were departing, according to the resignations, for professional reasons. Not revealed to the public or the board was the real reason. They were reluctant to be part of a college with a board tainted by scandal.

At 9:10 PM the meeting adjourned. The coalition fellows quickly disappeared, leaving Boeger, Jones, Steel and Zeitlin behind to exchange viewpoints with the Citizens for Triton and several press representatives led by Neil Mehler.

Jack Rossetter issued a bitter, caustic, sarcastic attack on the coalition: "It's completely incomprehensible to me why the board refuses to seek open bidding, unless there's selfish individual gain or some other financial gain by friends at stake. If the board remains bullheaded on this issue, legal action will be taken against them and the CFT will provide a vote of no confidence."

We left stunned by Jack's threat and marveled at his remarkable insight.

31

The Incredible Triton Story

O n August 19th the following editorial by Neil Mehler, editor and publisher, appeared in the *Franklin Parker:*

INCREDIBLE. That's the only word for the Triton College mess. Only a few months ago the college board was enjoying the greatest honeymoon with the press ever seen in these parts. We newspaper editors twice were treated to steak dinners while the college trustees outlined their plans for the building of a first-class junior college, first of its kind in Illinois to have its own campus.

We ate the steak, were charmed by the board members and wrote page after page of copy about how wonderful it all would be on the cozy little Triton campus in Leyden Twp.

What happened to ruin the honeymoon? Why is the Triton coat-of-arms in need of polishing before the first student ever sets foot in a class?

The answer is really very simple. The college board has acted in a manner directly opposed to the principles for which a good educational institution stands. If the board wants to build a college that will teach young men and women about government, make them responsible and decent citizens and encourage them to take an active part in public affairs, the board should start by setting an example of how it should be done.

If the recent bond sale had been discussed openly, its terms studied, its alternatives debated, the board would not now find itself in a corner from which it apparently cannot get out without spending more of the taxpayers' money than is necessary.

The trustees had only to do what they are now doing – WAIT FOR MORE INFORMATION – to avoid the mess they are In.

If, as has been charged (and never denied by the board), the interest rate to be paid is excessive, the attorney's fee on the bond sale is excessive, and the profit to the bond house is excessive, the trustees who voted for the sale should have done some more talking, some more telephoning and some more researching on the matter.

The community can only hope that Triton College itself will prove such an asset to the area that this incredible bond mess will some day be looked on as a mere birth pang, and that the baby will grow up to be a credit to its parents, the citizens of Leyden and Proviso Townships.

The following morning, Friday, August 20th, I visited Wade in his office to discuss the coming board meeting. On his conference table were nine critical articles that had appeared in August, in the *Elmwood Park Times, Suburban Life, Proviso Herald, Elmwood Park Herald, Franklin Parker* and the *Chicago Daily News.*

The headlines read:

SIXTH WEEK OF CONFUSION
LAWYERS HOLD BOND SALE KEY
BOND CONTROVERSY CONTINUES
FUROR RAGES OVER TRITON BONDS
STATE ATTORNEY CLARK ON BONDS
TOWARD OPEN BIDDING
ELMER CONTI'S LETTER
ROSSETTER, CONTI LOCK HORNS
THE INCREDIBLE TRITON STORY

Wade looked tired. In exasperation he asked, "Herb, will the press ever letup on us? If I were a student or faculty member, after reading all these articles I'd say nix on Triton. Now tell me, how many more resignations do you have this time?"

"Only two, Michael Soporin and Patricia Castro. No reason given. They just resigned."

"It was nice that they gave no reason. Had they spoken the truth, it would have meant fewer students selecting Triton."

"Back up a little, Wade. Two weeks ago I told you we had almost 700; today we have over 900. If we continue at the same pace we'll reach our goal of 1,000."

"This is quite a surprise. How do you account for this sudden surge?"

"Several factors were at work First, the mass mailing of schedules and the deans' distributing them to all our libraries helped a lot. And secondly, while the press continued to be critical of the board, they did help tremendously by printing all 27 press releases we submitted to them on faculty hired. Take a look at this bulletin of articles published by our newspapers."

I showed Wade the bulletin with the following headlines:

TRITON COLLEGE STAFF GROWS
EVENING REGISTRATION SET
DR. COX, H.S. PRINCIPAL, TO TEACH
CPA HIRED AS INSTRUCTOR
PUBLISHING ASSISTANT TO TEACH
KOVAL TO TEACH SCIENCE
HULL TO TEACH MACHINE SHOP
VERN MAGNESEN EMPLOYED
MELROSE PARK ATTORNEY TO TEACH
R. OLIVER TO TEACH FRENCH
LAWICKI TO TEACH BIOLOGY
MORRIS TO BE BUSINESS INST.
LANE TO INSTRUCT ZOOLOGY
RALPH SMITH TO TEACH MATH
MALCOLM BERD TO TEACH HISTORY
LOWELL HENRIKSEN - IND. REL.
BOARD APPROVES 18 INSTRUCTORS
VERWEIL - JOURNALISM
CLIFF WOODS TO TEACH BIOLOGY
HELEN MUMM – TEACH SHORTHAND
ARMY ENGINEER TO TEACH SURVEYING
SPINA TO TEACH ELECTRONICS
ODWAY TO TEACH ENGLISH & SPEECH
CAROLE WIDIGER - ASSISTANT LIBRARIAN
LOIS ROE TO TEACH ART AT TRITON
DE PAUL INST. TO TEACH ECO.
MATASAR TO TEACH HISTORY
COLON TO TEACH ENGLISH
GERENSTEIN PART-TIME TEACHER

"Wade, I'm sure that prospective students' interest in Triton increase when they read about the remarkable caliber of our newly hired staff. And don't forget the many students who can't afford to attend an out-of-town university. With its low tuition Triton is a lifesaver."

"Did you know that while your deans were distributing schedules to all the libraries, Neil Mehler was distributing free copies of the *Franklin Parker's* feature article, "The Incredible Triton Story"? Your deans were building Triton up while Neil Mehler's editorial was tearing Triton down."

"Wade, I don't see it that way. Neil gave a lot of thought to the editorial. He spoke the truth in well-chosen words with excellent analogies. I particularly liked his last paragraph, comparing the bond mess to the birth pangs of a baby that will hopefully 'grow up to be a credit to its parents,' our district's citizens. Wade, this is a beautiful analogy. Don't you think so?"

"Herb, that may be true and maybe it will lead to Neil's getting some award for superior journalism, but it will also result in the destruction of the *Franklin Parker.*"

"How is that?"

"I spoke to Don Dunahow yesterday. He's the most vindictive person I've ever met. He's vowed to destroy Neil Mehler."

"And how is he going to do that?"

"He, along with Collins and the Conti contingent, will do everything in their power to have all the *Franklin Parker* advertisers withdraw their ads. If that happens, and I think it will, Neil Mahler's paper will go bankrupt."

"Oh, that's horrible...but in my opinion Neil is a great journalist and some university or big newspaper will offer him new opportunities. I really don't believe his editorial did any harm to Triton. It enlightened the community on the facts. As a matter of fact Paul Harvey, in his daily radio news broadcast, heard by millions, made it a point to praise the editorial – and that's saying a lot."

"Yes, I know. Several folks have told me about it and now our local radio people have joined in the parade. It's now on the airways as well as in the papers. It just won't stop."

At this point Wade and I took off our jackets and reviewed each item on the agenda in preparation for the August 25th meeting.

There was tension in the air, no laughing or joking, as the trustees patiently waited for Babe Serpico and Joe Farmar to arrive at the meeting. They didn't show, so at 8:10 PM, with the five trustees present constituting a quorum, Wade called the meeting to order.

Don Dunahow, first on the agenda, read a long letter from Chapman & Cutler relating to HR 1710 and its effect on the sale of bonds. He raised several hypothetical questions, which no one answered. Wade requested that I contact several state officials to meet with the board ASAP to help in the interpretation of the bill. Dunahow said the three appraisals should be ready within a few weeks.

Following Dunahow's lengthy report, Bob Collins, as secretary of the board, made it a point to stand up and offer a lengthy address of adulation for the wise counsel Dunahow had given the board. On behalf of the board he expressed to Dunahow his deep appreciation for his great knowledge of the varying bond market.

Looks of disgust fell over the faces of the Citizens for Triton contingent and all members of the press while Steel, Jones and I remained pokerfaced. In rapid order the appointment of Lorraine Wilson and Maureen Pressy as office staff and several faculty members were approved, as well as the acceptance of the two resignations.

I reported that to date 939 students had enrolled and 42 classes were filled to capacity. The transfer students had expressed their preference of Triton to 47 other colleges. Mrs. Faye Lowe, one of the earliest supporters of the college, pleaded on behalf of the CFT for cooperation between the board and the Citizens. Wade thanked her for all her work in helping create the college. He then announced that, starting that night, at the midpoint of every meeting he would call a recess so that anyone could address the board.

After a 25-minute recess the board returned to the table to announce that Roy Jones, Fred Knol, Don Dunahow and I would attend a meeting of the Illinois Junior College Association in Moline on September 14th. Roy Jones, Wade Steel and I were urged to attend the Proviso Municipal League meeting on September 15th.

The meeting adjourned at 9:40 with Dunahow, Collins and Knol departing together immediately. That left Steel, Jones, Boeger and me to talk with the disappointed and saddened group of 43 about the incredible Triton story. Before leaving Jack Rossetter told us that he had contacted the office of the State Attorney General, William Clark, seeking his help in getting McDougal & Condon to break the contract.

In deep earnestness he said, "If it costs the taxpayers $20 thousand to break the contract it would be worth it. By advertising for competitive bidding on a smaller bond issue of $3 million, the district might save between $200 and $450 thousand in interest over the next 20 years."

The open session with the CFT ended at 10:40 because Jones and Boeger had promised their wives to return early. Wade asked me to follow him home since he had an urgent matter to discuss.

When we arrived at Wade's place, Millie ushered us into the finished basement, where beers and ham sandwiches awaited. Halfway through the snack I asked, "Wade, what's up?"

"Herb, I've been told that if Attorney General Clark doesn't help the CFT, Jack will be going one step higher."

"And what is that next step?"

"He plans to round up 100 to 200 citizens and march right into Governor Kerner's office and demand justice from the system."

"Do you think he'll do it?"

"I don't know. The press has lauded him as a rare find, highly intelligent with unimpeachable integrity. He's the Pied Piper for the do-gooders. Everyone listens attentively to him when he speaks."

"Do you think he's dynamic enough to find 100 to 200 people willing to take a day or two off from work to follow him?"

"It could happen if his message is loud and clear and delivered to angry people."

"What's his goal?"

"He wants to expose and put an end to corruption by slick politicians."

"Well, that sounds good to me. Why shouldn't we cooperate?"

"Personally, I don't think he could recruit a large enough force to make an impact on entering the governor's office. And such an event could hurt Triton further. Can you imagine what a ball the press would have? Just imagine the headline, 'Corruption Exposed at Triton College.' Do you want to see that happen?"

"Heavens no! It would ruin our chances of getting the one million plus grant from the federal government and prevent us from receiving North Central accreditation. Under HR 1710 the state junior college board might even terminate our trustees and take over the operation of Triton."

"Herb, all those things could happen if Jack Rossetter goes off halfcocked. While he's trying to help us, his actions may lead to Triton's destruction before we even get started."

"Well, what can we do to prevent this from happening?"

"Tomorrow night I'll be visiting Jack and Sue at their home. Perhaps I can convince him to run for the board as Babe's replacement."

"Wade, you've got it! Jack really wants status, and besides that it would be the beginning of the breakup of the Serpico coalition. Sounds good to me. Go to it and keep me informed."

It was well after midnight when I left Wade's home, feeling a little better knowing that he might have good luck with Jack and a new day would begin if he were on the board.

The following morning while having breakfast with Eugenia I received a long distance call from New York City.

"Dr. Zeitlin, my name is Benjamin Fine. I'm the education editor of the *New York Times.* Recently I heard Paul Harvey read on the air a fascinating editorial called, 'The Incredible Triton Story.' Could you tell me more?"

"No, I can't really. You already have the full story."

"Oh, come on now. There's more to it. Is the Mafia part of the corruption?"

"We have two lawyers as trustees, plus another lawyer who specializes in community college law. Anyone who prints a story implying that the Mafia is connected to the college will be subject to a big libel suit. Do you want that to happen to the newspaper that only prints 'all the news that's fit to print?'"

"Hey, wait a minute. I didn't say Triton was Mafia-connected. I just asked you – was it?"

"How would you like it if I asked you if the *New York Times* was Mafia-owned? Just suppose a few reporters from Chicago asked you the same question. The mere asking of such a question arouses people's curiosity to such a point that they ask another person, who in turn asks another, then another. By the time the sixth person is questioned, it's more of an answer: 'Do you know that the *New York Times* is owned by the Mafia?' How's that for a fast analysis?"

"Dr. Zeitlin, you make a good case. I completely withdraw my question. Before calling you I checked my files. You know, about nine years ago Dr. Robert Bush, a friend of mine from Stanford University, sent me the synopsis of your doctoral dissertation on high school discipline. I liked it so much that I wrote a feature article in the *Sunday*

Times, highlighting it as one of the best scholarly researches of the year. Do you remember that?"

"Yes, I do, but I didn't know you were the author of the article. As a result of your feature I received dozens of requests for the synopsis from high school principals throughout the United States. I want to thank you very much for helping me advance my professional career."

"Dr. Zeitlin, let me ask you one more question. At the time your dissertation was published you were the foremost authority on high school discipline in the nation. Why did you leave that area?"

"Dr. Fine, with one new junior college opening up every week or two, I felt it would be exciting to be instrumental in the founding of such a college."

"Well, is it?"

"Yes, it is. As you know there's a strong relationship between discipline and the curriculum. If the teacher is exciting and the course of study is practical, there are no disciplinary problems. Unfortunately, today the most talented people do not enter teaching, and so many curricula are outdated. As a counselor for seven years at the Phoenix Technical School I learned the worst students can become the best if taught vocational/technical subjects by competent instructors. I'm now in the position of creating the first community college and technical institute in the state of Illinois. Hopefully I'll make Triton the model for many others to follow. It's an opportunity of a lifetime. I believe the Triton students will have job offers before graduation, which is not the case for the thousands of university graduates with majors in art, music, psychology, journalism and theater arts."

"I'm fully aware of the unrealistic plans of so many of our college students today and that's why I, too, am excited about your new community college and technical institution. Please stay in touch as you weather the vicissitudes of Chicago politics."

After hanging up I thought for a while about the dialogue with Dr. Fine. At first I thought of him as a threat. Now I realized he was a true educator and journalist who reported only news "fit to print." If only the world had more journalists of his type!

32
Faculty Workshop

The air was filled with excitement, adventure and challenge as 22 full-time and many more part-time instructors met for the first time on August 30th for a week of orientation. All eyes of the experienced teachers and administrators were focused on Wade Steel as he opened the meeting with an introduction of each trustee. The faculty were impressed with the trustees' good physical appearance, educational background, fine articulation ability, rapid responsiveness to questions and sincerity. They were an instant hit and could have sold the Brooklyn Bridge had they wanted to. While no trustee mentioned the bond issue, they all praised the administration for recruiting a faculty of such high caliber and asked the teachers to make history as the founding staff. After an hour or more of wonderful dialogue Wade declared a 15-minute recess that lasted 25 minutes.

After the break I proudly introduced Dr. John Widergren, dean of admissions and guidance, with a summary of his education, experiences and family background. He in turn requested counselors Trudy Wilson, Dr. Victor Dye and the coordinator of student activities, Arthur Shearburn, not to summarize their background but to give the full story, which they did.

A similar sequence of events followed when Dr. Robert Darnes, Gordon Simonsen and Bob Dale were presented. After establishing a friendly, family-like atmosphere we adjourned to the Homestead Restaurant for a delightful luncheon. I requested that all trustees and administrators not sit together but with the instructional staff, and discuss their dreams for the future.

The audience was quite surprised when Wade introduced his wife Millie at a distant table. I promptly presented my wife Eugenia, who was seated nearby. Seated next to Eugenia was architect John Fox, whom I introduced as our luncheon speaker.

Fox stressed the fact that faculty input was vital to building the first community college campus in Illinois. At present there were to be no restraints if sufficient funds for construction were available.

The principal concerns of the faculty were: where? when? and how?

John's reply: the River Grove site; construction to start after one year of planning; and mode of construction to be decided at a later date. He assured the group that it would not be a high-rise since the land did not meet the requirements. Most of the buildings would have one or two floors; some might have three. He concluded by pleading with the board and me to purchase the site ASAP.

For the afternoon session John Widergren led the discussion regarding student registration, grading, program changes, counseling, adding or dropping a class, deficiency notices and, finally, graduation requirements.

On Tuesday morning the business office had the stage. Bob Dale reviewed purchasing procedures, paying bills, insurance and hospital choice, bookstore operation, college maintenance and college security.

In the fifth session, held on Tuesday afternoon, Arthur Shearburn distributed the student handbook and stressed the importance of student activities, whether held before, after or during school hours. He invited all faculty to the first college dance and encouraged faculty and students to be part of the lecture and forum series. While on that subject he proudly announced that the first lecturer was to be astronaut Lt. Commander. Eugene Cernian, a Proviso High School graduate from Bellwood. The topic: "Planning a Trip to the Moon."

When Art opened the floor for discussion he heard:

"It will never happen in our lifetime."

"A terrific waste of taxpayers' money."

"Hi, Ho, Buck Rogers, we'll meet you in space."

"A dream that will never be fulfilled."

"Who knows, maybe by the year 2000 it will happen. If not then, maybe 2500."

"How much is this astronaut being paid?"

"He's not charging us a penny. NASA has him on a speaking tour so the interested public will learn about space travel."

Art ended his discussion saying, "In this room we have some of the best brains in the state of Illinois. But on this subject there's still a wide difference of opinion. Gene Cernan's dream is that one day he'll walk on the moon. I hope that some of us will still be alive when it happens."

After the break John Swalec, athletic director and PE chairman, described the programs he was working on despite limited resources. He was peppy and filled with hope for the future on the new campus. Since the pool and gym were available in the late hours he intended to put them to full use. On the light side he invited the faculty to get into the swim as soon as the pool party was arranged.

On the morning of the sixth workshop day the faculty heard a different beat from the wisecracking prizewinning bandmaster from Oklahoma, Dr. Robert Darnes, the dean of instruction. With an erratic rhythm he discussed the articulation agreements reached with the University of Illinois and other colleges, preparation for accreditation, development of new programs, need for many faculty committees, formation of a faculty association and the grading and evaluation of faculty.

On Wednesday afternoon the seventh session was conducted by Gordon Simonsen, dean of technology, who emphasized the need for balance. With each occupational program there was a vital need for general education courses. With great pride he announced some of the names of prominent company executives who consented to serve on Triton's occupational advisory committees. In order for Triton to receive the additional reimbursement from the state vocational board, rigid requirements as to class size, equipment to be used and instructor qualifications had to be met.

Gordon estimated that Triton, the only community college in the state with 14 approved occupational programs, might receive over one million dollars from the state vocational board by the end of the year. Tom McCabe, the Notre Dame graduate and math instructor, asked, "Why is the state giving so much money for vocational training? Wouldn't it be better spent on math and science improvement?"

Gordon smiled as we all waited for his reply. "First of all, the money from the state comes originally from the federal government. For many years Illinois has returned millions of unused federal allocations."

"Why is that?"

"Because many high school and college boards and administrators shun vocational training, believing these programs are of lower status and should not be part of a respected institution. Fortunately for us we have a board and college president that are different. The board has encouraged and authorized President Zeitlin to offer as many voc/tech programs as the community needs, and we're just beginning. We'll fill a shameful and tragic vacuum that's existed for many years. On future agendas additional occupational programs will be developed, making Triton a major center for such training."

Gordon continued to field many questions. At the end of the session I felt he'd done a splendid job of communicating to a mixed faculty of academic and vocational instructors what a pioneering asset the community college and technical institute would be. The staff left better informed and enlightened, which had been the purpose of the workshop.

On Thursday morning, as we opened the eighth session with distribution of the faculty handbooks, I said, "This booklet has been prepared to answer most questions that instructors raise and to help you interpret college policy. Without this book you'd be left on your own in securing needed information, usually by word of mouth and possibly inaccurately."

Using the overhead projector I presented the college organizational chart. I pointed to the top box: *The People.* "Shortly after the district was formed these 280,000 people elected a board of trustees (Box 2), who in turn did a national search for a college president (Box 3). I was honored and delighted to be selected as the executive officer of the board and chief administrative officer of the college. Now, let's face it – no president can run a college without some help. Again, after a nationwide search help was found in the form of three deans, all of equal rank, plus a business manager. They in turn found you, the best of the best. In the weeks ahead you and the deans will appoint the division heads. Your day-to-day direction will be provided by your division chairs. Now, I ask you: What box is the most important one in this chart?"

Silence fell over the group. No one said anything until Tom

McCabe reluctantly spoke out. "We've all read the newspapers and are fully aware of the problems you're facing with the board. So if you ask me, I would say the power is with the board. They hire, fire, fix the tax rate and control our salaries. Do you agree?"

I said nothing, hoping for more faculty participation. Eventually a response came from John Collins, a history teacher, who at age 55 was the oldest faculty member present. "Regardless of the organizational chart, we as teachers have the major function of teaching. In order to teach we must have students. Without students we have nothing. Therefore, I would put in the top box STUDENTS, taught by TEACHERS in a box 2 directly below, guided by DEPARTMENTAL OR DIVISION CHAIRS in box 3, directed by DEANS in box 4, inspired by the goals set by the COLLEGE PRESIDENT, in box 5. I would always put the students in the first box."

"Thank you, John. I buy that viewpoint 100 per cent. Any other suggestions?"

Dr. Victor Dye waved his hand and said, "I think there's much merit to what Tom and John said. I joined this college because of its excellent salary structure and the opportunity to grow. Now tell us, Dr. Zeitlin, what means do you have for us to grow?"

"Dr. Dye, I'm glad you asked that question. Now let me take you to the tree that will grow as we grow. It's known as the college committee structure. This structure is the democratic way of getting things done. Every teacher shall be required to serve on one or more committees. You'll grow from active participation on committees, attending conferences, taking graduate courses, doing some research, holding office in the faculty association or state organizations and from sharing your experiences and knowledge with your students and colleagues."

With my pen on the chart I touched each committee box and explained its function, concluding with, "Please contact your dean soon and let him know the committee of your choice. We're loaded with talent in this room, so your input is highly desired. This chart was developed by me based on several years of experience with structures that work democratically. It is not forged and tempered in steel and is subject to change as new needs develop. During the first week of school I intend to drop in on every class for a minute or two just to say hello to you and your students, and then I'll be on my way."

Malcolm Berd waved his hand. "Dr. Zeitlin, may I commend you for inserting all these job descriptions and responsibility statements in this booklet. I've never seen anything like this before. Is this another first by you?"

"No, Malcolm, it's not. It's borrowed and refined from some excellent colleges of the past. Now everyone knows what everyone is doing. It should help. While we now have five full-time administrators for a college of 1,000, if the enrollment doubles in the second year, which I expect it to, then of course we'll be adding more teachers and administrators. I say this not to encourage you to leave the classroom but to let you know that if you're thinking about making a job change in the future, Triton will always give preference to the internal candidate if she or he is fully qualified."

"Does that mean we can continue to advance on the salary schedule even if we take graduate courses in school administration?"

"Yes, if approved by your dean. However, the opportunity of a 10, 20 or 30% salary increase through additional graduate work is offered so that you'll become more knowledgeable in your subject area. As a superior master teacher with a 30% increase in salary, you'd be earning more than a beginning administrator."

"So what you're saying is, you don't have to become an administrator to make more money! Is that correct?"

"Yes, definitely. If you're at the maximum on the salary schedule with summer school, plus an overload, it would mean you'd have to take a salary cut if you became an administrator. I don't encourage you to take that road. So decide early what road you want to be on."

"May I make an appointment with you?"

"Why, of course. Next week things will be a little tight since it's my intent to visit every class briefly, and I also have to get ready for the board meeting Wednesday night. However, the following week is wide open. See Maria and she'll set up an appointment. Incidentally, starting the first week of October and every Thursday thereafter I'll have an open door from 2 to 4 PM. No appointment is needed, just come and we can talk about anything. I believe the deans will also announce an open door schedule."

After several more questions we adjourned for lunch. An hour and a half later we reconvened for the final workshop. I introduced James Hannum, Assistant Cook County School Superintendent, and Dr. George Cox, Principal of the West Leyden High School.

Mr. Hannum briefly covered the resources of his office and asked that all teachers register their teaching credentials to avoid a delay in their first paycheck Dr. Cox, a heavy smoker himself, claimed he'd found the solution to converting a non-smoking high school facility from 7:00 AM to 3:30 PM to a junior college with ashcans from 3:30 PM to midnight. It was quite simple! At precisely 3:30 PM his afternoon maintenance crew would put out 20 big gallon tin cans, filled 3/4 with sand, in key locations. Around 11:30 PM the graveyard shift, in addition to cleaning the classrooms, would pick up the cans, clean them and store them away until 3:30 PM.

Stopping for a few moments and looking straight at the Triton faculty, he pleaded, "Please tell your students it's OK to smoke outside of the classroom only if they put their butts in the tin can. This is a major concern to us and we need your cooperation. Now, on behalf of all the high school teachers, we welcome you to our campus. Your mission is our mission and that is to work together to provide greater educational opportunities to all our people. Whether you stay here for two years or more, we're delighted that your president selected West Leyden as the first campus for Triton and look forward to a good partnership."

After Dr. Cox left I added, "Although I've only known George Cox for about six months I've learned to admire and respect him because he is no ordinary person. He never labels concerns problems but calls them challenges. No matter how difficult the challenge may be, he'll always come up with a solution. We're indeed fortunate to have this most cooperative principal as our partner. He is one prince of a man."

Before adjourning the session I made the following announcements:

"Dr. Widergren has informed me that these past four days have seen a surge in enrollments. We may even go over the goal of 1,000. Registration will continue all day tomorrow and next week we'll have four days of late registration.

"The keys to your rooms and the faculty centers may be picked up any time today. See Bob Dale. The faculty desks have arrived;

business and occupational teachers will occupy Center 12A. All others will be housed in Center 12B. Tomorrow you'll have all day to get organized in your new quarters.

"The Triton library, which occupies one half of a Triton wing, will officially open in two weeks. Carole Widiger will continue to take your orders for books and visual aids.

"All Triton offices will be closed to the public this Saturday as we vacate the premises so they can be converted back to classrooms. We'll be packing Saturday, moving Sunday and opening shop on Monday, which to many of us will be a real day of labor. Your days of labor will start on Tuesday. I have great faith in you as you live up to your reputation as the best teaching faculty in this area we could find. May your future be stimulating and gratifying as you open new worlds of knowledge and skills to our students. To quote a frequent navy command: FSA — *FULL SPEED AHEAD!*"

As the faculty started to leave, I saw, to my surprise, Bernard Verweil at the door distributing the first issue of *The Trident,* dated September 7th, the opening day of school. There was a gang up at the door where the instructors stopped to read. I grabbed a copy, sat down and avidly read, and then said "Wow!"

Bernard was smiling and murmured, "I loved doing it."

I grabbed his hand, shook it and said, "It's wonderful! Your creativity was beyond my expectations. On Wednesday night I'll publicly commend you in front of the board for this splendid contribution."

On Saturday morning, with a brown bag lunch in one hand and working gloves in the other, I joined a wide awake, similarly prepared group of hard workers. What had seemed earlier like an insurmountable task, really turned out to be rather simple. All boxes were packed, sealed and labeled by noon. It was so nice seated around the big conference table having a picnic luncheon with my new second family, all of us trying to make the birth of Triton a success. We talked about anything and everything.

For those on the quiet side I asked, "What do you usually do on Saturday morning?" Some of the responses brought laughter, some sympathy, but on the whole our interest in each other was apparent. With the exception of Dean Darnes, who delighted the staff with his jokes, there really were no stars. Everyone in his own way did shine and I was so proud of the highly select staff.

Inasmuch as so many of the group were churchgoers, it was decided to reconvene and unpack our belongings in the new facility on Sunday at 1:00 PM. Midpoint in the unpacking we all stopped working to take a break and share pleasantries as Eugenia arrived with a wide variety of home-baked cookies.

Monday morning, Labor Day, I met with the deans to review class sizes. Two of Darnes's and one of Simonsen's classes were over 44. I had requested that all three classes be split, creating the need for additional classrooms and three more teachers. The space was available but finding instructors at this late hour was challenging, if not impossible. At 5:00 PM both deans came into my office. Bob said, "Dr. Zeitlin, you asked us to do the impossible – well, we did it. We open tomorrow with no instructor having to teach an overloaded class."

"Fellows, on behalf of the three instructors and over 130 eager students, I thank you for your concern about reasonable teaching loads for all instructors."

I went home that evening and ate a heavy dinner, filled with anxiety over what tomorrow, September 7th, would bring.

33
School Starts September 7th for Six

September 7th, the day after Labor Day in the year of 1965, was a new beginning for the Elmwood Park family known as the Zeitlins. Clare, the youngest, age 6, had counted the days on the calendar since January 3rd while she waited to return to school, which she loved so much. The day before she kept saying, "ool tomor-row, ool tomorrow" and we kept answering her, "tomorrow you go, tomorrow you go."

So when tomorrow came we all got up at 6:30 AM and had an early breakfast. First to depart, at 7:30, was Eugenia, who had applied the previous week for a part-time teaching position at Wright Junior College. To her surprise Dean Ernest Clements had said, "There's nothing open for part-timers but we urgently need someone to teach two classes of English 1A and two of English 1B in the morning. Would you be interested?" The salary placement and hours were so good she couldn't resist saying yes.

Second to leave, at 8 AM, was son Mark, age 15, who was very excited that morning because he was trying out for the Elmwood Park High School junior varsity football team. After spending most of the summer catching my passes he felt sure he would make the team.

At 8:15 Joyce and Ann, wearing their neatly pressed uniforms, departed together to walk to St. Vincent's school on North Avenue. Joyce was starting her first day as the student supervisor of the cafeteria, while Ann was entering the class for the able and ambitious.

So at 8:25 Dad, holding Clare's little hand, waited near the curb for the special education bus to arrive. As we patiently waited I thought about what an active family we were, with Eugenia starting a new full-time job as assistant professor of English, Mark into football, Joyce a supervisor and Ann classified as gifted. And here I was, the oldest in the family, given the responsibility of seeing to it that the youngest and handicapped kid got on the bus safely every morning. The large yellow bus arrived promptly at 8:30. I lifted Clare up to give her a hug and kiss, which she resisted as she struggled to get down and on the bus. She ran and took a seat on the driver's side so I had to run onto the street to wave her good-bye. She ignored my shouting but I was taken aback when so many of the others shouted and waved back to me. They were a strange-looking lot. Then it occurred to me that they all seemed to have some sort of handicap. Did my darling little daughter belong with these strange people? I thought not! I must talk it over with Eugenia that night and make some changes.

The more I thought about it, the more disturbed I became. It was impossible for me to be at two places at the same time. I was also scheduled to be at Triton's opening. I picked up the *Chicago Tribune* and *Chicago Sun Times,* returned to the kitchen, finished my coffee and toast and read both newspapers. It was disturbing to read about another driver being killed as he started up his car. Would that ever happen to me? A terrible thought, but it kept flashing back to me. College presidents were often *fired* but hardly ever *fired upon.*

What I was looking for was some little article about the Triton opening. None appeared. Oh well, it may have been important to me and the thousand students who were attending, but according to the many editors it wasn't news.

Around noon I left home, drove west along North Avenue, took a right and went north on Wolf Road toward the college. I was jolted when the red light changed and a small child coming from the other side of the road ran into my car and fell down. I immediately got out and picked him up. He was OK but was so embarrassed he ran away without a word. It upset me. I told myself to calm down and thanked God that nothing had happened.

As I turned onto the campus I was pleasantly surprised to see a long line of students waiting to register with Trudy Wilson or Dr. Victor Dye.

Dr. Widergren said to me, "Herb, if this keeps up we may reach 1,100. There certainly are a lot of procrastinators."

Upon opening my office door I was overcome with a strong sweet smell. I couldn't believe it. There were six large bouquets of flowers signed with many pleasant congratulations from John Fox, our architect; Dr. David Byrnes, the new superintendent of the Leyden High School district; Dr. George Cox, principal of West Leyden; McDougal & Condon, the bond company; Maria and Tony Provenzano, my wonderful secretary and her husband; and lastly from my Mom, big brother Lester and his wife Rae.

I was quite touched when I read Mother's card: *"Dear Herbert, we are all so proud of you. Sorry Dad is not here to see the birth of your fifth child. Good luck and best wishes for the future. Love always, Mother, Lester and Rae."*

The lump in my throat grew larger and I had difficulty swallowing. Not bad for a mother of seven kids who dropped out of school at age 15 to become the piano player for the silent movies at Brooklyn's Halsey Theater.

She'd referred to Triton as my fifth child. I liked that because it eased some of my guilt feelings at not being home that night with the family to share an exciting day. What's a father to do? A newborn child needs your help and attention the most. I was there when the other four were born; tonight I was home in spirit but not in body.

I wondered how the parents of the 1,000 or more students were feeling today. They must have been very proud of their kids for taking the giant step to improve their lives through more education.

At 3:00 PM I went outside to see the exodus of the high school students. By 3:20 most of them were gone. A few minutes later a stream of different cars arrived. Fifteen minutes later we were packed, and the security officers were busy finding parking spots.

When 4:00 arrived, I left the car area to start my tour of the classes. It was wonderful to see classroom after classroom of eager students of all ages listening and taking notes from master teachers. When I arrived most of the instructors introduced me as the president of the college.

My first words were, "Welcome to Triton College. I hope everything is going well with you. If it isn't please tell me what I can do to help."

Instant feedback revealed that most students were happy to be at Triton. Several students said, however, that parking was difficult. I promised to do something about it soon.

Before leaving I asked each class, "Who is your best friend at this college?"

It was interesting to hear the wide variety of responses, from "my boyfriend" or "my girlfriend" to Mom or Dad or brother or sister or neighbor. I kept probing until I got the answer I was seeking. Eventually I heard, "My counselor."

I impressed upon the students the importance of working with their counselor, because he or she had a wealth of information that would be most helpful. "If you're not in the right course or field of studies the counselor will make adjustments for your benefit."

While it was my intent to spend only two or three minutes in each class, it didn't happen. Many times I extended the period to five or six minutes. As a former counselor I enjoyed immensely the flowing dialogue with the students, even if at times I had to cut it short to complete my mission. At 6:15 PM I stopped, after visiting only 21 classes instead of 37, for a couple of slices of pizza with the deans in the conference room. I managed to squeeze in a few minutes on the phone to talk to Eugenia and each kid briefly. All were happy and doing well.

Shortly thereafter I went out to Wolf Road to watch the invasion. Compared to the orderly movement in the afternoon, it was overwhelming. Horns were blowing, not from the invaders, but from those drivers forced to stop to let the invaders onto the campus. It seemd as though 100 or more cars arrived at the same time. At 7:00 there was still a line up so I went to the rear to locate the problem. I found a disorderly mess, since the officers was waving them in but not parking them in rows. I took over and had them park in straight lines. In twenty minutes all cars were parked and I started to make my rounds.

My first words to the students were, "We will have a parking problem if all 500 cars arrive at the same time. Please try coming 30 minutes earlier." The dialogue was similar to that of the afternoon group, except the parking discord was more intense in the evening.

The next morning I visited Dr. Cox and explained to him the parking challenge. He immediately got on the phone, called the minister of a nearby church and was given permission to use their parking lot. We then walked out to the back lot and decided it was time to put in white parking lines, thus creating more space.

I called Harry Behrman and he decided to increase the security force by two. By noon the parking challenge was solved and I felt good that the boys had come through rapidly.

On Saturday morning, before closing his cabin in Michigan, Wade informed me that he would not be at the Wednesday meeting and had asked Bob Collins to permit Roy Jones as vice president to chair the meeting. It would be a fast way to heal the wounds and prove to the public that the board was working together.

That night Bob Collins called the meeting to order. It was immediately moved, second and carried by Fred Knol and Babe Serpico that Joe Farmer would act as president pro tem in the absence of Wade Steel.

Under old business Don Dunahow stated he had arranged a 12:15 PM meeting on Friday with the appraisers to meet with the Triton board in Chicago to hear their final report. Everyone nodded they would attend. Given the floor, I reported that at the same time the first meeting of the state junior college board would also be held. I happily informed them that word had been received from Dr. Lyman Glenny, Jim Hannum and Dr. Eldon Lichty that they'd be glad to discuss the Class I versus Class II junior college status on Thursday, September 16th at 8:00 PM in room 220.

With joy I reported that as of the day before 1,205 students had enrolled, approximately half full-time, and 87 of the 175 class sections were filled to capacity. After the announcement I waited, expecting the administration to be commended for exceeding the projection of 1,000 by over 200. Silence was not golden; no one said anything.

Elmore Boeger broke the silence by lauding the administration for an excellent four-day faculty workshop, enjoyed by all the trustees.

Under new business Bob Dale presented a proposal submitted by the Victor May Company to furnish security officers on a monthly basis at an hourly rate. Jack Templin, the head security officer, was commended for his fine work on parking. During the discussion on a motion by Jones and Boeger to accept the proposal, Bob Collins read a letter he'd received from Lewis Case applying for the position of security chief.

I immediately interrupted the discussion and requested postponement of any action since the college staff was not informed about this new position. There was no job description and the board would be violating its own policy on hiring.

To this last comment Mr. Farmar loudly proclaimed, "Dr. Zeitlin, this person would not be reporting to you, the college staff or the board attorney. He'd be directly responsible to the board and no one else!"

"Mr. Farmar, what you just said is a violation of our policy on hiring."

After my statement the motion to accept the May Company as the security force for Triton was defeated. Moments later it was moved and seconded by Collins and Farmar to direct Dunahow to enter into negotiations with Mr. Case for the position of security chief at a salary not to exceed $10,000 per year. An attempt by Boeger and Jones to table Collins's motion went down to defeat instantly.

Seconds later Collins's motion to hire Case was approved by a vote of 4 to 2. It was agreed by all the trustees that the May Company would continue its service until a security chief was hired.

The trustees had been hotly divided on the last issue, so Joe waited a few minutes for each one to refill his coffee cup. Then with a smile and in a pleasant manner he asked me to continue. My request to hire additional faculty and student help was approved without comment.

The four informational bulletins were reviewed and accepted, with Joe complimenting me on the personnel directory. "It's a good directory. Now I know where our staff lives and I can call them if I have any questions."

After presentation of the student handbook all trustees were invited and encouraged to attend the first Triton dance, to be held on September 17th. I distributed copies of *The Trident* to the trustees and an audience of 49, and made it a point to compliment Bernard Verweil for his creativity. The trustees and the audience expressed their appreciation.

Before break at 9:30 PM Joe thanked me for my annual report and informed me that discussion on it would take place at the next regular meeting of the board. During the break the board members politely answered a variety of questions to the audience's satisfaction.

The only loud dissenting comment came from Jack Rossetter. "I just don't like hiring a new security guy when the present one has performed so well and so reasonably. What disturbs me most is that there is no job description and the board has completely ignored its own policy."

Before we reconvened several citizens praised me and the college faculty for creating what they hoped would be a wonderful college. That helped a lot. The remaining time was spent on accepting the IBM agreement, purchasing survey equipment, invoices to be paid, new offer to be made on the Carey site and adoption of the Triton budget for the coming year.

TRITON'S SECURITY

The four-to-three split on the Triton College board reflects more than just a difference of opinion on how things should be done to establish a college. It indicates deep and disturbing differences over what an educational institution really is and how it should operate. The college appears to be at another crossroad, and at this stage in its young history, a wrong turn in the road could be disastrous.

Board Secretary Robert Collins has proposed that the college employ a security officer who will investigate to see whether any "risks" -- moral or political -- have found their way on the faculty. What may seem to many to be a perfectly reasonable suggestion by Collins and his supporters on the board is in reality a very disturbing notion.

In the first place, in attempting to hire a former Oak Park police captain to head the security department, the 14-step personnel plan previously approved by the board was side-stepped.

SECONDLY, the duties of this security officer, as outlined in a contract read last week before the full board, give him broad powers to investigate everything and everyone at the school, thus making the security chief, in effect, independent of the administration and outside the "laws" established by the board. These actions would seem to indicate a lack of confidence in the administration. An investigating officer is an unusal part of a college campus where, normally, the board hires the administration and sets policy, and the administration hires the faculty and staff and runs the school.

It is doubtful that many self-respecting instructors will want to work at a college where they face constant "investigation." Triton is new, is not an accredited school, and pays no more than most others, in fact not as well as some suburban high schools. Why work under conditions of irritation when there are other jobs open in the teaching profession and at places where academic freedom and freedom from political pressures are considered part of the pay check?

Why Triton College needs a gestapo or a Royal Mounted Police force is difficult to understand. Many colleges and universities have police forces, but these are there to patrol the campus and regulate parking, not to investigate teachers. Teachers are no better or worse than the rest of the population, but they have a habit of resenting school boards that want teachers to be twice as American and twice as moral as everyone else. The University of California suffered for years following a controversy of a similar nature. Many of the faculty departed to other campuses in that dispute.

If, as Triton President Herbert Zeitlin told the board last week, Triton's chances to become accredited are harmed by the manner in which this security force was handled, the students and the taxpayers will have paid a high price for "security."

34
Eruption Over Security Chief

On Friday, September 9th Bob Dale burst into my office and said, "This is a strange one. There's a Mr. Case in my office who's requested a room and desks to open shop as the Triton security chief. Has he been hired?"

"Bob, this is a complete surprise to me. No one is officially hired until approved by the board and Mr. Case, though an applicant, has not been hired. Let me talk to him."

Standing tall but fidgety was a good-looking, dark-haired, athletic gentleman who introduced himself as Lewis Case. I gave him a hearty handshake and asked, "When were you hired and by whom?"

"The contract was signed this morning by the board secretary Mr. Robert Collins and attorney Donald Dunahow, with the request that I start today. So here I am. To begin with I need a room large enough for two secretaries and for my partner and me."

"Mr. Case, may I see your contract?"

"Sure, here it is." He pulled out a three-page legal document signed by Collins and Dunahow.

I read it slowly with great interest and commented, "This is the usual contract but it's not valid until the board officially ratifies it at the next meeting, which is scheduled for Thursday the 16th. May I make a copy?"

"Sure, go ahead. You know, Mr. Dunahow said I should start immediately."

"Mr. Dunahow is not the board or the chief administrator of this college, so you'll have to wait until next Friday. In the meantime we'll have to find a place to house you since we have no empty rooms."

"OK, may I suggest you rent a large trailer, the kind that

contractors generally use? It has to be large because our force will increase as the college grows."

Reading his contract left a bitter taste in my mouth. I was undecided on what to do. To oppose him would create an instant enemy, which I didn't want to happen. I decided to be friendly with him with the hopes of finding out what the boys were planning.

I said, "We need to find a place for your trailer. Come with me; perhaps a place near the fieldhouse would work"

As we walked along he told me he was a retired captain of detectives with the Oak Park Police Department and had recently developed a full security system for the Ford City shopping center.

"Why would you want to leave Ford City?" I asked.

"The pay at Triton is $3,000 more than at Ford City, and that's reason enough for me to change jobs. Besides, Dunahow told me that one day Triton will be big and I'd like to grow within the system. You should want me because I'll protect you."

"How will you protect me?"

"We all know there are a lot of crazy people out there, including those smart-ass Commies. I intend to be at your side at all public events and board meetings. Just like the security chief looks after the Chicago school superintendent."

"You mean you'll be my bodyguard."

"Yes, you can count on me. Plus, I'll chauffeur you wherever you go in my Lincoln Town Car. You'll be protected at all times by me and my 45."

We arrived at the fieldhouse.

He was quite pleased with the spot he selected because it was near the toilet and shower facilities. On the way back he insisted that I meet with his partner Hermie.

When Hermie got out of the twin Lincoln, he shook my hand strongly, and I asked him, "Have we met before?"

"Maybe, but I don't think so."

Lewis interrupted, "Hermie and I have worked together for years. He's arrested many more queers than I have and I've arrested quite a few."

"Please tell me, how do you know if a person is a queer?"

"It really is quite simple. I can tell by the way they walk, talk, act and how they dress."

"Really, please explain."

"I can spot a homo a block away just by watching his fairy-like walk, his high-pitched voice, his attempt to touch people and his long hair. And he's usually wearing something purple-colored."

"Is that scientific?"

"Oh, come on, now. I would say it's 80 to 90 per cent accurate. The other 10 to 20 per cent are leaning toward the gay life. By the way, how many gays have you hired?"

"I have no idea."

"It's a good thing you have Hermie and me. We'll find the sons of bitches and kick them out. Did you know they're found mostly in the art, music, theater and writing groups?"

"I didn't know that."

As they started to drive away in their twin Lincolns I noticed they had rifles stacked in the front near the driver's seats. Case called out, "We'll see you Thursday night."

I waved back but said nothing.

Upon returning to the office I called an emergency meeting with the deans and Bob Dale and presented them with copies of Lewis Case's contract. After reading it they all expressed shock and Bob Dale said, "He has half of my job if he's responsible for the inventory of all equipment and the recruitment and recommendation of all non-teaching personnel."

"That line was included so that the politicians could dole out jobs to their friends and relatives even if they're not qualified," Dean Widergren remarked. "He'd really be the czar of jobs."

Dean Darnes burst out, "I can't believe this. He's given the power to investigate all employees, keep records of them and reveal the contents only to the board. That sounds like Hitler's storm troopers. I deplore that paragraph!"

Dean Simonsen, the last to speak, said sadly, "This is horrible. We must all do what we can to prevent Case from being hired. I'm sure his presence on any staff would foul up the accreditation."

I then related to them our conversation about gays, to which Bob Darnes reacted bitterly. "I spent most of my life living with and teaching music. We have no more or fewer gays than any other profession. And what does it even matter, anyway?"

It seemed like a chorus sang out, "What are you going to do, Herb?"

"I'm going home to make a list of all the people who might help in some way, and contact them. Tomorrow morning I'll visit the Oak Park Police Department chief to see if I can find out anything about Hermie and Case. In the meantime if you hear anything on this matter or have any suggestions get back to me immediately. Before you all go may I tell you how proud I am of you for doing such a wonderful job these past few months."

Friday night, September 10th, was the first evening in the last five that I had the chance to eat dinner with Eugenia and the kids and hear their stories. First on was our baby Clare, who was asked about school, teacher and bus driver?

Her answer to the first two questions was "nice." But she hesitated in answering the last question, so I repeated it. "How is the bus driver?"

With a giggle she said, "Very nice. . .good-looking guy."

Ann said with excitement, "I have a new friend, Mary Jo Hicks, who lives near us so we walked home together. The teacher said I should write a story about my summer at Bonner's Lake."

Joyce also talked about her new friend, Ellen Hicks, Mary Jo's older sister.

Mark had made junior varsity but wasn't happy because instead of catching passes, the coach made him a line blocker, and that was hard work

"Is there any danger of getting hurt?" Eugenia asked.

"No, not much, because I'm protected with heavy gear. Boy, was I rolling in sweat!"

When it was Eugenia's turn, she reported, "With the exception of one caustic remark about Triton, I had a wonderful five days, with excellent students and a brilliant faculty. Now, Daddy, how was the opening of Triton?"

"Just fine," I replied. "Instead of 1,000 students we enrolled over 1,200, which created a parking problem. Thanks to Dr. Cox we solved it. This weekend I have to work on some other problems that just came up."

The kids were laughing and joking as they did their chores. Eugenia took a stack of papers to correct on the kitchen table, while I went into the den to compile my list of people to contact. The list included Wade Steel, Roy Jones, Elmore Boeger, Harry Behrman, the Oak Park Police chief, the Ford City Manager, the Illinois Attorney General, Illinois State Superintendent's office, Superintendent Joe Rindone, Chet DeVore, the Executive Secretary of the American School Administrators Association, Jim Hannum, Assistant Cook County School Superintendent, Dr. Leroy Knoeppel and my uncle, Frank Soff.

On Saturday morning I managed to get into the office of the Oak Park Police chief. He seemed amused by my desire to find out about Hermie and Lewis Case and said, "I can't tell you anything about those two retired police officers. Their personnel records are sealed."

"Would you like to know how much Lewis Case will now be earning?"

"Not really. How much has he been offered?"

"Ten thousand a year to start, with promises of raises each year."

"That's more than I'm making. No wonder he quit Ford City."

"How many years did he work in Oak Park? Did he ever cause any trouble?"

"I can't tell you, but he worked for us a long time. Trouble comes with the job."

"Have you had more or less trouble since Case left?"

"Less, but I can't be quoted."

"I understand. You won't be quoted. Would you take him back if he wanted to return to Oak Park?"

Looking straight at me with his eyes popping out, he rounded his lips and very quietly said, "No."

That was what I'd been waiting for. I'd managed to squeeze it out of the police chief that the department was glad Lewis was gone. Before I left the chief remarked, "I heard you're offering a degree program in police science. I may send a few officers to Triton to brush up on their skills."

"That's fine. We'd be delighted to have them. Have you given any thought to teaching one of our many courses? It would be great to have you."

"How would I get started?"

"See Harry Behrman, the coordinator of the program. I know he'd be happy to talk with you. Maybe you could become an adjunct faculty member."

Back in my office I telephoned Harry Behrman to discuss Lewis Case's contract. He was rather cool, asked me to describe Hermie, and immediately asked, "Do you know who I think Hermie is?"

"No, I don't. Please tell me."

"He fits to a 'T' my old friend Herman Furlong."

"If my memory is correct, that's guy who was eavesdropping at the restaurant. He had glasses and a mustache. Could that have been a disguise?"

"You bet your life it was. As I went by him I noticed his phony mustache and clear glasses. Remember, he was a rogue detective who liked to play Sherlock Holmes."

"I don't want him to be Triton's assistant chief of security. Is there anything you can come up with that I could use against him?"

"His gay-bashing is a known fact, but no one has filed a charge against him. His personnel records are sealed. In Chicagoland corruption is considered a local sport and the police, instead of protecting us, are often the ones we need to be protected against. If you don't want Case hired, you're the only one who can stop it. I'm with you in spirit and by the way, I look forward to the Oak Park chief joining our faculty."

When I spoke to Roy Jones and Elmore Boeger, they readily agreed not to approve Case's appointment. Unfortunately, I couldn't reach Wade at his cabin; Millie told me he'd deliberately not had a phone installed. She said he'd be back in time for the board meeting Thursday night. That was a good sign. My calls to the attorney general and the state superintendent of schools were put on hold since they were out of town.

My conversation with the assistant superintendent of Cook County Schools, Jim Hannum, was especially good. "Dr. Zeitlin, in my over 30 years in public education I never heard of a security chief having such unusual duties. I would fight it tooth and nail. You know, a few of your board members called me today and asked how I felt about Triton becoming a Class I college. I told them the truth. It's the best thing that could happen to Triton. They hung up after that; it wasn't what they wanted to hear. I'll see you Thursday night at the meeting and perhaps we could talk personally after adjournment."

My biggest support came from Dr. Leroy Knoeppel. "If you dare let that one in, you'll have no end of the patronage parade. Can't you just see him investigating anyone the board doesn't like and filing false reports? He's a rogue cop who'll distort things to set someone up. Do you know who'll head his list to investigate?"

"No, I don't know."

"You. If he becomes your chauffeur and bodyguard, you can rest assured he'll be making notes of everything you say and do and reporting it to Dunahow and Collins."

"Dr. Knoeppel, I'm fully aware of that. I know I'll be putting my job on the line Thursday night. I hope you'll be there."

On Tuesday morning I received a long-distance call from the executive secretary of the American Association of School Administrators.

"Dr. Zeitlin, I studied your security chiefs contract and it's bad from beginning to end. First of all I know of no good district having two administrators reporting directly to the board. Who is running the college? You or your security chief? Divided authority is a disaster. Get your faculty involved and get them to kill the contract."

I thanked him and gave some deep thought to what was said. If I involved the faculty, who'd been on the job only a week, they'd be jeopardizing their own future. This was a problem between the board and me, and it had to be resolved between us, and not the faculty. If the faculty were entangled, it would spread to the students and slow down their education.

Later that evening I called my Uncle Frank Soft, one of the many attorneys for the City of New York.

"Great to hear from you," he said. "Martha told me about the great job you're doing in Illinois. We are all proud of President Zeitlin. Now, what can I do to help?"

I slowly explained the situation to him. He interrupted me several times to ask significant questions. Finally he said, "My dear boy, you're a little green between the ears. You're in the big leagues now. Act like a big leaguer and not like a small-town hick. Become a Harry Truman."

"What do you mean?"

"Harry was a protégé of Tom Pendergast, the Democratic Party boss of Kansas City, and head of the largest political machine in the nation. He got Harry elected head of a county that doled out jobs and contracts to Pendergast's friends. Harry didn't like doing, it but to please Tom he did it. Don't you see the similarity?"

"I'm not sure."

"The politicians expect you, as the president of a college, to give them the right to award contracts and jobs."

"I can't do that! It's not right."

"Then resign. On the other hand, if you cooperate with the politicians your star will rise rapidly."

"I can't do anything dishonest."

"It's not dishonest to award contracts and jobs to friends. You're only returning favors. Believe me, in New York it's done all the time. It's only dishonest if you accept some monetary award for yourself. Don't ever accept money, cars, free vacations or expensive gifts for returning favors. Stay clean and in ten years you'll be on your way to Washington, just like Harry Truman. The only difference here is that Harry had Tom and you may have Mayor Richard Daley."

"I just don't feel comfortable awarding contracts without bids and awarding jobs to the least qualified instead of the most qualified."

"If you really feel that way, my dear nephew, then get out before you get sick."

"Two nights from now the board will meet and I intend to oppose with all my energy their appointment of this security chief."

"Do that and your career is finished. I suggest you talk it over with the board attorney and board secretary. If they are good politicians – and I'm sure they are – they'll be open for some sort of compromise.

"Thanks a lot for your advice, Uncle Frank. I do value it so I'll call Bob Collins tomorrow morning and see if we can work something out."

The following morning the usual exodus of the Zeitlin family took place. After I put Clare on the bus the phone rang and a panicky Eugenia spoke.

"I'm at the Elmwood Park police station. I've been arrested! The car has been impounded and I'll be put in jail unless I can post a bond in cash."

"Let me speak to your arresting officer."

A very rough voice got on. "Your wife has been arrested for driving without a valid license. Governor Kerner has requested all police departments to lock up dangerous drivers. Driving without a license is dangerous."

"But she has a valid California license."

"That doesn't count. She lives and works in Illinois and she must get an Illinois license within 90 days. We impounded her car because she doesn't have a parking permit for Elmwood Park."

"How much is the bail?"

"$500 in cash. We don't accept checks or credit cards and she's due in court in 30 days. Even if you are a college president, Dr. Zeitlin, you have no special privileges with the Elmwood Park police. If you're not here by noon, we'll lock her up."

After I bailed out Eugenia her first words were, "I can't believe this has happened to me. This police department doesn't serve and protect; they harass and fine innocent people."

"Eugenia, we're going over to City Hall right now to purchase a local permit so you can go to work."

"I'm so upset I don't know if I can teach today. I've already missed the first class."

"Pull yourself together. The best way to get your mind off this ordeal is to do what you do best: teach! Next week we'll go to the motor vehicle bureau and you'll get your driving license."

"Should I tell my students why I'm late, that I was arrested?"

"I'd advise you not to do so. It will spread all around Wright College. It might even reach the press and they'll attack the board again with a vengeance. Let's try to keep it quiet." I gave her a long kiss good-bye.

The more I thought about it the angrier I got. The police could have given her a ticket and let it go at that. But to impound her car and threaten to jail her was just too much. I knew the idea had come from Dunahow and Collins and been approved by Mayor Conti, all because I'd publicly disapproved the hiring of Lewis Case. If my phone lines were tapped, as Harry Behrman claimed they were, then they knew of all my calls for help.

Last night I was prepared to offer some kind of compromise to Dunahow and Collins, but now I changed my mind completely. The idea of hitting my wife instead of me hurt. It was foul play! Therefore, there had to be a showdown tomorrow night regardless of the consequences. I hated the thought of being fired publicly and having to leave abruptly after assembling such a superb administration, faculty and staff.

When I arrived at the office my mind was filled with so many mixed feelings. I was angry at Collins and Dunahow for the latest retaliation against my wife.

I was concerned about my kids and how their classmates would treat them after reading about my being fired. I realized how stupid I had been not listening to Waddie Deddah and what he had to say about Chicago politicians.

My feelings shifted to Maria. What a tightrope she had to walk these past twelve months. How could she be loyal to both Babe and me at the same time? Was she trying to convert Babe to my side? I liked to think so.

Maria snapped me out of my deep thought. "Dr. Zeitlin, all the deans and Mr. Dale want to see you immediately."

"Show them in." As they entered, they sat down quietly and said not a word. I wondered what was up.

Finally Bob Darnes spoke. "Dr. Zeitlin, we all know what agony you must have been going through these past few days and we want you to know we intend to share our thoughts and responsibilities with you. Please read this declaration:

> We the undersigned hereby declare we are opposed to the appointment of Lewis Case as Chief of Security. This direct violation of the board's own policy communicates to all that the board is lacking in professional ethics and furthermore, such an appointment would jeopardize the future accreditation of the college. The North Central Agency or faculty would never accept a nonprofessional with the duties of screening all personnel. A lack of accreditation would have a detrimental effect on Triton's future. Therefore, the executive committee of the college unanimously requests that Mr. Case not be hired.

The declaration was signed in large bold ink by G. Robert Darnes, Gordon Simonsen, John Widergren and Robert Dale, in that order.

"Would you like to sign this?" asked Dr. Darnes.

I took my pen, signed it in large letters and asked, "Do you fellows know what you're doing? The axe, if it falls, will not be on my head alone, but on all five of ours."

"Maybe so and maybe not," Darnes said. "When the board sees this declaration they'll know we're united in supporting our president. If he goes, we go with him."

"If I go, one of you will be named interim president, with a slight salary increase. Doesn't that appeal to you?"

"Not really," remarked Dr. Widergren. "Bob Darnes and I talked it over and concluded one of us would be approached because we have doctorates. We both decided we would turn it down."

"Why?"

"Anyone with anything between the ears would do the same. Who would want to be president of a college with a board of crooks? If the trustees dish out jobs to their unqualified friends, the college would very quickly earn a reputation as a Sleaze College or a Clout College. None of us wants any part of such an undertaking."

"Fellows, I'm overwhelmed by your support. *Unexpected support.* To my dying day I'll always remember this moment. You put your jobs and future on the line, not knowing what will happen."

A few moments of silence followed until Bob said, "Dr. Zeitlin, we intend to sit all together at tomorrow night's meeting and if the board doesn't rescind its previous action we'll stand up and cry out in unison, 'Oh no!' Don't you think that should rattle them a bit? To top it off I think the press and the Citizens for Triton will support us."

"Fellows, tomorrow night the adjourned session will start at 9:30 PM, much later than usual, so there won't be many people there. At 8:00 we're meeting privately with the promoters of HB 1710. Try to hold the audience together while I'm gone. We need an audience."

I left the deans fully elated, knowing that the following night would be a major turning point in my life's work. I felt I had a fair chance of correcting the board if only I could come up with the right words when I addressed them.

Thursday morning before leaving for work Eugenia gave me a very short kiss goodbye and said, "It would be nice some evening if you'd tell me what's going on between you and the board before I read about it in the newspapers."

"I'll do that only if you clear your desk of those many themes and let me take you out for dinner and a movie Saturday night."

"You're on!" she said as I gave her an extra long hug while Mark squeezed by and looked, but said nothing.

The first thing I did when I got to the office was call Millie Steel. She had spoken to Wade the night before and he'd promised to be back in time for the two meetings. I was disappointed since I wanted very much to discuss the plan of action before we met. Later I shared my thoughts with Boeger and Jones and received their support. To my annoyance I was unable to make contact with the four other trustees so I left messages with their secretaries.

The day went by very fast as I observed the orderly arrival of cars, well-run teaching and no lines in the bookstore or cafeteria. Dr. Darnes and I had a snack in the cafeteria before I left to await our higher education visitors. Jim Hannum arrived first in my office, followed by Dr. Lyman Glenny and Dr. Eldon Lichty. I quickly ushered them over to room 220 and introduced them to the board, where they received a somewhat cool reception.

Dr. Glenny, as the executive secretary of the Board of Higher Education, informed us that with the passage of HR 1710 the junior/ community colleges of Illinois would no longer be under the control of the state school superintendent, but instead would become part of the higher education family. The universities and state college heads heartily endorsed the new plan, hoping that the junior colleges would cater to the freshmen and sophomores while the universities would concentrate on the upper division and graduate students. To make sure this plan would work the state legislature had earmarked millions for junior college construction and financing.

Dr. Lichty, the principal author of HR 1710, joined in by first congratulating me on Triton's opening with the most comprehensive community college program in the state. He urged me and the board to apply at once for Class I status and become the first community college to be built in Illinois.

Jim Hannum, the county school official who had sworn in all the trustees a year and a half earlier, embarrassed me by congratulating the board for their wisdom in selecting a Californian for their founding president. I felt he did that just to let the board know they'd be making a mistake if I were fired that night. He stressed that besides filing for Class I status it was urgent that the college file for North Central accreditation.

Every trustee had a question or two for the specialists, mostly related to the sale of bonds. Their answers: Sell the bonds through competitive bidding ASAP as a Class I or Class II college. It didn't really matter. Buy a site and start building.

The meeting adjourned at 8:50 PM, giving us 40 minutes to get to the official Triton session. I insisted that Wade come to my office so I could tell him about the latest happenings. The other trustees, I assumed, headed toward the board room. Later, when I arrived at the board room and found only Boeger and Jones present, I realized my assumption had been incorrect. The room was packed and Jim Tarpey showed me the sign-in form with 66 names on it.

Wade got impatient at 9:40 and asked if he should cancel the meeting if the fellows didn't show soon. They'd been there 50 minutes earlier and now they couldn't be found.

Roy Jones injected, "Wade, don't you dare cancel this meeting; that's exactly what they want. They're around here somewhere. By waiting it out they hope the crowd will disappear. They hate those watchdogs and resent seeing so many of the press present."

A moment later Jack Rosseter stood up and addressed the crowd. "Mr. Steel, it's ridiculous to start a public meeting at 10:00 PM. However, my group will wait until 10:30. If those missing trustees don't show up, then we'll leave. I might add, you know the press will blast away at them tomorrow. You can imagine the newspaper headline: WHY DID THE TRITON TRUSTEES VANISH? WHAT ARE THEY HIDING?"

With that I left the board table, found Jim Tarpey and directed him *to find the missing trustees* and tell them to "get their asses over here."

"Where should I look?" Jim asked.

"Everywhere, but find them. You might start with the parking areas."

Ten minutes later Jim came back and said, "I found them and they're on their way."

The adjourned meeting opened with Dunahow giving a longer than usual detailed report on the meeting with the appraisers and concluding, "The official appraisal cannot be written up until the college has the money to pay for the land."

Wade immediately covered his mouth and whispered to me, "Dunahow is wrong on that. We must know what a property is worth before making any offer."

Continuing, Dunahow outlined in detail the condemnation procedures, a resolution offering $2,771,500 for the Carey site, letters to and from Bob Collins and the necessity for filing a mandamus suit. Such a suit could result in the court ordering Steel and Collins to sign the bonds and put them up for sale.

What followed was a long series of questions to Dunahow, to which he slowly responded. As six people left Wade whispered to me, "They're stretching this out, with the hope that many more people will leave."

At 11:30 PM the vote for filing a mandamus suit was approved by 4 to 2, with Bob Collins abstaining. Immediately after, I was directed to make a Class I application to the State Junior College Board. The higher education authorities had convinced the trustees that was the way to go, and I was happy to see my efforts had paid off.

After the vote was taken about a dozen or more of the audience left, leaving behind only four reporters and about 21 Citizens for Triton. Dunahow looked at Bob Collins and received the signal to go ahead. Dunahow slowly pulled out of his case a three-page document and read a resolution authorizing the employment of Lewis Case. Mr. Case stood up as he was introduced by Dunahow and told the audience he was a former captain of detectives at the Oak Park Police Department.

It was moved by Collins and seconded by Farmar to adopt the resolution as presented. In the discussion that followed Roy Jones did not question Mr. Case's qualifications or character, but objected to the by-passing of the board's policy on hiring.

Wade questioned the advisability of Mr. Case's working as a security officer despite the lack of job description. At this moment I informed the trustees of the meetings I had with Case and the executive committee on Monday, September 13th. In a voice loud enough for everyone to hear I read the declaration the executive committee had written, as intense, angry looks appeared on the faces of Dunahow, Collins and Farmar.

Staring at them with the same eyeball-to-eyeball intensity I said, "If Triton cannot be accredited, enrollments will sink and millions of much needed dollars will be lost. Do you want to see that happen?"

After my strongly worded statement, Collins attempted to defend the board's action. "The present security staff is inadequate. All we're trying to do is protect the students."

Babe Serpico boldly declared, "Dr. Zeitlin only has authority to hire the professionals. Our security chief is not a member of the faculty. He will report directly to the board and to no one else."

Serpico added that the night before he'd seen someone on the campus with a blackjack, implying that the campus was unsafe at night and better security was needed.

Mr. Steel picked up on Babe's remarks by reading two letters he'd received from the Citizens for Triton. They feared the new security officer would have too much power and it could be the beginning of a Nazi-like police state investigating anyone they didn't like.

Jack Rossetter was given permission to speak. "We just don't like the power given to this person and have a feeling his duties will go beyond the usual. I don't know of a single college president with the need for a bodyguard. Do you know of anyone?"

No one said anything.

Elmore Boeger suggested that the administration determine what types of security systems had been established in other colleges throughout the state of Illinois. I reported that a survey was already underway and the results would he known in a few weeks.

Wade firmly voiced his opinion. "It's wrong to have two chiefs reporting directly to the board; one the chief administrator and the other the chief of police. Triton should have only one chief administrative officer."

Elmore Boeger declared, "Unless this board puts complete confidence in our executive officers our accreditation will be jeopardized."

Finally, at Steel's urging, Collins read the contract under discussion. Included were provisions that Case *"is answerable to no one except the board," "should take an inventory of all college equipment,"* and *"should conduct security checks on all teaching and non-teaching personnel."*

Those provisions drew loud exclamations of shock from the audience. One individual shouted, "What the hell is this board trying to do?"

With much disdain the audience turned against Case and his cronies. You could feel the heat between the two, leading Case to stand up and say, "In the interest of avoiding controversy and for the sake of the college and the students I feel this matter should be studied further and no action be taken tonight."

Fred Knol, who maintained a poker face throughout the discussion and said nothing up to this point, moved that the motion be tabled. To everyone's relief the board unanimously approved his motion, thus avoiding a most embarrassing situation. As further evidence that the tide had turned in the audience's favor, Babe moved and Boeger seconded that the resolution to hire the security chief be tabled. At 12:06 Friday morning the meeting was adjourned.

Dunahow, Collins, Farmar, Serpico and Case disappeared together fast, leaving Fred Knol behind.

Fred commented to Wade, "I can't join them at this damn hour. I have to get up early tomorrow to make a living."

Wade proudly commended him. "Fred, you did exceptionally well tonight by bringing to a close what might have been a disaster to Triton's future."

"I know that, Wade, but I couldn't convince them to change their minds earlier this evening. Dunahow is not a good attorney." Fred left immediately.

Wade, Roy and Elmore, chatting away, left with the three deans as Bob Dale and I gathered our material together. After turning off the lights to the board room, I locked the door and we walked down the hallway toward the stairs, when all of a sudden two bodies intercepted us. It was Lewis Case and Herman Furlong. Case grabbed me by my tie and pulled me close enough to feel his spit as he yelled, "Who the fuck do you think you are? You'll get yours, you son of a bitch. Do you know who you're dealing with?"

In my nervousness I dropped my things on the floor. He released my tie so I could pick them up. While bent down I heard Herman say, "Not now, Lew – someone's coming."

The attackers hurriedly went down the stairs as a janitor with a vacuum cleaner approached. To Bob and me he seemed like an angel in disguise. We retreated with alacrity back to my office. Bob asked, "What the hell do we do now?"

"Don't panic we need time to think." I locked the door and then grabbed a phone. I held it for a minute or two, not knowing whom to call, and finally hung up without calling anyone. Bob and I realized if a match were to take place, it would be uneven. Who would you bet on if two 5'8" school administrators traded blows with two ex-policemen towering over 6'2"? Conclusion: Avoid a losing fight.

"Let's go now," Bob called out as we heard the vacuum cleaner outside our door. We hurried toward the front parking lot and suddenly stopped as we saw through the windows several people surrounding my little Skylark. Who were they? Dunahow, with Farmar and Collins at his side, was telling Case and Furlong what to do. I undoubtedly was the subject. I wondered what plot they were hatching up against me. We returned to the office and waited. Sometime after 1:30 AM we took another look outside. The gang had left so I automatically assumed it was safe to leave.

"Hold off, Dr. Zeitlin," Bob warned me. "They may be waiting for you on Wolf Road."

"Bob, they know my car but not yours. Could you drive out first and check Wolf Road as you leave to see if a big black Lincoln is parked nearby? Call me back on my hotline and let me know if it's OK to leave."

Twenty minutes later Bob called back. "They're waiting for you right outside of the high school. I wouldn't leave. Should I call the police?"

"Which police department do you imagine could help me?" I gave him my thoughts on the local departments.

"I suggest you wait it out until dawn. They wouldn't attack you in the daytime. It's less than five hours away."

"Thanks for your help. Maybe I will. I have to try one other resource." I hung up.

My watch showed 1:43 AM as I dialed another number. If he didn't answer in six rings, I would hang up. On the fourth ring I heard a sleepyhead say, "Who's calling?"

"Harry, you said to call you if I ever needed help. I need help right now." I explained to Harry Behrman, my coordinator of police science, the threatening situation.

"Don't worry, I have a good relationship with Richard Oligive, the Cook County Sheriff. I'll get a squad car over there to escort you home within five minutes."

If ever I needed a bodyguard to protect me from an enraged rogue cop, it was now. I couldn't believe it but I breathed a great sigh of relief when not one but two patrol cars arrived.

When we arrived at my house at well past two in the morning, the county officer told me he couldn't understand how any company would hire those two emotionally unstable ex-cops. One of the officers assured me that to ensure my safety they would keep my home under surveillance till dawn.

After having some cookies and milk I walked through the bedrooms to check on the kids and Eugenia. I almost choked up as I thought about what would happen to them if their father and husband were eliminated. I thanked God again for not only protecting me but for giving us the sheriff and his superior and honest officers. They really did *serve* and *protect.*

Shelves of Learning

It was a typical evening at Triton College outside Chicago. In Technology Center, Instructor Joe Kroc explained measuring instruments to his students in Basic Refrigeration and Air Conditioning 010. Inside a cavernous garage, machines whined and motors roared as a squad of grease-smeared men labored over disassembled cars for Auto Technology 036. And in a classroom in Liberal Arts Hall, students in Philosophy 102 discussed linguistic fallacies.

Triton exemplifies a new type of college that is redefining the concept for many Americans: the public community college. From The Bronx to West Los Angeles, these educational supermarkets are offering their varied shelves of learning to a growing clientele. Enrollment nationwide has more than doubled since 1965, to an estimated 2,689,000 this fall. The students are as diverse as the courses they take. Nine-year-old Triton's student body of 16,681 (up from 1,243 in 1965 and 13,034 last year) includes housewives, off-duty cops and laborers in their fifties, as well as pert teen-age coeds.

One Out of Ten. Like patrons of regular supermarkets, community college students generally live in the neighborhood. Nearly 90% of Triton's students come from a 58-sq.-mi. section of Cook County near O'Hare International Airport. An area that includes light and heavy industry, tract homes and old mansions, the district has a population of 422,000, spread among such disparate communities as stately River Forest and working-class Melrose Park.

Local taxpayers provide a third of Triton's funding (with tuition and state and federal aid making up the balance). For their money, the citizens of district 504 get a college that is everything they never thought a college could be: cheap, accessible and extraordinarily responsive to their specific needs. One out of every ten district residents has taken courses inside Triton's modern brick-and-glass buildings, which are open from 6:30 in the morning until 10 at night.

Triton's low tuition ($150 a semester for a full-time student) and closeness to home attract many students in the top ranks of their high school classes, as well as the less able who might find it tough going at other colleges. Triton also attracts adults who are trying to fill gaps in their education. More than half the students attend part time, and many combine their studies with full-time jobs.

There is a course or program to suit virtually every student need and ability. At each level the emphasis is on careers; in fact, Triton calls itself "the Career Center of the Midwest." Students can get associate degrees or one-year

EXERCISE IN WELDING

certificates in any of 104 career areas, from advertising art to police science to diesel or welding technology. Even for the 4,000 students in the university-transfer program, the focus is on the practical. An English course in children's literature, for example, is "recommended for elementary school and library science majors." Says Joseph Quagliano, a former Playboy Club manager who runs Triton's restaurant-training school: "There's no dabbling here. Everyone knows where he's going."

Alert, enthusiastic students and a brisk, businesslike atmosphere are part of the appeal for Triton's hard-working faculty. There are no academic ranks, and all teachers are called "instructor." The emphasis is on teaching, not research, and only a few of the 834-member faculty boast doctorates; many are working mechanics, cooks or other tradesmen and technicians by day, earning a flat $12 an hour in the evening at Triton.

Up to Date. In each career area, outside advisory committees help the faculty shape programs to keep them up to date. The electronics curriculum recently eliminated study of the vacuum tube and now concentrates on transistors and integrated circuits. When job openings slackened in optical technology and civil engineering, Triton dropped both courses. Among the newest programs: the training of staff for day-care centers.

The faculty prides itself on being able to patch up a student's background learning. Among the more popular offerings are remedial courses in basic writing and mathematics. "We take lower ability kids, yes," says Biology Chairman Don Giersch, "but we're able to instill confidence in a lot that might have bombed out elsewhere right away." Conversely, through the College Level Ex-

RESTAURANT TRAINING AT TRITON

DIESEL TECHNOLOGY
No dabblers here.

amination Program, older students can get credit at Triton for learning acquired outside the classroom.

Many legislators and establishment educators still treat Triton and its ilk like adolescent stepchildren. Although Illinois' community colleges enroll more than half the students in public higher education in the state, they receive only 13% of the higher-education budget. Similar slights are common across the country. Yet for many students who aspire to being something between ditch-digger and a nuclear physicist, the public community colleges are clearly filling an important void.

Triton's Zeitlin

The man behind a new educational concept

By JACK SPATAFORA

MEET Herbert Zeitlin — idealist and pragmatist, dreamer and doer, understanding adviser and exacting taskmaster, and, incidentally, president of Triton college.

Dr. Zeitlin heads one of Chicagoland's most provocative educational experiments, a fully-developed college and technical institute right in the community.

"THE JUNIOR college is an instrument of tremendous potential," according to Edmund Gleazer, executive secretary of the American Association of Junior Colleges.

"It can motivate youth who have had little hope of learning beyond the high school. It can lift the sights and strengthen the efforts of the generation wanting to go beyond their fathers' achievements. It can train for the new skills demanded by a changing technology."

In a pedagogical nutshell, that is Herbert Zeitlin's view of his mission at Triton.

"THERE ARE now over 300 courses in 45 different subject fields," he said. "And a student's past record in high school along with the results of his guidance and placement examinations is taken into consideration before a counselor a p p r o v e s his course of study."

Zeitlin, a native Californian, came to Triton in 1964 to shepherd the fledgeling institution. It has not been an easy undertaking, but President Zeitlin obviously relishes challenge. His opportunity to effect an educational revolution in Chicagoland's western communities seems to whet his appetite.

"All of us want the best in life for our sons and daughters," he declared.

WE WANT to see them develop to their fullest potential. For most young people this potential is realized in a satisfying occupation that will allow them to function as responsible members of the community.

"Placement in an occupation, business or profession depends upon . . . adequate education."

But, Zeitlin points out, many parents have learned." . . . there is no place for their son or daughter at crowded state universities . . . the family budget cannot be stretched to cover college at an out-of-state school . . . their senior's grades are just not high enough to gain admission to the college of his choice

DR. HERBERT ZEITLIN

Last of a Series

Triton college which serves Leyden and Proviso townships ends its first year of operation in West Leyden high school this year. The TIMES examines the success of this first year and finds what the students like about this new college and technical institute.

. . . they are parents of a late-starter who had no interest in college until recently."

THESE ARE the people President Zeitlin says Triton is especially here to serve.

"Like students in cities all over the United States," Zeitlin continued, "the Tritonite — that new breed of student, product of the American dream — follows an unusual daily schedule. He carries a full collegiate program, but often his classes are held during late afternoons and evenings or even Saturdays."

Zeitlin extolled the virtues and beauty that will accrue with the massive new Triton campus planned for the fall of 1968:

"VISUALIZE, if you will, the new campus. As you drive north on Fifth avenue, you will know you are in the Village of River Grove as you pass under the Triton College bridge.

"To the right of the bridge there is a beautiful wooded area of 200 or more a c r e s with the DesPlaines river smoothly flowing through the outer campus. To the left is a 67-acre site that the students refer to as the inner campus . . . a horseshoe-shaped road leads to . . . any of the nine beautiful buildings. . . .

"Two of the largest and most impressive on the campus, each three stories . . . are the Technology and Liberal Arts Centers. It is almost as if the architect were saying, 'These two buildings are of equal importance and one is no good without the other.' "

PRESIDENT Zeitlin was asked about his faculty and staff. "I am sure," he replied, "you are well aware that a learning center can have excellent buildings and modern equipment, but it isn't worth much at all if it doesn't have the prime motivator of students— the teacher.

"The Triton College Board of Education is to be commended because it has adopted as a policy a continuous endeavor to discover, attract and hold the best teaching talent available. A beginning instructor with an M.A. starts at $6,825 per year, an instructor with a doctorate degree and 17 years of experience will receive $15,465.

"We believe we have one of the best Junior college salary maximums in the country."

DR. ZEITLIN'S day begins early and ends late. It is a study in human dynamics filled by: executive meetings with his staff; reading, digesting, and responding to a myriad of reports and recommendations; maintaining active contact with associated institutions; keeping abreast of the exploding innovations in the field of education, and in general holding a sensitive thumb to the rapid pulse of the entire Triton operation.

President Zeitlin concluded by offering his overview of the Triton experiment: "The community college concept is an American social invention dedicated to the fulfillment of the American Dream."

457

West Cook County Press

★ *A Progressive, Independent Newspaper* ★

Published every Wednesday and Friday by The Press Publications, 112 S. York St., Elmhurst, Ill. 60126

ar No. 100 | Two Sections 40 Pages | Second Class Postage Paid at Elmhurst, Ill. 60126 | **Friday, December 18, 1970** | By carrier: 50c per month; $5.50 yearly By Mail: $6 per year in DuPage county; $9 outside DuPage county

'Do Something For Everyone,' Triton Head Advises Colleges

In a time of change and unrest in higher education, the teacher and administrator at the university should note the philosophy of the junior college staff, Dr. Herbert Zeitlin, president of Triton college, River Grove, said in remarks delivered to the Higher Education conference in Chicago this fall.

"For years, university presidents teaching graduate junior college courses would say to their students: 'Don't imitate the weaknesses of the university. Be innovative. Be a people's college. Serve the poor. Do something for everyone. Get into the community.'

"Perhaps some of this philosophy should be turned around and also applied to the universities," Zeitlin said.

Zeitlin cited the recommendations of the Carnegie commission on higher education in relation to the community college. Among the recommendations were that:

—Community colleges should be available to all persons throughout their lives.

—Community colleges should remain two-year institutions and not expect to become four-year or graduate universities ("This fall, for the first time, Triton college's enrollment exceeded 10,000," Zeitlin said. "Now, many people in the community are convinced we will be a public university within a few years.")

—Full transfer rights should be provided qualified graduates of community colleges by comprehensive state colleges and universities.

—Occupational programs should be given the fullest support and status within community colleges.

—Guidance, occupational, and personal, is a particularly important function for the community college, ("By 1980," Zeitlin commented, "I believe personal counseling will be available without cost to all who feel the need for this kind of service.")

—The community college should be an active center for art, music and drama and intellectual discussions.

—Financing should be increased and shared by federal, state and local government (The commission also recommended that the community college should charge no, or low tuition. Triton's per-hour tuition is $5; college of DuPage charges $7.) "I believe if the Carnegie commission recommendations are implemented," Zeitlin told the 136 Illinois public and private college presidents, "there will be much cooling down on many campuses throughout the nation and many more of our public will be pleased.

"Is incorrect education the real problem in higher education?" Zeitlin asked, "or is it

Dr. Herbert Zeitlin

One Edition

Because of the Christmas holiday there will be only one edition of The Press Publications newspapers next week. Distribution will be on Thursday.

overeducation? Are we preparing people to have a vast storehouse of knowledge that will eventually lead to frustration when they are unable to find a buyer?"

Zeitlin pointed to one one of the employment predictions for 1980, that a high school education will be sufficient for eight out of every 10 jobs, although the number of professional and technical workers will increase by 50 per cent.

"If 80 per cent or more of all the jobs will require less than four years of college and more likely just high school and a year or two beyond," the Triton president noted, "then are we not planting our own seeds for frustration, discontentment and rebellion by overselling the benefits of education?"

Last summer, he said, "in many communities it was easier for a community college graduate to get a job than it was a newly acquired Ph.D."

Zeitlin referred a comment by the Carnegie commission that "while supporting open access, (the commission) does not believe that all young people either want higher education or can benefit from it. "Many of those who can benefit from higher education and want it would be better off in other endeavors, for a time after high school, before entering college."

He further cited an article in "Ladies Home Journal" in which Dr. Hudson Armerding, president of Wheaton college, was quoted as saying: "A college education as it has been generally understood is not appropriate to all young people. To me, it is regrettable that vocational training and skills have been relegated to an inferior status in our culture."

Zeitlin has been president of Triton since its organization in 1964.

Wednesday
Nov. 19, 1975
22nd Year No. 89
Lincoln's Gettysburg
address was given on
this date in 1863.

Triton 'Brainstorms' Expansion

How Triton Has Grown Since 1965

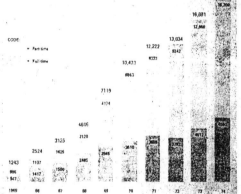

by GREG MAHONEY

A "five-year plan" that could result in more buildings and facilities on the Triton college campus is being studied and "brainstormed" by the college administration, staff and board of trustees.

Implementation of the plan would require voters' approval of a bond issue to augment state funding.

"Details, cost estimates and the bond size and timing are now being worked on by the staff, the board and our architect," college President Dr. Herbert Zeitlin said in an interview this week.

Some of these things may come about, some may not," he added. "We're now in the process of brainstorming the ideas and concepts."

The only bond issue requested by Triton was the $8.9 million approved in March, 1965, enabling the college to acquire the campus land in River Grove and develop it, with state aid, in a 14-building master plan.

"But now we're looking beyond 14 buildings," Zeitlin said.

Contractors' bids for the 13th building — the Community Career center — may be opened by board next March."

The major portion of the $8.2 million cost will be paid by the state ($5,180,000), with Triton matching the rest. The college's other facilities have been built with the 75 per cent (state) - 25 per cent (local) funding.

The two-story Community Careers center will be built on the college

land east of Fifth av. (former drive-in theater land).

Suggested for the center are: physical education facilities; rooms and therapeutic labs for the elderly and handicapped; police and fire science training facilities; a child care center; an allied health careers center; and possibly a swimming pool.

Final approval of specific items in the center must be given by the state's Community College board, the Board of Higher Education and the Capital Development board. The college is also taking "input" from the board of trustees and the staff, as well as community organizations and residents.

Triton has received the first-step approval for funding of the 14th campus building — the Center for Performing and Creative Arts. The site of the building — either on the main campus or east of Fifth av. — is still undetermined, Zeitlin said.

The Community College board has recommended that the Board of Higher Education approve state funding of $8.7 million for the $12 million project.

"If all goes well," Zeitlin said, "the state funds could be available sometime in the 1977 fiscal year (July 1, 1976-June 30, 1977)."

Zeitlin said that the center would include a 3,500-seat auditorium.

"It could be the Arie Crown of the suburbs," Zeitlin said in reference to the theater in Chicago's McCormick Place. "It would bring most of the

cultural aspects of Chicagoland right here."

The center would be the last building on the original campus master plan and the first on the new "five year plan."

Also proposed in the plans are renovations on the main campus.

"We've been here nearly eight years," Zeitlin pointed out, "and we need more shop space, more faculty offices, more parking and greater flexibility in operations."

College officials project that Triton's total enrollment will reach 30,000 by the early 1980's. The current enrollment is 22,184, a 12 per cent increase over the 1974 count of 19,799.

Triton's full-time enrollment increased from 4,590 last fall to 5,346 this year and Zeitlin projects that 6,000 full-timers may be enrolled by 1983.

"If the enrollment continues to increase, and we expect it to, we'll need additional facilities as proposed in the five-year plan," Zeitlin said.

In designing the campus, college officials expected that 3,000 parking spaces would be sufficient, "Zeitlin said. "Adequate parking has been one of the keys to our success."

Improved public transportation is a priority item, he added, noting that a college committee is working with the municipalities, the Regional Transportation authority and West Towns Bus Co. to improve frequency of service.

A bridge linking the main campus with the east side of Fifth av. would be an essential part of the Community Careers center, Zeitlin indicated. The bridge would carry pedestrian traffic into the second level of the center.

Architect John Fox has proposed that the bridge could be widened to accommodate a snack bar and catered function area, manned by the restaurant training students.

The bridge - with - snack bar would cost an estimated $1.6 million, Fox has told the college board, while a simple, unheated pedestrian bridge would cost an estimated $200,000.

Traffic signals have been installed

(Continued on Page 3)

A progressive independent newspaper published every Wednesday and Friday
By the Press Publications, 112 S. York St., Elmhurst, Ill. 60126

20 Cents

West Cook County Press

By Carrier 75¢/Mo. $8.00/Yr.

2 Sections—40 Pages

Last Man on the Moon Honored By
Mayors, Congressman Hyde and President Zeitlin

Triton President Herbert Z. Zeitlin welcomes Captain Eugene Cernan (center) as Mayor Howard Moore of Forest Park, IL, Congressman Henry Hyde of Cook County and Mayor Siegel Davis of Bellwood join hands. Captain Cerman was honored by Triton College when the school's new space center was named after him.

Triton comes out a loser in Bakalis lawsuit

By TAMI JENSEN
STAFF WRITER

Triton College Board President Mark Stephens is among the four people found guilty of breaching the contract of former Triton President Michael Bakalis and denying him due process when they fired him in 1992.

A federal jury returned a unanimous verdict Nov. 25, more than five years after Bakalis filed his lawsuit against Stephens, Trustee Merrill Becker and former Trustees Jenny Golembeski and James Durkin.

Bakalis, who has been teaching public policy and public management at Northwestern University's Kellogg Graduate School of Management in Evanston since 1994, was awarded damages estimated to be upward of seven figures.

"The issue is not about money, though I was certainly entitled to money under my contract," said Bakalis, who would not disclose how much money he was awarded by the jury.

"It is a matter of principle. I feel vindicated. I feel the blot on my reputation has been removed. Unfortunately, I can't recover the past five years of my life."

The only comment made by Triton officials, including Stephens, comprised a two-sentence statement.

"We are extremely disappointed with the jury verdict and we respectfully disagree with the jury verdict. The college attorneys are currently exploring all options, including appeal."

Worst experience

Neither Stephens nor Sean Sullivan, Triton's associate vice president of business services, would elaborate on the statement.

Bakalis said after five years, he is glad to put "the worst job experience" he'd ever had behind him.

"It was not a professional experience," said Bakalis, the former state superintendent of public instruction and former state comptroller who was hired in 1991 to help the floundering college get off academic probation and not risk losing its accreditation.

"It was the worst educational experience of my career."

Bakalis blames the experience on the administration, not the faculty or students.

"I have high regard for Triton teachers and students," he said. "There are some fine people working there.

"But you can't let people in power use an educational institution as a political playground and trash your reputation in the process. I spent 37 years building what I felt was a good reputation. You can't let people trample all over it."

Board influence

Bakalis said he was aware of Triton's troubled past when he was applying for the job, but was not aware of its extent until after he was hired.

He claims that the four trustees named in his lawsuit attempted to influence his hiring and firing decisions and interfered with the day-to-day operations of the college.

He says when he refused to buckle under the pressure, he was fired.

"They hurt me, and they totally disrupted my career path," he said. "My objective was to stay here for three or four years before moving on to become the president of a small, four-year liberal arts college.

"They destroyed that dream when they fired me. It's hard to get a job when you've been terminated, you've filed a lawsuit against your former employer and it's all over the news."

Bakalis says two years passed before he was hired full time to teach at Northwestern University.

"They wasted five years of my professional career," said Bakalis, who in the interim worked part time as an independent contractor."

Even worse, says Bakalis, is college politics nearly cost students careers.

"When a college is put on probation, it is one step away from losing its accreditation," he explained. If a college loses its accreditation, credits are no longer transferable to other colleges and financial aid is sacrificed.

"They played games with the people they were elected to protect," he said. "My instinct is to stay as far away from Triton College as I possibly can."

Relevance—the secret of success

By ALLAN G. PILGER

When Herbert Zeitlin, president of Triton College, talks about his school's whirlwind growth, he talks about relevance:

"Triton is relevant to what's happening in the American scene," he says, explaining that the state's largest junior college not only offers an extensive university transfer program but also the most career education programs (150) in the state, possibly in the nation.

In fact, Zeitlin considers career education, which trains people for specialized fields from beauty culture to industrial technology, as the "greatest strength of Triton College." It's the college's biggest drawing card.

Career education students finishing one-year certificate or two year degree programs at Triton generally find a bonanza of employment opportunities because more and more specialized jobs are being created each year, says Zeitlin, an Elmwood Park resident. Often the career education graduate gets a bigger

For a story on Mrs. Herbert Zeitlin, wife of the Triton College president, see Living, Elmwood Park Style section in next week's issue of Elm Leaves.

starting salary than the holder of a four-year degree, but still enjoys many opportunities for advancement.

TRITON ALSO offers 26 university transfer programs for students wishing to continue schooling at a four-year institution after being graduated by Triton. "We offer the same courses for the first two years as the universities do. If the student takes courses recommended by our advisors, he won't lose a single credit when he transfers," Zeitlin says.

As a college "for all the people," Triton has attracted thousands of out-of-district students, including 812 from Oak Park, 376 from Forest Park, and 116 from River Forest. The Triton district covers the Proviso, Leyden, and Elmwood Park High School districts.

The large enrollment from outside the district enables the college to expand its programs.

"OUR COLLEGE is not just for people immediately out of high school. There are many adults enrolled in all of out programs, especially continuing education courses."

August 25, 1971

Last year's enrollment of in-district students include May wood, 952; Elmwood Park, 856; Bellwood, 845; Melrose Park, 752; Franklin Park, 682; River Grove, 474; Northlake, 469; Broadview, 346; Hillside, 339; Berkeley, 234; Stone Park, 112; and unincorporated areas in the Triton District, 567.

These totals are based on Triton's 1970-71 enrollment of 10,473, with nearly 4,000 full-time students. The remainder are part-time students, including adults in a continuing education program encompassing both career education and university transfer programs.

ENROLLMENTS at Triton, which was built in 1964, have grown from 4,605 in 1968 and 7,119 from 1969, two years in which Triton had the largest enrollment increases of any college in the state, Zeithlin says.

Even greater growth is projected: 14,714 students by 1975 and 20,972 by 1979. But such size is not a positive indication that Triton will become a four-year institution, says Zeitlin, who came to Triton from California School systems.

"In the master plan, Triton was designed as a community college, not a university," he says. "We emphasize the strong instructional program, but do not have the facilities for independent research by teachers and graduate students that the universities offer."

Universities' emphasis on research and graduate programs has produced an oversupply of doctoral-degree holders in many fields. "Universities are in competition of turning out PhDs on the faculty is a great status symbol for many of them," says Zeitlin.

So while career education students from Triton have little trouble finding jobs, many holding doctorates from other schools are unsuccessful job hunters. "Some come to Triton seeking teaching jobs and admit in interviews that they are applying only because they can't find jobs in industry," Zeitlin reports.

"If their backgrounds show they are not interested in teaching, but consider it only a last resort, then we're not interested in them," says Zeitlin.

DESPITE HEAVY publicity about oversupplies of graduate- and bachelor-degree holders in certain fields, including teaching, colleges and universities show no significant drop in enrollment in these curriculums, according to Zeitlin.

"Status motivates people. I have found as a counselor that many parents push their children into the professions. And the white-collar parents aren't the only ones doing this. The union people want their children to go through college and enter management," says Zeitlin.

But he notes that career education jobs carry much responsibility and prestige. Some at Triton are management training programs.

For instance, when the Triton College Center building opens in the fall of 1972, a two-year restaurant management training program will be started, with students operating the cafeteria and faculty dining room. "The managerial trainee will be involved in all restaurant functions," says Zeitlin.

He considers the restaurant program indicative of Triton's desire to prepare people for fields in which there are shortages of trained personnel. "There are many great restaurants in the Chicago area, a major convention center," he says.

Triton several years ago became only the third college in the nation to offer training in numerical control, which is a new development in industrial automation. Punch cards and tapes "tell"

"CAREER EDUCATION has developed into our greatest strength, but we give equal weight to university transfer and other programs."

lathes and other industrial tools what to do. The machines function automatically, which eliminates thousands of semi-skilled machine operator jobs, but creates many skilled jobs.

IF A NUMERICAL control course is available to him, the displaced worker can train for a newly created draftsman job, Zeitlin points out.

That's why Zeitlin considers it important for communities to offer extensive career education programs. Triton attracts many students who move into the Triton district specifically to attend the college.

And Triton is becoming more and more attractive to west suburban residents both inside and outside the district, Zeitlin says.

Elmwood Park High School District residents voted against formation of Triton College in a 1963 referendum, which was successful due to substantial majorities in the Proviso and Leyden Districts. But last year Elmwood Park was the second biggest student-producer for Triton.

An Oak Park citizens committee reported in 1963 that there would be no need for the village to join in formation of the Triton district. Then two years ago, Oak Parkers approved a referendum to join the district, but Triton district residents voted against accepting Oak Park.

So Oak Park students must pay $30.50 per semester hour as out-of-district students at Triton, compared to $7 for in-district students. Students from out-of-state pay $48.50. All tuitions rates are subject to change prior to registration for the 1971-72 year.

IN ADDITION, the Oak Park-River Forest High School District must pay Triton a certain sum for each student from its district student attending the college. district residents pay property taxes to Triton.

(Continued on page 9)

"WE HAD NEVER SAID we were the largest junior college in the state. Someone else said it first, but we didn't fight it."

Staff photos by Fred Hutcherson

7

35
Shots That Missed

Even though I had only four hours of sleep I felt blessed on Friday morning to have breakfast with such a lively family on a beautiful day in September. If I were to tell Eugenia about last night's eruption, I felt sure she would immediately take the kids out of school and return to California. I didn't want this to happen, so I said nothing to my Eugenia, even though she knew I came home at a rather late hour.

I was now faced with the greatest challenge of my life: how to survive when targeted by a rogue cop and crooked politicians. I feared Lewis Case and his cronies. How could I protect myself? An immediate must was to trade in my Skylark for a more powerful and safer car, one with a hood that unlocked from the inside. I made an appointment for Saturday at Jacobs Twin Buick to look over some used cars.

After breakfast I drove over to Wade's office to post him on the latest. He was not surprised, since he'd heard so many ugly stories about Case and Furlong. He said, "I still can't understand why no one has ever filed a suit against those two."

"Well Wade, we can. Should we?"

"I think we should, but we need more evidence before doing so."

Reluctantly I accepted Wade's advice and added, "I only hope that with Harry Behrman's help we can obtain enough solid evidence to put those boys away."

"In the meantime, Herb, keep me posted on your whereabouts all the time and don't ever meet with any member of the coalition unless you have one of your deans with you."

"Wade, after last night how do you think those boys will react to me now?"

"Inside they're steaming but on the outside they'll be cool and act as if nothing has occurred. Just be on your guard all the time. Incidentally, I have an extra rifle you can have if you wish to borrow one."

"I certainly could use it, but Eugenia would strongly object. With our four kids around something could go wrong. You know, I lost a very dear uncle when a rifle his Dad gave him while in a boat accidentally discharged and killed him."

"How horrible! If it ever develops into a shooting match, I'm a very good marksman."

"Wade, thanks very much. I'll keep it in mind," I said as I left.

When I arrived at the office at 11:00 AM Widergren, Simonsen and Dale congratulated me for the part I'd played the night before and said, "This should put an end to your troubles with the board, now that they know the accreditation is a must."

"I hope so," was my reply. "Where is Bob Darnes? He's usually the first one in every morning. I'll give him a call right now."

As we waited there was no answer. "That's strange. I'll call later."

I called again at 11:30 and at noon, with the same result. Just as I was about to leave for lunch Bob walked into my office carrying a black attaché case, with a very serious look on his face.

"Bob, we won last night. You should be very happy. Your declaration did it. Is something wrong?"

"I'm not too sure we won. Those guys play hardball. This may be the beginning of something far more serious."

"Such as?"

"Open warfare! Last night around 3:00 AM Alma and I were suddenly awakened when we heard what we thought were two shots into our bedroom. After I heard a car drive away I peeped through the broken glass and saw nothing."

"What did you do next?"

"What anyone would who thought his life was in danger. I called the Elmwood Park police. No answer. I kept calling until finally someone answered. He asked me if anyone was hurt, and I told him no one was, but we were scared stiff. He told me to relax, someone would come over as soon as they handled a few other emergencies. Three hours later, as dawn was breaking through, a patrol car arrived. One of the officers picked up two slugs and put them in his pocket. I didn't know for sure whether their late arrival was deliberate or not, but one thing is sure. I don't think much of the Elmwood Park police."

"Did the officer say anything about the slugs?"

"He looked at them very closely and said, 'We'll get them to the lab today for further examination.'"

"What do you think the lab will find?"

"The small marks on the slugs or the shells the officers later picked up will help identify the make and kind of rifle used."

"And suppose the marks match a rifle from the Elmwood Park police department arsenal. What happens next?"

"The police department would be in hot water and then some arrests would be made."

"I don't think so; that's wishful thinking. You must remember, Don Dunahow is a mastermind of evil plots and at the same time the prosecuting attorney for the city of Elmwood Park. I believe when those rogue cops failed to pursue me at two in the morning, Dunahow probably authorized them to scare the hell out of you at three o'clock by firing into your upper window."

"You know something, I think you're right. But how in the hell did those guys know my address and that I lived on the second floor?"

"They got it from the faculty bulletin I distributed at the last board meeting, or else Virginia Sybilla gave it to them. To some extent they have tails on all of the administrators."

"My God, it's worse than I thought. It's scary to work here."

"Bob, stop where you are. Let's get the deans and Bob Dale in here right away."

When the five of us reassembled Bob and I gave them a full account of the past night's scary encounters. Darnes said, "You know, I thought we were only dealing with two rogue cops and a few crooked politicians. But when the politicians hire hoodlums to do their dirty work they're no longer politicians but gangsters, and that's what we're dealing with today."

"I don't ever want to deal with gangsters," Dr. Widergren reflected. "Therefore, I think we should all quit right now."

"How do you think the public would react to that?" Simonsen asked.

Dale responded, "They'd be surprised, and some might even be shocked, but it would cool off in a matter of days. I just wonder what the board would do."

Simonsen continued, "In a way the board might even be glad, because it would give them the chance to make five temporary emergency replacements. You can rest assured such replacements would be lackeys to the trustees and Herb's dream of making Triton the career center of the midwest would vanish."

Dale added, "I'm staying at least to the end of the college year. I don't think you fellows realize that we have those boys on the run. And we have the public and the CFT behind us. What's more important, there are over 1,200 students that want this college to continue. Those shots fired last night were aimed at Darnes mainly because he was the declaration's author. They were intended to scare the hell out of us. Are we scared?"

"Yes, I am," I replied. "I'm scared as hell. I know if Case and Furlong had worked me over last night, Eugenia would have me on the way out today! But they didn't, so I'm staying, and I hope you'll all do the same. If my phones are tapped, as Harry Behrman says they are, then the coalition knows that the FBI has been fully informed. If anything ugly happens to any of us, the FBI will know where to look for the guilty ones."

Silence fell over the group for a few minutes, until Simonsen lifted his head and said, "I'll stay. You must all remember God is on our side."

Dale echoed the minister's son. "I'm with you, Gordon."

The four of us looked at John Widergren and waited for his reply. With some reluctance he said, "I'll stay, but only to the end of the college year. My wife and I have heard some weird tales about Conti, Dunahow and Serpico and we don't feel comfortable working for them. All I have to say is, you fellows have a lot of guts even though you may lack some sense at times – and this is one of those times."

We all stared at Bob Darnes, wanting him to say something unusual. He did. "Fellows, I wouldn't be here now if I didn't intend to stay. I am not leaving. I don't have another job and they are damned hard to find at the beginning of a semester. I will go as soon as I find something good and I hope it won't be too long. These past six months have been exciting and creative ones for me. I only hope that Herb lives to see his dream come true. He certainly turned us on. This morning I was turned on by my old friend from Oklahoma. I'm sure glad he never left me."

Dean Darnes clicked open his attaché case and fuddled around a little as we waited. He pulled out a brown under-the-arm holster containing a black revolver.

We all gasped a little as he said, "It's loaded and will stay with me as long as I'm at Triton. If any one of you fears danger is approaching, just call me. My second title will be the Lone Ranger, with a side arm known as Silver. My grandfather, who was one of the early pioneers in Oklahoma, has told me good tales about bad guys in the olden days. Now I'm about to add a few of my own in Chicagoland."

We were awed by Dr. Darnes's bluntness and pugnacity and hated the thought that he might be leaving us. What would Triton be without Darnes? Before leaving I urged the deans to update their confidential files at the universities. I'd be very happy to write confidential letters for all of them to help them get better jobs in the future.

As Darnes left I asked him, "Do you have any idea how the boys knew you lived on the second floor of your apartment house?"

He thought a while and said, "I'm not positive but I think we have three fifth columnists on our staff."

"What do you mean?"

"Virginia Sybilla was the only one who knew I lived on the second floor. Since she's a dear friend of attorney Dunahow I'm sure my whereabouts were transmitted to Case and Furlong."

"You may be right. She seemed exceptionally quiet today, and a little flushed. Who are the other fifth columnists at Triton?"

"You should know. It's your secretary, Maria Provenzano, and our press agent, Jim Tarpey."

"Bob, I think you're wrong about Maria. Although she is Serpico's sister-in-law she nevertheless is loyal to me. All she's trying to do is get Babe on the might track. But you're probably right about Jim Tarpey. After all, he is Collins's lifelong friend. His sugar-coating the minutes reveals his loyalty to Collins."

As Darnes and the boys left I thought long and hard about Maria and Virginia. Was I the stupid one when I recommended hiring those two, knowing their connections? Maybe so, but they were hired for their superior secretarial skills, not their connections.

On Friday night, while having dinner with the family, I told Eugenia I might trade in the Skylark for something a little better the next day at Jacobs Twin Buicks.

"You know Mark will be 16 soon and he wants to drive now," she said. "Don't you think we should keep it for him?" I then told her the engine was burning oil and the car needed new brakes, tires and a paint job.

"After 90,000 miles it's ready for retirement. I only hope I can get a few hundred for it."

"If you get another used one, promise me you'll get it washed regularly. It's shameful the way you treated the Skylark. It looks like it hasn't been washed in months."

"You are absolutely right, my dear," I told her, not letting her know that I inspected a small piece of tape over the hood every time I drove – my method of playing it safe. On Saturday morning Mark earned a dollar making the Skylark squeaky clean inside and out before I took it to Twin Buicks.

The salesman gave me the keys to a clean three-year old V8 Buick Electra, recently traded-in, with low mileage. I drove it along the Eisenhower Expressway for five miles. It was perfect, with a hood that locked from the inside. Within an hour I signed all the papers for a two-year loan and drove it away happy. That evening I took my beautiful wife out in my near-new car to a beautiful restaurant and a movie.

We enjoyed *The Sound of Music* with Julie Andrews. To us the movie was better than the stage show, which we'd seen at the Starlight Theater in San Diego over a year before.

Eugenia remarked, "I loved that movie! It should be nominated for an Academy Award."

"What did you like about it?"

"It was a fine musical, with a story. Baron von Trapp was to be admired. Rather than fight for the Nazis he despised, he fled the country with his family."

"Are you sure that was the right decision? He gave up a huge estate worth many millions. He could have stayed."

"Stay and work for the Nazis? Never. Even if he didn't join the Nazi party his life there would have been miserable. When people are bad, the further away you stay from them the better. He did the right thing, absolutely."

As Eugenia was speaking my mind was comparing the von Trapps and the Nazis with the college president and the Triton coalition. They weren't the same but there were some similarities. Eugenia felt Baron von Trapp was right to leave rather than associate with bad people. While I knew Dunahow, Collins and Farmar were doing bad things, I was determined to stay, hoping to reform them. If I told Eugenia what had occurred Thursday night, I knew she'd insist we leave Chicagoland. I didn't want to go at that time, so I decided not to tell her.

Before we went to bed Eugenia told me the kids were enjoying living in Elmwood Park and she was extremely happy to be part of Wright Junior College. She'd been readily accepted by the bright and well-informed members of the English department, the students were great and the pay was extremely good. The kids and she agreed life in Chicagoland was far more exciting and varied than the quiet, restful life in Chula Vista.

As we cuddled up for sleep I told her how proud I was of her. Within the space of one year she had gotten the kids to adjust to a new life, and found happiness in her new challenges. What a remarkable wife, mother and lover I'd married, I thought, as we fell into a most blissful state.

On Monday morning Dean Widergren came into my office to give me the latest on our enrollment. "I'm happy to inform you that enrollment exceeded the projection by over 24 per cent, nearly 1,250. Do you know why?"

"I believe it was the excellent recruitment efforts of the staff. Is that right?"

"Yes and no. The recruitment helped a lot but to me the biggest surprise was the great number that came from out of the district"

"How many, John?"

"Over 20 per cent from 42 different cities in Illinois. Mostly from Chicago and the many communities in Du Page County."

"Tell me, did any students come from Oak Park/River Forest or Riverside/Brookfield, the cities that rejected Triton?"

"Oak Park/River Forest sent us 21 students and Riverside/ Brookfield honored us with eight scholars. Isn't that interesting?"

"Yes, it is. In the future those same students and their neighbors will recommend Triton as the place to go. I'm sure that one day those two school districts will recognize they made a big mistake."

"Do you think those two districts will ever want to join us?"

"Yes, I'm sure they will. What surprised me is that we did nothing to recruit students from any of those 42 out-of-district cities. Why did they come to Triton? I guess they heard about us from the many news articles. Even though we had ten weeks of bad publicity the students didn't seem to care. They were turned on by our staff and the variety of our programs."

"You know something, Dr. Zeitlin? I think you're right This is a case of bad events putting Triton in the headlines and those headlines helping increase the enrollment."

"This is an odd twist of events. I think Samuel Goldwyn was right when be said it didn't matter what they said about him as long as it got in the newspapers."

With John's announcement I was more determined than ever to see it through. My dream of Triton becoming the most comprehensive community college in Illinois was more than a dream. It was reality on the horizon. I called Wade to tell him about it.

"Dr. Zeitlin, that's very good news. I wonder how the superintendents of those two districts will feel when we send them charge-back bills for their students. Do you have any idea what we'll charge them?"

"I can't be precise at this moment but Bob Dale tells me it will be the cost of educating the students minus their paid tuition of $5 per semester hour and the state reimbursement."

"Well, how much will that be?"

"About $20 per credit hour."

"Since half of your class sections were filled to capacity, I think the first registration priority in the future should be given to our own students. The out-of-district students may take whatever is left."

"That sounds like a fair and good idea. Hopefully the board will adopt it as new policy for the next college year."

As I left I thought how lucky we were to have Wade as the board president. He was the most knowledgeable and honest school person in the state that I had met. I always left him feeling a little wiser. Although he'd been retired only a few months, I felt when the time came to name buildings after trustees he should be the first to be so honored. What building should it be? I could envision the *WADE A. STEEL SCIENCE CENTER.*

The trustee with the most guts, and a fighter against great odds, was Roy Jones. He'd had the nerve to take on the whole coalition and their political protégés. Way back he'd told me the coalition consisted of a bunch of crooks. I hadn't believed him then. Now I realized how naive I had been. I wondered if there would ever be the name ROY JONES BUSINESS HALL in bold letters on a building.

My Thursdays at Rotary were always pleasant. Why? I usually arrived somewhat tense but the camaraderie and well-cooked meals by the sisterhood created a climate of relaxation and fun. Talking with Elmore Boeger the day after a board meeting gave me a different perspective on the many vital issues. In his unassuming manner Boeger came across as a most intelligent and honest man. He was the epitome of a good Rotarian and I treasured his comments. With luck and much perseverance I might get the Rotary International involved in establishing a house for visiting students: BOEGER ROTARY INTERNATIONAL HOUSE.

The four other trustees were relatively good men who'd been led astray in get-rich schemes promoted by attorney Don Dunahow. I felt he was the bad one and if Triton were to survive, Dunahow had to be dismissed. When I heard Fred Knol comment that Dunahow was not a good school attorney, a new hope hit me. It would take only four votes to make it happen. Could we get Knol to break with the coalition? That would be my new goal in the months ahead.

My greatest disappointment was Bob Collins. Here we had a young, active, likable fellow, with so much to offer, who had gotten on the wrong road. Why? Was it the $50,000 bonus Dunahow had promised him? Maybe. Or was he being blackmailed by Dunahow, who must have had photos of him having fun with nude call girls? If I could only separate him from Dunahow, the tide might turn and Collins would be on his way to eventually becoming River Grove's youngest mayor. I wanted to forget his part in the March incident when Farmar had nearly beat me up for refusing to hire Neil Neuson as business manager. Bob had pushed hard on me to accept Joe's lackey and I'd been lucky to get out without any physical bruises. As hard as I tried to forget, the image of Bob's part in the chicanery stayed with me.

Babe Serpico, as the tax assessor, had one of the most important jobs in Cook County, besides being Mayor Daley's strongest vote getter in the Democratic Party. He was so busy that the mayor had requested that he quit the Triton board, which he intended to do as soon as his term of office was up. Now, if only I could persuade him to change his vote and go for open bidding on the bonds, then the Triton board would again be in the good graces of the public. My strongest ally in this effort would be Maria Provenzano. It was quite possible that the all-American football player, if he reformed, might one day have the football field or gym named after him.

My last hope for a reformed trustee was Joe Farmar. While I personally liked him for his great sense of humor and sharpness, I also feared him for his sudden, potentially violent outbursts. When he was high he got out of control and became someone to stay away from. He would be the hardest one to change because he needed that extra $50,000 to maintain his high living standards. It was readily evident to most who knew him that he was an alcoholic; he spent much of his money on this expensive habit. If his dream of becoming a judge were realized, the coalition would be broken, though that possibility seemed rather remote.

As I looked at the whole picture after spending a full year with the board I still felt beneficial changes were possible. It was not hopeless, as several others proclaimed. I was determined to keep at it for at least one more year; however, it was paramount that I protect myself.

My known physical enemies were Farmar, Dunahow, Case and Furlong, plus any of their cronies. Wade offered to lend me a shotgun or one of his rifles. I gave the idea some thought but rejected it, fearing if it got into the hands of one of my kids I might regret it for the rest of my life.

Dr. Darnes, on the other hand, felt that to feel safe he needed a gun with him all the time. I just didn't know what to do. I slept on it for several nights. Was my life really in danger or was my imagination running wild? I knew if Lewis Case had been given the opportunity Thursday night he would have beaten me up. From his heavily armed Lincoln it would have been easy at two in the morning to shoot at me or my car. Maybe not to kill me but to cause a serious enough auto accident. Who knows what might have happened? I was just lucky having a friend named Harry Behrman to get me a county police escort to my home.

Would these boys try it again? I hoped not, but they might. I made up my mind and got out the yellow pages to look for a gun shop away from the district. I located one on Central Avenue in Cicero.

Guns and Herb were not strangers, even though my Mother forbade anyone in our family to have a weapon. In my senior year at Jamaica High School I enrolled in the ROTC. I felt it might help me in the future if, as Germany rearmed under Hitler, troubled Europe erupted. We drilled daily with the exception of target practice on Fridays, which I liked very much. My weapon was the heavy World War I rifle, the Springfield. By the year's end I had earned a citation for superior marksmanship. I was ready to fight the Nazis, come what may.

During my three years in the Army Air Force during World War II, I fired a .45, a .38 and the light rifle known as the carbine. On rare occasions I fired a Browning and Sharpe machine gun, which had a tremendous backlash. The ideal gun for inside coat pocket concealment was a .22. I wondered if the shop carried such a weapon.

When I arrived near the gun store, I made it a point to park my car two blocks away so I couldn't be identified. Instead of opening the door to the shop I walked around the block, returned to the shop and then returned to my car. I needed more time to think! If I carried a .22 to school every day, would I be safe? Would I and my dean of instruction be the only college administrators in the nation to arrive at work every day fully armed? If I made a survey of the 3,100 college presidents in the United States, would my colleagues think I was nuts to ask such a question? These questions remained unanswered. What to do? What to do? Please God, help me!

I returned to the gun shop, walked in and asked to look at a .22. To my disappointment the clerk responded, "Sorry, sir, we no longer carry those babies. The communities were outraged about that gun, now known as the *Saturday night special.* Can I sell you a .38? It's a helluva lot better. When you hit someone with that baby, they're gone. The .22 doesn't always do the job. If you want a one shot knockout, go with the .45 or .38."

He proceeded to show me a variety of .38's and .45's, which I slowly rejected after thinking it through. There was a two- to three-week waiting period before the purchase could be completed; I would have to be fingerprinted and investigated before a permit could be issued. That was a disappointment. Looking around the shop I noticed a rather nice pocketknife – not what I'd come for, but it could be a substitute weapon. So I bought it. I left the shop not fully armed, but at least with a small, concealed weapon, which I could use if ever it became necessary.

36
Ten Commandements for Trustees

Late in the afternoon on September 28th Maria called me from the conference room. "Dr. Zeitlin, you better get over here right away. It's serious!"

I immediately stopped what I was doing and raced through the hallways to see what was up. Upon opening the door to the conference room I found it in complete darkness, most unusual for this time of the day, when all of a sudden a chorus of voices rang out, "Happy birthday to you, happy birthday, Mr. President – and may you have many more!"

As the lights went on I saw a room full of people. In front of me and laughing all the way were the classified staff, all the administrators and the full *Trident* staff with its advisor, Bernard Verweil.

Very strange, I thought. My birthday is in January. I stopped wondering who goofed when Ed Sexton, the bookstore manager, rolled in a big cake. In the middle of the cake was an extra large single candle flickering away.

Maria explained, "Dr. Zeitlin, you've forgotten. You arrived at Triton a year ago today. Happy anniversary."

To my surprise Ed put a large knife in my hand and shouted, "Blow out the candle, Mr. President, and re-energize us with the cake Maria spent all weekend baking for us."

Everyone was in a light and happy mood as I gave each person a slice, chatting along with an exchange of pleasant words. The *Trident* photographer took many pictures to be included in the next issue. Here we had a classified staff of twelve, none of whom had ever worked at a college before. But all were pleased to be part of the founding and excited about the future. They expressed their heartfelt feelings to their president and the deans.

Strange as it may have seemed, no one mentioned the problems with the board, all assuming they were birth pains soon to be resolved and forgotten.

That evening after dinner I told Eugenia how good I felt about having Maria and the excellent classified staff. Without their help Triton would not have made such a good beginning.

After the kids had gone to bed Eugenia asked, "Well, Mr. President, what's next?"

"The deans are presently working on the Spring schedule. It should be ready next week. We anticipate the usual drop in enrollment of 10 to 20 per cent during the second semester. Next, it's urgent to sell the bonds through competitive bidding, purchase the site and build the college campus."

"What have you learned this past year that you didn't know before?"

I hesitated for a while and slowly responded. "First, I learned I was mistaken in believing that you could tell the character of the board members by what they said and by the degrees they held from elite colleges. Second, I learned that if you went against the coalition, they would soon be out to get you."

"If that's the case, then you know they'll go for you and Jack Rossetter, and our future in Chicagoland is in jeopardy."

"Not if we can break up the coalition. Boeger is already out and if we can get one more the tide will change. In addition we have two newfound friends: the Citizens for Triton and the press."

"That may sound good but remember the board hired you, not the Citizens or the press."

"I know that, but I feel the board will not go against public opinion, which right now is on our side. How long that will last I don't know."

"Have you thought about quitting?"

"Yes, but I don't want to. This college and the community have so much potential."

"What does the coalition really want?"

"They want jobs and contracts for their friends. I remember well the reprimand Dunahow gave me when I recommended the printing contract go to Hammand Press instead of to Babe's friend, who had submitted a bid over twice the lowest."

"Is Dunahow the voice of the board?"

"At the moment it appears so. He's out to pick up tips that far exceed the usual 10 to 20 per cent given to waiters. He arranged the bond sale in which he promised $50,000 to the four coalition members and $100,000 to the Republican and Democratic Parties."

"Is he evil?"

"Yes. He pushed me to write individual contracts for every teacher hired and intended to give me $100 on the side for each contract written. With 87 teachers now hired that would have amounted to $8,700 of rotten hush money. I have no idea what he paid the call girls he hired to go on his boat. However, I do suspect that he's blackmailing Bob Collins and at least one other trustee."

"Well, what do you intend to do about it?"

"Wade and I have agreed Dunahow cannot be reformed. Dunahow believes that when one is in power he should go all the way to solicit illegal money. He delayed and lied to us about the bond sale because he needed the time to make the right connection with a bond company. Merrill Lynch and Dean Witter declined his request for big contributions to the political parties, but he found a smaller company willing to go along."

"How is this all going to end?"

"I don't know for sure, but Wade and I do agree that Dunahow has to go before he does more damage to Triton's future. In the meantime I managed to hire all the qualified administrators and faculty that were needed, despite the uncalled-for efforts of the coalition to get some of their own in."

The following morning I heard glowing reports from the deans. No question about it, the faculty we hired were superior and well-accepted by the students. Dean Simonsen was working on adding beauty culture, nursing and several other programs for the next year. Dean Darnes encouraged the faculty to elect their own officers and to develop a constitution. At the same time he was preparing papers to submit to the accrediting agency. Business manager Bob Dale was snowed with purchase orders from the faculty and had to hire extra help. Even though we were mostly an evening college Art Shearbnrn, coordinator of student activities, had found student leaders who were planning a full extracurricular program. The admissions office was humming with student inquiries and counseling. I was so pleased to find all the administrators optimistic about the future despite the problems with the board.

Bob Darnes summed it up: "Dr. Zeitlin, we have the makings of a great college here if only we could have a different board."

All the deans nodded in agreement. "I would stay if that happened," remarked Dr. Widergren. "But seriously, I don't think it will. These suburbs are no different from Chicago. They're tainted. You can't reform a way of life that's existed for generations. The suburbs have not only imitated Chicago they've developed new and improved varieties of corruption."

"You know, Dr. Zeitlin, there's much talk among the political experts that you'll be out before the year is over and one of us will replace you. Have any of you heard this?" Dean Simonsen said.

"Yes, I heard it," Bob Dale said. "It's a tossup whether it will be Dr. Widergren or Dr. Darnes. It has to be someone with a doctorate."

"You can rest assured I'll have no part of it," Darnes responded instantly. Widergren followed with, "Ditto for me!"

Dean Simonsen, looking first at me and then long and hard at each dean, spoke very quietly. "You know, fellows, I believe if we all support Dr. Zeitlin we can beat the odds. The old saying 'united we stand and divided we fall' is very true. If we all stick together, the board will never fire all of us at the same time. Don't you agree, Dr. Zeitlin?"

"Yes, I do. I don't want to quit. Despite all the negative publicity, the students came. They love the faculty and the programs. My wife and I are willing to put all our energy into making Triton a success. I need you and I hope I can count on you."

Moments later Bob Darnes responded, "You can count on me," and shook my hand.

Then Simonsen, Widergren, Dale and I joined in for a quadruple handshake as Darnes proudly proclaimed, "This administration is united behind its president. And fellows, may I suggest that anytime a board member calls or visits any one of us we report instantly the nature of the call to Dr. Zeitlin. Are we in agreement?"

I felt very good when I heard a chorus of, "Yes, we'll do just that.

However, big questions still remained.

Would Dr. Zeitlin still be on the job next year or would the conniving political board take over?

I wondered if I had heard the last of Lewis Case and Hermie Furlong. Would they appear again? I feared them ever since the plan to beat me up was foiled.

How many other chief school administrators had their lives threatened while carrying out the duties of their job? Naive as I was, I thought probably very few.

I did recall the time in 1958 when Dr. Roy Knapp, the superintendent who had hired me as the dean of the evening division of Antelope Valley College, arrived at a board meeting with two county policemen at his side. Over the phone he'd received threats on his life should he continue to campaign for a $12 million bond issue to build a new college campus. He was pale and shaking but determined to continue speaking to the public. Only this time, he'd brought along two bodyguards.

After tirelessly conducting a most stressful campaign, he achieved a successful bond approval from the public. He did age much during the campaign and retired a few years later in poor health, loved by many but despised by the powerful tax haters and politicians. He survived the vicissitudes of school administration for over 25 years, did his job honestly and built a great school district despite hundreds of personal attacks that undoubtedly affected his health.

It's a sorry fact of life that those who hate tax increases take out their hostility on the agency receiving the biggest bite of the tax dollar, the schools! I quickly learned that a chief administrator, the superintendent or college president, is the frequent target of vicious reprisals. The public is generally not aware of this. I wondered if I would go the way of Dr. Knapp, but at a much younger age.

Now that I was about to begin my second year, the local politicians let it be known to their precinct workers that I was on my way out. I was amazed when three realtors, unaware that I was a renter, called me about listing my home in Elmwood Park. Many a time inaccurate news travels faster than the truth.

I had always found teaching a very rich and satisfying experience but I'd never imagined that being a chief school administrator would carry so many risks. Was Chicagoland different from the rest of the country? As a newcomer I hesitated answering that question. It certainly was a lot more scary. So many horrible stories. Were they true? If only the frozen bodies at the bottom of Lake Michigan could talk. I didn't know what to expect in the coming year. I welcomed the challenges of starting a new college but feared the retaliation of my enemies.

I humbly asked God to protect Jack Rossetter and the wonderful Chicagoland Citizens for Triton. They had taken on City Hall and at the moment appeared to be winning.

Although I felt somewhat sorry for the trustees, so ruthlessly attacked by the press, I nevertheless thought the press's zestful search for the truth remarkable. Would the trustees succeed in selling Triton's high interest, tax free bonds despite the public's outcry? The bankers constantly calling me, willing to pay above par, to get their hands on those bonds.

Would Dunahow's efforts to kill Neil Mehler's paper be successful? Would Neil's brilliance and integrity be rewarded with bankruptcy?

How long could I retain the services of the highly efficient administrators? If more shots were to fly I was quite certain the exodus would be rapid.

A new ray of hope suddenly appeared on the horizon when Ed Gleazer, President of the American Association of Community and Junior College, mailed me a copy of the *Ten Commandments For Trustees* with the comment, "Herb, if you can get your board to change, this is the way to go."

As I read those beautiful words it hurt very much when I realized the Triton Board ignored all of them. While not biblical in nature, the commandments were short and sweet:

1. Don't conduct any board meeting without the college president.
2. Don't have more than one person, the college president, responsible to the board.
3. Don't solicit or encourage staff gripes.
4. Don't become an advocate for someone seeking a job at the college.
5. Don't conduct personal investigations.
6. Don't act like a trustee except when meeting as a board.
7. Refer all questions pertaining to administration to the college president.

8. Don't speak for the board except when authorized by the board to do so.
9. Don't form standing committees
10. Insist on written policies.

Later that night Wade Steel, while sipping a Budweiser with me, gleefully commented, "Herb, I'll do everything in my power to get the board to accept the *Ten Commandments* as part of the Triton policy.

"Can we make that a major goal for Triton's second year?"

"Yes, it will be very difficult but not impossible! Those tainted trustees must become untainted or else they have to leave. We succeeded in getting Elmore Boeger to see the light. He is no longer part of the coalition. If only we can get one more to change then the coalition will collapse. Babe is under pressure from Mayor Richard Daley to leave as soon as possible. And can you imagine how the picture would change if Joe Farmar were appointed a judge by Governor Kerner and Bob Collins became Mayor of River Grove?"

"Who would replace these boys?"

"I don't know, but the board has to replace them within 90 days in accordance with county law. If they don't, a special election must be held."

"Wouldn't it be smarter for the board to appoint one or two known supporters of Triton as trustees rather than hold an expensive election?"

"It certainly would be, but whom shall we appoint?"

"It's easy. You could make the general public and the Citizens for Triton very happy by appointing Jack Rossetter and Neil Mehler. I am certain the attacks against the board would stop immediately."

"I would love to see that happen. If only I could convince Mayor O'Connor to step down and Jim Kirie to step up his drive with Governor Kerner to make Joe a judge."

"You know something? I think I am beginning to understand Chicago politics. To prevent the worst ones from doing further damage, you kick them upstairs. Is that correct, Wade?"

"In this hypothetical case it may be true. Much depends upon the relationship between the Governor Kerner and Jim Kirie, the Leyden Township political boss. If Kirie's voting machine can produce enough votes to re-elect our governor for another term, then Kerner will honor

Kirie's request."

"Ever since Kerner wrote his famous report, over one million copies have been sold and his star is shining brighter. Do you think President Johnson may select him for a big Washington post?"

"I don't know. If he does it is the start of a new ball game for the people of Illinois."

"Tell me this, Wade. In all your years as a superintendent have you seen much corruption in the school districts?"

"To the best of my knowledge and recall in my 20 years as a superintendent I have not seen any corrupting practices in the Leyden, Proviso or Elmwood Park schools. There were just a few times when I was put under pressure to hire a trustee's relative, but there were never any corrupting money payoffs."

"Is that the usual or are our districts the exception?"

"There is nothing unusual about our practices. We are honest people. Small districts like ours are close to the people. We really are community high schools with board meetings well attended. Everyone seems to know his neighbor. The smaller the district the less corruption or none at all."

"What do you have to say about New York City, Chicago, Philadelphia or Los Angeles?"

"The bigger the district the greater the corruption. As the population increases, more schools are built, district offices grow and the chief administrators become detached from faculties. It is the damnation of growth!"

"Is there any way we can prevent this damnation?"

"Yes, of course. Whnever the district population exceeds 400,000, it should be cut into two separate governing entities, thus assuring a continuance of local control. Not to do so will encourage the building of a huge bureaucracy."

"Is there much difference between the trustee of a small district and a trustee of a big city?"

"Yes, there is. A trustee hoping to be elected to a small school district may spend a few hundred dollars to become elected or nothing at all. When a man or woman decides to run for school trusteeship in a city of one, two or three million people he or she will need money. Not just thousands but hundreds of thousands of dollars."

"Where does he or she get this money?"

"The candidate's first approach is friends, neighbors and companies. Companies that are doing or will be doing something for the district such as building contractors, suppliers, real estate developers, consultants, lawyers, financial specialists, unions, political bosses and bonding companies. There is no such thing as a free lunch. All who help the candidate out expect some favors in the future. That, of course, leads to awarding contract to friends without bids, frequently done in large districts without informing the public."

"Wade, is that the reason the coalition voted to sell our bonds without bids?"

"Yes, however, our boys went a little further than repaying favors. They thought they could get on the gravy train without anyone knowing it. The plan backfired on them when Neil Mehler discover the bonds were secretly sold two weeks before the board vote."

"If it had not been for Neil, Leroy Koeppel, Jack Rossetter, Roy Jones, Wade Steel and concerned citizens the plan might have worked. I owe much to you for your wisdom and support."

"Herb, the community admires your courage for taking on city hall. Roy, Elmore and I are convinced that your dream of the future for Triton will come true if you stick in there. Don't you dare consider leaving even if the coalition requests your resignation. I don't know what is going to happen in the months ahead but I still have hopes to convert one more trustee to our cause. If that happens Chicagoland corruption at Triton will collapse."

I left Wade feeling optimistic about Triton's future and determine to run a extra clean ship. Early reports from the faculty about the progress of our 1,200 students were very good.

Bernie Verweil candidly stated, "Dr. Zeitlin, most of our students are not aware of the tainted trustees and those that are have accepted it as part of Chicago lifestyle. My family and I have lived here many a year. No one can change it, not even you."

I suddenly realized my biggest challenge was in front of me. Could I change the Chicagoland lifestyle in higher education?

EPILOGUE

What happened to the first Board of Trustees and their attorney years later? This, in a sense, is the rest of the story.

BOB COLLINS never became mayor of River Grove. Found guilty of tampering with a board election, he was forced to resign. Had he refused he would have faced a jail sentence. Sometime later, his son, upon receiving his driver's license, took Mrs. Collins for a ride. A news report stated that the car stalled on a railroad crossing. The son got out in time, while his mother, unable to free herself from the safety belt, was killed instantly. Bob was forced to take an early retirement from the phone company. He later remarried and moved to Arizona.

RALPH (BABE) SERPICO, the leader of the coalition, was embarrassed when a lead story in *Chicago Today* linked him to the mob. Babe had traveled on a free junket to San Juan, Puerto Rico with a group of politicians and gangsters, including Tony Accardo, chief of the crime syndicate. Mayor Richard Daley fired Babe after he was found guilty of soliciting a bribe. After serving time in prison, Babe returned to civilian life in Melrose Park, where he entered the concrete mixing business.

JOE FARMAR never became a judge, his lifelong ambition. He accepted a job in the Cook County Attorney's office as a prosecutor. He died an early death. Shortly after he died, his wife Ceil became totally blind. As she faithfully followed certain church rituals, her sight returned. She claimed it was a miracle from God.

FRED KNOL, during his second year on the board, separated himself from the coalition and supported the administration. Upon his retirement from the board and his job, the board named the technology center after him. He has continued to teach Sunday School in Westchester, his home town.

ROY JONES, after serving two terms on the board, retired from the gas company and moved to Fish Creek, Wisconsin, where once again he became very active on local affairs. Prior to his leaving the board, the business building was named after him.

ELMORE BOEGER, who became chairman of the board after Wade Steel retired, was defeated in his fourth election by a new coalition of politicians. The board named the fine arts building after him. He retired from law practice to spend his remaining days traveling and enjoying life with his wife.

WADE A. STEEL, who served with great distinction, was the first trustee to have a building named after him. Later, four other trustees were so honored. Upon his retirement the board unanimously voted to have the college president award him the honorary degree of Doctor of Humanities. He retired to Neoga, Illinois, the birthplace of his wife Mildred. When he died on October 21, 1981, Dr. Zeitlin flew from California to delivery an eulogy on behalf of the Triton board.

DON DUNAHOW sued the college and its president for over a million dollars. It was settled for $45,000. After losing a hard-fought battled for a Triton board seat, he retired as attorney for the city of Elmwood Park and attorney for Elmer Conti.

LAUSD nailed!

Probe finds massive wrongdoing, incompetence, deceit, possible crimes in Belmont school scandal

THE BLAME

Audit finds a culture of lying

By Beth Barrett
Staff Writer

The Belmont Learning Center harbored a systematic, pervasive culture of lying, finger-pointing, power games, disregard for the law and wholesale shirking of responsibility that permeates top management of the nation's second-largest school district, the Mullinax report concluded Tuesday.

For years, the Los Angeles Unified School District has tolerated improper violations of policies and procedures without calling employees to account, disciplining them or even monitoring employees by name, said Don Mullinax, director of the district's internal audit and special investigations unit.

"No one was ever held responsible or accountable for their actions," he said. "A report I would read, in a procedure was not followed, next time follow the procedure. No names were ever mentioned, no one was held accountable, no discipline was given out.

"We're hoping today that will change, but it's not going to happen overnight."

The report validated what many critics have said is at the heart of the district's failures in many areas.

"This is what we've been saying about the school district for two decades," said Day Higuchi, president of United Teachers Los Angeles. "Its practice at that's been in place for 30 years or more. Now the people who should be properly overseeing the project and catch things didn't act. The culture

By Greg Gittrich
Staff Writer

Exposing massive wrongdoing and a career of incompetence at Los Angeles Unified's highest levels, an internal audit of the Belmont Learning Center released Tuesday called for criminal investigations, civil lawsuits and the possible dismissal of many top officials.

Mullinax, the district's inspector general, charged that officials — including Superintendent Ruben Zacarias, former school boards and consultants — are responsible for allowing the Belmont Learning Center to be built on a potentially explosive oil and gas field.

This culture developed a practice denying responsibility, deflecting their responsibility, accepting or blaming someone else, who planned and executed LAUSD actions with regard to Belmont.

Mullinax wrote in the report on a $200 million project that may never be completed.

The 200-plus page report, supported by more than 4,000 pages of evidence, concludes that former school boards were hindered by a lack of experience in the development of school facilities and consequently vulnerable when alerted to the nation's costliest high school.

Finding an absence of policy and procedures to protect the public's health and safety, investigators recommended overhauling the district's environmental and legal departments and revamping its site selection process for schools.

Mullinax advised one district to use several consultants, including the district's top outside legal counsel, O'Melveny & Myers, the lead architect, Mitchell, Mulkana and Winters, and possibly the project developer, Temple Beaudry Partners, led by Kajima Urban Development.

O'Melveny and Myers and Temple Beaudry Partners issued statements denying wrongdoing.

THE PROBLEM

Patterns of failure:

▶ Former school boards were uninformed, indifferent to safety rules, denied responsibility and broke state environmental laws in the Belmont project, and broke state oversight and were "generally rudderless."

▶ Current and past LAUSD administrators lacked accountability, failed to provide proper oversight, broke state environmental laws, succumbed to internal bickering and failed to fulfill their professional duties diligently.

▶ The state Department of Education and Governor's Office of Planning and Development failed to exercise their legal duty to properly oversee the Belmont project and catch serious environmental problems.

THE REMEDY

KEY RECOMMENDATIONS:

▶ Set up systemwide ethics, conflict of interest and other key policies.

▶ Provide disciplined leadership, promote excellence and ensure integrity.

▶ Develop new environmental, health and safety policies.

▶ Restructure property and building departments.

▶ Discipline or fire nine managers found responsible for Belmont failure.

▶ Pursue lawsuits against architect, law firm and other contractors.

▶ Negotiate with sue developer over undisclosed environmental hazards.

▶ Strengthen school safety team.

▶ Meet all state health and safety requirements

Investigator Calls for Staff Penalties in Belmont Case

■ **Education:** Report urges discipline, even termination, for top business managers involved with construction of the high school on environmentally plagued land.

By DOUG SMITH and RALPH FRAMMOLINO, TIMES STAFF WRITERS

The new chief investigator for the Los Angeles schools called Tuesday for a sweeping housecleaning of the district's senior business staff for failure to supervise construction of the environmentally plagued Belmont Learning Complex.

Nine high-level district employees, including general counsel Richard K. Mason, Chief Administrative Officer David Koch and former facilities general manager Beth Louargand should receive discipline up to termination, a 200-page investigative summary said.

The report said that former school boards violated state laws in approving the half-completed high school west of downtown with inadequate environmental review and that their decisions were "ad hoc, uninformed by reference to any policy and generally rudderless."

The Board of Education received the long-awaited report from its top auditor, Don Mullinax, on Tuesday morning. Although members gave no indication how quickly they would respond, pressure was already building for decisive action.

"The district is not competent to be building schools," said Barry Groveman, attorney for the district's environmental safety team that raised the red flags about Belmont. "They cannot take on those responsibilities as they are presently constituted."

No immediate discipline was recommended for Supt. Ruben Zacarias, who was a deputy superintendent when the Belmont project started. But the report said his "failure to supervise the Belmont project in a diligent, professional and effective manner" should be taken into consideration in his next evaluation.

On Tuesday, Zacarias denied responsibility for the project's problems, as did several others named in the report.

Explosive methane and toxic chemicals, including hydrogen sul-

LAUSD Files Suit Against Developers of the Belmont Complex

By DOUG SMITH
TIMES EDUCATION WRITER

The Los Angeles Unified School District filed a civil lawsuit Tuesday, charging developers of the abandoned Belmont Learning Complex with submitting millions of dollars in excessive billings and failing to complete work the district paid them for.

The lawsuit names the project's developer, Temple Beaudry Partners, as well as two major construction firms that formed the development partnership—Los Angeles-based Turner Construction and a U.S. subsidiary of the Japanese construction giant Kajima International.

Also named in the lawsuit is Bel-mont's architect, McLarand, Vasquez & Partners, which the district accuses of design errors and a failure to ensure that the downtown site had been adequately assessed for environmental hazards.

Joseph Cotchett, an outside attorney who filed the lawsuit for the district, said he could not specify the amount of alleged excessive billings because district accountants are still examining project records.

However, Cotchett said he believes the amount will exceed the $2-million figure cited by district Inspector General Don Mullinax in his December report probing Belmont's finances.

"Our belief is that it's much more," he said.

Cotchett said he submitted a copy of the lawsuit Tuesday to ry Partners; declined comment Atty. Gen. Bill Lockyer, a move that would precipitate a state investigation into the alleged loss of taxpayer money.

The Los Angeles County district attorney's office is still reviewing allegations of excessive billings. However, the district attorney's office declined to file criminal charges after examining an earlier report by Mullinax that blamed nine district employees and several contractors for their roles in the Belmont fiasco.

The school board aborted the $200-million project in midstream-early this year after environmental experts warned that underground methane could result in an explosion.

A spokesman for Temple Beaud-Tuesday. The spokesman said the "design and construction" of Belmont because of bad advice the district received from O'Melveny & Myers.

According to the lawsuit, O'Melveny & Myers attorney David Cartwright told the district that terms of the contract the drafted provided "less reason for the district to perform an intensive review of the invoice documentation."

In reviewing payment applications since January 1997, the lawsuit said, the district last discovered "substantial overbilling and excessive payments . . . as well as incomplete and defective work . . . represented as complete."

The lawsuit filed Tuesday alleges that the contractors—and 14 subcontractors also named in the court action—were able to engage in "a pattern of overbilling and incompetence during the design and construction" of Belmont because

Tuesday; declined comment on the lawsuit. The spokesman said the "design and construction" of Belmont because of bad advice the district received from O'Melveny & Myers.

Myers, the city's largest law firm, the district alleges that it received faulty legal advice that allowed the project to begin in 1997 without adequate environmental assessments.

Later investigations have shown pervasive seepage of methane and small quantities of toxic hydrogen sulfide in the ground below the school site which is on a former oil field west of downtown.

Several environmental experts have said the campus could be made safe by placing plastic membranes under buildings and some open areas. Estimates for the repairs have ranged from $10 million to $60 million. The board voted in January to cancel the project, on which approximately $175 million has so far been spent.

In its suit against O'Melveny &

"What's happening at Triton College, Mr. President?"
asked Chicago's renowned interviewer, Studs Terkel.
Radio Station WFMT.